Capitalism and the State in U.S.–Latin American Relations

Edited by Richard R. Fagen

Capitalism and the State
in U.S.–Latin American Relations

This book was sponsored by the Joint Committee on Latin American Studies of the Social Science Research Council and the American Council of Learned Societies

Contributors

CYNTHIA ARNSON

ANGELA M. DELLI SANTE

PETER EVANS

RICHARD R. FAGEN

ROBERTO FRENKEL

IRA KATZNELSON

MICHAEL T. KLARE

ANTHONY P. MAINGOT

HENRY R. NAU

GUILLERMO O'DONNELL

OSCAR PINO-SANTOS

KENNETH PREWITT

EARL C. RAVENAL

JERRY SANDERS

BARBARA STALLINGS

STEVEN S. VOLK

ALAN WOLFE

Capitalism and the State in U.S.–Latin American Relations

Edited by Richard R. Fagen

STANFORD UNIVERSITY PRESS
STANFORD, CALIFORNIA 1979

Stanford University Press
© 1979 by the Board of Trustees of the
Leland Stanford Junior University
All rights reserved
Printed in the United States of America
LC 78–65394
Cloth ISBN 0–8047–1020–1
Paper ISBN 0–8047–1040–6

Acknowledgments

In an enterprise such as this, lasting over several years, indebtednesses —of the good kind—accumulate rapidly. While this project was in its most preliminary stages, Stanford University supported a series of planning activities. Subsequently, while I held a fellowship from the Rockefeller Foundation and was a visiting fellow at the School for Advanced International Studies of the Johns Hopkins University, I was able to do much of the organizational work for the conference at which the papers contained herein were first presented—as well as most of the work on my own essay with Henry Nau. The conference itself, in all of its various stages, was generously supported by the Joint Committee on Latin American Studies of the Social Science Research Council and the American Council of Learned Societies through its Research Planning Program. This Program, in turn, has been supported by grants from the Ford and Tinker Foundations. Finally, the Woodrow Wilson International Center for Scholars of the Smithsonian Institution was a most cordial and cooperative host for the week-long conference in March 1978.

My greatest pleasure, however, is in acknowledging the multiple contributions of more than 100 colleagues from Latin America, the Caribbean, and the United States. As critics of and contributors to the planning stages of the conference, leaders of workshops, commentators, participants, and friends, their mark is indelibly on this volume. Only sixteen are directly represented in the pages that follow, but dozens more have left their imprints on the essays, on the topics discussed, and on all of us who were privileged to have their company and counsel.

R.R.F.

v

Contents

Capitalism and the State
in U.S.–Latin American Relations

Introduction

RICHARD R. FAGEN

In a much-quoted passage about the United States, José Martí once said that he had lived in the bowels of the monster and he knew it well. His brilliant newspaper articles and essays from the late nineteenth century support the truth of his claim; but at the same time they also suggest how fragmentary and time-bound any claim to knowledge about politics and society must always be. Knowledge of the world in which we live is clearly constrained by the location, vision, and values of the observer.[1] Moreover, it is constantly under assault by new information and perspectives generated by "events" that are themselves only the outcroppings of larger forces at work in both national and international systems. The frequency with which we confuse the "events" with those larger forces attests to the difficulty of generating knowledge in an epoch when the rate and profundity of social change clearly exceed our capacity both to understand and to manage that change.

People interested in the conduct of public affairs in the final two decades of the twentieth century cannot help but be troubled by this situation. Theoretical constructs, intended to order, clarify, and simplify certain basic relationships, are constantly under assault by the upwellings of observed social change. The predictions of the allegedly knowledgeable are frequently swept away with what some would say is alarming (and others would say is reassuring) frequency. The social sciences necessarily reflect the times. In economics, sociology, and even political science the dominant paradigms of the postwar period are almost everywhere being challenged. Theoretical confusion and conflict are reflected in the work and lives of both younger and older scholars.

In this context, one raises the banner of the social sciences only with

---

Richard R. Fagen is Professor of Political Science at Stanford University, and is the author or co-author of eight books, most recently *Rich and Poor Nations in the World Economy* (1978). He has taught in Chile and Mexico and is currently working on a study of U.S.-Mexican relations.

1. Without wishing to enter into a lengthy epistemological discussion, I should make it clear that I am using "knowledge" in its commonsense meaning of an ordered, truthful understanding of some set of phenomena.

some trepidation. To do so implies a leap of faith, a not-always-easy commitment to rationality in politics, and a belief that knowledge correctly generated, framed, and presented will have some impact on the conduct of public affairs. The leap is perhaps a bit longer in the field of international politics and foreign policy than elsewhere. There the gulf that separates knowledge (as here understood) from policy-making— at least in the United States—is very large indeed.[2]

It was in this climate of both hope and skepticism that we began planning for a conference on "The United States, U.S. Foreign Policy, and Latin American and Caribbean Regimes."[3] From the outset it was intended that the study of the United States, very broadly conceived, would be put at the center of the effort.[4] In a working paper circulated in February 1976, this central concern was expressed in the following fashion:

There is a widespread consensus among students of Latin America and U.S. foreign policy that the context in which interhemispheric relations is conducted has changed and continues to change in important ways. There is much less of a consensus on assessments of U.S. reactions to this changing context, and the possibilities and limits to U.S. reponses and initiatives. For many years in Latin America, and increasingly among certain scholars in the United States, the dominant understanding of the United States has been of a nation that is structurally committed to opposing basic changes in political and economic arrangements in the Americas. From this point of view, the basic dynamics of the oppositional role of the United States are not to be found in "bad men" or "mindless bureaucracies"—although both may abound.

2. This topic is immense, well beyond the scope of this Introduction. The basic point, however, is that the foreign policy process (again, at least in the United States) tends to define useful knowledge as *intelligence*: names, dates, statistics, who is doing what to whom, or who is trying or intending to do what to whom. There is a resulting vulgarization of the concept of knowledge, a closing-off of alternative understandings of reality, and a confusion of data on "events" with knowledge of the more enduring forces at work both domestically and internationally.

3. The "we" in this instance refers to myself and the staff and members of the Joint Committee on Latin American Studies of the Social Science Research Council and the American Council of Learned Societies. From the outset, "U.S. foreign policy" was understood very broadly to include both governmental and nongovernmental influences on official programs and policies. It was also understood by all concerned that limiting the geographical focus of the conference to Latin America and the Caribbean was perhaps a necessary but certainly also a somewhat artificial constraint. The non–Latin American aspects of the study of U.S. foreign policy are reflected in several of the papers and much of the discussion that follows.

4. Slightly earlier, the Joint Committee had initiated a series of complementary studies on Latin America, to be published by Princeton University Press as *The New Authoritarianism in Latin America*, under the editorship of David Collier.

Rather, as dependency theorists and others have often reminded us, they are to be discovered in the structural properties that characterize contemporary center-periphery relations, and particularly the political-economic properties of the United States. Big-power status, massive military spending, institutionalized anti-Communism, high mass consumption and waste, the logic of the market and unequal exchange—all undergird and reinforce these dynamics. In the case of Latin America, historically and geographically close to a hegemonic United States, the dynamics are, if any thing, stronger and more mutually reinforcing than in other parts of the Third World. They will not quickly or easily be turned around.

As an orienting perspective toward the prospects of and limits to change in U.S. foreign policy, this understanding of how the hemisphere works is useful. There is, however, a second optic—not necessarily incompatible with the first—through which these issues can be viewed. Here the emphasis is on the meaningful room for maneuver that does exist in the foreign policy arena. Large fissures have appeared in the hegemonic facade. Cross-national cooperative ventures are increasing in Latin America and the Third World. The edge of consciousness is changing in the United States after Vietnam, Watergate, and the CIA revelations—even though the material base of that consciousness is changing more slowly. Demystification occurs concomitantly with clearer understandings of the contradictions inherent in continuing the "American Way of Life."

What both of these perspectives lack (and what in part explains the pessimistic cast of the former and the guarded optimism of the latter) is a serious and detailed attempt to model the structural characteristics of the United States—and changes in those characteristics—hypothesized to determine or set limits to foreign policy. Stated most simply, the elaboration of a model of how the hemisphere works has far outrun elaboration of a compatible model of how the United States works. I stress the question of compatibility because the age of North American innocence in foreign policy analysis is passing. No longer is it acceptable to "explain" or "predict" U.S. foreign policy as simply the product of intragovernmental struggles—however important such struggles may be at particular moments. The policy process involves deeply rooted economic, social, and governmental interests in the United States, interests that are themselves affected by what is happening in the hemisphere and elsewhere.

As planning for the conference continued, it became increasingly clear that the search for the "deep sources" of U.S. foreign policy was an ambitious task indeed. Not only was a more profound understanding of the United States needed, but a more thorough mapping of U.S. global relations and the nature of the contemporary world system was also essential. In short, as conceptualized, the awkward and relatively innocent-sounding title of the proposed conference implied an agenda of theorizing and research that extended far beyond our modest possibilities. Some cutting back was necessary.

At that point, a decision was taken to approach this thicket of concerns by commissioning a series of case studies, each of which would give its author or authors an opportunity to explore themes of more general interest.[5] For example, the manner in which banks and international financial institutions serve particular interests and classes both in the United States and abroad was to be explored in the context of case studies of Peru and Argentina. Similarly, the continuing Cold War matrix of much policy formation and implementation in the United States was to be examined in case studies on the transfer of repressive technology to Latin America and the origins and ideology of the new anti-Sovietism personified in the Committee on the Present Danger. The tradeoffs involved in this approach were understood and accepted: systematic theoretical discourse would be subordinated at many points to detailed discussions of politics and economics; holistic understandings of the United States would be partially lost in a scattering of cases, which, though they might illuminate parts of a system, would not by themselves suggest its integrative features; speculations about the future and explorations of preferred alternatives would give way to a concentration on past and current realities, no matter how unpreferred and/or contradictory these might turn out to be.

Thus the list of cases grew, reflecting not only an attempt to achieve geographical, substantive, and disciplinary diversity, but also a conscious effect to select studies that would shed light on the multiple sources of U.S. foreign policy and the consequences, direct and indirect, of those policies for and on the hemisphere.[6] We went even one step

5. This decision was taken after extensive consultation with Latin American colleagues as well as potential U.S. participants. The general feeling was that at this stage of the evolution of the study of the United States and Latin America, priority ought to be given to research rather than to orienting *marcos* or frameworks. In turn, this research commitment led quite naturally to a case-study-disciplined-by-theoretical-concerns approach to the generation of knowledge. In this and a number of other ways the present volume continues the work begun earlier under the auspices of the SSRC-ACLS and reported in Julio Cotler and Richard R. Fagen, eds., *Latin America and the United States: The Changing Political Realities* (Stanford, Calif., 1974). (The volume was also published in Spanish by Amorrortu, Buenos Aires, 1974.) See particularly the Introduction to that volume.

6. Efforts were made to involve Latin American and Caribbean scholars as authors, although with a few exceptions this proved difficult because so few persons from the region have worked seriously and extensively on the United States

further by actually framing each case in terms of the more general theme or problem that it was intended to illuminate. That authors often strayed from these themes attests not only to their independence of mind but also to the multiplicity of theoretical and thematic purposes to which cases of this sort can be put.[7]

Nevertheless, in the final analysis, what is striking about the studies assembled here is the extent to which they are mutually compatible and reinforcing—the extent to which various authors return again and again to common topics and common issues. In part this is, of course, a function of the like-mindedness of the writers, for despite the geographical, substantive, and disciplinary diversity mentioned above, most of the authors share certain key assumptions about U.S. foreign policy, its sources, and its consequences. But that is not the whole explanation. More important are the commonalities induced by the cases themselves, by the "events" through which the more elusive deep sources of foreign policy are expressed.

What then do we see when we step back from the details of the cases and attempt to look at the whole? What is most immediately obvious— and not particularly surprising—is that two basic issues or *problemáticas* dominate all others. The first is the nature of contemporary capitalism; the second is the nature of the contemporary state. Related to these two fundamental issues is a series of subordinate but separable topics: North American exceptionalism in a changing world; institutions, actors, and alliances; ideology and legitimacy; and values, choices, and policy. Let us look briefly at each in turn.[8]

---

in the case study tradition that we embraced. At the conference at which these papers were discussed, held at the Woodrow Wilson Center of the Smithsonian Institution in March, 1978, approximately half of the persons in attendance were from Latin America and the Caribbean. In an effort to encourage future work on U.S. foreign policy by those in attendance and others, the final two days of the five day conference were devoted to six substantive and methodological workshops: Human Rights and U.S. Foreign Policy; The Executive Branch and U.S. Latin American Policy; Congress and Foreign Policy; Military and Security Affairs; The Mass Media and Foreign Policy; and The Transnational Corporation.

7. Originally, three general thematic essays were envisioned. For various reasons, only one reached final form and is included here—the paper on constitutionalism, class, and U.S. foreign policy by Katznelson and Prewitt.

8. It would be indecently immodest to imply that in a few pages I could do justice to *problemáticas* such as these. I simply mean to alert the reader to the fact that the studies which follow raise these issues and thus should be read with them in mind. The studies also raise a series of methodological questions, some of which were foreseen and discussed in the Introduction to Cotler and Fagen, eds., *Latin America and the United States*. See in particular the section on "Theory and Cases, Wholes and Parts, Continuity and Change," pp. 9ff.

CONTEMPORARY CAPITALISM: NORTH, SOUTH, AND GLOBAL

Even persons with little or no sympathy for Marxist modes of analysis would agree that an understanding of contemporary capitalism in the United States and elsewhere is essential for an understanding of the workings of the international system. We live in a world dominated to such an extent by market mechanisms that even self-proclaimed communists behave like "good capitalists" out of necessity if not belief on many occasions. Buying cheap and selling dear is close to a universal norm at this particular historical moment. As a preliminary guide to understanding international economic, and at times political, relations, explanations based on this norm serve better than most other hypotheses; and they have the additional virtue of appearing hard-headed and nonsentimental in circles that value *Realpolitik*.

The analysis of contemporary capitalism as approached in these essays, however, addresses more complex and subtle issues. Above all, the essays taken together ask "What are the mechanisms by which capitalist accumulation and distribution continue in environments, both national and international, that are not as simple and perhaps not as propitious as they were even as little as a decade ago?" There are multiple answers, which in turn are partial and thus necessarily incomplete. Some examples will help to clarify and substantiate this point.

Steven Volk, in a detailed analysis of recent trends in the U.S. electronics and steel industries, suggests how a changing structure of production reflects changes in factors of production such as labor and technology. In such circumstances, capital seeks to defend itself in various ways from competition and falling rates of profit. In electronics, production has been decentralized with many operations going overseas in search of lower labor costs. In steel, this is more difficult, and thus consolidation and protectionism are "logical" responses of management—and in some cases of labor. Roberto Frenkel and Guillermo O'Donnell, on the other hand, are concerned with recent attempts to breathe life into a politically troubled and economically crisis-ridden peripheral capitalism in Argentina. Operating under International Monetary Fund guidelines that define economic "health" largely in terms of balance of payments, the unencumbered entry of foreign capital, and reduced government deficits, the military junta has been able to restore substantial international "confidence" in the Argentine economy. The toll paid in human suffering has been immense, with economic and political repression necessarily focused on the organized working class.

More surprising, although well explained by the authors, is the extent to which the middle class and many national entrepreneurs have also been hurt by the programs imposed. Related developments of peripheral capitalism are illuminated by Barbara Stallings's case study of Peru, by Peter Evans's study of Brazil, and in more muted form by the Angela Delli Sante and Richard Fagen—Henry Nau studies of Mexico.

A second major point on which several essays converge is the question of distribution. This, of course, is a direct extension of the previous point, but with specific emphasis on who profits from and who pays for the kinds of programs instituted in the name of the new needs of capital. The most obvious losers have been wage earners both North and South—a point emphasized by Ira Katznelson and Kenneth Prewitt, Anthony Maingot, and all of the other authors just mentioned. But also hurt in various degrees have been sectors of national capital both in the United States and abroad (Evans uses the example of shoe manufacturers in the United States), as well as broad sectors of the consuming public whose incomes do not keep up with rising prices in situations that run from the mildly inflationary to the conflagrational. But of at least equal importance for understanding the foreign- and international-policy implications of these changing patterns of accumulation and distribution is a mapping of who profits. In general, transnational corporations are well equipped and located to take advantage of the structure of contemporary capitalism—after all, they helped to create it! At least equally advantaged are the large private banks (themselves a special kind of transnational corporation) as well as a host of financial intermediaries, speculators, and national entrepreneurs with the right kinds of links to the state both at home and abroad.

The foreign-policy implications of these patterns of gain and loss in a changing environment of capitalist accumulation are immense, if not immediate. For example, it is impossible to understand the multiple pressures for and against protectionism exerted on the executive and the legislative branches of government in the United States without a more basic understanding of the way in which both the domestic and the international economies are changing (see, for example, the essays by Katznelson and Prewitt, Volk, and Evans). Similarly, the conflicted political situations of countries such as Argentina, Brazil, Peru, Mexico, and the English-speaking Caribbean all reflect crises of accumulation and distribution in the local economy as well as the linkages of those economies to the international system. These conflicted political situations in turn resonate in the foreign-policy process in the United States in ostensibly "noneconomic" domains such as human rights and the East-West confrontation.[9]

THE NATURE OF THE STATE: NORTH AND SOUTH

No discussion of contemporary capitalism would be complete without acknowledging the profoundly important role of the state in the process of accumulation and distribution touched on above.[10] An important part of the history of contemporary capitalism could be organized around a description of the way in which various classes, groups, and economic interests attempt to use state power to give themselves advantages in a world in which the "free market" is even less operative than it was a few decades ago.[11] Whether in ostensibly technocratic questions such as interest rates and import quotas, or in openly political struggles such as the smashing of workers' organizations, the state is everywhere involved as an active participant in deciding who wins and who loses. The fiction that the state is actually a neutral arbitrator of the continuing contest for material advantage is probably not now believed by most serious observers of social reality. Conservatives and others often wish to see the hand of the state removed from one or another arena of economic activity, arguing that it is tilting the balance in ways inimical to the "general welfare." But this very argument is an open admission of the critical and perhaps inevitable role played by the state in contemporary capitalism.

This basic truth about the essential role of the capitalist state in the process of accumulation and distribution, however, is so broad that at best it can only serve as an orienting idea. The really interesting questions are to be found much closer to the grain of specific countries and historical circumstances. Thus Stallings recounts the central role of the

9. For an elaboration of this point see Richard R. Fagen, "The Carter Administration and Latin America: Business as Usual?" *Foreign Affairs*, 57, no. 3 (1979), pp. 652–69.

10. Without getting enmeshed in an endless theoretical debate about the concept of "the state," it is essential to reaffirm that we are not simply talking about governments or administrations. The concept of the state refers to the architectonics of a regime, its forms, purposes, and instrumentalities of rule. This is well expressed in the epigram "governments change; the state endures." Like all such epigrammatic sayings, however, this one is not invariably accurate. The 1973 coup in Chile, for example, destroyed or subordinated most of the historic forms, purposes, and instrumentalities of rule. The nature of the Chilean state changed at that time.

11. An equally important part of the history of contemporary socialism could be written in much the same terms, although in this case the battle against the continuing operation of market forces would occupy center stage.

Peruvian state first in incurring massive indebtedness to private banks, and then in having to enforce the harshest sorts of austerity measures—implying very substantial repression—in order to secure new loans and have some possibilities of repayment. There is substantial irony (some would say tragedy) in the spectacle of a regime forced to turn against large sectors of its own population in an effort to pay its debts and thereby not perturb the orderly functioning of the international monetary system as presently constituted.

In a situation that is in some respects the mirror image of the Peruvian case, Katznelson and Prewitt suggest how the lack of central planning in the United States (of the sort common in Western Europe) makes the spreading of the costs associated with more liberal foreign economic policies difficult. Easier access to U.S. markets for Latin American manufactured goods, for example, means real difficulties for certain sectors of labor and capital in the United States—whatever the benefits for Latin America and U.S. consumers in general. In the absence of a centralized planning apparatus—one more consequence of what the authors call the "low stateness" of the U.S. political system—the policy process is inordinately exposed to political pressures generated by special interests. In this context, strong protectionist reactions to more open borders are inevitable and have a high probability of being implemented. The point is not that groups and interests should not attempt to use the instrumentalities of the capitalist state to secure what they perceive to be their most immediate advantages. It is both proper and predictable that they should do so. Rather, what is being emphasized is that the permeability of the U.S. state makes certain solutions to this political-economic struggle highly probable and simultaneously encourages the myth that the state is merely refereeing social conflict rather than helping to determine who wins and who loses.

The *problemática* of the state, however, as approached in these essays is not confined to explorations of the manner in which it mediates conflicts of accumulation and distribution. Several authors also address directly the question of the state-as-independent-actor in foreign policy. This is, of course, an old and continuing theme in historical and political analysis, the source of much theorizing and debate. To a greater or lesser degree the state (or its instrumentalities) is seen in this tradition as having an autonomous capability of action, which is expressed through, if not always generated wholly within, executive leadership, legislative mandate, and/or bureaucratic behavior. Emphasis is frequently placed on the schisms between state and society, the manner in which governments—for at this point the focus of analysis is usually on specific governments—take actions that cannot be explained by, or do not respond to, the activities of powerful nongovernmental groups and interests.

Thus Fagen and Nau describe how and why the Carter Administration turned down the purchase of Mexican natural gas in late 1977 despite the fact that the U.S. corporate and banking communities were wholeheartedly in favor of it. Volk chronicles the largely unsuccessful attempts of the U.S. steel industry to achieve the levels of protection and government support it sought. Evans recounts the tangled history of the shoe industry and the Overseas Private Investment Corporation to illustrate how difficult it now is for certain sectors of North American business to achieve the support they seek from the U.S. government. The study by Michael Klare and Cynthia Arnson, the essay by Alan Wolfe and Jerry Sanders, and Anthony Maingot's paper on the Caribbean all suggest how perceptions of U.S. national interest among elites—essentially national security perceptions—condition foreign policy decisions relatively independently of the structure of economic interests. And at a more general level, Katznelson and Prewitt emphasize the pull over foreign policy exercised by constitutionalism in the United States —constitutionalism understood in part as a doctrine that intentionally fragments state power and aids in obscuring the covert, imperialist aspects of U.S. foreign relations.

Is a synthesis possible? That is, can models of the foreign policy process be constructed that combine in more or less harmonious fashion understanding of the workings of capitalism, both nationally and internationally, and understanding of the workings of the state—with all its intricacies, peculiarities, and contradictions? If the essays in this volume are taken as representative, the answer to this question is "No," at least not at this time. The only author who reaches directly toward this synthesis is Oscar Pino-Santos in his comment on the Wolfe and Sanders essay. Pino-Santos's core explanatory concept, "state monopoly capitalism," suggests a bridge between the two analytical terrains. But as he would be the first to admit, this bridge by itself is not now sufficiently elaborated or strong enough to sustain the empirical and theoretical work that is needed.[12]

In sum, we are still a long way from having generated the frameworks necessary for analyzing the new political economy of U.S. foreign

12. Not surprisingly, the possibility of such a synthesis was also under discussion at the conference mentioned earlier. See in particular, "Models of Politics: Class, Institutions, Government," in Cotler and Fagen, *Latin America and the United States*, pp. 6ff.

policy—frameworks that would take full cognizance of contemporary capitalism, on the one hand, and link the insight gained there to detailed understandings of the contemporary state, on the other. The following essays, however, do provide useful leads and challenges. The remainder of this Introduction will be devoted to exploring some of them.

NORTH AMERICAN EXCEPTIONALISM IN A CHANGING WORLD

In reading these essays it is hard to escape the conclusion that historically specific models of the political economy of the United States are needed if social-scientific knowledge is not to float too far above the realities of power and politics. The general notion that the United States was and is different from other developing or developed capitalist societies is, of course, an enduring theme. The founding fathers, Tocqueville, Woodrow Wilson, and every presidential memoir written since the Second World War emphasize some aspect of American exceptionalism, often differentiating the young (or not-so-young) republic from its allegedly less vigorous or less moral European brethren. Very different perspectives on the question of exceptionalism are to be found in the abundant critiques of U.S. politics and society originating in both conservative and radical thought at home and abroad. The United States appears, in these writings, not just as one more crassly materialistic or imperialistic state, but rather as *the* epitome of materialism and/or *the* incarnation of imperialism.

The exceptionalism suggested in the following essays, however, has a somewhat different cast. The essays do not in general seek to locate the United States in the broadest comparative context.[13] Rather, they seek the conjunctural, the changing, and the specific. All are set in the 1970's—although some authors, like Maingot and Stallings, root their analyses in several decades of recent history. What binds them together is that all cut into the international system and U.S. foreign policy at a moment when the hegemonic reach of the United States is less than it was a decade or two ago and when new modes and rules for the management of the hemispheric development crisis are being formed. Thus, in one fashion or another the essays attempt to come to grips with the

13. A partial exception to this generalization is the Katznelson and Prewitt essay. As noted above, this was commissioned as a thematic paper and not as a case study. The authors were specifically asked to analyze U.S. political culture and political processes in a way that would illuminate special features of U.S. foreign policy, emphasizing what makes the United States different from other advanced capitalist democracies.

exceptionalism of the United States in the specific context of the 1970's. How, they ask, should one understand the dominant power in the hemisphere at a moment when many of the old policy instruments are no longer as viable as they once were yet when few of the basic structural features of the U.S. political economy have changed?

The essays respond to this analytical challenge largely through the search for "telling examples." Thus Delli Sante's study of the American Chamber of Commerce in Mexico highlights the manner in which U.S. and Mexican business firms, in consonance if not actually in conspiracy with the U.S. Embassy, attempted to protect themselves from what they perceived to be a rising tide of nationalist and anticapitalist feeling. It is quintessentially a story of the 1970's, and equally an episode in which U.S. corporate interests "had to" take a leading role given their stakes and prior activities. Similarly, the Wolfe and Sanders study underlines the uniquely North American staying power of the anti-Soviet theme in foreign policy, while also emphasizing the way in which the Committee on the Present Danger is a particular product of post-Vietnam, post-Watergate America. Again, the continuity, the change, and the specificity are all seen as important for an understanding of the events. In fact, just about every other case study—each in its own way—can be read as an illumination of these same three factors, as a comment on the changed circumstances of foreign and international politics and the way in which the United States, as the historically leading power, is involved as both actor and reactor.

Although at first glance the exploration of this through the use of case studies and telling examples might seem to avoid if not resolve a host of problems, it really only postpones the day of reckoning. Just as ultimately one must join an understanding of contemporary capitalism to an understanding of the contemporary state in the ongoing search for a political economy of foreign policy, so one must embed an analysis of the United States in this larger matrix. It is undeniably true, for example, that the U.S. Congress plays a very special role in the foreign policy process. It is equally true that there have been changes in this role since Vietnam, Watergate, and Chile. Additionally it is true that certain Senators and Representatives, by the force of their ideas, congressional assignments, and parliamentary skills, are inordinately important in shaping foreign policy outcomes. The challenge is to take these and a hundred other changes in and peculiarities of the U.S. political system into account while not losing sight of the larger forces that move foreign policy. Thus assessed, an example is "telling" to the extent that it illuminates these larger forces. The larger forces in the 1970's are in turn clarified to the extent that they are seen in their specificity as well as in their historical and structural continuity. Not surprisingly, none of the cases moves easily across all these levels of analysis.

INSTITUTIONS, ACTORS, AND ALLIANCES

The cast of characters that marches across the following pages is largely familiar. In no particular order, the dramatis personae include transnational corporations, banks, the military-in-power (and occasionally out-of-power), organized and unorganized labor both north and south of the Rio Grande, local producers of goods and services, the executive and legislative branches of the U.S. government, incumbent governments of Latin America and the Caribbean, business organizations and assorted lobbies, political parties (where they still exist), and a host of protagonists, knaves, and villains—the characterization depending in large measure on one's political and social values.[14] It would be a mistake, however, to assess the cases solely in such terms. It is not the cast of characters that is ultimately important, but rather the roles they play and the drama that unfolds. When viewed in this fashion, the case studies suggest a substantially changed and still changing set of relationships.

Perhaps most striking is the enhanced role of the private banks and the international financial institutions.[15] As Stallings and others point out, it is only in the 1970's—and particularly after the OPEC-induced price increases of 1973–74—that the banks moved back to center stage in development financing in Latin America and the rest of the Third World. What she calls the "privatization" of capital flows is a central feature of North-South relations in our time, with vast implications for the development process, for the "who wins, who loses" questions posed earlier, and ultimately for such closely related issues as human rights. And where the banks are so deeply involved, can the International Monetary Fund be far behind? The answer for Peru is clearly "No," and in somewhat different fashion the answer for Argentina, Jamaica, Mexico, and other deeply indebted countries is the same. Furthermore, as the studies make clear, the role played by the IMF "this time around" is

14. Heroes, it should be noted, are strikingly absent.

15. As a simple quantitative indicator, the International Monetary Fund was mentioned only once in Cotler and Fagen, *Latin America and the United States* (p. 386). In contrast, the IMF is here central to the Argentine and Peruvian case studies, while also at least of passing importance in the Maingot and Fagen-Nau studies.

different both in intent and consequence from what it has been before.

Other agencies, institutions, and groups also have different and enhanced roles. As Klare and Arnson suggest, the programs of arms transfers from the United States to Latin America that were so characteristic of the 1960's and early 1970's are now much diminished quantitatively. Support for the military and police of selected Latin American governments continues, however, through the official arms "pipeline," commercial sales, the International Narcotics Control Program, and supply arrangements with Latin American weapons producers. Many of the same goals are pursued, but the modalities of U.S. support for repression in Latin America have changed. Related arguments about new varieties of pressure and involvement are made by Delli Sante with regard to business organizations, Fagen and Nau with regard to transnational corporations, and Volk and Evans with regard to aggrieved sectors of national capital and labor in the United States and elsewhere.

The most striking new feature on the hemispheric and international stage, however, is not the actors themselves, but the alliances they form. We live, it might be said, in the age of the unholy alliance. The wolves are seen to lie down with the sheep, and the politicians make common cause with those whom just a few short years ago they were denouncing as enemies of the people. Thus, Fagen and Nau sketch the manner in which the Mexican government allied itself with the international banks and U.S. gas transmission companies in an attempt to secure a price and import agreement from the U.S. government. Maingot, following Norman Girvan, predicts that even for relatively progressive governments like the Jamaican there will be "a new alliance between the corporate managers of the transnational aluminum companies and the buro-political managers of the Caribbean bauxite-producing states." Frenkel and O'Donnell explain why a political alliance between repressive military rulers and some sectors of the population who are badly hurt economically by the military's policies "makes sense" in the context of Argentina's recent history. Less initially surprising, but equally important in understanding the new context of foreign policy, are alliances of the sort pointed out by Evans (the triple one between the entrepreneurial Brazilian state, a segment of the largest owners of local capital, and the transnational corporations), by Stallings (between a rightward-turning Peruvian state and the international banks and the IMF), by Wolfe and Sanders (between Cold War liberals in the United States and important organizations on the right), and by Delli Sante (between U.S.-based transnational corporations and Mexican entrepreneurs).

How is this continuing process of alliance-making to be understood?

Not all alliances have the same explanation or the same dynamics, but two general characteristics should be noted. First, many alliances of substantial importance are not really struck between institutions or actors in any formal sense. Rather, they are what might be called "alliances of affinity," relationships that emerge from the logic of situations—sometimes but not always in consonance with class-based interests. An example would be the alliance between the military junta and financial speculators in Argentina, as described by Frenkel and O'Donnell. No memo of understanding was ever signed to consummate this alliance. The military junta and the IMF did not specifically set out to restructure the Argentine economy for the benefit of the speculators. But in practice they did create the conditions for the enrichment of the speculators and finance capital in general, and in the process an alliance of affinity with both political and economic dimensions was forged. So too in the United States: protectionist sectors of labor and capital, for example, often move in tandem to defend their interests in Congress and elsewhere. But only on rare occasions is this multiclass alliance formalized. More usually, it operates somewhat spontaneously, energized by a shared sense of beleaguerment and the search for survival strategies in an increasingly transnationalized world.

Second, a high percentage of the newer alliances involve private capital *and* the state, both North and South. This is an expected corollary of what was said earlier about contemporary capitalism and the processes of accumulation and distribution. It is increasingly difficult in today's world to "do business," nationally or internationally, without the active cooperation or participation of the state. This being the case, alliances between sectors of capital and the state—often involving international financial institutions as well—are really not surprising unless there is reason to posit a prior and basic antagonism between the partners. In some instances the form, duration, or intensity of the alliance may be unexpected, and certainly alliances often reflect rather than resolve other contradictions. But that there should be a continuing movement toward alliances that link the state (or groups and sectors within it) to economic actors is hardly startling.[16] Only the inordinately powerful can sometimes afford the luxury of operating outside the mantle of

---

16. Although not developed here, the more general theoretical point is important: In an era of declining U.S. hegemony in the hemisphere and elsewhere, these complex webs of alliances are a principal mechanism for integrating Latin America into world capitalism. Speaking somewhat metaphorically, they substitute for the threats, gunboats, and marines of yesterday, stabilizing and making more predictable complex and otherwise problematic relationships.

the state. And by definition the very weak have few opportunities to wrap themselves in the flag—while having many reasons to make the attempt.

IDEOLOGY AND LEGITIMACY

Perhaps no area of contemporary political and economic analysis is as confused and controversial as the study of ideology. The dictionary notion of ideology as "the body of ideas characteristic of a particular individual, group, or culture" would be accepted by many, although the majority if not all of the authors represented here would judge such a characterization to be analytically incomplete. So too with the concept of legitimacy. Its common sense meaning of "acceptance by those who are governed or ruled" at best captures the static aspects of the concept, leaving untouched the processes by which legitimacy (of states, governments, institutions, and policies) comes into being or disintegrates. Finally, the relationship between ideology (viewed most globally as a body of ideas) and legitimacy (understood as the values and perceptions validating a particular set of institutions or actions) is both complex and open-ended: a given universe of ideological discourse opens the way for certain means of legitimizing rule, but the former does not "determine" the latter in any direct sense. Even within a common ideological universe, fierce struggles to legitimate alternative institutions and modalities of governance can take place. The United States, for example, offers multiple examples of this process. There is a very high level of ideological consensus in the United States—and concomitantly minimal ideological debate. There is also, however, constant and sometimes fierce competition to appropriate a shared body of ideas and symbols and transmute them into support for particular policies and programs.

We cannot here attempt to bring order to this vast topic. It is important, however, to underline the central role played by the *problemática* of ideology and legitimacy in the papers that follow. For example, most of the case studies that deal directly with Latin America put ideological analysis close to the core of the investigation. This is particularly true for Delli Sante and for Maingot. The former asks how a national and transnational business community in Mexico, feeling threatened by a nationalistic and occasionally antibusiness climate during the Echeverría presidency, mobilized itself to conduct an ideological campaign (and by extenstion a legitimizing campaign) to change that climate. The study suggests that at that particular moment in Mexican history the political and economic conditions confronting business "required" the waging of a no-holds-barred ideological battle. Maingot, using many of the same analytical elements, underlines the international and national roots of the ideologies of West Indian socialism in Jamaica, Guyana, and Trinidad-Tobago. He argues convincingly that it is impossible to understand the particular forms that socialism has taken in the English-speaking Caribbean today without a deep appreciation of race, class, and the genesis of political parties and labor organizations. Although the different historical situations and cases lead the two authors to locate the ideology and legitimacy issues at different places in their investigations and explanations, they share a common commitment to attempting to understand the complex linkages between ideas and politics.

In somewhat different fashion, the Frenkel-O'Donnell paper on Argentina and the Stallings paper on Peru also explore the same linkages. As both make clear, the International Monetary Fund operates with a well-defined ideology, a body of ideas incorporating both a preferred set of outcomes and a favored way of achieving those outcomes. But what both papers also suggest—and what is ultimately more important—is the manner in which those ideas become articulated with and incorporated into ideologies *and* programs of national development.[17] The structure of repression, present from the time of the 1976 military take-over in Argentina and increasingly evident in Peru after the debt crisis began to surface in 1975, is closely linked to the austerity measures integral to the IMF-dictated programs undertaken in the name of the restoration of international "confidence." The IMF's ideas were critically important in creating a climate in which—and the machinery by which—the costs of restructuring the economy could be and were distributed in a certain way. So too, although less directly, with the question of legitimacy. In Argentina, as the authors point out, certain ways of viewing the ongoing political-economic crisis—ways that receive substantial encouragement from international financial institutions and foreign governments—lend credence and thus some legitimacy to continued military rule and repression. Somewhat to the contrary, the inability of government authorities in Peru and their friends abroad to articulate an acceptable explanation for the crisis and their handling of it has created

17. The capacity of the IMF to put its ideas into practice is all the more impressive because its control over capital flows (its major carrot and stick) is in large measure indirect. As both papers make clear, the "legitimizing function" of the IMF—giving a stamp of approval to the plans and practices of a national government and thus giving confidence to other lenders and governments—is a critical arm in its arsenal of control.

massive disaffection from military rule—expressed whenever the political process functions with some degree of openness.

In the examination of U.S. foreign policy, the essay that is most direct in posing the *problemática* of ideological analysis is Katznelson and Prewitt. In a discussion of "constitutionalism" in American politics, they link the ideological question directly to the conduct of foreign policy:

These special features of the U.S. regime modify, shape, and also obscure basic imperatives of the political economy in a number of important ways. They form the group and class actors who pay attention to foreign policy. They fashion a powerful ideology that organizes public discourse about foreign policy. The language of policy discussions between groups and classes in constitutionally defined arenas is ideological not only in the sense of masking exploitative relationships but also in the sense of creating a policy-relevant political culture that shapes apparently contradictory initiatives like support both for authoritarian regimes *and* for the promotion of human rights. The character of the arena of U.S. politics and of the relevant contending groups defines "legitimate" choices that policymakers can consider in public. It also compels them to operate covertly where this political culture does not permit open activity.

This is a rich and some would say controversial set of statements. Certainly it suggests an agenda for research designed to specify the manner in which the ideology is linked to structural features of the U.S. economy, the way in which the policy contradictions are worked out in practice, and the occasions on which—and the extent to which—policy implementation "goes covert" because the political culture will not easily sustain a public display of wrong-doing.

The same cluster of issues is raised in the Wolfe and Sanders essay on the Committee on the Present Danger, and the comments by Earl Ravenal and Pino-Santos on that essay. All four authors would agree that the Cold War as a continuing and central feature of U.S. foreign policy has to be understood in both ideological and structural terms.[18] Where they would begin to part ways is on how one models or understands the relationships between an ideology, changing circumstances nationally and internationally, the men and women who have responsibility for making decisions in such changing environments, and the essentially *unchanging*

18. Klare and Arnson also touch on this theme when they discuss the manner in which national security ideology in the 1960's—and the fear of "other Cubas"—led to the arming and training of Latin American police and military forces.

features of the political economy of the United States. A preferred ordering of these elements of understanding is stated most clearly by Pino-Santos. Basing his critique on a classical Marxist approach to the study of ideology and material interests, Pino-Santos comments that Wolfe and Sanders's "interesting and very important study would improve substantially if its authors, while not ignoring the superstructural manifestations of certain historical processes . . . would ponder the real importance of the phenomena that take place in the base, in the relations of production and the corresponding structures, behaviors, and class struggles." Wolfe and Sanders would probably not disagree with this as a checklist of the factors with which a fuller analysis ought to deal—nor most probably would Ravenal. But what such general agreement again highlights is the great difficulty of combining multiple levels of analysis in a case study of ideology, legitimacy, and the structural determinants of national policy. In fact, the closer to actual case materials, the more difficult it seems to be to keep the underlying structural factors at the center of the analysis. This is not a counsel of despair, only a reminder of the kinds of challenges sure to be encountered when one insists that the study of foreign policy must include not only an analysis of ideas but also an understanding of the forces that give birth, sustenance, and staying-power to those ideas.

VALUES, CHOICES, AND POLICY

The study of international and foreign relations is, among other things, the examination of values made manifest in choices and policies. The cases that follow are, in this sense, profoundly normative. They deal with value-laden topics; and as a rule the political and social preferences of the authors are discernible, if not always overtly argued. This is as it should be, for nothing is gained and much is lost by attempts to obscure the normative components of this subject matter.

These normative components, as should now be clear, are not something "tacked onto" the topics. They are built into the choice-making and policy-making features of contemporary society. As emphasized at the outset, in both rich and poor nations, state action is constantly conditioning processes of accumulation and distribution—tilting outcomes in favor or against other nations, classes, groups, and persons. Issues of social justice cannot be separated from these basic economic processes as mediated by the state. Less immediately evident to some, but equally real, are the values embedded in the policies promulgated by the ostensibly "nonpolitical" international financial institutions. Perhaps most obvious of all as normative issues are the multiple degradations visited on citizens of the Americas by repressive regimes and the common condition of grinding poverty that affects tens of millions of people even in the so-called "middle income" countries.

In closing, therefore, it seems fitting to sketch the main political/ normative concerns that pervade the essays: the East-West struggle, national security, and developmental alternatives. In so doing, we will necessarily lose detail and nuance in an attempt to synthesize; but the price is well worth paying. By asking the "big questions" we remind ourselves that the social sciences gain importance to the extent that they inform choices and illuminate alternatives and their consequences. In turn, we emphasize that these choices, alternatives, and consequences profoundly affect the lives, freedoms, and futures of real men and women—in this hemisphere and beyond.

Despite the optimistic assumptions of some, détente between the United States and the Soviet Union did not signal the end of the East-West struggle or challenge the basic assumptions of national security thinking in foreign and domestic policy. Although some of the rules of the game have changed, the contest continues. Recent events in the hemisphere, involving Panama, Cuba, and Nicaragua, all quickly became enmeshed in the net of Cold War perspectives. And at least half of the case studies that follow provide insights into the manner in which the national security preoccupations of the 1950's and 1960's continue into the 1970's—albeit partially transmuted by changed circumstances.

The normative issues raised by a national security approach to foreign and domestic politics are not limited to the immorality of the interventionist and murderous scenarios that have so often accompanied that particular way of viewing and acting upon the world. Ultimately, there is no way to control these scenarios without restructuring the criteria by which policy initiatives and responses are judged. As Ravenal points out in his comment on Wolfe and Sanders, national security politics cannot be humanized by gathering more and better information on the persons and systems that are allegedly threatening. There is always the strong possibility, and in many instances the certainty, that in so informing yourself you will discover that "they" are even *more* threatening than you had previously imagined. At that point, consistency and "responsible" politics dictate a stronger reaction against the threat, often implying more vigorous intervention and heightened repression. Rather, what is needed is a sharp break with the past, a reordering of decisional criteria. Such a reordering is a political and normative act, one that clearly subordinates national security concerns, as presently understood, to other and more humane values.[19]

Earlier it was suggested that "the question of distribution" is central to an understanding of, and debates about, the workings of contemporary capitalism, North and South. This is clearly a question that does not fit neatly into disciplinary boxes, involving as it does not only technical economic subjects but also the classic political issues of "who gets what, when, and how" (as well as the mirror image "who suffers what, when, and how"). Additionally, distributive issues are preeminently normative, implying complex linkages between visions of what "ought to be" and alternative possibilities for moving from a less preferred present to a more preferred future. In sum, there is no escape from the value dimensions of developmental dilemmas viewed as distributional problems and challenges.[20]

If failures of distribution are central to a normative critique of contemporary capitalism, however, the question of alternatives to capitalist development naturally suggests itself.[21] To some extent the Maingot case touches on this issue in the English-speaking Caribbean, but in general the case studies only hint at alternatives to present political-economic relationships. In the main this is because it is impossible to do a case study of something (alternative development models) that does not really exist in the hemisphere—with the exception of Cuba. Nevertheless, what is suggested by the studies taken as a whole is the manner in which the political-economy of the United States, and the larger global system of which it forms a key part, impedes the emergence of alternative developmental experiments. It is at this point that the national security approach to foreign policy and the commitment to

19. I am not suggesting that such reorderings can be accomplished in voluntaristic fashion, by an act of will that overcomes structures of interest and power in the United States and elsewhere. As current controversies over human rights and foreign policy suggest, national security approaches to decision-making benefit important sectors of U.S. society—including the public and private bureaucracies that manage the far-flung American empire. Nor again—referring to the human rights controversies—is there reason to believe that a reordering of priorities would come easily, quickly, or without associated costs. I simply mean to emphasize the value-choice components of a move away from national security approaches to policy.

20. This is true both in the Third World and in the United States and elsewhere. Despite much higher levels of aggregate wealth, questions of who will benefit from and who will bear the burdens of "development" in the United States are very much in evidence in several cases.

21. I have dealt with this and a number of related topics in some detail in "Equity in the South in the Context of North-South Relations," in Albert Fishlow et al., *Rich and Poor Nations in the World Economy* (New York, 1978).

capitalist or state-capitalist patterns of development are seen to be intimately related. Socialism remains a dirty word among U.S. elites concerned with the hemisphere, not just because it potentially "opens the door to Soviet and Cuban influence," but also because it threatens to upset the current patterning of national and international winners and losers. "One cannot stand idly by," as Henry Kissinger once said about Chile under Allende, while the structure of power is so radically altered. One of the virtues of these cases is that they suggest the meaning of that statement in a hemisphere where the Marines have not left their barracks since 1965, where significant changes in national and international relations have occurred, yet where the basic patterning of those who profit and those who lose remains much the same as it was two decades ago. In this stagnation in the midst of change, and misery in the midst of plenty, are found two of the key ethical challenges of our time.

Part One

Understanding the United States
and U.S. Foreign Policy

Constitutionalism, Class, and the Limits of Choice in U.S. Foreign Policy

IRA KATZNELSON AND KENNETH PREWITT

As an object of explanation, U.S. policy toward Latin America has been more diverse and more changeable than many analysts have allowed. Latin America is an unwieldly unit for analysis. The immense differences between nation-states—in size, wealth, geopolitical capacity, character of regime, and independence from U.S. direction—and the vast range of alternative policies practiced by the United States at any one time—including disaster aid, counterinsurgency training, credit, economic "destabilization," immigration control, drug traffic management, and, on occasion, direct military intervention—make it difficult to speak in unitary terms about U.S. policies toward the hemisphere as a whole. This difficulty is compounded by the obvious oscillations in emphasis in both the rhetoric and the performance of U.S. policymakers, who have alternated over time between "soft" policies associated with being a Good Neighbor and with the Alliance for Progress and "hard" policies such as the Bay of Pigs, the Dominican invasion of 1965, and the unremitting hostility to the Allende experiment in constitutional socialism.

From Kennedy to Carter the overall trajectory of U.S. policies has been one of less overt intervention, some economic disengagement, and more rhetorical concern with human rights and the quality of life. No marines have landed since 1965. With the obvious exception of Chile, U.S. administrations have worked hard to transmit a more benign image of their activities in the hemisphere.

Neither the complexity of U.S.–Latin American relations nor the

Ira Katznelson chairs the Department of Political Science at the University of Chicago. He is the author of *Black Men, White Cities: Race, Politics, and Migration in the United States, 1900–1930, and Britain, 1948–1968*, and *City Trenches: The Patterning of Class in the United States* (forthcoming). Kenneth Prewitt is President of the Social Science Research Council and has taught political science at the University of Chicago and Stanford University. He is the author of *The Recruitment of Political Leaders: A Study of Citizen-Politicians*, and co-author of *Labyrinths of Democracy: Adaptations, Linkages, Representation, and Policies in Urban Politics*.

changes in administration emphases, however, should be allowed to obscure a very high degree of fundamental continuity in U.S. policy. Two underlying principles have been most important: first, the maintenance of a skewed pattern of north-south geopolitical capacity; and second, the maintenance of a skewed pattern of distribution of economic opportunities and rewards. The whole gamut of U.S. policies concerned with aid, trade, activities of international organizations, investment, and military security has been directed, at least since the end of the Second World War, at "the preservation and extension of North American political, economic, and cultural influence and domination in the hemisphere, at the lowest possible cost."[1] These practices have maintained dependent industrialization characterized by growing foreign control over industrial development, competitive advantages to foreign firms, a deformation of local industry, planned expansion in harmony with the needs of external purchasers of exports rather than with those of the home market, and the outflow of profits. In addition, they have supported the formation and dominance of clientele local classes with a vested interest in such patterns. The varied policies of the United States have been vital to the maintenance of this status quo in a number of ways. The United States has set clear and widely understood limits to the acceptable behavior of Latin American governments. In so doing, it has provided regimes willing to operate within these bounds with the means to survive in spite of their shaky legitimacy. The United States also provides the security necessary to insure the capacity of its firms to participate in the bounty of dependency.

Policy analyses of U.S. activities in Latin America have generally proceeded at two very different levels: on the one hand, political economy explanations have made sense of the overriding goals of dominance and the maintenance of a structure of dependent inequality; on the other hand, ad hoc treatments have made sense of alterations in policy over time, stressing changing situational factors. Neither approach is wrong so much as insufficient. Each fails to describe "middle-range" characteristics of the U.S. regime that are special in the universe of capitalist democracies yet more enduring than the monthly or yearly flow of events.

Concretely, we argue that two closely related features of the U.S. regime are basic to an understanding of the pattern of oscillations in foreign policy within a consistent set of hegemonic goals. The first of

    1. Richard R. Fagen, "Commentary on Einaudi," in Julio Cotler and Richard R. Fagen, eds., *Latin America and the United States: The Changing Political Realities* (Stanford, Calif., 1974), p. 262.

these characteristics is the "low stateness" of the polity. Though the size and functions of the state have grown enormously in this century, and especially since the Second World War, the United States is a peculiar democracy with an ideology and practice of divided and circumscribed government. One keen observer, J. P. Nettl,[2] went so far as to say that at the domestic level the United States lacks a state in the German or French sense. There is, in short, a paradox of big but diffuse government.

The second characteristic is the "low classness" of social and political life in the United States. The country is the most developed of all the capitalist societies and thus is divided objectively between collective capital and collective labor more fully than any other. Yet with the partial exception of workplace relations, U.S. politics is organized on a plurality of affiliations of a nonclass kind, and the country lacks even the modest kind of social democracy associated with Great Britain or West Germany.

The impact of these distinctive features of the regime on domestic politics and policymaking is overwhelming; in various ways, to be sure, virtually all modes of social and political analysis deal with them when internal U.S. affairs are being considered. Their relevance for a consideration of foreign policy obviously is more opaque. Accordingly, we wish to complement work in the political economy tradition as well as ad hoc case studies by exploring connections between the state as an actor in the international system and those of its durable features that may condition and limit foreign policies.

First, we will explore the middle-range characteristics of the U.S. regime and specify the dynamic relationship between the character of state and class relations over time. Second, we will suggest ways in which these middle-range features in fact act importantly, if mostly at the margin, to inform the content of U.S. foreign policy.

STATE, CLASS, AND THE U.S. REGIME

The term "capitalist state" has been the subject of much theoretical and historical discussion within the Marxist tradition, revolving around the question, How can democracy and capitalism be maintained and re-created simultaneously? Virtually all the answers—whether they emphasize differential recruitment patterns, the special capacity of capital

2. J. P. Nettl, "The State as a Conceptual Variable," *World Politics* 20 (July 1968), pp. 559–92.

as an interest group, the "selective" character of the mechanisms that link society and politics, or the dependence by the state on a revenue surplus generated by successful capitalist accumulation—share with Nicos Poulantzas the formulation that it is the state that manages the tensions between capitalism and democracy by functioning as the "factor of political organization of the dominant classes" and as the "factor of political disorganization" of the working classes.[3]

This approach rightly understands that the state is not simply a passive recipient of class and group pressures but an entity whose very structure conditions whether and how class will be made politically relevant. This process and its effects cannot be understood, however, at the generic level of the "capitalist state" except to indicate or project broad tendencies. Rather, within the structural logic imposed by industrial capitalism, individual states with their own form of government are connected to social structures conditioned by different historical traditions. If the ideal-typical capitalist state tends to organize the dominant and disorganize the subordinate classes, we still must ask, How do distinctive states actually perform these functions? With what mechanisms and with what degree of success? How does the state shape the unequal and competing capacities of classes as historical social groups?

Our discussion of the regime in the United States revolves around these issues. The pattern of class formation, one of "low classness," developed before the Civil War and was caused largely by the constitutional organization of the polity. In turn the pattern of class relations has contributed to the reproduction of the "low stateness" of U.S. democracy. Over time these mutually reinforcing elements have fashioned a regime distinctive in the West, one whose key features inform and constrain the making of foreign policy.

The United States is characterized by an extraordinary diversity of collective affiliations. Class does not provide the central theme organizing political conflict. Class relations do not seem as simple or transparent as elsewhere in the industrial capitalist world. The links between categories of individuals shaped by their places in production and social and political behavior appear more remote, or at least less obvious. Given that the United States has the most developed of the capitalist economies, this anomaly has been very puzzling.

As in all the other capitalist states, the "economic motion" of capital underpins struggles at work, in residence communities, and between

---

3. Nicos Poulantzas, *Pouvoir politique et classes sociale* (Paris, 1971), vol. 2, p. 116.

citizens and the state. But more than in any other capitalist society, each of these arenas of conflict has been unusually enclosed and encapsulated in the United States. The links, especially between work and community, have been tenuous. Each locus of conflict has had its own vocabulary and form of institutional expression—residence and groups, local parties, churches, and voluntary associations; workplace and unions. Class has been lived and politically expressed as a *series* of *partial* relationships and is experienced, therefore, as one of a number of competing bases of social life.

The differentiation of social life into work, community, and state relations is, of course, an objective feature characteristic of all capitalist (and perhaps all industrial) development. Because life outside the workplace is free from the authority of capital or management and because workers, unlike slaves, sell their labor time and not themselves, patterns of life and culture in residence communities constitute in large measure an autonomous sphere of private life. Here the worker is a consumer, a member of a family, a resident of a territory, a person interacting with others, sharing ethnicity, race, and interests. Such interactions may be affective or instrumental or both. It is hardly surprising to find that work lives and community lives may be perceived as unconnected. What is distinctive about the experience of the United States, however, is the extent to which the linguistic, cultural, and institutional meanings given to this differentiation have taken such an extremely serial character *in the polity* for so long.

What has been exceptional about the experience of class in the United States, in short, is that the split between work and community has been reproduced ideologically and institutionally in ways that have fragmented patterns of class in qualitatively distinctive fashion. Elsewhere in the West the tendency to parcelization has been partly countered by competing "global" institutions, which provide understandings of class. Such interpretations are to be found in the history, rhetoric, programs, and organizational strategies (joining work and home) of social democratic, socialist, laborist, and communist parties, and of voluntary associations. They often, but do not necessarily, entail revolutionary interpretations of capital and the class structure. It is the virtual absence of even moderate global approaches to class—and the massive resistance to such attempts in the past—that is so striking about the U.S. experience.

As early as the Civil War, the American working class, at the level of class formation, had become labor; it has remained so to the present. The nonwork aspects of the lives of working people have been organized into politics on other bases, including those of race, ethnicity, and territoriality. Because workers are not structured into political life in terms that produce a coherent working class at the level of dispositions, workers lack the capacity to counterpose the interests of capital as a whole to those of the working class as a whole. Rather, workers affect political life as members of interest groups that sometimes utilize the language and grammar of class and sometimes the language and grammar of other group identifications.

The sources of this unusual pattern of class relations may be located in the intersection of the dynamics of capitalist development and citizenship in the three decades before the Civil War. In this period the creation of a modern working class, principally in the older, predominantly mercantile cities of the East, which entailed the physical and social separation of work and community, was accompanied and given meaning by the culmination of a number of reinforcing *political* trends that collectively defined the terms by which workers would be linked to the polity: federalism, franchise extensions, a modern national party system, and its neighborhood (not yet centralized) machine affiliates. Citizenship intersected community, not work. In this way citizenship and its bases were given communal meanings separate from work relations. The segmented pattern of class understandings in the United States thus was caused principally by features of the polity created by the operation of a federal constitutional system. The constitutionalism of the regime has continued to matter, not only for the character of class relations but also for the ways constitutionalism has shaped a polity of "low stateness."

From the perspective of the international system, "the state is the basic irreducible unit, equivalent to the individual person in a society."[4] The salience of a state—"stateness," in Nettl's term—is highest where foreign affairs are concerned. However, not all nations exhibit the same degree of stateness. The salience of a state is highly variable, depending in large measure on the character of its organization, the autonomy of other sectors of society, the degree of plurality in modes of representation, and the language and idiom of political life. "Low stateness," paradoxically, is compatible with big government and with an assertive foreign policy; and such is the case in the United States.

The "stateness" of the United States in the international arena is at least as great as that of any other nation-state. The growth in the size and capacity of government is also not in doubt. Total government expenditures accounted for only about 7 percent of the GNP at the turn

4. J. P. Nettl, "The State as a Conceptual Variable," p. 563.

of the century, compared to 37 percent today. Yet, understood comparatively, the state—the autonomous organized sector of society that authoritatively taxes, preserves order, potentially conscripts, makes foreign policy—is less tangible, more diffuse, and more interpenetrated by nonstate actors than virtually anywhere in Western Europe. "Low stateness" in the United States is foreshadowed in the design of the constitutional system and can best be described by turning to the originating document, the Constitution itself.

Now in existence for almost 200 years, the Constitution proclaims a theory of government, popularizes a language of politics, establishes decision rules and institutional arrangements, and creates a political regime accepted largely without question. To be sure, there have been serious political conflicts about the interpretation of the Constitution, the most violent of which became a full-fledged civil war; but with the exception of the Civil War era, major political movements have not been organized around a demand for a different constitution.

The Constitution is more than a set of political rules; it was designed to be compatible with an economic framework under which citizens expect to find happiness by maximizing private gain. The Constitution does not establish a state that in turn manages the affairs of society toward some clear conception of the public welfare; rather, it establishes a political economy in which the public welfare is the aggregate of private preferences. The constitutional order has benefited quite directly from the impressive standard of living provided many citizens by U.S. industrial capitalism. Consumer satisfactions in a materialistic society shade over into commitment to the "American way of life," which in turn translates in the public mind as loyalty to the constitutional order.

There are additional and more "political" reasons for the stability enjoyed by the constitutional regime in U.S. history. For example, it is hard to rebel against "low stateness," for there is not much of a target for rebellion. This does not mean that every segment of the population is necessarily satisfied with public policy. But dissatisfaction most frequently takes the form of trying to force a new and more favorable interpretation of the Constitution. Black anger, for example, has been directed not at the dissolution of public order but at racist public policies and laws, at making the Constitution work. Social movements, especially when fueled by egalitarian or redistributive demands, tend to express anger at those public policies that get in the way of some group's ability to maximize private interests (upward mobility for blacks, equal treatment for women). Public policies neutralize this anger by improving the access of the deprived group to the rewards of a consumer-oriented capitalism. That this may deprive some other group (white male workers, for instance) only calls forth another round of policies to ameliorate their discontent. Never in this endless shuffling does the Constitution itself become the target. Rather, constitutional principles legitimate claims for a fair share of "the American way of life," and constitutional interpretations and reinterpretations are the means for forcing reallocations.

The design of the Constitution was not merely an attempt to create a framework for the pursuit of gain. It was an experiment with unprecedented political forms aimed at avoiding political tyranny and establishing real, if limited, popular sovereignty. The fear of centralized authority and the search for democratic safeguards led the designers of the new government to the principle of limited powers, which was to be realized primarily through dividing and diffusing sovereignty. The United States was the first nation to self-consciously experiment with the heretical doctrine that sovereignty need not be established with a single pyramid of power. There was to be no unified state at the apex of public life in the United States.

The writers of the Constitution identified their primary challenge as the creation of a government that would have sufficient powers to control the governed while also being obliged to control itself against the tendency toward tyranny. This was to be accomplished, according to *The Federalist Papers*, "by so contriving the interior structure of the government so that its several constituent parts may, by their mutual relations, be the means of keeping each other in their proper place."[5]

A government of divided powers was established in two steps. First, formal government powers should be divided between two layers of government—national and state, or central and regional. The second dimension of divided powers is the doctrine that the different branches of government—legislative, judicial, and executive—were autonomous in their own spheres, each being given the constitutional means to resist domination by the other two.

Together the two dimensions of divided powers significantly lowered the salience of the state. Nettl understands this point precisely in his review of the separation of political authority among different layers and branches of government. "Hence in the United States," he writes, "the real boundaries of autonomy fall not between the state and other institutions but within and between the complex of institutions that

5. *Federalist Paper* No. 51.

elsewhere would be encapsulated within the collectivity of the state.
. . . This internalization of distinct areas of institutional autonomy is
the fundamental implication of the separation of powers."[6]

Limited government was to be achieved not only through separation
of powers but also through the application of such doctrines as "a government of laws, not men." The independent judiciary is particularly
critical here. In addition to adjudicating civil and criminal transgressions
against society, the judiciary measures the actions of government itself
against the principles of the Constitution. Stated more generally, the
United States is a government of legislation and litigation. Where the
political order is legitimate, as U.S. constitutionalism is, politics becomes
the struggle to translate social and economic interests into law. Once
group interests become law, they cease to be group interests and appear
as those of society in general. The government then assumes the task
of getting others in society to do things in a manner that promotes the
interests of the group. If legislation is at the core of those processes that
translate group interests into general law, *the political culture defines
political power as getting a law passed.* Though starting from a different point, Nettl reaches a similar conclusion. In his description of the
United States, he notes that "in practice only law is sovereign, and probably the 'function' of sovereignty can indeed best be taken as being fulfilled and institutionalized by the law."[7]

Constitutional democracy and the sovereignty of law, together with
the segmented character of workplace and community bases of affiliation, constitute the idiom of U.S. politics. Political business could not
be conducted without such terms as "citizen participation," "majority
rule," "due process of law," "accountable leaders," "regular elections,"
"civil rights," "civilian control of the military," and "free press." Except
in rare instances and in small numbers, U.S. citizens do not question
whether they are governed by democratic procedures, let alone whether
democracy is the best form of government. Group and class conflicts,
tensions, and struggles are refined in this crucible.

THE LIMITS OF CHOICE IN U.S. FOREIGN POLICY

The regime elements of "low classness" and "low stateness" affect
U.S. foreign policy not by providing the basic impetus for the international activities of the state but by creating a context for policymaking

6. J. P. Nettl, "The State as a Conceptual Variable," p. 569.
7. *Ibid.*, p. 574.

that is distinctive among the advanced capitalist democracies of the
West. These special features of the U.S. regime modify, shape, and also
obscure basic imperatives of the political economy in a number of important ways. They form the group and class actors who pay attention
to foreign policy. They fashion a powerful ideology that organizes public discourse about foreign policy. The language of policy discussions
between groups and classes in constitutionally defined arenas is ideological not only in the sense of masking exploitative relationships but also
in the sense of creating a policy-relevant political culture that shapes
apparently contradictory initiatives like support both for authoritarian
regimes *and* for the promotion of human rights. The character of the
arena of U.S. politics and of the relevant contending groups defines
"legitimate" choices that policymakers can consider in public. It also
compels them to operate covertly where this political culture does not
permit open activity. Finally, the "low classness" and "low stateness" of
the regime make it very difficult, if not impossible, to fashion the political agency required to make even modest progressive changes in current U.S. practices in Latin America. Let us take up these matters in
turn.

All the capitalist democracies of the West act to reproduce a capitalist
order because they cannot do otherwise. These states depend in the first
instance—whatever their aims apart from the recreation of capitalism—
on the productive apparatus to generate a surplus that can be taxed to
provide revenue for state activities. Making the economy work is both
the primary goal and the political test of incumbent governments. Dictates of political prudence thus reinforce the imperatives of the political
economy to make the needs of business the chief business of government.
Virtually everywhere in the West, however, these powerful imperatives
are modified by working-class organizational and ideological capacities.
Yet the distinctive "low classness" of political and social life in the
United States largely precludes these working-class pressures from playing an important role in the making of domestic and foreign policy. As
a result, the U.S. state possesses an unusually strong capacity to insulate
class-interested policies from the countervailing pressures of an organized working class, and to make many public policies appear technically and politically neutral with solutions beneficial to all members of
the society. Intense public attention to issues is thus limited largely to
those matters that directly affect highly organized groups and associations. The very pluralism of American life outside the workplace
thus fashions a degree of freedom for the relations between the state
and capital virtually unknown elsewhere.

Given the absence of a socialist or social democratic ethic, ideology, and definition of the working class as a whole, workers appear in the political process almost exclusively as organized labor. The capacities of organized labor to affect domestic and foreign policy are considerable. In the area of social welfare expenditures, for example, precisely those programs in the relatively emaciated American welfare state that directly affect the material well-being and security of the unionized 20 percent of the workforce—especially programs of social insurance—have been the ones to grow the fastest and to show the least discrepancy with expenditure patterns in Western Europe. With respect to foreign policy, organized labor is a member—albeit the least important member —of a specialized coalition whose other members are transnational capital and the national security managers of the state. Once policies are considered in terms not of class conflict but of a cross-class, hegemonic interest-group framework, labor by and large joins with capital and the state in the role of interest group. Organized labor, then, fully shares with its coalition partners an interest in current relationships of domination, for it harvests with its partners the fruits of the structure of dependency. Most of labor's activities in Latin America in the past half century, including its close cooperation with U.S. intelligence agencies, are comprehensible only in those terms.

The plurality of nonwork identifications and affiliations in the United States produces much intense attention to domestic policymaking. Clients of specific state programs, for example, together with those who administer such programs develop a stake in their continuation and expansion.[8] Such collectivities—along with organized labor, traditional interest groups, and racial and ethnic groups—all press with varying degrees of success to shape government activity. By contrast, the freedom of the state to act in foreign affairs is much greater, because those outside the foreign policy coalition rarely pay much attention to international matters. Indeed, unless a foreign relations issue cuts close to questions of economic well-being (more often than not defined in hegemonic terms), it is unlikely to draw widespread public notice. Selective inattention leaves the foreign policy coalition relatively unconstrained, except in cases where particular subpublics closely monitor particular issue arenas, as is the case with pro-Israel groups and Middle East policies. On the whole, such subpublics do not exist with respect to Latin America, the main exceptions being associations like Amnesty International, concerned with civil and political rights.

8. Morris Janowitz, *Social Control of the Welfare State* (Chicago, 1977).

"Low classness" and "low stateness" also fashion an idiom of politics that makes an active role in foreign affairs very difficult for the public. The ordinary democratic, constitutional grammar of U.S. political discourse has no place for terms like "imperialism," "military aggression," "covert operations," "puppet regime," and "subversion." The absence of an appropriate vocabulary and language does not mean that U.S. citizens support military aggression, such as the Bay of Pigs, or covert operations, such as the undermining of the Allende regime; but these acts, even when recognized for what they are, are dismissed as temporary deviations.

Consider Vietnam. There was a brief period during which the antiwar movement called into question the benign nature of U.S. foreign and military policy. But the general public, even when it began to question the wisdom of the war, never adopted the language of the antiwar movement. Moreover, the end of the war quickly removed the rhetoric of the antiwar movement from public discourse, dismissing it to the left-wing journals and scattered academics where and among whom it had originated. American foreign policy was scarred by Vietnam, but the democratic idiom so central to the political culture remained intact. Even in more routine periods the democratic idiom disguises the imperialism of much of U.S. foreign policy. As we noted earlier, it also plants in the political culture the lesson that politics is primarily law-passing—not a lesson easily applied in the international setting.

The language of U.S. politics, however, does not merely contribute to a masking of state activities; it also helps shape them. This "positive" effect takes two forms. First, the routine grammar of political life makes it important for policymakers to emphasize those features of their activities that mesh with the constitutionalism of the regime: the United States acts to promote liberty and human rights abroad, to alleviate suffering, to help the poor help themselves. Though hardly the only cause of "soft" side to U.S. policies abroad, the need to explain and legitimate state activities in terms of the ordinary language of a regime of "low stateness" and "low classness" should not be underestimated. Those features of foreign policy most easily apprehended in the language of democracy—as in the case of individualistic human rights—are the most clearly recognized by the public at large, thus placing limits on what government can do.

Second, the language and understandings of constitutionalism help define the boundary between overt and covert activity. Obviously, a "constitutionally dominated" foreign policy is hardly the whole picture. Many features of U.S. policy are clearly incompatible with the rules and spirit of the constitutional game. The image of a "limited government" cannot easily mesh with the realities of a national security state that include a far-flung intelligence network, support for military regimes around the world, a propaganda program aimed at audiences within the United States and abroad, active promotion of and participation in regional military-security alliances, and sustained research and development in weaponry. Such ideas as legislation-dominated political processes, and such doctrines as separation of powers, are in apparent contradiction with an executive-centered foreign policy process and descriptions of the "imperial presidency" that have become fashionable in the United States.

More strikingly, how can it be said that constitutional principles guide a foreign policy that makes extensive use of covert operations, repression of dissident opinions, bribery, secrecy, and the like? Alan Wolfe has suggested that the United States has been governed by a "Dual State": "In domestic politics, there existed a state that was popular, democratic, constitutional. . . . Centered in the legislative branches of government, it was based on rules that were reassuring: executives executed, legislators legislated, and judges judged. Certain standards of conduct—like due process of law, democratic representations, and appeals to history and tradition—were expected to receive homage."[9] Wolfe argues that these constitutional principles were impotent in the 1960's and early 1970's, at least in foreign policy, as they increasingly were replaced by authoritarian and secret government. "At some point during the 1960's, then, a fully developed Dual State had come into existence. Because it was secret, very few were aware of its creation. . . . Because it had no public accountability, it was arrogant and ruthless. . . . Because it considered itself omniscient, it developed its own language, its own code words, its own rules of proper reality."[10] Wolfe is arguing that in an effort to protect its commercial empire and to extend its means of accumulating capital, the United States suspended the rules of the Constitution in order to pursue a repressive foreign policy.

Borrowing from Wolfe, we can conclude that a more inclusive picture of the foreign policy process would have to understand the conditions under which there is constitutionally dominated policy and the condi-

9. Alan Wolfe, *The Limits of Legitimacy* (New York, 1977), p. 179.
10. *Ibid.*, p. 203.

tions under which the Constitution is for all practical purposes suspended.[11] The suspension of the Constitution no doubt occurs when there is a crisis. We suggest that foreign policy oscillates between being constitutionally dominated and being crisis-dominated.

Of course, this only begs the question. The analysis would have to deal with what a crisis is and who gets to do the labeling. Such an analysis would too greatly extend our discussion, but in preliminary and tentative fashion we can suggest a distinction between "real crises" and "manipulated crises." A "real crisis" might be a complete oil embargo, invasion of Taiwan by Communist China, Soviet-supported coups across Africa, and so forth. Attentive publics in the United States would probably be willing to tolerate suspension of certain constitutional constraints, as they did with the Tonkin Gulf resolution or the internment of Japanese-American citizens at the beginning of the Second World War. A "manipulated crisis" might occur when some special interests abroad needed to be protected, such as American business interests when Allende was elected. There might be a suspension of constitutional constraints, but covert action would be much more likely, because it would be difficult to sustain a suspension. One way to think about foreign policy under different presidents is to ask how much room there is for "manipulated" crises. Certainly there is less room under Carter than there was under Nixon.

Finally, the middle-range features of the U.S. regime make progressive reforms in Latin American policy more difficult to achieve than in other capitalist democracies. There is no dearth of concrete policy proposals that would assist more progressive forces in the hemisphere. One such list includes changes in the present pattern of trade preferences and commodity arrangements; debt rescheduling; the normalization of relations with Cuba; the cessation of police and counterinsurgency aid; the liquidation of the Overseas Private Investment Corporation, which protects U.S. investors from market risks; and a shift from loans to grants in development assistance.[12] None of these changes would require revolutionary transformations in U.S. capitalism or democracy. Nevertheless, they are highly unlikely to be implemented (even by an administration anxious to project benign intentions to the Third World)—first because of the features of U.S. politics and society discussed above, and second, because of the absence of state capacity to direct the internal distribution of costs entailed by a less imperialist foreign policy. The

---

11. Wolfe raised this point in discussion at the conference where an earlier draft of our essay was presented.

12. Fagen, "Commentary on Einaudi," in Cotler and Fagen, eds., p. 260.

constitutional doctrines of limited government, divided powers, and individual liberty, coupled with the practices of a market economy and the absence of a working class at the level of class formation, put a limit on the type of central authoritative agency that can emerge in the United States.

The "low stateness" of the regime is especially demonstrated by the absence of a centralized planning function. Central government planning with respect to land use, regional distributions, labor market trajectories, and industrial policy are common in virtually all of the capitalist democracies. In the United States, by contrast, although individual state policies and clusters of policies have important ramifications in each of these areas, national economic planning on the European model does not exist. The absence of a planning tradition or function in the United States makes it difficult (some say impossible) for the United States to absorb the costs of any substantial reform in foreign policy toward Latin America. These policies are constructed upon and maintain asymmetric power relations and skewed distributions of economic resources between the north and the south. The consequent U.S. advantages work to the benefit of nearly all segments and classes of U.S. society. The high consumption standards of advanced industrial capitalism, it should be remembered, produce a standard of living even for its poorer classes that easily outdistances the subsistence-level conditions of the majority of peasants and workers in the Third World.

A progressive foreign policy toward Latin America (or, more generally, toward the nonindustrialized, low-consumption nations) would have equity as one of its goals and would include some attempt to reduce the enormous disparity between the hemispheres. At a minimum this would involve tolerance of Latin American regimes committed to equity within their own societies—exactly the regimes that present U.S. policy consistently subverts. What impedes the development of a more progressive foreign policy is suggested by the larger point we have made about "low stateness" and the absence of a planning function in the United States: any policy that would close the relative gap between the north and the south would involve some reduction in economic growth and consumption in the United States. The costs of this reduction would have to be allocated across the different regions and classes of U.S. society. In the absence both of any larger views about the appropriate levels of production and consumption and of some planning function to implement these views, the allocation of such costs becomes exceedingly difficult. Given the diffuseness of power, the democratic controls, and the hold of marketplace values in the United States, any attempt to allocate the costs of reduced consumption would impose heavy political costs.

The fate of affirmative-action programs is instructive. Affirmative action was introduced and promoted as a way to overcome several centuries of racism, but once understood by the public as a policy to redistribute rewards (jobs and schooling for jobs) from the classes that have controlled those rewards to the classes that have not, it aroused political opposition with a forcefulness that has attenuated it, if not dismantled it. An analogy to foreign policy is not far-fetched. It took a century of internal strife for the majority of white Americans to acknowledge the racism that they lived with every day. To recognize the more distant imperialism and exploitation in foreign affairs is obviously a much more difficult task. Without this recognition, however, "affirmative action" in foreign policy is not likely.

Assume for the sake of argument that the U.S. public could be made to understand that it shares responsibility for the exploitation of Latin American societies. Should we then expect "affirmative action" in which some deliberate attempt to atone for that exploitation would be made? The question is obviously rhetorical. Given the sharpened competition for the rewards of the international marketplace, the United States will not voluntarily forgo its "rightful" share, measured by its present standard of living. The regime of "low classness" and "low stateness" is not compatible with the emergence of the kind of "agency" in the United States that could internalize and politically allocate the costs of an international order based on global equity.

We thus reach the conclusion that political processes internal to the United States will not generate a major transformation of foreign policy toward Latin America, though there will continue to be oscillations in policies depending on the character of different presidential administrations and the access enjoyed by different elements within the foreign policy elite. Oscillations from "hard" to "soft" policies, however, will occur within limits set by the policy goals of maintaining geopolitical hegemony and hemispheric inequities. If there is to be serious challenge to current foreign policies, it will come from outside the United States, most likely from Latin American nations themselves.

Resurgent Cold War Ideology: The Case of the Committee on the Present Danger

ALAN WOLFE AND JERRY SANDERS

INTRODUCTION

On Veterans Day 1976, three days after Jimmy Carter's election to the presidency, a group calling itself the Committee on the Present Danger held a news conference to unveil its founding statement, "Common Sense and the Common Danger." The statement warned of a "Soviet drive for dominance based upon an unparalleled military buildup" and suggested as a countermeasure that the United States take a tougher stance in its policy toward the Soviet Union, spend more for the buildup of military forces, and accelerate the development of new weapons systems. The Committee's leaders included such venerable Cold War hard-liners as Paul Nitze, Eugene Rostow, David Packard, Dean Rusk, and Henry Fowler. They in turn spoke for a broad-based coalition of 141 persons ranging from *Commentary*'s editor Norman Podhoretz to erstwhile presidential hopeful John Connally. Among the Committee's founders were ten prominent labor leaders, including AFL-CIO Vice-President Lane Kirkland and Albert Shanker, President of the American Federation of Teachers. Also listed were numerous literary and academic figures—among them Nobel Prize winners Saul Bellow, Eugene Wigner, and W. F. Libby. A platoon of retired military commanders was led by Kennedy's adviser General Maxwell Taylor, and Nixon's Chief of Naval Operations, Admiral Elmo Zumwalt. And as one might expect, a whole host of Cold War architects and long-time presidential national security advisers—including Leon Keyserling, Gordon Gray, Charles Burton Marshall, Arthur Dean, and Douglas Dillon—graced the membership rolls of the Committee on the Present Danger (henceforth shortened to CPD).

Alan Wolfe is a Visiting Scholar at the Institute for the Study of Social Change, University of California, Berkeley. Jerry Sanders is an Acting Instructor in the Department of Sociology, University of California, Berkeley, where he is writing a doctoral dissertation on Cold War militarism.

Though the timing of the CPD's statement was meant to serve as a message to the newly elected president, it was not fear of the impending Carter Administration that prompted the group's formation. Its roots went back to the disintegration of the foreign policy consensus during the Vietnam war, and its purpose was to reverse the erosion of American power and to give new life to the doctrine of "containment" that Vietnam had shattered. By the summer of 1974, a number of key figures in the Committee's subsequent formation had decided that the nation was virtually catatonic in the wake of Vietnam while its leaders were mesmerized by détente even as the Soviets were embarking on a massive buildup of nuclear and conventional forces. Eugene Rostow, former Undersecretary of State during the Johnson years and unreconstructed hawk on Vietnam, probably had more to do with organizing the CPD than did any other individual. Rostow headed the Coalition for a Democratic Majority's Foreign Policy Task Force, which in the summer of 1974 released a paper critical of the Nixon-Kissinger strategy of détente. (The Coalition [henceforth CDM] had been born two years before in the ideological strife surrounding McGovern's nomination as the Democratic Party's standard-bearer in the 1972 election.) Many of the key members of the CDM followed Rostow into the CPD. In all, 13 of the 18 members of the Foreign Policy Task Force were also founders of the CPD. After his Task Force experience, Rostow became convinced of the need for putting together a broadly based committee to awaken the nation of "the Soviet threat" and to return the United States to the expansive international role characteristic of the years between Korea and Vietnam.

Another major force behind the formation of the CPD was Paul Nitze. Nitze, head of the State Department's Policy Planning Division during the Truman Administration, was the principal author of NSC-68, the secret document that outlined the politico-military strategy for the Cold War. Nitze had become one of the most respected figures within the national security establishment, and over the years had served in numerous capacities. Since 1969 he had been a member of Nixon's SALT delegation, but he resigned his post in June 1974, citing his disgust with the Nixon-Kissinger negotiating position. He followed up his resignation by going before the Senate Armed Services Committee with the warning that the Administration was promoting a "myth of détente." Nitze's testimony gave perennial détente critic Henry Jackson, then serving as co-chairman of the CDM, all the information he needed for a new round of attacks on Nixon-Kissinger diplomacy, which had already been undermined by the Watergate disclosures on the domestic front. Meanwhile, James Schlesinger, who was in contact with Rostow and Nitze, kept up the pressure against détente inside the Administration from his post as Secretary of Defense.

In November 1975, the founders of what would be christened the Committee on the Present Danger decided that the time had come to formally launch their plan. Schlesinger, the conduit of the hard-line view within what by this time was the Ford Administration, had just been fired for his opposition to Kissinger's diplomacy. The question became not whether to go public, but when and how. After all, 1976 would be an election year, and though Democratic Cold Warriors dominated the CPD, there were Republicans among the founders as well. Moreover, it was by no means clear that the Democratic nominee would be sufficiently hard-line to warrant the CPD's support. Thus the strategy became one of forcing candidates to address "the Soviet threat," hedging one's bets as it were, in an effort to push the entire primary and presidential battle to the right. The strategy was a success. Reagan forced Ford and the Republicans to adopt a jingoistic foreign policy platform, and such Democratic moderates as Fred Harris and Morris Udall were shunted aside in favor of the enigmatic Carter. But the election campaign proved to be not the final drama that would shape the next four years, but only the prologue to the ideological and policy battles to come. In what follows we hope to elucidate the difficulties of the first year of the Carter Administration by analyzing how the principal protagonist of resurgent Cold War ideology—the Committee on the Present Danger—was able to confound any thought of new directions in U.S. foreign policy, even though the realities of the post-Vietnam world called for radical departures from Cold War orthodoxy.

THE COLD WAR IN TRANSITION

Domestic political controversies undoubtedly shape foreign policy options, but how and to what extent they do so is very much open to controversy. Two polar notions on the relationship between domestic events and foreign policy decisions can be discarded at the outset. The first views something called "public opinion" as an invisible hand, establishing limits on foreign policy elites and ensuring the success of democratic restraints. Among the many conventional wisdoms destroyed by Vietnam was this one. But one can also discard the notion that an indivisible and coherent "military-industrial complex" uses the foreign policy machinery to promote without opposition its self-serving ends. In its own way, Vietnam destroyed that canard as well, for it revealed an elite unsure about its objectives, divided over tactics, and either unwilling or unable to obtain its articulated goals.

The breakdown of the foreign policy consensus over Vietnam interacts with a breakdown of the consensus on the study of foreign policy, each reinforcing the other. In this paper we hope to use the former to shed light on the latter: that is, we plan to examine attempts to reestablish an ideological basis for U.S. foreign policy in the face of the fallout over Vietnam, because such a fluid situation is perfect for trying to sort out the various influences that shape and constrain foreign policy options.

The historical context of our argument is as follows.[1] At the end of the Second World War, fundamental differences existed within the United States over this country's objectives in the world. Walking narrow lines between free-trade liberalism, conservative isolationism, Wilsonian idealism, and strategic *realpolitik*, a new consensus was achieved that structured U.S. foreign policy for nearly a quarter of a century. That consensus can be described as Cold War liberalism. Joining domestic liberals who saw defense spending as a macroeconomic stimulant to economic growth and strategic thinkers who were arguing that an expansionist Soviet menace constituted the greatest threat to American civilization, Cold War liberalism constituted a brilliant political maneuver that laid the groundwork for a centrist foreign policy able to appeal to influential members of both political parties. Although Eisenhower was reluctant to implement the Cold War liberal strategy, Kennedy showed no hesitation in doing so and brought to the national security apparatus men who saw the world almost entirely in those terms. Before long, however, Cold War liberal assumptions led to Vietnam; and over time that war undermined the integrity of the ideas and the political interests that had coalesced around Cold War liberal notions.

By 1968, three key assumptions of Cold War liberalism were in disarray. First, expenditures for defense were hurting rather than stimulating the economy, contributing to a negative balance of payments, inflation, and investment in unproductive methods of manufacturing. Second, overseas adventures, far from binding the country together, were resulting in dissent and even insurrection. Third, Vietnam indicated that, strategically, Cold War interventionism might reduce rather than en-

1. The following four paragraphs summarize part of a chapter from a forthcoming book by Alan Wolfe and David A. Gold on the rise and fall of Cold War liberalism tentatively entitled *America's Impasse*.

hance the credibility of American power. Clearly Cold War liberalism had had its day.

The disenchantment with Cold War liberalism was strongly reflected in the 1968 election, when the archsymbol of the coalition, Hubert Humphrey, was defeated—both because of his liberalism *and* because of his Cold War attachments. Living up to his mandate, Richard Nixon did in fact repudiate Cold War liberalism during his presidency. First, through détente and the China trip he undermined the image of a unified totalitarian Communist menace so essential for defense-spending rationales. Second, even his Administration's strategic doctrines were a repudiation of the key assumptions of the Cold War liberals. The national security ideas of Defense Secretary Schlesinger were based on the idea that the credibility of American power had failed during Vietnam, forcing us to up the ante in order to prove how sincere we were. These notions would necessitate the subordination of nearly all domestic objectives to national security goals; yet the essence of Cold War liberalism had been the opposite, that we could have our national security but our welfare state as well. By the time of Watergate, the Nixon presidency had put the last nail in the coffin of the Cold War liberal coalition.

But while Nixon was president, influential national security managers,[2] always more comfortable with the Democratic Party, used their enforced exile to formulate a foreign policy strategy of their own. Successive issues of *Foreign Policy*, the "1980's project" of the Council on Foreign Relations, the Aspen Institute of Humanistic Studies, and the Trilateral Commission all began to address the shape of a post-Vietnam world.[3] With Carter's election, this homework began to pay off. A new generation of foreign policy professionals, many of them archcritics of Cold War liberalism, took over key positions in the National Security Council, in the State Department, and on the president's staff. If a post–Cold War liberal foreign policy could be developed, it was up to them to develop it.

Changes in a country's stance to the rest of the world, however, do not come about because a new group of men and women come to positions of power. Little of the debate surrounding the new foreign policy questioned the most fundamental features of the American face toward the world, such as the assertion of hegemony or the need to

2. This term comes from Richard Barnet, *The Roots of War* (Baltimore, Md., 1973).

3. For some material on this reassessment see Laurence Shoup and William Minter, *Imperial Brain Trust* (New York, 1976).

protect vital interests. Our point is that with the election of Carter, changes in the directions of U.S. foreign policy might have been expected because the material reality of the U.S. position had shifted. The interventionist thrust of Cold War liberalism had been developed at a time of economic expansion. Growth led by the state sector stimulated prosperity; balance-of-payments problems did not interfere with foreign adventures; the dollar, as the world's currency, allowed cheap methods of financing expensive projects; inflation was under control; and neither allied countries nor Third World resource-owners were in a position to challenge U.S. economic strength. By 1976, in part because of Vietnam, all this had changed. The reevaluation of U.S. foreign policy was in reality a debate over the economic capabilities of the United States. The long-range perspective of the critics of Cold War liberalism emphasized that high defense budgets, outflows of military equipment, and a vigilant interventionist posture would conspire to fuel inflation, tamper with international stability, and contribute to the fiscal crisis of the state. If any segment of the national security elite was class conscious and understood what was necessary to manage the economy successfully, it was that faction that argued for retrenchment—meaning a reduction of Cold War tensions, a continuation of détente, a tolerance for North-South rhetoric, some efforts at arms control, and a laissez-faire stance toward intervention that emphasized long-run economic stability over short-term strategic considerations.

The critics of Vietnam that took power with Carter were in a sense riding the wave of history. Their analysis not only had economics on its side but also was in accord with a public sentiment that was weary of foreign entanglements. Yet even though there were grounds for predicting major changes in the direction of U.S. foreign policy under Carter, what is most interesting is that so many new directions were ignored. Instead, the United States saw a resurgence of the very ideas and political interests that by 1968 had seemed dead beyond resurrection. Strong public support for defense spending, the emergence of a phalanx of Senators hostile to the SALT talks, the warnings of a Soviet military threat by intelligence-gatherers, the one-vote margin for a Panama Canal treaty, and the creation and strength of Cold War lobbying groups such as the Committee on the Present Danger—all breathed life into Cold War militancy. Faced with a strong Cold War ideology on his right, Carter played down new initiatives. He promised to increase the defense budget rather than to trim it, and allowed his Secretary of Defense to make extremely hawkish speeches, such as the September 15, 1977, outpouring to the National Security Industrial Association.[4] And most importantly, rather than trying to isolate groups like the Committee on the Present Danger by seeking to build public opinion against them, Carter has decided to work with them and to keep their influence within the Democratic Party. This was dramatically illustrated in the president's March 17, 1978, speech at Wake Forest College, warning the Soviet Union that the United States would match its military spending and parry Russian thrusts wherever they might occur. Hard-liners found little to quarrel with in this bellicose expression of American policy.

The problem we want to explore in this paper is how this resurgence came about. We assume that conventional theories about the relationship between domestic events and foreign policy are unable to explain it. Those who argue, for example, that material interests determine foreign policy options must confront the proposition that increased defense spending and a militant foreign policy would be as harmful to American capitalism now as they once were stimulatory.[5] On the other hand, those who see the foreign policy machinery as a response to public opinion—which is generally viewed as strongly anti-Soviet—must consider the reaction against Vietnam and the subsequent attempts to shape a quality as nebulous as public opinion to one perspective or another. Finally, those who argue that foreign policy is the product of ideas hatched in elite organizations like the Council on Foreign Relations must deal with the fact that in this struggle the elite organizations are losing.[6] Indeed, no existing set of ideas seems capable of making sense of the resurgence of Cold War ideology at this time. This has forced us to abandon our own pet theories and search for explanations in new places, however tentative.

Our methodology must be as tentative as our approach. In seeking

4. "Remarks by the Honorable Harold Brown, Secretary of Defense, at the Thirty-Fourth Annual Dinner of the National Security Industrial Association, September 15, 1977," News Release, Office of the Assistant Secretary of Defense (Public Affairs).

5. Whether defense spending is harmful or beneficial to the prosperity of American capitalism has been much debated. The former perspective is argued by Seymour Melman, *The Permanent War Economy* (New York, 1974), and the latter by Paul Baran and Paul Sweezy, *Monopoly Capital* (New York, 1966). Our view is that these positions are not necessarily mutually exclusive; defense spending may have stimulated the economy until the 1960's, but it is now slowing it down. Certainly, many business leaders have concluded that this is the case. See, for example, the pamphlet *Controlling the Conventional Arms Race*, published by the United States Committee on the United Nations. We have found discussions with David Gold to be most helpful in clarifying our views on this question.

6. This is the weakness of the analysis by Shoup and Minter in *Imperial Brain Trust*.

answers to the question of why Cold War militancy is resurfacing, we
first decided on a case-study approach and then selected as our case the
most important of the new organizations, the Committee on the Present
Danger. Each of us went to Washington and interviewed not only the
officers and directors of the CPD but also prominent policymakers in
the Carter Administration to determine their reactions to the CPD. But
rather than present a descriptive report on our findings, we decided instead to organize our material around what we considered to be the
major themes that help explain this revival of Cold War ideology.
Among these themes are what we call the perversion of the social-democratic experience in the United States, the nature of inner-elite struggles
when one side can launch a Bonapartist appeal to the masses and the
other cannot, and the consequences of a particular kind of power that
stems from not holding the power of the state. An elaboration of each
of these themes should shed light on the puzzling phenomenon of how
an ideology can persevere long after the conditions for its demise have
manifested themselves.

THE PERVERSION OF SOCIAL DEMOCRACY IN THE UNITED STATES

In the aftermath of the Second World War those European societies
that had not already realized it finally concluded that capitalism was too
important to be left to capitalists. On the one hand, elites learned that
unplanned, spontaneous business decisions resulted in an economy that
performed in a manner unable to achieve stable economic growth. On
the other, pressures from below to recognize and accommodate working-class demands for social justice were difficult to deny given working-
class support during the war. Between them, these factors made a social-
democratic solution to postwar capitalist contradictions essential. A
planning apparatus combined with a strong welfare state—both administered either by a socialist-based political party or by a reformed
capitalist one—became the rule, not only in Scandinavia but through
most of Europe.

The United States was not immune to those pressures toward social
democracy. But because American capitalism was different from the
European version, America's social democracy would be different as
well. Instead of a commitment to planning and social equality, reformers
in the United States tried to achieve the twin goals of economic growth
under stable conditions and redistributive government spending through

a process compatible with America's unique values and ideology. The solution involved defense spending and the generation of a Cold War ideology. The forces pushing toward social democracy in Europe, when transplanted to the United States, transformed themselves into military Keynesianism.

Cold War liberalism cannot be understood unless its liberalism is taken seriously. In the postwar period the American right was against such liberal innovations as high defense spending, a system of military conscription, and an ideology of permanent crisis necessitating permanent response. On the other hand, reformist beliefs in government spending as a macroeconomic stimulant and in the need to generate jobs in the public sector were opposed by a capitalist class that did not have the long-range vision of its European counterpart. Cold War liberals like Paul Nitze and Leon Keyserling, who together produced NSC-68, the founding document of the new *Weltanschauung*, understood this before most. Nitze discovered that by bringing in the liberals he could secure a base in the Democratic Party for a Cold War foreign policy and thereby counter opposition from the right. Likewise, Keyserling found that by tying government spending to defense he could broaden the basis of Keynesian ideas and win business support for ideas they would otherwise denounce. In this context, the social-democratic goal of centrist state management of capitalism combined with moderate reform to harmonize all social classes became the basis of a consensus that would make the Cold War rival the New Deal as the foundation of the Democratic Party's postwar political unity.

Paul Nitze and Leon Keyserling are both now on the board of the Committee on the Present Danger. Here we have our first clue to the success of the Cold War resurgence after 1976. By understanding Cold War ideology as the American version of the social-democratic experience, we begin to realize a major source of its political longevity.

Joseph Schumpeter argued in his essay on "Imperialism" that capitalists prefer pacifism and lend their support to military adventures only when they have no other choice.[7] In a peculiar way, an organization like the Committee on the Present Danger can take on an anticapitalist perspective. For example, one prominent CPD member with many years at the top of the national security bureaucracy told us: "Schumpeter was so correct. You can never rely on businessmen. They operate out of a very narrow frame of reference. Generally speaking the smart ones can

7. Joseph Schumpeter, *Imperialism and Social Classes* (Cleveland, Ohio, 1953).

think about the balance sheet for the year after next. The ordinary ones can't even think that far. I wouldn't rely on them any more than I would the editors of *The New Republic*."[8]

This feeling is reinforced by the experience of détente, which the Committee on the Present Danger views as being rooted in capitalist naiveté. Another member of the CPD board told us that "businessmen, not being politically astute," were taken in by the promise of trade: "U.S. businessmen would go to Moscow and come back supercharged from vodka parties and the promise of hundreds of millions of orders. They came back and lobbied for MFNs [most-favored-nation trading status] for the Russians."[9] This notion that the establishment of commercial relations with the Soviet Union will not only bail that country out of its economic woes but compromise American business investors besides represents a deep-seated fear among CPD members. The Foreign Policy Task Force of the Coalition for a Democratic Majority—another Cold War liberal organization whose members, as we have noted, formed the nucleus of the CPD—suggested that "in dealing with the Soviets, private pecuniary gain and the American public interest may not always coincide."[10]

One of the dominant ideological themes of European social democracy was that capitalists could not be trusted to pay due regard to the national welfare. Some restraints on private accumulation were essential, or else businessmen would trade away the country's most precious asset. If one defines national security as an asset, and understands that fear of invasion is considered by many the single most important component of the national welfare, then one finds that the national security managers of extreme Cold War persuasion often mimic, even if unconsciously, the social democrats of the 1940's. For example, the sociologist Peter Berger, writing in *Commentary* (the main intellectual organ of the Committee on the Present Danger), defined the problem this way: ". . . the economic elite operated on the notion that the maintenance of American power in the world was in their interest. Vietnam changed all this . . . it has given rise to the idea that the maintenance of American world power is *unprofitable*." The question in Berger's mind is, "What if Marxism had been wrong all along? What if American world power comes to be seen as an economic disadvantage by the 'ruling circles' of the American

8. Interview, August 25, 1977.
9. Interview, August 22, 1977.
10. Coalition for a Democratic Majority, Foreign Policy Task Force, *The Quest for Détente* (Washington, D.C., 1974), p. 5.

economy?" Completing his portrait of "the greening of American foreign policy," Berger concludes: "If the proposition is to diminish American world power, the intellectuals make it seem morally right and the businessmen make it appear realistic."[11] Thus does Peter Berger, an outstanding sociologist with roots in a social-democratic tradition, find himself using anticapitalist language to support the ideology of Cold War liberalism.

If Cold War ideology is the U.S. perversion of social democracy, then one would expect a strong input from organized labor. This is certainly the case with the Committee on the Present Danger. Besides the membership of Lane Kirkland, heir apparent to the AFL-CIO presidency, the list of CPD members includes President Sol Chaikin of the International Ladies' Garment Workers Union (the closest union in American history to the social-democratic tradition when presided over by David Dubinsky); Evelyn Du Brow, Legislative Director, ILGWU; William Du Chessi, Executive Vice President of the Amalgamated Clothing and Textile Workers; Albert Shanker, President of the American Federation of Teachers (the closest thing to a social-democratic stereotype at the present time); Rachelle Horowitz, Director, Committee On Political Education, AFT; Martin J. Ward, President of the Plumbers' and Pipefitters' International Union; John H. Lyons, President of the Ironworkers' International Union; J. C. Turner, President of the International Union of Operating Engineers; and professional anticommunist Jay Lovestone, Consultant to the AFL and ILGWU on international affairs.

The CPD's close ties with labor are readily apparent in a speech by prominent Committee member Frank Barnett, who sang the praises of labor before the D.C. League of Republican Women, a group not given to prolabor sentiment. In his address, "Alternatives to Détente," Barnett mounted a scathing attack on American business while applauding labor's hard-line foreign policy views: "Some of our leading businessmen and bankers, whose salaries are well over $100,000 per year, flock to Moscow as if they were penurious Polish peasants beseeching the Czar for economic favors." In contrast, Barnett pointed out: "It was George Meany and the American labor movement, not America's businessmen and lawyers, or the Republican White House, who gave Alexander Solzhenitzyn a forum for freedom in this country."[12]

11. Peter Berger, "The Greening of American Foreign Policy," *Commentary*, March, 1976.
12. Frank R. Barnett, "Alternatives to Détente," speech before the D.C. League of Republican Women, Washington, D.C., April 5, 1976, p. 4.

In addition to his affiliation with the CPD, Barnett is Executive Director of the National Strategy Information Center (NSIC), another Cold War lobbying organization that works closely with the CPD. One of the stated goals of NSIC is "to train young American labor leaders in the critical issues—philosophical, military, and political—that divide the free world from the Communist States."[13] This effort is being undertaken by means of "educational" seminars conducted in cooperation with Georgetown University, itself a stronghold of Cold War ideology. Georgetown lists seven of its faculty on the CPD membership rolls. The director of Georgetown's International Labor Program, Roy Godson, is both a staff member of NSIC and a prominent member of the Coalition for a Democratic Majority, having served as secretary of the latter's Foreign Policy Task Force. When NSIC moved to Washington from New York to set up what Executive Director Barnett described as a million-dollar "interface operation" designed to "crank up an all-out effort to meet the current and growing threat from the USSR,"[14] it was Godson who became NSIC's Washington representative, working out of the CDM office until NSIC moved into its own facilities a few blocks away.

In addition to its labor ties, the Committee on the Present Danger has won the support of numerous American intellectuals. It is the role of intellectuals not just to join political movements but to use their ideas to give those movements coherent ideological shape. This need became vital to Cold War liberals as power began to slip away from them in 1968 with the popularity of Eugene McCarthy and Robert Kennedy. When George McGovern received the 1972 Democratic nomination, the crisis was clear. Looking back on those events, a staff member of the Coalition for a Democratic Majority noted that the insurgent forces had "ideas and ideals. The Democratic establishment had neither."[15] These "ideas and ideals," which the Cold War liberals found so disconcerting and antithetical to their own notions, seemed to be sweeping wider circles of opinion beyond college campuses, as numerous intellectuals abandoned the Cold War shibboleths of the Democratic establishment and increasingly contributed to the emerging "new politics." Enter the intellectual defenders of the old order, writers like Ben Wattenberg and Richard Scammon, who wrote *The Real Majority*, an ideological tract that attempted to give a new coherence to conservative

13. National Strategy Information Center, *Purpose and Policy*, p. 8.
14. Personal correspondence from Frank Barnett to Eugene Rostow, May 24, 1976, p. 1.
15. Interview, September 1, 1977.

forces within the Democratic Party.[16] Interestingly enough, the thrust of their ideas was a classic social-democratic attack on "do-gooders" and "reformers." In the world view of the Cold War militants, the trouble with the McGovern forces was not their progressivism but their "elitism." Like social democrats of another era, the Cold War liberals saw themselves as leading an attack on privilege.

In the view of these men, being privileged meant belonging to the middle class, not to the highest reaches of wealth and power. Therefore, Cold War intellectuals leveled their charges against the most recent arrivals to the middle class, as well as against the rebellious youth movement and aspiring minorities. Embittered Cold War liberals like Michael Novak discovered a "new ethnicity" as the basis for a conservative movement.[17] Sociologists like Nathan Glazer and Seymour Martin Lipset (both board members of the CPD) put together some respectable-sounding ideas. By 1976, social-democratic intellectuals were the major forces attempting to give the revival of Cold War liberalism ideological coherence. That coherence was achieved around the notion that the promotion of growth and continual expansion was the *sine qua non* for the perpetuation of the American liberal tradition. Not all those interviewed went so far as one CDM staffer and ex-Moynihan aide, who told us "antigrowth is antihuman";[18] most preferred the more ideological parlance of Senator Moynihan, who in a 1977 article suggested that America's declining birthrate of late represents a decline of America as a civilization.[19] Moynihan's close friend and fellow social-democratic ideologue Norman Podhoretz agreed, maintaining that "certain cultural tendencies such as zero-economic-growth and zero-population-growth express in the broadest sense a failure of nerve in the culture as a whole." Podhoretz also described American business's eagerness to trade with the Soviet Union as similarly motivated by "failure of nerve."[20]

Those who questioned such notions of growth and expansion—whether in international relations, the economy, or the size of the family—were accused of being elitists. In the backlash climate of the 1970's, the social-democratic intellectuals were thus able, in an ironic political twist, to turn the egalitarian ideals growing out of the upheavals of the 1960's to their own uses——impugning the efforts of those who would

16. Ben Wattenberg and Richard Scammon, *The Real Majority* (New York, 1970).

17. Michael Novak, *The Rise of the Unmeltable Ethnics* (New York, 1972).

18. Interview, September 1, 1977.

19. Daniel Patrick Moynihan, "The Most Important Decision-Making Process," *Policy Review*, Summer 1977.

20. Interview, August 12, 1977.

limit the size of the military, the family, or the economy as attacks on both the traditional values and the material security of working people. It was a brilliant ideological coup. But the new ideology by itself was not enough. It was one thing to attack the "new politics" at home as elitist and another to warn of the danger of a Soviet threat. But how could each theme be related to the other? In this context, the Mideast War of 1973 was a godsend for the Cold War liberals. Writing in *Commentary*, Eugene Rostow of the CPD argued that the October War (which he later referred to as the Arab-Soviet military attack) "was like a Pearl Harbor. . . . Like a flash of lightning it illuminated the contours of a landscape large sectors of European and American opinion, in particular, were firmly resolved to ignore."[21] The flash of lightning was the fact that the events in the Middle East provided a rationalization for large sectors of liberal opinion, especially among Jews, to concentrate on foreign policy at the expense of domestic goals. What was needed in order to resurrect Cold War ideology was a crisis that could enable "realistic" and "hardheaded" domestic liberals to shift their attention from attacks on the New Politics to world affairs.

The shift of important Jewish intellectuals after October 1973 indicates the success of this transformation. It was at this point that *Commentary* stepped up its already strident attacks on détente and that prominent intellectuals like novelist Saul Bellow and historian Oscar Handlin joined the Cold War liberal campaign and gave it added respectability. More recently, these same Cold War liberals formed the Jewish Institute For National Security Affairs (JINSA), expressly for the purpose of reaching the American Jewish constituency and getting that substantial voting bloc behind its militaristic program. JINSA's founding "Statement of Purpose" in effect wed Israel's survival to the size of the Pentagon budget, arguing in unequivocal language that "Israel's existence could well depend on American recognition of Soviet intentions and America's willingness and ability to defend its own interests."[22] The founders of this latest Cold War lobby include CPD/CDM luminaries Eugene Rostow, Norman Podhoretz, Rita Hauser, and Max Kampelman. The president of JINSA is Richard Schifter, law partner of Kampelman and a member of both CPD and CDM.

When one combines antibusiness sentiment, strong support from organized labor, an appeal to ethnicity, and an intellectual posture em-

21. Eugene V. Rostow, "America, Europe, and the Middle East," *Commentary*, February 1974, p. 40.
22. Jewish Institute For National Security Affairs, *Newsletter*, June 1977, p. 1.

phasizing resentment against privilege, one has all the essential elements of a social-democratic movement. This is one important explanation for the tenacity of Cold War notions after 1976. If Cold War liberalism had been simply an elite strategy, unconnected to masses of people and their interests, then its staying power would have been minimal. Political coalitions and their ideologies desperately need legitimation, and Cold War liberalism has been able to generate its own legitimating momentum. Because of its ties to defense industries, it has significant support from some important vested interests and geographical regions. But even more vital than this, the social-democratic component of Cold War liberalism gives it an appearance of fairness and a link to the "masses." The forces around Carter that are trying to develop an alternative strategy, as we shall see, have a good deal of support from prominent interests but little to offer the people. Thus they appear "elitist," whereas Cold War liberals are able to portray themselves as being on the side of the common man against the interests. It all may sound peculiar given the Cold War liberal ties to one vested interest after another, but the strangeness is due only to the perverse form that the social-democratic experience has taken in the United States.

ELITES WITHOUT MASSES

The tenacity of Cold War militancy after 1976 also results from the nature of the intra-elite struggle in which it has been engaged. Ideological battles inevitably involve legitimation, the ability to appeal to the people for support of one's position. If both sides in a struggle neutralize each other's ability to make such an appeal, then outside forces such as public opinion will not play a role in determining who wins. Such a standoff has not occurred in the disputes between the Cold War liberals and their opponents currently within the Carter Administration: the latter have consistently refused to make a mass appeal, giving their more militant adversaries a flexible position in the battle for legitimation.

A recapitulation of the important events in Carter's first year indicates how the Administration became locked into an impossible position because of its refusal to appeal to the people. Postwar American foreign policy has been dominated by two images, dubbed the "Riga" and "Yalta" axioms by Daniel Yergin.[23] The former is named for the Latvian city from which U.S. diplomats watched Russia with great suspicion in the 1920's and concluded that the Soviet Union was a potential world

23. Daniel Yergin, *Shattered Peace* (Boston, 1977).

dictatorship that had to be contained at all costs. The latter, named for the meetings held between Churchill, Stalin, and Roosevelt in Crimea in 1945, stands for the opposite premise that the USSR behaves internationally in a traditional balance-of-power manner despite its ideological Marxist-Leninism. Yergin's book *Shattered Peace* is a brilliant account of how the Yalta image was submerged by the Riga one in the first year of Harry Truman's presidency.

Although there were always rumblings beneath the surface, the Riga axioms dominated Democratic Party thinking from Truman to Johnson, and it was the Riga mentality that produced the overextension of American power in Vietnam. As a result, official American policy slipped back into a Yalta perspective under Nixon and Kissinger. The latter, for example, explained the impact of the Yalta axioms on his approach in a letter to Eugene Rostow: "We have sought to rely on a balance of mutual interest rather than on Soviet intentions as expressed by ideological dogma. In dealing with the Soviets, we have, in a sense, appealed to the spirit of Pavlov rather than Hegel."[24] Such ideas were heretical to the Cold War liberals. They engaged in a determined effort to restore the viability of the Riga axioms in the face of Kissinger's betrayal. Rostow wrote to Kissinger: "We deny that relaxation of tensions between the two countries has in fact occurred. And we think it is not only wrong, but dangerous to lull public opinion by proclaiming an end of the Cold War, a substitution for confrontation, and a generation of peace."[25] When the Committee on the Present Danger was launched, it began with a reassertion of the Riga axioms in the strongest possible language: "The principle threat to our nation, to world peace, and to the cause of human freedom is the Soviet drive for dominance based upon an unparalleled military build-up. The Soviet Union has not altered its long-held goal of a world dominated from a single center—Moscow."[26]

Once Nixon, Ford, and with them Kissinger were removed from power, little seemed to stand in the way of a return of Riga principles. After all, Carter had campaigned against Kissinger and therefore could not so easily adopt his principles. With some confidence key officials of the CPD, the CDM, and the AFL-CIO presented Carter with 53 names

24. Personal correspondence from Secretary of State Henry Kissinger to Eugene V. Rostow, August 19, 1974, p. 1.
25. Personal correspondence from Eugene V. Rostow to Secretary of State Henry Kissinger, September 4, 1974, p. 1.
26. Committee on the Present Danger, *Common Sense and the Common Danger*, p. 2.

of men to serve in key Administration positions. They were stunned when Carter rejected them all. At least initially, Carter seemed determined to take an unprecedented action: to abide by neither the Riga nor the Yalta axioms and to adopt ideas that did not place the Soviet Union in the center of world conflict at all.

Carter's appointments went to men who had been critics not only of the war in Vietnam, but also (and this was less widely understood) of *the assumptions that produced the war in the first place.* Consider the views of Leslie H. Gelb, currently the director of the Bureau of Politico-Military Affairs in the State Department. Noting that the foreign policy of the whole postwar period had been based on the doctrine that the Soviets were the main enemy, Gelb told a seminar at the U.S. Army War College in June 1977 that "I had no special wisdom prior to 1967—the doctrine was in my head, too. My views just changed. It is very hard, looking back at it, to see how Vietnam was important, save in terms of that doctrine. I think it is easy to see that its importance was attached solely to our sense that everything happening in the world would impact directly and severely on U.S.-Soviet relations. It was a zero-sum game." It does not take long for Gelb to reach the appropriate conclusion: "fewer and fewer things had to do with the Soviet-American connection."[27] In short Gelb and such others as Anthony Lake and Richard Holbrooke were abandoning the one point that both the Riga and the Yalta axioms had in common: that all events must be interpreted with respect to their impact on Soviet-American relations.

If the Carter people were serious about this idea—which meant confronting over 30 years of doctrine—they would have no choice but to develop a new doctrine, one that would give ideological credence to their views. Many possibilities were available. There was the notion of interdependence, developed by Harlan Cleveland, a major figure in the Kennedy Administration; or there was the notion of a new world order, strongly articulated by Joseph Nye, who became a high Carter appointee; or there was the notion of a North-South cleavage, developed by the Council on Foreign Relations and the Trilateral Commission. The point was not which doctrine or doctrines were chosen, but that a choice had to be made. "Ideology is the door through which the people enter the closed room of the realm of interests," Schurmann has written.[28] The creation of a counterideology not only would have worked to undermine the legitimacy of both the Yalta and the Riga axioms but also would have

27. Leslie Gelb, "National Security and New Foreign Policy," *Parameters,* Journal of the U.S. Army War College, November 8, 1977, p. 10-F.
28. Franz Schurmann, *The Logic of World Power* (New York, 1974), p. 39.

provided some sense of the rules of the game to participants in the struggle.

But the Carter Administration explicitly refused to develop a new doctrine. As Gelb explained:

The general approach of this Administration in the first four months was not to try and mass this disparate, diverse, and sometimes incomprehensible foreign policy universe into a new strategy. There is no Carter Doctrine, or Vance Doctrine, or Brown Doctrine, because of a belief that the environment we are looking at is far too complex to be reduced to a doctrine in the tradition of post–World War II American foreign policy. Indeed, the Carter approach to foreign policy rests on a belief that not only is the world far too complex to be reduced to a doctrine, but that there is something inherently wrong with having a doctrine at all.[29]

Gelb's words, however noble sounding, reveal the fatal flaw of the Carter Administration's approach to foreign policy: the failure to develop a "doctrine" has placed the Carterites at the mercy of Cold War militants like those in the Committee on the Present Danger. A Carter State Department official acknowledged to us that the Administration was not prepared to battle the CPD but denied that this would cause problems. Others we interviewed, however, were clearly upset by the CPD's mastery over doctrine.

There are doctrines and there are doctrines. If one is talking about an intellectual straitjacket that distorts reality beyond recognition, then of course Gelb is correct. But if one means a body of ideas that organizes an elite strategy and can be used to win support for that strategy among the general population, then Gelb's naïveté is in full view. Cold War militants have understood since 1946 that in a formally democratic society no ruling group can hope to stay in power long without making substantial efforts at creating a legitimating ideology; documents like NSC-68 are full of references to the necessity to win popular support. And legitimating ideologies, once created, do not roll over and play dead just because conditions in the world change. Cold War ideology still lives on in the hearts and minds of most Americans; so long as that remains the case, the failure of either a ruling faction or a radical movement to develop a counterexplanation of world events will structure any battle over foreign policy in its favor. An example should help indicate the importance of ideology in this context.

Our illustrative case involves the CIA's annual assessment of Soviet

29. Gelb, "National Security," p. 10-F.

military capabilities and intentions, which serves as the official national intelligence estimate (NIE) by which U.S. foreign policy, including arms negotiations, is bound. These NIEs had over a number of years been the target of mounting criticism both from participants in the process of their creation (e.g. Air Force generals George Keegan and Daniel Graham) and from outsiders like Paul Nitze and Richard Pipes of Harvard (also a member of the CPD), who felt the conclusions of the intelligence establishment showed a pattern of being "soft on the Russians." Graham told us in an interview that from his years in the CIA's Office of National Estimates he could only conclude that they were "antimilitary." Moreover, he charged, "There are more liberals per square foot in the CIA than in any other part of government."[30] Finally in the spring of 1976, with Reagan making national security an issue in the primaries, Gerald Ford followed the recommendation of his Foreign Intelligence Advisory Board and appointed a group of outsiders known for their hard-line views to a panel that would conduct an independent analysis of Soviet strength based on the same classified data available to the CIA's analysts. The Advisory Board included six names that also appeared on the membership list of the Committee on the Present Danger. Similarly, the seven outsiders chosen for the adversary procedure included CPD members Paul Nitze, Foy Kohler, William Van Cleave, and Richard Pipes. Pipes served as chairman of what came to be known as the Team B panel. The other three members were also well known for their hard-line convictions. Thus the stage was set. Whereas in the Nixon years the fundamental struggle between Riga and Yalta manifested itself in the battles between Schlesinger and Kissinger, the latest chapter was to take the form of the Team B outsiders versus the CIA regulars.

Once the estimating process had begun, one CIA regular described it as a "rather unfair setup" in which the outsiders felt they had a somewhat broader mandate and used it.[31] The broader mandate was, of course, to reinstate the Riga doctrine as the raison d'être of American foreign policy. The restoration of the Soviet Union as the implacable foe was essential to this larger task. One need look no further than the participants' own statements to discern who had the upper hand in the controversy. "Sometimes we left them speechless," one member of Team B recounted. "We had men of great prestige, some of them with memories

30. Interview, August 29, 1977.
31. David Binder, "New CIA Estimate Finds Soviet Seeks Superiority in Arms," *New York Times*, December 26, 1976.

going back 25 years or more, and they made devastating critiques of the Agency estimates."[32] In other words, what Team B had on its side were the arguments, as well as the architects, of an ideology that had governed American foreign policy in the generation of its greatest influence in the world. A CIA official summed up the adversary process by calling it "an absolute disaster for the Agency."[33] Working in a doctrinal vacuum, the CIA estimators had no counterframework with which to make sense of their findings and to defend its conclusions. Thus in the frequent controversies over differing interpretations of the same classified data, the Agency regulars were systematically put on the defensive, forced to justify their analysis and fit it into the confines of a hostile world view, one already preempted by the Riga hard-liners.

High-ranking officials of the CIA referred to the new NIE that would be waiting on Carter's desk when he arrived in Washington as the most "somber" in more than a decade.[34] A top-level military intelligence officer who had read the estimate commented: "It was more than somber—it was grim. It flatly states the judgment that the Soviet Union is seeking superiority over United States forces."[35] After the inauguration, the new president responded to these charges by saying "we're still by far stronger than they are in most means of measuring strength."[36] Moreover, Brown and Vance, unlike their predecessors at Defense and State, were not at odds with their boss or with one another on this controversial point. Even the Joint Chiefs agreed, refuting General Keegan's publicly aired charges of Soviet superiority. Yet despite the notable absence of hard-line ideologues in the new Administration, the Cold Warriors had by their domination of the intelligence estimates left behind a legacy that could not easily be ignored. As the *Washington Post* explained: "The new NIE, plus the Pipes Report, plus the encouragement given to pessimists or 'worst case' theorists on Soviet intentions inside the government, is regarded as a high barrier for the Carter administration to overcome to carry out its own broader objectives for US-Soviet nuclear arms control."[37]

Thus, though Carter's answer to the running battle between the ideological supporters of Riga and Yalta was to appoint to his Administration pragmatists wedded to neither doctrine, it soon became apparent that

32. *Ibid.*   34. *Ibid.*
33. *Ibid.*   35. *Ibid.*
36. Banning Garrett, "The Coming Battle Over Defense Policy," *International Bulletin*, January 14, 1977, p. 3.
37. Murray Marder, "Carter to Inherit Intense Dispute on Soviet Intentions," *Washington Post*, January 2, 1977.

changes in policy do not follow ipso facto from changes in personnel. Although the pro-Riga ex-insiders had lost out in the appointment process, they had still managed to have their views prevail in the multivolume intelligence guidelines that circumscribe the conduct of foreign policy. Unwilling or unable to mount a concerted effort against such entrenched ideological precepts, Carter in his efforts to achieve an arms agreement with the Soviets soon played into the hands of Riga's contemporary adherents in the Committee on the Present Danger.

Given this intelligence advantage of the Cold War militants, damage to arms control prospects was inevitable. In his inaugural address, President Carter said: "We will move this year toward our ultimate goal—the elimination of all nuclear weapons from this earth."[38] Two and a half weeks later, at his first press conference he once again struck this bold theme by suggesting that if both the United States and the USSR compromised a bit, an early accord could be reached on SALT II. By the end of March, the Carter people had devised a formula for Soviet consideration. But when the Vance-led team unveiled the Carter plan in Moscow the Russians were taken aback, charging that Henry Jackson, Cold War liberal *par excellence*, "had so much influence in shaping the U.S. position that he possessed an invisible chair at the talks."[39]

A perusal of the substance of the proposal as described in the press suggests that it was an effort to placate the Cold War coalition as well as to accommodate the so-called arms control community. Neither had been happy with the high ceilings allowed on nuclear weapons in the Vladivostok interim agreement engineered by Henry Kissinger, who, in the spirit of Yalta, had sought to institutionalize the status quo in nuclear weaponry much as one might ratify territorial spheres of influence in geopolitical negotiations. Someone in the Carter Administration must have reasoned that both hawks and doves could be united around the idea of scrapping Vladivostok and lowering the threshold of nuclear weapons. Accordingly, the proposal offered arms control supporters the prospect of a major cut in the development and deployment of nuclear weapons; but in addition, it called for most of the cutting to come from the Soviet Union's heavy land-based missiles in order to make "arms control" acceptable to the Cold Warriors. Not surprisingly, Russian sensibilities were ruffled by this abrupt departure from Vladivostok, Foreign Minister Andrei Gromyko calling an unprecedented news conference to

38. Jimmy Carter, "Inaugural Address," January 1977.
39. David K. Willis, "Why Détente Is Freezing Over This Summer," *Christian Science Monitor*, June 27, 1977.

denounce the proposal as "unrealistic . . . [and] questionable, if not cheap."[40]

The severity of the Soviet rejection was seized upon by the CPD as an opportunity both to etch the Team B analysis even more deeply into American policy and to persuade Carter to become the standard-bearer of a "Soviet threat" campaign. There was an urgency in gaining Carter's endorsement of the Riga position at this time. As Paul Nitze explained: "The American public has changed its mind and opted for a stronger defense. It's concerned. . . . [But] obviously if the President says there's no problem, and the Secretary of State says there's no problem, and the Joint Chiefs of Staff say there's no problem, then the people may not feel there is one."[41]

Consequently, soon after the Moscow rebuff, with Carter badly embarrassed in his first major foreign policy initiative, the CPD released "What Is The Soviet Union Up To?" The answer and supporting arguments, right out of earlier CPD statements and the Team B report, emphasized world conquest. Interestingly, at the news conference where this latest CPD effort was unveiled, Nitze praised Carter's leadership and his approach to arms negotiations but added that he "doubted whether Moscow would accept it . . . because it is an equitable deal, and that's what they don't want."[42] Thus the public was treated to the spectacle of Riga hard-liners like Paul Nitze, after having been left completely out of the Administration, backing the mercurial president even as the beginnings of dissent against his SALT stand began to be heard within the ranks of Carter appointees. Similarly, it was the Cold War social democrats who applied "human rights" to the Soviets (another Carter policy that bore the unmistakable markings of Henry Jackson) against the liberal wing of the Democratic Party, who thought the term applicable only to Latin American dictators. Joining with the liberals were foreign policy professionals and others within the Administration who worried that Carter's "moral strategy" would likely worsen relations and lead to an escalation of arms competition. To counter this growing sentiment, the Coalition for a Democratic Majority released a letter applauding Carter's position on human rights and arms negotiations. The open letter encouraged him to continue the direction

40. David K. Willis, "Soviet Rebuff Opens New Arms Issues," *Christian Science Monitor*, April 1, 1977.
41. William Greider, "U.S.-Russian Arms Debate At Crossroads," *Washington Post*, February 20, 1977, p. 18.
42. David Binder, "Group Warns On Soviet Expansion," *New York Times*, April 4, 1977.

he had begun, and thus in effect to ignore his liberal critics both outside and within his Administration. It ended by painting Carter favorably in pro-Riga hues and urging him to "Hang tough, Mr. President." At the same time, it revealed the Pandora's Box Carter had opened for himself: "You have set off on a long, challenging course, but it is the right course. We promise to do all we can to rally the public support that will enable you to pursue it."[43]

And if you should waver from that course we will do all we can to alert the public of that, too, the letter might have added, as Carter soon discovered when he dispatched Vance to Geneva in May with the outlines of a conciliatory proposal designed to revive the moribund arms talks. But if the Russians were happier with the May outline, the return to the Vladivostok framework only served to confirm the hard-liners' suspicions that Carter's "toughness" was constructed on a rather shaky ideological edifice. On the other hand, even the Administration's fallback position could be used to the hard-liners' advantage—i.e. by portraying the Russians as warmongers who would not accept peace at any price, which the CPD's statement "Where We Stand on SALT" in fact argued. Released on July 6, the statement, largely drafted by Paul Nitze, attacked the Soviet Union as expected but also harshly criticized Carter for waffling in his bargaining stance. The president was reportedly very angry with the CPD statement and the broader hard-line criticism set off in its wake. Yet despite the fact that the Cold Warriors portrayed the Soviet Union as intransigent and characterized Carter's efforts as inexperienced and overeager, the president's only response was to invite the executive officers of the CPD to a White House meeting to discuss their widening differences with himself, national security chief Brzezinski, and Defense Secretary Brown.

The question posed by this example is why the Carter Administration refused to take the debate out of the hands of the foreign policy professionals and appeal to the general population on the basis of a counterideology. The answer may be that Bonapartism can only work once in any generation. We can explain this by noting that both sides in the debate over the direction of U.S. foreign policy face the same problem: each must take a strategy that objectively serves the narrower interests of ruling elites and transform it into subjective appeals that satisfy the political and emotional needs of large numbers of people. This task is so difficult that it is possible that the very success of the Cold War

43. Coalition for a Democratic Majority, Open Letter to President Carter, May 14, 1977.

liberals in accomplishing it the first time around may be the reason why
the Carter Administration cannot accomplish it now.

The problem is complicated by the fact that the men around Carter
cannot build a doctrine with popular appeal because of the very nature
of their foreign policy goals. Their objective, it should be recalled, is to
transcend both the Yalta and the Riga axioms by downplaying the cen-
trality of Soviet motivations in the world political situation. This gives
them more of an economic perspective on the world than a politico-
strategic one. In their view, both the Yalta and the Riga axioms demand
a perspective on world events that subordinates trade and the expansion
of capitalist industry in favor of questions involving military strength
and flexibility. In searching for an alternative to both Riga and Yalta,
advisers close to Carter have already indicated their attraction to the
option that dominated State Department thinking before 1946: a *multilateralist* perspective that saw in free trade the solution to the problem
of world order. Like Wilsonian liberals, or Cordell Hull and Will Clayton, the Carterites are developing an approach based on the assumption
that American domination of multinational corporations will preserve
American hegemony better than any emphasis on military capabilities.
But like them as well, they are also discovering that such an approach is
difficult, if not impossible, to "sell" to the American public.

The economic approach of the men around Carter has three immediate applications. First, the Soviet Union should be treated as not so much
a military threat as an economic entity that requires both cooperation
and competition. The Soviets, in debt to Western banks, have set up
profit-oriented companies throughout the West in order to expand their
exports and solve what is by all accounts a severe economic crisis facing
their society. Second, the United States should pursue arms control
through SALT because it makes economic sense. Reductions in the arms
budget would not only allow the economy to grow by reducing unproductive investment, it would also leave more room for domestic spending in case of revolt at home. And third, the United States should substitute economic devices—encouraging or withholding trade, extending
or not extending loans, subsidizing or not subsidizing development—for
large troop commitments or pledges of military assistance.

Yet each of these objectives, however worthwhile, has elitist implications that make a legitimating strategy cumbersome. The theme of out-
trading the Russians, though it gave us the Nixon-Khrushchev "kitchen
debates," cannot sustain popular interest for long. There is no economic
counterpart to the notion of totalitarianism, and so long as the Cold War
militants can wield the image of a "totalitarian threat," they will retain

control over popular allegiance. In addition, the call to cut back arms, given the social-democratic nature of American defense spending, makes the free-traders appear elitist—unconcerned about jobs, and clearly anti-labor. This image, which the supporters of arms control around Carter have done little to counter, seriously undermines their ability to keep important interest groups lined up behind their foreign policy strategy. Finally, movements away from a military outlook on the world and toward an economic one—e.g., the Panama Canal treaties—cannot be legitimated unless they can be shown to benefit ordinary people. So long as the issue is posed in terms of trade, this does not happen—hence the enormous popular opposition to even so small a step as the Canal treaties. Once again, the free-traders around Carter find themselves on the defensive in the ideological war against the Cold War militants.

Thus a second important factor behind the resurgence of Cold War militancy after 1976 has to do with the importance of legitimating ideologies. Hemmed in by an economic approach that is inherently elitist, the Carterites find themselves put on the defensive by an even more elitist group, but one that has convinced the public that it represents their interests. The only way to break this link would be for Carter to lead a campaign for a new doctrine, one that would make foreign policy issues comprehensible to people and convince them of the need for alternatives. For example, since the theme of national security is so obviously important to people, the president could try to build a campaign around the notion that an increased arms race, a capacity to intervene, and a foreign policy concerned exclusively with the Soviet Union would bring about not security but its opposite. There is no reason why the Cold War militants should have a monopoly on issues involving security. But to conduct such a campaign Carter would have to repudiate the history of, and some of the key individuals in, his own party, and this he is clearly unwilling to do. So long as that remains the case, movements away from Cold War liberalism cannot be expected from a Democratic president but will have to be the result of either popular pressure from below or attempts by Republicans to form a new governing coalition for the United States; both alternatives seem unlikely at least for the immediate future.

THE POWER OF IMPOTENCE

A final explanation for the success of Cold War ideology after the Carter election lies in a peculiar kind of power that can flow to those who are outside the formal structure of the state. Part of the frustration of the Committee on the Present Danger is that its leading lights assume an almost hereditary right to exercise state power. Paul Nitze, for example, has worked for every Democratic president since Roosevelt, and the board of the CPD reads like an honor roll of ex-policymakers: Eugene Rostow, Henry Fowler, Dean Rusk, David Packard, Leon Keyserling, Gordon Gray, Arthur Dean, Douglas Dillon, Maxwell Taylor, and Richard Allen. These men are natural "insiders," possessed of an extreme loyalty to the man in charge and preferring at all times to exercise their influence through internal debate. "If you're working for a president, then goddammit you are working for him, and you maintain discretion even if he doesn't accept your recommendations,"[44] Nitze told us, and his attitude reflects the insider mentality that the men of the CPD prefer.

But though the CPD people prefer to be insiders, the fact is that they have now been excluded from state power, which naturally leads to expressions of bitterness. Yet what these men may have discovered is that being out of power conveys a power of its own. When insiders become outsiders, they can, if they play their cards correctly, have the best of both worlds. To the extent that a president does what they advocate, they can claim credit for it. To the extent that he does not, they are free to "leak" material to the press and disavow those actions. In this way the CPD has found itself in the unique position of being insiders and outsiders at the same time—having access to high officials within the Carter Administration, yet being able to attack the Administration in the press at the same time. This is a risky place to be; the CPD can either have the best of two worlds or expose itself as hypocritical and untrustworthy. The outcome depends in part on the political skill of the CPD, which makes the question of its political direction a central one.

There are two possible political directions that the Committee on the Present Danger can take: it can remain within the Democratic Party establishment and work quietly toward pushing Carter in its direction; or it can form a public link with other Cold War militants, particularly those from the right end of the political spectrum. At this point (mid-1979) the Committee is engaged in doing both. As mentioned earlier, the CPD had a formal meeting with President Carter and his chief advisers, Brown and Brzezinski, on military matters on August 4, 1977. The CPD was never extended an invitation as an organization; but when the Committee's director, Charles Tyroler II, began to receive word of the invitations extended individually to meet with the president, he

44. Interview, August 24, 1977.

reported that he thought to himself, "My God, that's our power structure," adding with obvious delight in relating the story, "This is something we hadn't anticipated quite so soon." [45] In attendance at the afternoon session (and identified by the White House press release as simply "a group of leaders from private industry") were Paul Nitze, Eugene Rostow, Henry Fowler, Lane Kirkland, Elmo Zumwalt, David Packard, Rita Hauser, and Melvin Laird. Laird, Secretary of Defense in the early years of the Nixon Administration, was the only invitee not a member of the CPD. Dean Rusk of the Committee was invited but was unable to attend.

The meeting apparently began with the president listening attentively and even showing some sympathy for the CPD's contention that the Soviet military buildup presented a grave danger to the United States. However, the meeting quickly grew tense and heated when Carter told the group that public sentiment in the United States would not support a large defense budget. Explaining the consternation this caused the CPD leadership, *Washington Post* columnists Evans and Novak wrote: "He [Nitze] and others present were dismayed to hear the President echo the dubious judgment of his national security subordinates about what the American people will or will not accept." [46] Carter's assessment of the public mood rankled the gathered CPD leadership as much as "Where We Stand on SALT" had unglued Carter. "No, no, no," Paul Nitze was overheard murmuring as Carter explained his views. "Paul," the president complained to Nitze, "would you please let me finish?" Evans and Novak reported that "that mood of exasperation dominated the one-hour meeting (twice the time scheduled) that left everybody ill at ease." [47]

There are conflicting accounts of Carter's purpose in calling the meeting. One source speculated that the president called the Committee's leadership in to explain that the best the Administration could expect to achieve in SALT II was an agreement along the lines of the one Kissinger had been close to obtaining before he was interrupted by the 1976 election. What Carter wanted from the CPD was its support, or at least its abstention from virulent public criticism of his efforts. Evans and Novak reported that over the course of the session Carter's "repeated refrain" was, "I am the President trying to do his best and

45. Interview, August 24, 1977.
46. Rowland Evans and Robert Novak, "A Touchy Carter: Shades of Former Presidents?," *Washington Post*, August 13, 1977.
47. *Ibid.*

achieve goals we all agree on; why don't you support me instead of picking on me?"[48] To this end, Carter invited the Committee to establish channels of communication with Brown and Brzezinski to express its judgments of Administration policy rather than to "go public" as it had done with "Where We Stand on SALT." Thus the Committee would seem to have been in a strong position after the August meeting to translate its hardline ideology into policy recommendations assured of a hearing at the highest echelons of policy formulation.

Yet, despite these ties to the Administration, the Committee remains uneasy about the relationship and is also keeping alive the possibility of an alliance with right-wing movements, which indeed might become essential if its efforts are to succeed. This dual strategy is apparent from the conflicting reports of the meeting's outcome. In a *Christian Science Monitor* account, supposedly based on Administration sources, the Committee was said to have made substantial progress in getting its point of view across to the president. One CPD member said of this version: "It didn't come from us. It made it sound like we had a tremendous impact on the President, that we turned the President around."[49] That this was the last thing the Committee wished the public to believe is evident from Evans and Novak's rendition of the August 4 session. Well-known partisans of the Cold Warriors' cause, they reported that the Committee left worried that Carter was overeager to achieve an arms agreement and that he wrongly believed that the American public was unwilling to spend more for defense. Why would the CPD shun an image of success for one of disappointment? The answer is that the CPD simply could not afford to come out of the meeting expressing confidence in Carter's leadership without jeopardizing its own source of strength as a group of outside Cassandras. Since proponents of the CPD's hard-line position are practically nonexistent within the Administration's foreign policy and national security network, the CPD's only leverage is to invoke the legitimacy of public support for its views. If the CPD leaders gave the impression of being satisfied with what Carter told them, public alarm might decline precipitously and with it the power of the Committee to influence Carter's policies. Conversely, an outpouring of public concern about "the Soviet threat" would increase the CPD's effectiveness because of its peculiar status. Increased effectiveness, too, would be facilitated by an alliance with the American right. The Cold War social democrats have indeed warily begun to form such an alliance, however unwieldy it might at first seem to be.

48. *Ibid.*
49. Interview, August 24, 1977.

Already, despite their considerable philosophical differences, the social democrats and the right have demonstrated the potential strength of a coalition. The occasion was the intense opposition to the nomination of Paul Warnke as head of the Arms Control and Disarmament Administration and as chief delegate to the SALT talks. Early opposition to Warnke was fueled by a widely circulated memo written under CDM auspices and by the lengthy and virulent testimony of Paul Nitze during hearings before first the Senate Foreign Relations Committee and then the Armed Services Committee, which had decided to hold hearings on the nomination as well because of its oversight interest in military matters. The leading force behind this move by Armed Services was its second-ranking member, Cold War liberal Henry Jackson. On the heels of Nitze's testimony to Foreign Relations, and in anticipation of the Armed Services hearings scheduled for a few weeks later, an all-out effort to stop Warnke surfaced. It was led by an ad hoc organization called the Emergency Coalition Against Unilateral Disarmament.

It did not seem at all surprising to find the Emergency Coalition working out of 1721 DeSales, the offices of the CDM, nor for that matter to find ubiquitous Team B member Daniel Graham as its chairman. But it was a shock to run down the list of the officers and steering committee of the Emergency Coalition and discover the new bedfellows of CDM, an organization that Norman Podhoretz proudly proclaimed to be the home of "Cold War liberals." The steering committee was laden with such representatives of the ultraright as James G. Roberts, Executive Director of the American Conservative Union; Charles R. Black, until recently Chairman of the National Conservative Political Action Committee (NCPAC), and in 1978 campaign director for the Republican National Committee; and Howard Phillips, National Director of the Conservative Caucus. Conservative Caucus was described by Andrew Kopkind in a September 1977 article on right-wing movements as "the key connection" of New Right grass-roots organizing efforts for candidates and causes.[50] Another prominent right-winger on the steering committee was Paul Weyrich, Director of the Committee for Survival of a Free Congress. Weyrich's group is credited with having sent out 600,000 letters urging voters to lobby their senators against Warnke. (Weyrich had formerly been with the Heritage Foundation, a fairly new right-wing think tank and publishing house established with money from beer baron Joe Coors.) Still other organizations whose directors

50. Andrew Kopkind, "America's New Right," *New Times*, September 30, 1977, p. 29.

were on the steering committee included Young Americans for Freedom, the Young Republican National Federation, and the American
Security Council. The last-named organization, a long-time Cold War
lobbying group, has been called by one investigator "the soul if not the
heart of the military-industrial complex."[51] Its recent activities have
included a suit against CBS charging the network with biased reporting
on national security matters, and the production, along with the AFL-
CIO, of a controversial film on "the Soviet threat" entitled "The Price
of Peace and Freedom." Finally, Morton Blackwell, the Executive Director of the Emergency Coalition and the man who actually led the anti-
Warnke assault on a day-to-day basis, represents perhaps the heart (and
probably the soul as well) of the ultraconservative dimension of the
burgeoning Cold War coalition of the 1970's. Blackwell is contributing
editor of *Conservative Digest* and editor and assistant publisher of *The
Right Report*, both of which are produced from a hub of right-wing
activity in Falls Church, Virginia. The titular head of the Falls Church
complex is one Richard Viguerie.

Viguerie, who first gained notoriety as a fund-raiser for George
Wallace, describes his own conservatism as the combined influence of
"the two Macs—Senator Joseph McCarthy and General Douglas Mac-
Arthur."[52] Viguerie's Falls Church center is reportedly the largest political mail operation in the country. By virtue of its computerized
access to millions of names and its expertise in mobilizing this vast network, the complex represents a key institutional link in getting the Right
behind the "Soviet threat" campaign with the same fervor it has shown
for the so-called pro-family (anti-ERA, anti-gay, anti-abortion) movements in recent times.

An opportunity to extend its operations from the domestic into the
international arena was presented by the Panama Canal debate during the
early months of 1978. Indeed, for ideological purposes the Canal linked
the two. Viguerie's direct-mail operation dispatched anywhere from
seven to nine million letters and was largely responsible for raising
three million dollars in a nearly successful attempt to block Senate ratifi-
cation of the Canal treaties. Though their efforts in this case fell short,
two of the leaders who spearheaded the campaign, Representative Philip
Crane (Rep., Ill.) of the American Conservative Union and Howard
Phillips of the Conservative Caucus, indicated that they would subse-

51. Harold C. Relyea, "The American Security Council," *The Nation*, January
24, 1972, p. 114.
52. Mary McGrory, "The Panama Treaty Foes," *San Francisco Chronicle*, October 1, 1977.

quently point the anti-Canal-treaty juggernaut toward the SALT negotiations, unleashing their direct-mail and traveling "truth squad" tactics once again in an effort to derail an arms limitation agreement. While Viguerie claimed that the Panama campaign added between 250,000 and 400,000 new names to the conservative cause, Phillips cautioned that "raw numbers alone won't do the job when you're up against something like the American foreign policy establishment. People look to experts for answers, not to a group of outsiders."[53]

Thus, a marriage of convenience between the *déclassé* experts of the CPD in search of a popular base and the mass-based New Right in search of authoritative backing for its hard-line conviction would seem to be in the offing. Signs have surfaced in recent years that conservatives, tired of sectarian purity and ignominious defeat, have begun to see the possibility of long-term gains for themselves in such an alliance. Both Viguerie and conservative ideologue William Rusher, for instance, have editorialized in favor of conservative participation in the Democratic Party. The lines of such a strategy (pre–Panama Canal) were revealed in a *Conservative Digest* interview with the publicist for Anita Bryant's successful anti-gay campaign. The conservatives' goal, as explained in the course of the interview, is to begin with the nucleus of people who are conservative on "the family" and to get them to "go to work together for other issues and other candidates." Specifically tapped for this new conservative coalition are "Democrats, blue-collar workers, and Jewish voters."[54]

If we substitute "foreign policy" for "the family," the strategy becomes an apt description of the social-democratic position; the targeted groups are virtually identical to Wattenberg's "new majority." Nor are these parallels between the Right and the Cold War social democrats matters merely of appearance. The parallels run much deeper, tapping the same theme of *security*—the one manifesting itself as concern over internal breakdown, the other as concern over external attack. Similarly, both the pro-family forces on the Right and the Cold War liberals share a mutual antipathy toward "sixties culture," which they hold responsible for our loss of security, described on the one hand as "the decline of traditional values" at home and on the other as "the loss of will" abroad. Though these ideological currents have yet to come together into one cohesive movement, the potential for synthesis is very real, as evidenced by Norman Podhoretz's article "The Culture of Appeasement."[55] In it, Podhoretz brought together, however tenuously, the anti-gay fight in the domestic arena and the anti-communist battles in foreign policy. In so doing, he provided the ideological rationale for a fusion between the mass-based "pro-family" forces currently in vogue and the "Soviet threat" effort of elite groups led by the Committee on the Present Danger.

The gist of Podhoretz' piece is that an unhealthy pacifism has pervaded the nation since the Vietnam War, similar to that which characterized England in the 1920's and 1930's. This is a common theme in the CPD/CDM literature, which is replete with analogies of the United States today and Europe in the 1930's, punctuated with frequent cries of "Munich!" But Podhoretz takes the case one step further, arguing that at bottom the root cause of this erosion of will is homosexuality! In making such an argument, and suggesting that this was similarly the case of England in the earlier period, Podhoretz closes the circle, tying both types of insecurity together into a small if not neat package of demagoguery that will surely find its way into *Readers' Digest*—especially since the chairman of that mass-circulation magazine is a member of the CPD. Podhoretz concludes his article with the warning that "the parallels with England in 1937 are here, and this revival of the culture of appeasement ought to be troubling our sleep."[56] His overtures to Phyllis Schlafly (anti-ERA) and Anita Bryant strike a new mood in American political life.

These examples of how the Committee on the Present Danger is attempting to walk in two different political directions at once indicates something about the power that comes from impotence. Freed from the responsibility associated with the exercise of state power, the CPD finds that it can be as "Cold Warriorish" as it chooses without having to pay the costs. After all, Vietnam did force such Cold War militants as Walt Rostow and Dean Rusk to retire, if not dishonorably, then at least into relative obscurity (for them, potentially a worse punishment). Their crime was not that they believed what they did but that they attempted to put their beliefs into practice and failed. Now out of power, they can believe anything they want and lay the blame for failure elsewhere. It is only a matter of time before the Committee overcomes its anger at being passed over for high policymaking positions and realizes its opportunity to criticize a timid president who has neither the courage nor the flair the CPD members once possessed. Clever political maneuvering may give the CPD influence far beyond its outsider status.

55. Norman Podhoretz, "The Culture Of Appeasement," *Harper's*, October 1977.
56. *Ibid.*, p. 32.

Yet the stakes are high, and other forces are in play that could have the effect of isolating the Committee from main currents in American life. We do not wish, in other words, to leave the impression that the success of the CPD in walking this two-direction political path is guaranteed or inevitable. Within the CPD there is bound to be disagreement over an alliance with the Right, with opposition to be expected from organized labor and social-democratic intellectuals. If the Committee moves to the right to maximize one advantage, in other words, it minimizes another by isolating itself from very powerful ties to a social-democratic tradition. Outside the Committee much depends on Carter and his advisers, who are engaged in their own game of trying to contain the Committee's influence and strengthen themselves in the eyes of the CPD's natural constituents. As the Committee moves closer to power it must downplay its allegiance with the Right; as it moves away from power it must build it up. This requires astute political sensitivity, and the task is so difficult that it may be beyond even the political skills of Cold War liberals like Nitze, Rostow, and Podhoretz.

CONCLUSION

The breakdown of Cold War liberalism after Vietnam provides a unique opportunity to assess the forces that shape and determine American foreign policy options. Policy is made through a complex dialectic among the interests of political elites, material conditions, and struggles over legitimation. It would be an error to conclude by arguing that business leaders at crisis points simply reassess their alternatives and lead the campaign for new foreign policy initiatives. They do, but that is only the beginning of the story. Once those reassessments are made, they must be translated into policies and then convincingly presented to the public. Our case study teaches us how difficult this process can be.

In the aftermath of Vietnam, conditions were about as ripe as they could be to bring about a significant change in the direction of U.S. foreign policy. First, the expense of maintaining a capacity to intervene throughout the world had resulted in a decision on the part of a significant sector of the business elite to sponsor reductions in defense spending and a less cumbersome imperial presence. Second, disenchantment with war had become pervasive in the general population, although this sentiment was complex and could not be reduced to support for either pacifistic or anti-imperialist goals. Sensing the changing times and responding to this new mood in the presidential campaign, Jimmy Carter promised a fresh direction in world affairs that would at once ennoble the American spirit and restore American power. To this end, the new Administration was staffed from the ranks of the one faction of the national security elite that was most convinced of the need to reassess the entire direction of postwar foreign policy. Yet under even these seemingly optimal conditions, it appears that no great changes will be made. Indeed, it could be argued that U.S. foreign policy will become more militant over the next few years rather than less so. What can explain this surprising failure of the Carter Administration to strike out in new directions?

We conclude that real opportunities for policy reevaluations occur rarely and that when they arise, it is owing to a fortuitous combination of circumstances that make immediate action essential before the opportunities contract. It was precisely such a fluid situation that Carter entered in 1977. When right-wing Republicans had lost in their bid for the presidency and Cold War Democrats had failed to gain a place in the Administration, each became more strident in their opposition to a reduction in East-West tensions. The election seemed to accelerate their momentum, the Carter appointments to bring them together in common purpose. Yet it was at this early juncture that Carter had the best opportunity to strike a fatal blow to Cold War ideology and perhaps have his name enshrined as the man who brought a stable peace to the world. (Nixon had sought this reputation, but will be denied the credit for his effort for other reasons.) Upon taking office Carter was in a position that will never again be duplicated during his presidency. Though not overly popular, as a new president he had much good will to count upon. Moreover, many of his supporters within the elite, particularly from the multinational corporations, were in favor of a major reevaluation. But Carter vacillated. Rather than fulfill his pledge for a fresh course in world affairs by proclaiming a bold new ideology that could combat the resurgence of the discredited doctrines of the Cold Warriors, Carter chose instead to seek an accommodation with his critics on their own ideological grounds. This placed the burgeoning forces of Cold War militarism, led by the Committee on the Present Danger, in the position of being both inside advisers and outside critics. And it has left Carter's cabinet appointees on the defensive ever since, forcing them to adjust their designs for post-Vietnam realities to a conceptual framework built for the post–Second World War period.

Moreover, since the end of the Second World War important changes have taken place in the nature and direction of the American ruling class. Though it was true that until the war the American state tended to act as the unmediated representative of big business in its pursuit of foreign policy goals, the coming of the Cold War gave rise to a group (we hesitate to call it a class) of state managers who created and ran the national security policies of six presidents. Part of the reason for the success of this national security elite was that its policies were in accord with the wishes of large corporations. But such an accord was possible only in conditions of economic growth. When those conditions altered, the first reaction of much of large-scale business was once again to seek policies that were based on cheap budgets and an avoidance of balance-of-payments problems. Yet in thinking along these lines, class-conscious businessmen aroused the opposition of a firmly entrenched national security elite. Brought into being by Cold War liberalism, the state managers were not easily removed from power when conditions changed. They have used their control over the state, even from "private" positions, to wreak havoc on any plans to relax Cold War tensions. In the face of such opposition, business support for new initiatives has collapsed. Business will now go along with the resurgent Cold War ideology and, as usual, extract its price. Carter, in short, was in a position to exploit a potentially major split between the business elite and the national security managers; but when he hesitated the split was avoided, and he now faces general unity on the issue of increasing defense budgets.

What the Committee on the Present Danger understands, whereas Carter apparently does not, is that ideology is central to the successful exercise of political power. By preserving its basis in the American version of the social-democratic experience, by waging a campaign for public support with undiminished enthusiasm, and by walking the narrow line between insider and outsider status, the Committee has shown a political acumen that enables it to maintain influence beyond the point of its historical glory. Those are the elements that are difficult to reconcile with simple theories of foreign policy formulation, but those are also the elements that determine whether an Administration will capture momentum or be captured by it.

State Monopoly Capitalism: A Comment on Wolfe and Sanders

OSCAR PINO-SANTOS

As will be seen in the following, my perspectives on the problem dealt with by Wolfe and Sanders differ significantly from theirs. Nevertheless, I still consider their essay a valuable and in several ways a positive contribution to the theme of the Cold War. In this light, it certainly would have been desirable to do a more profound analysis than time and circumstances have permitted me.

There is one aspect of the presentation by Wolfe and Sanders that deserves to be emphasized: the basically healthy and progressive point of view that pervades the entire paper. Moreover, the presentation by Wolfe and Sanders—apart from the differences one might have with the conceptual framework that determines their analysis and conclusions—has the notable merit of being the bearer of a political message so significant that we are obliged to point out its full importance: the factors and the ideology that promoted the Cold War in the United States have not disappeared, they are still alive and not only latent, but already organizing a new offensive—charged with tragic omens—as reflected in the case of the so-called "Committee on the Present Danger."

The thesis of Wolfe and Sanders can be summarized as follows: after the Second World War, a consensus arose in the United States among the "liberals" (who were seeking economic growth through a program of defense spending) and the "strategists" (who saw everything revolving around the alleged Soviet threat). The result was the beginning of a "centrist" policy in foreign affairs that would be called "Cold War liberalism."

Nevertheless, Cold War liberalism reached a crisis toward the end of the 1960's owing to the following factors: (1) it was understood that the policy of defense spending damaged the North American economy

Oscar Pino-Santos is one of Cuba's leading economic historians. He has been Cuban ambassador to China and more recently an adviser to the Cuban Prime Minister. He is currently director of the Havana-based Center for the Study of the Americas.

more than it benefited the economy; (2) the hawkish adventures abroad created a domestic atmosphere of dissent and near-rebellion; and (3) Vietnam raised the question of the credibility of the United States. This crisis appeared to culminate in the rise of the Carter Group. Nonetheless, recently Cold War tendencies have begun to reemerge, a trend appropriately represented by the so-called "Committee on the Present Danger."

According to Wolfe and Sanders, this resurgence of the Cold War cannot be explained by the use of traditional theories such as those that apply to the role of public opinion and the "military-industrial complex." In their place, they propose to interpret these developments in the light of the following hypotheses: (1) the "perversion" of North American social democracy (based on the theory of military Keynesianism); (2) the struggles between elite factions wielding doctrines that must be legitimized through mass support; (3) the existence of a system of power that consists of "not having the power of the state."

In my judgment, these are Wolfe and Sanders' fundamental ideas. Since I have tried to summarize them briefly and simply, surely I have not presented the nuances from every angle. The authors to whom I refer can clarify whether I have erred about the essence of their argument, which is what matters. But on this—which I consider to be the fundamental argument—I would like to make some critical observations which might possibly be useful for a later reconsideration of certain aspects of their essay.

It seems to me essential to begin with an extremely condensed—and therefore schematic—version of the way in which we interpret the historical process that culminated at the end of the 1940's and early 1950's in the North American policy of the Cold War. Nevertheless, to accomplish this it is necessary to go back still farther and to set out a historical framework that extends beyond the purely North American. In this spirit, it seems relevant to our analysis to sketch, however briefly, the theory of "state monopoly capitalism." How did this particular kind of capitalism come about? What is it? What is its contemporary role?

The monopolistic tendency of capitalism—which as we know was seen by Marx and Engels in the middle of the nineteenth century—began to predominate at the end of the nineteenth and the beginning of the twentieth centuries. Competitive or free-market capitalism, through the action of its own laws, gave way to monopoly capitalism, and this in turn was subsequently converted into state monopoly capitalism. This later development took place through the ever-increasing intervention of the state in the economies of the developed capitalist countries. This was a process that was initiated with the First World War, and—as progressively closer ties to the large monopolies evolved—accelerated notably with the crisis of the 1930's and the Second World War, becoming even more evident in the postwar period.

State monopoly capitalism is usually defined as the joining of the monopolies with the power of the state for the purpose of trying to resolve the contradictions of the system, consolidate the hold of large capital, and augment its profits. There are, of course, other ways to conceptualize and/or express the phenomenon—including some that would reject the term. But the fact of its existence is beyond doubt, and its central importance as a characteristic of contemporary capitalism cannot be denied.

The modern capitalist state has not, of course, lost its class character nor some of its formal structural characteristics. Although dominated by a hegemonic monopolistic class fraction, the state continues representing the interests of the bourgeoisie as a whole and it still maintains its classic institutional forms—legislative, executive, and judicial powers —as well as its armed forces and the rest of the apparatus of repression. Nevertheless, during the last few decades, the state's economic (and political) role has been significantly enhanced. Earlier, the economic role of the state was primarily restricted to fiscal, budgetary, and administrative tasks, and—since the establishment of central banks—to certain monetary controls. After the First World War, this situation changed. That conflict accelerated and sharpened the transformation of capitalism into state monopoly capitalism, a phenomenon, as we noted above, that was accentuated even more with the crisis of the 1930's and the Second World War. In that period, the concentration of production and the centralization of capital—and, above all, the increasing internationalization of capital at the end of the 1950's and the beginning of the 1960's—took place in the context of an accelerating increase in economic intervention by the state in capitalist countries. We are not dealing with parallel processes, but rather with closely linked phenomena, interpenetrated and reciprocally conditioned.

State intervention has assumed diverse forms, varying from country to country. For years one of its most important mechanisms has consisted of anticyclical policies, of Keynesian inspiration, based essentially on a set of regulatory fiscal and monetary policies. Public spending, intended to support effective demand, has been particularly important. In the United States, this has particularly taken the form of military spending. Also, especially in Western Europe, direct state control of productive enterprises, including important industrial complexes and entire sectors of the economy, has been important. In Great Britain, enterprises that were only marginally profitable or actually losing money, like railroads, utilities, and mines, were nationalized in order to subsidize private industry. In some cases, such as France, successive projects of state economic planning have been attempted. In sum, by the early 1970's, public spending represented 25 percent of gross domestic product in the United States (taking only the federal government into account), approximately 45 percent in West Germany, and more than 50 percent in Great Britain.

The state, however, applies its anticyclical policies, takes charge of important sectors of the economy, and spends enormous amounts on infrastructure, research and development, and education under the prodding of and in relation to the interests of monopoly capital. *Basically, what characterizes capitalism in its present phase of monopolistic and imperialistic development and its general crisis is that the process of accumulation cannot continue except in the form of state monopoly capitalism.*

At the same time, state monopoly capitalism sharpens the contradictions of the system because *it is itself constructed on contradictory bases.* Monopoly capitalism does not completely eliminate competition; in fact it sharpens competition among the capitalist powers. But growing state intervention, in the service of monopoly capitalism itself, goes against the principle of competition. At root, the increasing functions and property of the state have a limited objective, beyond which they begin to endanger the very existence of the capitalist order. Thus state monopoly capitalism sharpens even more the fundamental contradiction of capitalism: the contradiction between the social character of production and the private appropriation of the benefits of that production.

In pointing this out, we note that North American capitalism, despite certain specific features of its development that we all recognize, did not by any means escape the working out of the aforementioned general laws of this system. Consequently, it passed through the free market stage, entered the monopolistic and imperialist stage, and began, after the First World War, to become state monopoly capitalism. This North American state monopoly capitalism gained decisive impetus in the crisis years of the 1930's (under New Deal policies) and accelerated enormously during, and above all after, the Second World War. It had, in addition, special features which differentiated it from Western European and Japanese state monopoly capitalism. In the United States it was not based on the nationalization of industries or on programs of economic pseudoplanning; rather (as Wolfe and Sanders comment, using an apt term), it tended to emphasize a sort of "Keynesian militarism." Nonetheless, fundamentally it has still been state monopoly capitalism—and moreover an aggressive form of it.

The theory of state monopoly capitalism allows one to explain perfectly the internal political developments in the United States in the postwar period in a context that takes into account the peculiarities of the mature capitalist development of this country (in its imperialist phase) and the behavior of its dominant classes. The theory of state monopoly capitalism, as a methodological guide for analysis, would surely enable a well-aimed study of the current resurgence of certain "Cold War" trends on which Wolfe and Sanders' concerns have so rightly focused.

The absence of a more scientific viewpoint, which would take into account the characteristics of the socioeconomic development of North America, the behavior of its dominant classes in a process of an ever-intensifying (at the national and international levels) process of class struggle, and other features that follow from any rigorous analysis which considers the real historical developments in the United States is, perhaps, the major weakness of the paper we are discussing.

One might, of course, also point out inconsistencies that are, in a way, only terminological ones. For example, the term "Cold War liberalism" may or may not be appropriate. But its interpretation as a consensus between "liberals" and "strategists" which resulted in a "centrist" (!) U.S. foreign policy would seem debatable. To be sure, in the 1950's especially, there was a consensus between the representatives of the dominant North American classes that controlled the leadership of the Democratic Party and the Republican Party. But it was a consensus between "neo-liberals" and "neo-conservatives," a reactionary, aggressive, and imperialist consensus (a reflection of the interests of the hegemonic monopoly groups) based on the most regressive principles of domestic and foreign policy. Therefore, the mere reference to a consensus between "liberals" and "strategists" (Cold War liberalism) does not help much to explain the class background against which this North American historical period developed, running from the unharnessed, bellicose anticommunism of the Truman-Dulles era to the period of Kissinger's *realpolitik*.

The authors of the article of course allude to the crisis of Cold War policy that took place during the Nixon-Kissinger years. Nevertheless, the explanation they offer for the corresponding change that took place in North American foreign policy—damages imposed on the economy by defense spending, dissent, and domestic near-rebellion because of the bellicose adventures and loss of credibility for the United States in Vietnam—seems insufficient, even adding, as the paper does, the role of Kissinger's ideas (the "Yalta" line vs. the "Riga" line). In effect, the authors forget the determinant role played in this entire process by the changing world balance of power, the growth of Soviet military power, the USSR and socialist community policy of détente and peace, the rise of national liberation movements, and other factors.

By way of conclusion, one tends to think that a paper such as the one we are commenting on, the product of such an interesting and *very important* study, would improve substantially if its authors, while not ignoring the superstructural manifestations of certain historical processes (although *not* examining them from the point of view of narrow theories of "elites"), would ponder the real importance of the phenomena that take place in the base, in the relations of production and the corresponding structures, behaviors, and class struggles. Specifically, the theory of state monopoly capitalism should be taken into account as a valuable and irreplaceable conceptual tool for interpreting cases such as the Cold War: its origin, development, crisis, and new attempts at resurgence.

Wolfe and Sanders, using such an approach, would see the weaknesses of a theoretical position which begins by not taking into account the role of monopolies; they would also see the danger of an underestimation of the role that those directly or indirectly associated with the "military-industrial complex" play within the totality of those monopolies. This is what truly represents the "perverse" face, not of North American social democracy as the authors say, but of state monopoly capitalism in the United States.

Foreign Policy Made Difficult: A Comment on Wolfe and Sanders

EARL C. RAVENAL

Alan Wolfe's and Jerry Sanders' paper, "Resurgent Cold War Ideology: The Case of the Committee on the Present Danger," has little bearing on Latin America. But no matter; it is a perceptive and unusual analysis, and it raises some important points about the motives and processes of American foreign policymaking. Yet among its points of interest are some crucial misconceptions of how policy is made.

We have here a case study of the rise of the Committee on the Present Danger as a challenger and a competitor to the foreign and national-security policymaking of the Carter Administration. What is the encompassing question that is presented by this case? We can get a sense of this question, as well as some of the authors' critical assumptions, from a series of formulations and statements in their paper. They wonder "how the principal protagonist of resurgent Cold War ideology —the Committee on the Present Danger—was able to confound any thought of new directions in U.S. foreign policy, even though the realities of the post-Vietnam world called for radical departures from Cold War orthodoxy" (p. 43). Again, they note "the puzzling phenomenon of how an ideology can persevere long after the conditions for its demise have manifested themselves" (p. 48). They observe that "the new Administration was staffed from the ranks of the one faction of the national security elite that was most convinced of the need to reassess the entire direction of postwar foreign policy." But they conclude that "under even these seemingly optimal conditions, it appears that no great changes will be made," and go on to ask: "What can explain this surprising failure of the Carter Administration to strike out in new directions?" (p. 74). And finally: "Even though there were

Earl C. Ravenal is a Fellow of the Institute for Policy Studies in Washington, D.C., and a professor of international relations at the Georgetown School of Foreign Service. His articles have appeared in many professional and scholarly journals, and he is the author or coauthor of five books on international relations and foreign policy.

grounds for predicting major changes in the direction of U.S. foreign policy under Carter, what is most interesting is that so many new directions were ignored. Instead, the United States saw a resurgence of the very ideas and political interests that by 1968 had seemed dead beyond resurrection" (p. 46). And so Wolfe and Sanders set out their task: "The problem we want to explore in this paper is how this resurgence came about" (p. 47).

I will agree that we have here a piquant—indeed a critical—problem in understanding the derivation of public and elite attitudes and the making of foreign policy. But you cannot fathom the causal process very well unless you have the basic facts straight. The way you present the initial evidence inspires the questions you ask, and the shape of the questions points to certain kinds of answers.

Who are these new foreign policy elites of the Carter Administration, from whom so much was expected and so little has been forthcoming? As the authors say: "A new generation of foreign policy professionals, many of them archcritics of Cold War liberalism, took over key positions in the National Security Council, in the State Department, and on the president's staff" (p. 45). And "Carter's appointments went to men who had been critics not only of the war in Vietnam, but also (and this was less widely understood) of *the assumptions that produced the war in the first place*" (p. 57; the breathless italics belong to Wolfe and Sanders). The authors are referring to such rising bureaucrats as Leslie Gelb, Director of the State Department's Bureau of Politico-Military Affairs, and Anthony Lake, Director of Policy Planning at State.

I think this is the place to dig in: None of these people criticized the underlying assumptions of American foreign policy. As I will put it later, none dissented from the "major premise," the large paradigm that has ruled our foreign policy for the past thirty years, and still does. They just made bold and suggestive noises (ambiguous ones, it turns out, because ultimately inconsistent) about everything: human rights, arms transfers, alliances, intervention, the defense budget, military force structures, international economics, the American-Soviet relationship. But policy is not made of noise. Of course these new foreign policy elites are articulate. That's just the trouble. "Mod" scholarship is getting to be like journalism—lots of raw material, not very thoroughly cooked; and such large portions. Scholars talk to too many people, policymaking types. They get to know what's in their heads, or off the top of their heads. But how much does that tell you about what those people are going to do, especially in circumstances that differ from the ones they predict, posit, or wish—in short, if there is a "threat." Better for scholars to meditate than to interview—or, in another image, to triangulate from a few crucial and correct compass readings.

The obvious answer to the question of why this Administration has not done what it "should have" done is that it never wanted to do it in the first place. The irony that puzzled Wolfe and Sanders, that provided the point of departure of their paper, that inspired their search for deep and sophisticated explanations—that all these nice, liberal people would end up executing hawkish, expansionist, dangerous, expensive, and ultimately illiberal foreign policies—turns out to be no irony at all.

We can see this by examining the nature of the "dissent" of these liberals from the policies of a succession of American governments in the Vietnam war. (I hesitate even to say a succession of governments, since all of these supposed dissenters defected at some point in the Nixon Administration, and not entirely for reasons of principle.) Look, for instance, at their criticism of Kissinger, which leaned heavily on alleged aberrations of personality. Indeed, to them the whole Vietnam war was an aberration, a "mistake." They invented the "mistake" theory of Vietnam, publicized it, popularized it, saw to it that it became the prevailing liberal explanation of Vietnam and the whole era of Vietnam. (Look, again, at the "Vietnam obituary issue" of *The New Republic*, May 3, 1975, which is rather a mass grave of liberal retrospection on the war.) To the liberal critics, Vietnam was a product of errors. Some of them were relatively trivial misperceptions of the nature of the regimes in Saigon and Hanoi; others were faults in the organization of the American bureaucracy to process information; and, somewhat more serious, still others were exaggerations of the strategic importance of Vietnam. But to none of the liberal critics was the disaster of Vietnam the result of fundamental American objectives and purposes.

Their point was precisely the opposite: that we did not have to worry much about, or learn much from, the defeat or frustration of American designs in Vietnam, because Vietnam was unique, and therefore not replicable. They trivialized, isolated, and buried the case of Vietnam in order to gain freedom from precedent in future cases. No retrospection, no remorse, no lessons, not even any useful recriminations, certainly no fundamental reevaluation of foreign policy. This was the liberal critics' dowry to the new Administration, their early intellectual gift to the emerging new elite consensus.

A related theme in the Wolfe and Sanders paper is the now-familiar observation of "the disintegration of the foreign policy consensus during the Vietnam war" (p. 44). No; the consensus never disintegrated—

certainly not down to its foundation or anywhere near that. In any event, the elite consensus is now reconstituted. It has coagulated around a range of acceptable, though not entirely coincident, positions that constitute a spectrum of orthodoxy—shapes of the world and appropriate modes of U.S. foreign policy that can be "responsibly" advocated. Briefly, these positions may be set out as follows. First, there is the notion of "managed interdependence"—an invocation of global condominium, extended détente, a collusion of the superpowers and other powerful nations in the collective management of functional issues and problems. This is the contemporary equivalent of the earlier vision of universal collective security. Second, there is "trilateralism"—a lapse into bipolar confrontation, with the addition of Japan to the essential alliance and the economic nexus, and with the grafting of "North-South" and "global" issues (such as money, resources, food and population, and pollution) onto the political-military structure. Finally, there is the concept of the "balance of power"—the five-power or many-power world of Nixon and Kissinger, which still has its respected partisans.

Several things can be said about this revived elite consensus, this range of orthodoxy. First, it embraces the basic paradigm of American foreign policy—deterrence and alliance—though these elements have different meanings, and function differently, in the various foreign policy schemes. Second, disagreements among the positions are only about the "minor premise" of a large syllogism of which the major premise is a kind of universal proposition, a hypothetical "if-then" statement (if we are challenged by certain events or conditions in our external environment, then we must respond in certain ways), and the minor premise is simply a fact, a statement of what happens to be the problem, the challenge, the "threat." Third, all the positions within the range of orthodoxy imply ample military postures, large defense budgets, and periodic wars. They are all interventionist, though the mechanisms for insuring world order, allocating security responsibilities, policing spheres, and enforcing minimally correct conduct vary appropriately among the orthodox positions.

Most of the foreign policy disagreements aired these days have been on the minor premise—different judgments of Soviet capabilities and intentions, different opinions of the strategic importance of some threatened object, different conceptions of the most effective method of combating aggression or revolution (including the debate within the Carter Administration on the wisdom of "linkage"). It is rare for critics—even liberal ones in their most heightened moments of disaffection—to defect from the major premise. And it is virtually unheard of for someone to accept, or grant, fairly hawkish intelligence about hostile capabilities and threatening events and yet deny the "obvious" conclusion of a belligerent American response—because he had denied the major premise in the first place. But only that would have constituted the serious dissent that Wolfe and Sanders expected, and sought in vain, from the liberal foreign policy practitioners of the Carter Administration.

In terms of this analysis we can even understand how a working consensus could be constructed between the Administration and its "ideological" opponents in the Committee on the Present Danger: all it would require is a truce about the threat and a compromise on the implementation of our response, since the major premise, the fundamental American foreign policy paradigm, has never been brought into question. By any reckoning, we have to say that the Carter Administration is implementing, rather faithfully, even gratefully, the foreign policies of its predecessor, the Nixon-Ford-Kissinger Administration—region by region, function by function. Of course, if intentions could easily become perfected actions, the Carter Administration would have retreated a way from Nixon's and Kissinger's cold pursuit of the multipolar balance of power to a policy it thought the American people would support more intuitively and generously, a policy involving, once again as in the early 1960's, a flourish of morality, alliance loyalism, and ideology—in other words, a policy of bipolar confrontation. But intentions do not dictate or produce actions. The model is more complex than that, and the conditions are tighter. Thus, by the middle of its first term, the only remaining friends of the Carter Administration were those who never took its promises seriously in the first place.

Now we can take up the matter of "ideology" (or "doctrine," if you will), the mode in which Wolfe and Sanders prefer to explain the evolution of, and the conflict over, U.S. foreign policy. The authors take far too seriously the notion advanced by Administration members such as Leslie Gelb that the Carter government has eschewed "doctrine." This is because both the authors and Gelb see "doctrine" as a parade of beliefs, a string of verbalizations, instead of seeing it as something more akin to "policy," which is (or should be) defined as a nation's, or an Administration's, predictable pattern of response to challenges. In these more operational terms, the Carter Administration has its doctrines; if they do not yet have names, that is the fault more of the president's speech-writers than of the president.

In a related vein, the authors are also overimpressed with the intellectual odyssey of Leslie Gelb, as related to the colonels at the Army War College in May 1977. (This is not a pursuit of personalities; quite the contrary, it is worth mentioning precisely because it neatly illustrates the pattern of rationalization of "the brightest and the nicest" of the Carter Administration.) Gelb said that sometime during the Vietnam war, which he confessed originally to have supported, he came to the conclusion that we did not have to be doing those things, because "fewer and fewer things had to do with the Soviet-American connection." Wolfe and Sanders take comfort from that sensible realization. But should we? How reliable is such a change of heart and mind? How useful in a more recent challenge that *does* have something "to do with the Soviet-American connection," because the source of it is the Soviet Union—a fact that does not take the unique insights of the Committee on the Present Danger to make us grasp? Was it not Brzezinski's National Security Council that put the president up to warning the Russians about Zaire, Rhodesia, and the Horn of Africa? And was it not Gelb's own Bureau of Politico-Miliary Affairs that regarded Somalia as a growth opportunity for American influence and arms shipments? In other words, ask not why people acquire attitudes and beliefs in the first place; ask rather why they give them up when the logic of objectives and challenges catches up with them.

So those nice young liberal careerists of the Carter Administration will implement the policies of the hawks—but, they beg us to believe, reluctantly. But when has foreign policy ever changed because people wanted it to? There has always been the plea of "necessity." And in a sense it is a just plea—though the necessity has to be understood not as absolute but as conditional. The authors profess perplexity over such questions as "why the Carter Administration refused to take the debate out of the hands of the foreign policy professionals and appeal to the general population on the basis of a counterideology" (counter, that is, to that of the Committee on the Present Danger) (p. 63). The answer is not that the Carter Administration lacked an ideology. It had one, the same one as the Committee on the Present Danger: the continuing major premise, the large and constant paradigm of postwar American foreign policy. Initially, this Administration differed from its hawkish opponents in its assessment of the threat, but it did not take long to come around to the notion that it had better hedge by moving toward the Committee's apprehensions. Perhaps we should stop worrying about our hawkish opponents, who hector us and goad us, and start worrying about our liberal friends in the Administration, who asked first for our trust and later for our sympathy.

But what sort of "counterideology" could the Carter Administration have promoted? The authors project a "multilateralist perspective that

saw in free trade the solution to the problem of world order," positing
that "American domination of multinational corporations will preserve
American hegemony better than any emphasis on military capabilities"
(p. 64). That sounds suspiciously like all that "new era" talk put about
by the same Carter people several years ago, when they were critics.
But would it work? Probably not. For the proposal to substitute "nonmilitary means" such as economic dominance confuses the salience of
these items with the logic of problems and situations. By logic I mean
that, in situations, a factor that is not on the surface—not salient—can be
invoked by circumstances and become the pivotal point of the action.
And in most critical cases that factor will be political or military, not
economic. If we are challenged on such a strategic dimension, we might
have a choice of whether to respond or not; but we do not have the
choice of substituting irrelevant means simply because they are trendy
and reassuring. That is why economics does not constitute the basis for
a counterideology, any more than the "domination of multinational
corporations" obviates the need for "military capabilities." In fact, the
latter two terms are intertwined; one can invite or occasion the other.
The "need" to preserve one can invoke the "necessity" of using the
other.

The main trouble with the authors' thesis, in seeing postwar political
history as a competition and alternation of ideologies and doctrines, is
that it ignores the tangible play of challenges and responses. It almost
asserts that Cold War reactions (the old Cold War and its current re-
crudescence) are not just expensive, misguided, and sometimes disastrous, but fictitious; that is, not just bad but not even real, not even
contingently "necessary" in terms of objectives and challenges. But—
and here we could refer specifically to Latin American cases—what if
there is revolution, political competition, denial of strategic and commercial access? What about sharp and unfriendly political change in
resource countries, such as Venezuela, Mexico, Peru, Chile, Jamaica?
What about hegemonic thrusts by Brazil? What if favorable conditions
cannot be reestablished by peaceful persuasion, multilateral diplomacy,
economic aid?

The radical view (as opposed to the liberal view) has always been
that problems are concrete, threats are real, choices are hard, solutions
are costly. The alternative foreign policy of nonintervention, even
though it is preferred, is not taken to be free. But it is a real alternative,
because it represents a change in the major premise, a distinct shift in
the fundamental American foreign policy paradigm. And it would invoke a rather unfamiliar coalition in its support: the left, the peace-

seekers, many ordinary businessmen, the remnants of those nasty "isolationists" out there somewhere beyond the right that is discernible in our generation. This coalition would be willing to give up some of the rest of the world to our geopolitical competitors and to assorted local revolutionaries. Wolfe and Sanders have captured something of these possibilities when they remark: "In the postwar period the American right was against such liberal innovations as high defense spending, a system of military conscription, and an ideology of permanent crisis necessitating permanent response" (p. 49). And they are perceptive in noting an essential statist and antibusiness bias among the Committee on the Present Danger.

Yet I doubt that we will get major foreign policy change—that is, change in the major premise—with those attractive liberals who succumb to the logic of the hawks in moments of military or political pressure. Periodic reassessments of "the threat" and discrete decisions about individual weapons systems or annual defense budget levels do not add up to reliable and lasting changes in patterns of political and military response. And ideologies and counterideologies can be insubstantial—just a screen of verbiage.

Real foreign policy change would have to be based on the premise of nonintervention, because nonintervention (war-avoidance, self-reliance) constitutes the logically minimum condition for cutting the linkage between perceiving challenges and going to war. Two essential items of linkage would be severed: first, the relevance of strategic challenges that are remote in time or space; and second, our Wilsonian universalist sympathies for other nations. Some would call that "indifference"; but in an era when the big people are wrong about the big things, the heroes might be the ordinary businessmen who only want to make their deals, get their materials, and sell their goods, and the ordinary citizens who only want to live, eat, and keep some of their money in their own pockets.

The International Competitiveness of the U.S. Economy: A Study of Steel and Electronics

STEVEN S. VOLK

In 1971 the AFL-CIO noted, "It is a fact of our international economic life that we must export more than we import. It is a further fact of U.S. international economic life that the one area of exports in which we have traditionally excelled is manufactured goods."[1] Six years later, however, the United States ran up a whopping $26.5 billion trade deficit, a figure more than four times the 1976 deficit and $20 billion higher than the previous record deficit established in 1972.[2] Furthermore, the major imports adding to this deficit were machinery, transportation equipment, and manufactured goods—not oil, which is so often blamed for our recent trade imbalances. In fact, during the ten-year period between 1961 and 1971—before the increase in oil prices—imports of manufactured and semimanufactured goods had risen from 44.1 percent of total U.S. imports to 66.8 percent.[3]

Trade balances with traditional buyers have also been upset. Latin America, for example, historically has run a negative trade balance with the United States. In 1977, however, the United States was more than $3 billion in the red in its merchandise trade with the Latin American republics. In the first six months of 1977 only Argentina, Chile, and Peru ran deficits in their trade accounts with the United States.

Steven Volk has been a staff member of the North American Congress on Latin America (NACLA) since 1973, has written extensively on the internationalization of capital in a variety of industrial branches, and is currently completing a Ph.D. in history at Columbia University. He would like to thank the members of NACLA, Tom Seidl, Cheryl Payer, and Mike Van Waas for their helpful critiques of earlier drafts of his paper.

1. Industrial Union Department, AFL-CIO, *Needed: A Constructive Foreign Trade Policy* (Washington, D.C., 1971), p. 14.
2. *New York Times*, Jan. 31, 1978.
3. José de la Torre, "Latin American Exports of Manufactures to the United States: The Outlook for the Future," in Robert B. Williamson, William P. Glade, Jr., and Karl M. Schmitt, eds., *Latin American-U.S. Economic Interactions* (Washington, D.C., 1974), p. 51.

To understand the trade problems that currently plague the U.S. economy, one must go *beyond* trade to appreciate the basic shifts in the nature of production currently challenging the international competitiveness of the U.S. economy. Two factors in particular form this challenge: the loss of technological competitiveness and the shift of productive capital, especially in labor-intensive manufacturing industries, from the United States to low-wage areas abroad.

Once indisputably first in technology and scientific innovation, the United States is rapidly falling behind. U.S. industry maintains its technological superiority only in three high-technology areas: computers, aerospace, and certain branches of electronics. Furthermore, each year a smaller percentage of the U.S. Gross National Product is spent on basic research and development. The failure of U.S. technology seems to be indicated in the trade in capital goods between the United States and other advanced industrial countries. With the index of competitiveness defined as the ratio between capital goods exports to developed countries and imports from them, we find that between 1963 and 1973 the ratio slipped from 2.6 to 1.0. In Japan, by contrast, the trend was reversed, with Japan exporting more capital goods to developed countries than it imported by the end of the ten-year period.[4]

Losing its technological edge, U.S. industry has already lost its ability to compete with less developed countries in terms of labor costs. As the productivity of labor relative to capital increases, countries with an abundance of low-wage labor and an increasingly sophisticated industrial infrastructure—such as Brazil, Mexico, Singapore, South Korea, and Iran—attract labor-intensive manufacturing industries, bank loans, and other direct investment from the advanced capitalist countries. This shift of investment in plant and equipment to overseas locations has cost U.S. workers an estimated 2 million jobs over the last decade, has increased the tax burden on U.S. citizens through the added costs of defending the U.S. overseas empire, and has exacerbated current U.S. trade problems. In 1976, for example, fully one-third of all U.S. imports originated in sales from majority-owned U.S. subsidiaries abroad. Furthermore, that same year, while the United States exported a total of $115 billion in merchandise, majority-owned foreign affiliates of U.S. companies exported (from their host countries) nearly $144 billion in sales.[5]

---

4. Cited in Fernando Fajnzylber, "Multinational Enterprises and the Economy of the United States: Possible Topics for Research," unpublished manuscript, 1978.
5. *Survey of Current Business*, Apr. 1978.

We are, *Business Week* recently remarked, poised on the brink of "an emerging new world economic order."[6] And though this assessment may be both premature and exaggerated, the structures of the world economy *are* shifting and the consequences of these changes are being felt acutely on the streets of New York and Des Moines, Youngstown and Miami. Manufacturing jobs are flowing out of the United States, leaving behind higher levels of unemployment and an increasingly service-oriented economy. Workers, who along with people on fixed incomes suffer most from high levels of inflation and a weakening of the U.S. economy abroad, are now increasingly blamed for creating the conditions of their own unemployment by pricing themselves out of the market. Corporations have stepped up their assault on labor costs, vigorously opposing unionization by shifting production to the so-called "right-to-work" states or by lobbying to block passage of pro-labor legislation. Even the delicate equilibrium of municipal finance has been upset by these changes, as cities lower corporate tax rates in order to attract or hold business and raise taxes on small property owners in order to pay for social services.

In this paper we will examine the international competitiveness of two U.S. industries, steel and electronics, with particular concern for the factors of technological competitiveness and the internationalization of productive capital. We will discover that though the current U.S. trade imbalance reflects the growing uncompetitiveness of the domestically based U.S. economy, trading practices *by themselves* have not led to this situation. Rather we must look to changes pertaining to the organization and structure of production.

Standing on opposite ends of the historical-industrial spectrum—steel having laid the foundation for U.S. industrial growth in the last century, electronics having paved the way for a second industrial revolution in the next—steel and electronics represent important branches of the U.S. economy that have been sorely tested by international competition. We will examine the basis of this challenge in the technological backwardness and overseas investments that have undermined the productive base of these two industries in the United States.

The paper is divided into three sections. The first examines factors of production in steel and electronics, describing developments in the technical and social relations of production that have molded each industry. Having described the problems each industry faces and why each is becoming uncompetitive, we will examine in the second section

6. *Business Week*, Jul. 24, 1978.

industry and government plans to restructure them as well as the implications of these restructuring plans for the economy as a whole. Finally, in the third section we will analyze what the growing uncompetitiveness of U.S. industry means for U.S. workers, how the new international division of labor will affect job structures, wages, working conditions, and the collective bargaining process in the United States, and how unions have responded to this challenge.

INTERNATIONAL COMPETITION IN STEEL AND ELECTRONICS

Steel: An Industry in Crisis

Within the past decade a number of primary manufacturing industries in the United States have faced increased competition from imports. Textiles, apparel, shoes and leather products, televisions, radios, tape recorders, and CBs have all been severely affected. George Meany has seen in the imports flood a second Pearl Harbor. "Foreign trade is the guerrilla warfare of economics," he declared at the 1977 AFL-CIO National Convention, "and right now the United States economy is being ambushed."[7]

Attention recently has focused on imports in the steel industry. Though this is not a particularly new issue, the threat that imports would capture more than a fifth of domestic industry shipments and a heated public relations counterattack by the steel companies brought the issue home to million of Americans. "Name a foreign steel producer," Bethlehem Steel demanded in its advertisements. "We'll get in the commercial ring with him and battle it out for America's steel market. And if we both fight by the same rules, we're confident we'll hold our own. But that isn't the way this 'competition' works. When a Japanese or European steelmaker climbs into the ring, his government almost always climbs in with him. That's bending the rules of 'free' trade, and we don't think it's fair."

The relevant question here is not whether imports of steel have gone up in recent years. Even though steel imports only captured 17 percent rather than the predicted 20 percent of domestic industry shipments in 1977, that figure is still significant. The question we pose is What can the patterns that emerge in the level of steel imports tell us about the nature of the problem?

In the first place, though imports of steel mill products have increased,

7. *New York Times*, Dec. 9, 1977.

industry output in the United States has gone through lengthy periods of growth and decline. U.S. steel companies produced less raw steel in 1977 than in 1955, for example. (See Table 1.) This pattern is related to a secular decline in the demand for steel in the United States—between 1955 and 1973, GNP increased by 88 percent in real terms, but steel

TABLE I

U.S. Raw Steel Production, Production as Percentage of Capitalist World Production, and Imports as Percentage of Apparent Steel Supply, 1955-77

Year	U.S. production (Millions of net tons)	U.S. production as pct. of capitalist world production	Imports as pct. of apparent steel supply
1955	117.0	50%	1.2%
1956	115.2	48	1.7
1957	112.7	47	1.5
1958	85.3	41	2.9
1959	93.4	40	6.1
1960	99.3	37	3.3
1961	98.0	36	3.2
1962	98.3	36	4.1
1963	109.3	35	5.5
1964	127.1	37	6.4
1965	131.5	37	10.4
1966	134.1	37	10.8
1967	127.2	33	11.5
1968	131.5	32	18.0
1969	141.3	31	14.0
1970	131.5	29	13.4
1971	120.4	28	18.3
1972	133.2	29	17.7
1973	150.8	29	15.1
1974	145.7	27	16.0
1975	116.6	25	12.0
1976	128.0	26	14.3
1977	114.0[a]	n.a.	17.0[b]

SOURCE: American Iron and Steel Institute, Annual Statistical Reports.
[a] Preliminary.
[b] New York Times, Feb. 5, 1978.

consumption grew by less than 50 percent—as well as to a cyclical decline in world steel demand linked to industrial recessions.[8] The current three-year downturn in U.S. steel production is directly related to the fact that, according to *Business Week*, "the world economy . . . is, as a whole, in serious trouble. Hardly any of the countries of the world have fully emerged from the last great recession of three years ago."[9]

Second, the increase in imports is linked to the resurgence of European and Japanese steelmakers following the Second World War, a revival that occurred at the same time as the discovery of large iron ore deposits and a fall in the world price of raw materials. Whereas in 1957 U.S. steelmakers commanded a two-to-one price advantage in the cost of raw materials over the Japanese, by 1972 the Japanese enjoyed a 6 percent advantage. (See Table 2.) Along with a relative decline in the cost of raw materials for foreign producers, foreign steelmakers also enjoyed a lower wage bill than their U.S. counterparts.

Finally, it should be noted that steel imports into the United States have risen irregularly since the late 1950's, with the largest jumps occurring in 1959, 1965, 1968, 1971, 1974, and 1977. This pattern correlates to the expiration dates of the steel industry's collective bargaining agreements with the United Steelworkers of America (USWA). Domestic producers turned to foreign steelmakers during these contract years to assure themselves a steady supply of steel in case strikes shut down the industry. Curiously, the pattern has persisted even though there have been no national strikes in steel since 1959 and few local work stoppages.[10] It would seem that the specter of the 116-day strike of 1959 still dances before the eyes of most domestic consumers of steel, despite the USWA's subsequent acceptance of a "no-strike" clause in their basic contract. As we will see, the issue of import competition has been used by both the steelmakers and the leadership of the USWA to bring the union into a passive position. If labor militancy in the 1950's led domestic steel consumers to turn to hedge-buying of foreign steel, the increase in imports that this occasioned became one of the major factors encouraging officials of the USWA to put a lid on worker militancy through the 1973 Experimental Negotiating Agreement.

---

8. Council on Wage and Price Stability, *Report to the President on Prices and Costs in the United States Steel Industry* (Washington, D.C., 1977), p. 12.
9. *Business Week*, Oct. 3, 1977.
10. David Gordon, Joseph J. Persky, et al., "Appendix 'A' to Plaintiffs' Trial Memorandum on Hearing for Preliminary Injunction: Economic Consequences on Steel Workers of Strikes and the Right to Strike in the Basic Steel Industry (1949–1970)," (mimeo., 1976), p. 6.

TABLE 2

Total Raw Materials Cost for Steelmaking,
United States and Japan, 1956–75
(Dollars per net ton of input)

Year	U.S.	Japan	Percent U.S. advantage
1956	$24.15	$41.39	71.4%
1957	24.22	48.41	100.3
1958	22.74	33.44	47.1
1959	23.42	30.52	30.3
1960	22.27	30.08	35.1
1961	23.18	30.86	33.1
1962	21.54	28.44	32.0
1963	21.21	27.72	30.7
1964	22.82	27.90	22.3
1965	22.76	27.90	22.6
1966	22.19	27.40	23.5
1967	22.08	27.19	23.1
1968	22.30	25.70	15.2
1969	23.37	26.47	13.3
1970	26.61	30.00	12.7
1971	28.12	27.98	(0.5)
1972	30.87	29.00	(6.1)
1973	36.12	37.94	5.0
1974	57.05	59.37	4.1
1975	58.16	63.45	9.1

SOURCE: Federal Trade Commission statistics, cited in
Council on Wage and Price Stability, Report to the President on Prices and Costs in the United States Steel Industry (Washington, D.C., Oct. 1977), p. 44.
NOTE: Raw materials include iron ore, scrap, and coking coal.

A Question of "Dumping." Most steelmakers charge that "unfair" foreign competition (not competition in itself) is at the root of the industry's problems. Given slack worldwide demand for steel—so the argument runs—many governments have subsidized their steel industries, thereby permitting below-cost exports of steel into foreign markets. The steelmakers claim that this "beggar-thy-neighbor" policy has been adopted for two reasons. The first is social: by maintaining steel production at high levels, governments avoid high unemployment in both the steel industry and those industries that depend on steel. The second reason is that most steelmakers argue that it is too costly to turn steel plants on and off, particularly in Europe and Japan, where labor is almost a fixed cost.

Steel "dumping" (setting export prices below the cost of production together with allowances for shipping and profit), then, becomes a method of exporting unemployment from one country to another, and U.S. steelmakers charge that they are on the receiving end of the dumping. "The U.S. is the greatest steel market anywhere in the world," according to Lewis Foy of Bethlehem Steel. "So the foreign producers have shipped steel here and sold it at any price that they can get anyone to pay. In the case of Japan and the European Community producers, we are certain steel is being dumped here at prices that don't cover their production and sales costs, and don't allow any profit."[11] Dennis Carney, president of ninth-ranked Wheeling-Pittsburgh Steel, agreed, noting that "almost all foreign producers are operating with heavy losses, and tonnages they are dumping in this country at prices below cost are inflicting further losses."[12]

The steelmen's charges were bolstered by an extensive study of the problem commissioned by the American Iron and Steel Institute (AISI), the industry's major trade representative. Not unexpectedly, the study confirmed the steel companies' worst fears: "Throughout the late 1960's foreign producers did not have sufficient cost advantages to account for the difference between their prices on U.S. shipments and the price of comparable domestic shipments. The unavoidable inference from this fact is that foreign producers were selling below their full production costs."[13] Furthermore, the AISI study places most of the blame on the Japanese, who are charged with consistently dumping steel on the U.S. market.[14]

Others strongly disagree with the AISI conclusions. Some of these reactions were predictable, such as that of Charles Stern, the president of the American Institute for Imported Steel, who called the steelmakers' charges part of a "fantastic propaganda campaign."[15] Other versions have come from less immediately interested parties. For example, Sanford Rose, a respected editor at *Fortune*, recently wrote that "Japan's export success, which is causing such consternation in the

11. Quoted in *U.S. News & World Report*, Nov. 21, 1977.
12. *New York Times*, Dec. 19, 1977.
13. Putnam, Hayes & Bartlett, Inc., *Economics of International Steel Trade: Policy Implications for the United States. An Analysis and Forecast for American Iron and Steel Institute* (Newton, Mass., 1977), p. 39.
14. *Ibid.*, p. 44.
15. Quoted in *U.S. News & World Report*, Oct. 24, 1977.

United States these days, does not depend to any appreciable degree on
such illegal trade tactics as dumping."[16]

The heated controversy has given birth to a series of studies examining the question of prices and costs in world steel.[17] Though these mono-
graphs do not rule out dumping, they arrive at a substantially different
conclusion from the AISI report: Assuming that a ton of finished steel
in the United States cost approximately $326 in 1976, these studies
found that Japanese steel could undersell U.S. steel by anywhere from
$61 to $83 a ton. Furthermore, most of these studies concluded that, in
general, the Japanese were not dumping steel on U.S. markets to any
appreciable extent. The Council on Wage and Price Stability determined
in its report that "the evidence available to us suggests that export
markets are quite competitive and that prices are sensitive to demand
changes. Japanese data demonstrate that the price of exported steel has
been above the domestic price since 1974."[18] And Charles Bradford of
Merrill, Lynch agreed that the Japanese were not setting export prices
below domestic prices. Even the Treasury Department, which calculated a 32 percent dumping margin by Japanese producers during a
preliminary hearing of an October 1977 suit brought by the Gilmore
Steel Corporation, has revised its figures substantially downward.[19]

Of course, one of the major differences between U.S. and Japanese
steel companies is to be found in the return each pays out to stock-
holders on invested capital. Japanese corporations raise a much higher
percentage of their capital needs through banks than through sales of
equity, contrary to standard U.S. corporate practice. Even in bleak
years in the steel industry, U.S. steel companies still press up their earnings and dividend payouts through price increases. For example, between
June 1977 and April 1978, U.S. Steel's earnings rose 53.7 percent and
Bethlehem Steel's 143.7 percent. Yet during the same period, their shipments either remained level (U.S. Steel) or actually declined (Bethlehem).[20] Although some of the increase in profits could be attributed to

16. Sanford Rose, "The Secret of Japan's Export Prowess," *Fortune*, Jan. 30,
1978, p. 56.

17. These studies include the one by the Council on Wage and Price Stability
cited in n. 8; Charles A. Bradford, *Japanese Steel Industry: A Comparison with Its
United States Counterpart* (New York, 1977); International Ventures Management,
Documented Japanese Steel Production Costs, Prices and Business Procedures (Pitts-
burgh, 1977); and, for earlier data, Kiyoshi Kawahito, *The Japanese Steel Industry,
with an Analysis of the U.S. Steel Import Problem* (New York, 1972). The International Iron and Steel Institute has also published data on the topic.

18. Council on Wage and Price Stability, *Report* . . . , p. 69.

19. *Wall Street Journal*, Jan. 10, 1978.

20. *New York Times*, Jul. 31, 1978.

greater efficiency in the plants, most was really due to price increases.

One final note on the question of dumping. Most studies of prices and costs in the world's steel industries have found that European steel costs are much closer to U.S. costs, and that in all probability the current recession has led Europeans to dump some steel on U.S. markets. This is underscored in the 1977 steel import statistics, which reveal that Japanese exports of steel to the United States fell 2.1 percent below their 1976 level whereas European shipments to the United States rose by 114 percent.[21] Nevertheless, the popular conception spawned by the nation's press is that the Japanese, not the Europeans, are dumping. Robert C. Christopher referred to this practice as "Jap-bashing." It seems it is easier to blame the Japanese for U.S. economic problems than the Europeans.

Based on this evidence, we would conclude that the current crisis in the U.S. steel industry does not originate in "unfair" trading practices, but in a higher degree of competition in general. We must look into the sphere of production for the causes of the crisis in U.S. steel. In particular, we will find that the U.S. steel industry has lost its technological lead to other advanced capitalist steelmakers and, on top of this, will soon be challenged by steelmakers operating from low-wage countries.

Technology and technical change in the steel industry. The record of technological developments by U.S. steelmakers is, in a word, abysmal. Not one major steelmaking innovation was developed in the United States. Of the most important technological advances in steel, most were adopted quite late by U.S. producers and, at first, only by relatively small producers.[22] The research and development budgets of U.S. steel producers reflect this neglect of technological change. In 1972, for example, steel companies spent an average of 0.26 percent of sales on research and development, substantially below the 2.3 percent average for all manufacturing industries.[23]

Steel is produced by one of two basic methods, the "hot-metal" or the "cold-metal" method. The former involves two processes. First, iron ore, in the form of either sinter or pellets, is fired with coke in a blast furnace to produce molten iron. Then the molten iron is refined along with scrap steel to produce molten steel. This second process occurs either in an open hearth furnace or in the more modern, more efficient,

---

21. *New York Times*, Jan. 31, 1978.
22. Craig R. MacPhee, *Restrictions on International Trade in Steel* (Lexington, Mass., 1974), pp. 11–13.
23. *Ibid.*

Basic Oxygen Furnace (BOF). BOFs were first installed in the United States in 1954. The "cold-metal" method obviates blast furnaces and coking ovens, since it refines scrap steel directly into molten steel in an electric arc furnace. The electric arc method—which requires a large amount of scrap steel—has become a popular secondary method of steel production in the United States and is the mainstay of many of the nation's "mini-mills."[24]

BOFs and electric arc furnaces are substantially more cost efficient than open hearth furnaces. Whereas open hearth furnaces require 9-10 hours per sequence ("heat"), heat times for BOFs are less than one hour, permitting up to 16 or more heats per day. Furthermore, BOFs produce a generally higher quality of steel than do open hearth furnaces.

In 1960 almost 90 percent of U.S. steel was produced by the open hearth system. This figure had been reduced to approximately 50 percent by 1968, with the remainder produced by BOFs (37.2 percent) and electric arc furnaces (12.8 percent).[25] George Stinson, chairman of National Steel, recently argued that if U.S. steel producers were relatively disadvantaged in relation to Japanese producers, the difference was due to capital costs, not technology. Nevertheless, as of 1977, the Japanese, the West Germans, and the French all produced more steel in BOFs (80 percent, 72 percent, and 68 percent, respectively) than did U.S. steelmakers (63 percent).[26]

Furthermore, we can find a similar technological advantage for foreign steel in the second major process of steelmaking, shaping. The facilities that shape and form molten steel compose the heart of most steel plants. In a hot-rolling mill, the molten steel is poured into ingot molds, where it cools and is then reheated and shaped by a system of rollers into semifinished shapes (blooms, billets, and slabs). Cold-rolling mills reform sheets and other semifinished forms without a second heating.

The most important recent advance in the field of shaping is in the process known as "continuous casting." This allows the molten steel to

24. On technology and the process of steelmaking, see Dale L. Hiestand, *High Level Manpower and Technological Changes in the Steel Industry* (New York, 1974), pp. 10-11; William T. Hogan, *Economic History of the Iron and Steel Industry in the United States* (Lexington, Mass., 1971), vol. 4, chap. 41; Bureau of Labor Statistics, *Technological Change and Manpower Trends in Five Industries, Bulletin 1856* (Washington, D.C., 1975), pp. 21-25.

25. Anthony Cockerill, *The Steel Industry: International Comparisons of Industrial Structure and Performance* (London, 1974), p. 16.

26. *Business Week*, Sep. 19, 1977.

be poured directly into a caster at a controlled rate. The steel solidifies as it moves down the long caster and is cut into proper lengths for further rolling or fabrication at the end of the process. Since continuous casting eliminates approximately half of the steps of hot-rolling mills, it is estimated that its application can save 30-60 percent of the capital costs of shaping.[27] As with Basic Oxygen Furnaces, continuous casting is not as common in U.S. plants as in foreign steel mills. In 1977, 10 percent of U.S. steel was shaped by continuous casting as compared with 31 percent of Japanese steel, 28 percent of West German steel, and 18 percent of French steel.[28]

Capital expenditures by U.S. steelmakers to improve plant and equipment have been inconsistent. A Bureau of Labor Statistics (BLS) study found that expenditures for new plant and equipment rose to a peak in the first half of the 1960's but dropped back steadily from 1966 to 1972.[29] Capital expenditures per production worker rose by an annual rate of 7.6 percent between 1960 and 1966, and then dropped by an average of 6.3 percent per year between 1966 and 1972. And this drop is even more significant, according to the BLS: "Although prices of steel plant and equipment are not available, the very sharp rise in general machinery and equipment prices over this period suggests that real capital outlays in the steel industry increased considerably less than is shown by the current-dollar data and that the decline in recent years has been greater."[30]

Furthermore, whereas U.S. steel firms have spent approximately $2 billion to meet government pollution-control requirements, Japanese steel firms have spent slightly more in order to meet even more stringent standards. Japan's biggest new mill, the Ogishima Works, has 20 percent of its construction capital assigned to pollution-control equipment.[31] Thus the comparative costs involved in meeting pollution-control standards, according to the State Department, "do not appear to be a major factor in relative levels of cost competitiveness" between U.S. and Japanese steel firms.[32]

The results all point to the fact that U.S. steelmakers, though making technological advances and still able to produce steel more economically than many other steelmakers, are rapidly losing ground to Japanese and,

27. Hiestand, p. 18; Hogan, vol. 4, chap. 41; and Bureau of Labor Statistics, *Bulletin 1856*, pp. 21–25.
28. *Business Week*, Sep. 19, 1977.
29. Bureau of Labor Statistics, *Bulletin 1859*, p. 27.
30. *Ibid.*, p. 27.
31. *The Nation*, Mar. 4, 1978.
32. Department of State *Bulletin*, Nov. 21, 1977.

to a lesser extent, European steel producers. A 1974 study of the international steel industry found this to be the case in comparing the "estimated efficiency ratios" of integrated steelworks in nine countries in the mid-1950's and the late 1960's.[33] The study rated both U.S. and Japanese steelworks as "highly efficient," meaning that more than 60 percent of their facilities produced at efficient levels. However, the efficiency ratio for U.S. integrated steelworks fell by 8.5 percent between the mid-1950's and the late 1960's, whereas the ratio for Japanese steelmakers increased by 94.6 percent during that same period.[34]

Productivity levels in steel. Productivity indexes provide a second measurement of change in the steel industry. Since productivity data relate labor time to output, they serve to indicate both the technical relations of production that govern the industry and the social relations of production. Productivity reflects changes in technology, installation of new plant and equipment, and capacity utilization as well as factors of overt class struggle on the shop floor, such as the effort by foremen to speed up the pace of work, the assignment of more tasks to a single worker, and the intensification of labor.[35]

Between the end of the Second World War and 1959, productivity in steel lagged seriously behind the average level for industry, increasing by an average of only 1.1 percent per year.[36] To a large extent, this reflected the virtual monopoly U.S. producers maintained over steel production in the capitalist world. With little incentive to increase production and find new markets, producers tended to divide market shares and collect administered, rather than competitive, prices.[37]

As we have seen, capital expenditures in the industry began to rise in the first half of the 1960's; productivity figures also began to increase in this period. Between 1960 and 1965, employee-hours per ton of steel shipped in the United States dropped from 15 to 12.2, reflecting a 4.1 percent yearly increase in productivity rates.[38] With a general decline

33. The data considered include average sizes of blast furnaces, types of furnaces used, shaping facilities (for hot-rolling mills), timing of production runs, capacity utilization, uses of scraps, etc. Cockerill, p. 97.

34. *Ibid.,* pp. 93–100.

35. Karl Marx, *Capital,* vol. I, chap. 15 and 16. For the methodology of the Bureau of Labor Statistics in measuring productivity, see Bureau of Labor Statistics, *Handbook of Methods, Bulletin 1910* (Washington, D.C., 1976).

36. Bureau of Labor Statistics, *Productivity Indexes for Selected Industries, 1977, Bulletin 1983* (Washington, D.C., 1977), pp. 94–95.

37. Tom Seidl, "Working Paper on the 'Steel Project': Economic Consequences on Steel Workers of Strikes and the Right to Strike in the Basic Steel Industry (1949–1970)," unpublished manuscript, 1976, pp. 24–25.

TABLE 3

Indexes of Output Per Hour in Basic Steel,
1964 and 1972–76
(U.S. = 100 at maximum levels of output)

Year	U.S.	Japan	France	Germany	U.K.
1964	100	53	52	60	51
•••					
1972	100	101	70	85	54
1973	100	111	66	84	50
1974	100	113	68	88	45
1975	100	123	67	91	46
1976	100	126	69	90	49

SOURCE: U.S. Department of Labor, Bureau of Labor Statistics, Office of Productivity and Technology, "International Comparisons of Productivity and Labor Costs in the Steel Industry: United States, Japan, France, Germany, United Kingdom; 1964 and 1972–76," Unpublished report, Nov. 1977, p. 2.

in spending from 1966–71, productivity increases leveled off as well.[39] Finally, productivity levels increased at a rate of 1.3 percent per year between 1971 and 1976, below general manufacturing levels and less than half the generally anticipated rate of growth.[40]

Productivity has been climbing at much faster rates in foreign steel plants. During the 1964–72 period, when U.S. output per employee-hour increased by an average of 1.2 percent per year, productivity in the Japanese steel industry rose by 14.3 percent, in the French steel industry by 6.2 percent, and in the German by 6.0 percent.[41] By the early 1970's, Japanese steelworkers were producing a relatively higher output per hour than were U.S. steelworkers. (See Table 3.)

Labor costs and the development of steel in less developed countries. Foreign producers, particularly the Japanese, have revolutionized the

38. Hogan, vol. 5, p. 2090.
39. In his massive *Economic History of the Iron and Steel Industry in the United States*, William Hogan argues that productivity did not increase during this period because the industry was producing lighter steels and, therefore, the amount of total shipments did not increase in tons, the measure of productivity. He also argues that the new capacity installed during this period took a long time to break in, and that a substantial amount of investment went into pollution-control devices and facilities to insure quality rather than increase tonnage.
40. Bureau of Labor Statistics, *Bulletin 1983.*
41. Bureau of Labor Statistics, *Productivity: An International Perspective, Bulletin 1811* (Washington, D.C., 1974), p. 74.

technology of steelmaking, allowing them to produce at greater economies of scale, for larger markets, at lower costs. They apply a principle
of manufacturing efficiency which maintains that real unit costs will
decline with the accumulation of "production experience."[42] In other
words, production costs should decline as a company produces an increasing number of units, as its experience grows. Japanese corporations apply this principle by rapidly expanding their markets at the expense of short-run high profits. This drives their unit and total costs
down, gives them good market position, and opens the possibility of
again recouping profits.

Recently, however, competition in steel has come from producers
with an advantage in terms of labor costs rather than advanced technology or marketing techniques. In the last decade a considerable number of less developed capitalist countries have brought their steel plants
on stream. With important government backing, these countries have
been able to purchase up-to-date technology and construct new "green-
field" plants near deep water. Most importantly, however, since steelmaking is still a labor-intensive process even given technical advances,
with wage rates averaging one-twelfth the U.S. level and one-sixth the
Japanese level, the world's newest steelmakers can undercut both of
these more technically advanced manufacturers.

At the close of the Second World War, steel was produced in 32
countries. Since then 35 more countries have entered into production.
"Third World" countries have quadrupled their output of steel since
1960, and by 2000, according to a United Nations estimate, they will
produce 25 percent and consume 24 percent of the world's steel.[43] As of
1973 these countries produced 34 million tons of steel and consumed
more than 70 million tons.[44]

The development of steelmaking in Latin America, in particular, raises
three issues for U.S. producers. First, Latin America represents a potential market for U.S. steel exports. Latin American countries purchase
approximately one-third of U.S. steel exports at present, and the estimated growth rates for steel consumption are particularly high for
Latin America. The only areas where they are expected to be higher
are China and other Asian countries, with the exception of Japan.[45] U.S.

42. See Rose, pp. 57–58.
43. *Business Week*, Sep. 19, 1977.
44. Donald B. Thompson, "Developing Nations: A Developing Steel Problem?"
Industry Week, May 12, 1975, p. 31.
45. Kenneth Warren, *World Steel: An Economic Geography* (New York, 1975),
p. 308.

steelmakers would like to fill the growing Latin American demand for steel, and thus would hardly favor the rapid development of steel production in the region.

Second, since most Latin American steel imports now come from Japan and Europe, these producers could be expected to divert an even greater percentage of their exports to U.S. markets if Latin American countries began to fill their own demand for steel.

Third, some countries, notably Mexico, already represent an "import threat" to the United States. Many less developed capitalist countries have found that steel production requires their having "access to markets greater than their own [in order to achieve] economies of scale," according to Alonzo L. McDonald, U.S. ambassador to the Geneva trade talks. This means building steel mills that produce more steel than local demand would dictate.

Though Mexican steelmakers already produced approximately 5.5 million metric tons in 1977 and doubled their exports of the previous year, the merger of Mexico's three largest steel plants (Altos Hornos de México, Siderúrgica Lázaro Cárdenas, Fundidora Monterrey) into a new firm, Sidermex, with a collective capacity of 6.5–7.1 million tons, will likely make Mexican steel a very serious competitor in Gulf and West Coast markets. As it is, Mexican steel plate already undersells both U.S. plate (by $40–$50 a ton) and lower-cost imported Japanese plate.[46]

Mexico is not alone in seeking to develop its steel industry. Both Venezuela and Brazil have placed an extraordinary emphasis on the development of steel. For both, steel is the epitome of capitalist development. To develop steel is to *be* developed. Under its current five-year development plan (1976–80), the Venezuelan government plans to invest the equivalent of $3.6 billion in order to boost steelmaking capacity to 15 million tons a year by 1990.[47] The Fondo de Inversiones de Venezuela expects that by 1984 the country's steel plants will have generated some B3,000 million worth of exports.[48]

More than 70 percent of all government investment in Brazil in 1976 went into the expansion of steel output.[49] With more than 9 million tons output in 1976, Brazil was the tenth-largest steel producer in the capitalist world. Nevertheless, it still had to import 10 percent of its steel requirements.[50] CONSIDER, the government agency that administers

46. *Mex-Am Review*, Jun. 1977, p. 19.
47. *Business Latin America*, Apr. 27, 1977.
48. Latin American Newsletters, *Special Report: Venezuela*, Jan. 1978, p. 6.
49. *Business Latin America*, Mar. 2, 1977, p. 68.
50. *Latin America Economic Report*, Jun. 17, 1977, p. 92; and *Brazilian Business*, Mar. 1977, p. 26.

the state-run steel plants, predicted 1977 output at 11.1 million metric tons owing to new capacity coming on-stream.[51] It also calculated that Brazil would become self-sufficient in steel by 1980, with an export capacity of 3 million tons.[52]

Still, it is doubtful that Latin American countries, with the exception of Mexico, will seriously compete in the U.S. steel market for many years. Yet few question that these countries will become steel exporters by the late 1980's. (See Table 4.) With efficient technology—most of the larger plants are equipped with BOFs and electric arc furnaces—low labor costs, and advantageous locations, Latin American steelmakers will increasingly show themselves a force to be reckoned with.

The current crisis in the U.S. steel industry originated not in the "illegal" trade practices of other countries, but rather in the U.S. steelmakers' neglect of technological developments. More than anything else, today's crisis in the U.S. steel industry is rooted in the growing cost inefficiency of an important percentage of U.S. mills. This, in turn, is directly related to the industry's virtual monopoly of steel production for many decades, freeing them from the necessity of upgrading their mills. When competition finally arose from foreign producers, U.S. steelmakers found themselves seriously behind. Furthermore, the crisis will only get worse, if all else remains the same, when steel from Latin America and other low-wage areas begins to compete for a share of the U.S. market.

Electronics: Waves of the Future

In the mid-1960's a group of Harvard Business School economists led by Raymond Vernon developed a model to explain why "corporate managers have felt, and will continue to feel, that pressures for foreign economic expansion are much more a compelling need or even an in-

51. *Commerce America*, Aug. 1, 1977, p. 10.
52. *Economist*, Feb. 12, 1977, pp. 85–86. Most observers doubt these projections. A recent confidential report from the World Bank noted that investment in the mills was too low to reach the goal. Administrators at two of the mills criticized in the report suggested that the inspiration behind the World Bank report (which has since created a series of difficulties for the Brazilians) was the fear of steel producers in advanced capitalist countries that, with Brazil reaching self-sufficiency in steel, they would lose their best customer in Latin America. While this is no doubt true, inefficiency and the difficulties involved in bringing new facilities up to capacity has forced the cancellation of the 1980–85 expansion plans for all three state-owned mills. See *Latin America Economic Report*, Jun. 17, 1977, p. 92, and *Business Latin America*, Mar. 2, 1977.

TABLE 4
*Latin American Raw Steel Production 1948, 1970, 1975, and Projected
Production, Selected Countries*
(*Thousands of tons*)

Country	1948	1970	1975	Projected
Argentina	17	1,824	2,440	4,000 by 1981; already exports.
Brazil	552	5,368	9,237	11,000 by 1977; 18,000 by 1979; export capacity by 1985.
Chile	14	547	560	620 capacity in 1977.
Colombia	—	239	418	2,900 by 1985; export to Ancom countries.
Ecuador	—	—	—	500 by 1981.
Mexico	176	3,845	5,911	9,890 capacity by 1978; already exports.
Peru	—	94	484	2,250 by 1982; 4,000 by 1988.
Trinidad-Tobago	—	—	—	450 exports to U.S.
Venezuela	—	927	1,172	15,000 capacity by 1990; exports by 1980.
TOTAL	759	12,844	20,516	Steel consumption to grow at est. 7.1 percent per year, 1970–85. Est. capacity additions of 37.2 million metric tons by 1980.

SOURCES: 1948 and 1970, Kenneth Warren, *World Steel: An Economic Geography* (New York, 1975), p. 269; 1975, American Iron and Steel Institute, *Annual Statistical Report*, 1975; projections, *Latin America Economic Report*, *Business Latin America*, *Economist*, and *Fortune*, various issues.

stitutional necessity than merely a profitable convenience."[53] Discarding both Marxist analyses of imperialism and more orthodox theories of the growth of firms, Vernon argued in his "product life cycle" approach that foreign investments would occur when the investor realized that "once the production process was free of its dependence on the spe-

53. Theodore H. Moran, "Foreign Expansion as an 'Institutional Necessity' for U.S. Corporate Capitalism: The Search for a Radical Model," *World Politics*, 25, no. 3 (Apr. 1973), p. 372. See also Raymond Vernon, "International Investment and International Trade in the Product Cycle," *Quarterly Journal of Economics*, 80, no. 2 (May 1966); Louis T. Wells, Jr., "Test of a Product Cycle Model of International Trade: U.S. Exports of Consumer Durables," *Quarterly Journal of Economics*, 83, no. 1 (Feb. 1969), pp. 152–62; and Robert B. Stobaugh et al., "U.S. Multinational Enterprises and the U.S. Economy," in Kujawa, pp. 82–126.

cialized inputs of the U.S. economy—once the conventional costs of capital and labor came to dominate the calculation—foreign locations might be more attractive than U.S. production sites."[54]

The product life cycle model argues that, because of its large population and high per capita income, the United States offers the world's largest market for most new products. Responding to market stimuli, firms closest to that market will develop most new products. This tendency is reinforced since early in the development of a new product production runs are short, irregular, subject to constant changes, and geared to ill-defined markets. It is most likely, therefore, that the manufacturer of this new product will set up shop close to the market and the innovator/entrepreneur, i.e., in the United States.

In this first stage of the cycle, U.S. producers enjoy a virtual monopoly over the production of the new commodity. As demand grows, production becomes increasingly standardized. Production runs become longer with the introduction of mass production technology, which raises the ratio of capital to labor. It is also likely, at this point, that technology will be exported, along with the product, to other countries.

With the diffusion of technology, foreign firms begin to produce the commodity, soon challenging the monopoly of U.S. firms. At this point, U.S. producers must decide whether they will give up the foreign market (since production costs should be lower for local firms) or challenge foreign producers directly by establishing operations inside the tariff barriers of that country.[55]

Cost considerations become more important as more producers enter the market. Producers begin to move their manufacturing lines to those countries where costs are lowest (i.e., countries with the lowest wages), and there they produce for local consumption, export to third countries and re-export to the United States.

In short, the product life cycle approach argues that U.S. firms invest abroad because they are *forced* to; investments are defensive measures designed to maintain the investor's place in the world market. "If U.S. firms tried to continue operating only in the United States, they would lose their markets to foreign firms, usually large enterprises from Europe and Japan."[56] Aside from this, three other conclusions emerge from the product life cycle approach: (1) there will be a steady tendency for low-technology, large-market items with stable production

54. Vernon, *Sovereignty at Bay* (New York, 1971), p. 3.
55. Moran, p. 374.
56. Stobaugh, p. 114.

runs to leave the United States for low-wage areas; (2) there will be a steady de-skilling (homogenization) of the labor force in the United States that goes hand-in-hand with the development of mass production technology; and (3) there will be an ever-widening gap between high-skilled jobs and de-skilled jobs, with de-skilled jobs shipped abroad in increasing numbers.

The product life cycle approach may serve as a useful descriptive model of foreign investment, but it falls short as a comprehensive theory of the internationalization of capital. In the first place, by locating itself at the level of the firm, it loses its ability to explain the social expansion of capital. Analysis at the level of the firm can describe a form of the self-expansion of social capital, but not the logic of this self-expansion process itself.[57] One is left with the tautology that firms expand as a defensive reaction against other firms that are also expanding, and so on; since there is no theory of competition, there is no exit to the argument. In the second place, the model breaks down to the extent that productive capital becomes increasingly internationalized, since it posits reaction to stimuli that exist at the national rather than the international level.[58]

In our examination of the electronics industry, we will see that the product life cycle approach can be fairly accuate in describing how executives make the decision to invest abroad. To reach a fuller under-standing of the process of the internationalization of electronics, how-ever, we need to develop a discussion of competition, the nature of technical and social changes in the industry, and the manner in which the internationalization of capital in electronics affects the domestic U.S. economy.

The internationalization of production in electronics. Though elec-tronics traces its history to Thomas Edison's work on the incandescent lamp in the late nineteenth century and to J. J. Thompson's "discovery" of the electron in 1897, as an industry it is exceptionally young.[59] The

---

57. See Christian Palloix, "The Self-Expansion of Capital on a World Scale," *Review of Radical Political Economics*, 9, no. 2 (Summer 1977), p. 4.

58. See Vernon, *Sovereignty*, pp. 107–8, and Herbert Souza, "An Overview of Theories of Multinational Corporation and the Quest of the State," *Latin America Research Unit* (Toronto), Working Paper No. 19 (Feb. 1977), pp. 9–12.

59. Electronics is a difficult industry to define since, more precisely, it is a sci-ence. It is a natural offshoot of the earlier electrical industry. While both deal with the flow of electricity through circuits, electronic products also include tubes and semiconductors that can discharge, direct, control, or otherwise influence the flow of electricity. There is no one definition of the electronics industry that is

industry concentrated on radio production until the Second World War, but then brought electronics into the trenches with a massive upsurge of military products. Following the war, both industry and consumers began to take more notice of electronics as computers and television started to play an increasingly active role in our lives.

These postwar developments filled out the four major production areas in electronics: consumer, industry, government/military, and components (the transistors, diodes, resistors, etc. that form the basis of the three other areas of production). Altogether, electronics represents an industry with 1977 sales near the $60 billion mark. According to the vice president of one large electronics firm, it is an industry that has "served as the basis of a 'second industrial revolution.' "[60] Electronics is a constantly expanding industry. This year it will sell millions of dollars worth of products that did not even *exist* five years ago. As a leading industry representative remarked, in electronics "you don't project future markets—you go out and invent them."[61]

Within electronics, the semiconductor industry stands out in terms of technological developments, sales, and the development of markets. The semiconductor industry produces the millions of "bits and pieces" that form the central nervous system of all electronic equipment. A $6-billion-a-year industry, it continues to operate on "the frontiers of technology," as *Fortune* has put it. Other sectors of the U.S. electronics industry, particularly the field of consumer electronics, have gradually fallen behind technologically and lost their markets to foreign producers. Not semiconductors: "Clobbered from all sides by foreign goods," wrote *Business Week*, "U.S. industry can now count on few markets where it is clearly the world leader, much less a major exporter. But the semiconductor industry still qualifies on both counts. Although Japan is quietly preparing an all-out assault, the U.S. will easily maintain its leadership position in semiconductors in 1978 by growing 10 percent or more in sales."[62] According to Dataquest, Inc., an industry analysis

---

accepted by all sources. According to the *Electronics Marketing Directory*, the industry is spread across 37 SIC categories in 12 major groupings and 244 product classifications. In this study, I have adopted the classification system used by the U.S. Department of Commerce, which includes the following SICs: 3573 (Computers and Related); 3574 (Calculating and Accounting Machines); 3651 (Consumer Electronics: Radio and Television); 3662 (Communications Equipment); and 367 (Electronic Components and Accessories).

60. *Business Week*, Jul. 5, 1976.
61. Quoted in Simon Ramo, "Revolution in Electronics," *Comments on Argentine Trade*, Sep. 1976, p. 5.
62. *Business Week*, Jan. 4, 1978.

firm in Menlo Park, California, the worldwide semiconductor industry doubled sales in the last five years. And U.S.-based firms control 60 percent of those sales.[63]

The semiconductor industry is a prime example of an internationally integrated industry. There are a number of reasons why this is so. Manufacturing in the industry is easily divisible into high-technology work (development, design, engineering, testing) and labor-intensive work (assembly); therefore, geographic separation of the two aspects of production is quite simple. Second, the industry produces components that have a high value in relation to their weight and that therefore can be shipped easily and inexpensively. Third, since components are an intermediary product, they can escape high tariffs, entering the United States almost duty free under Items 806.30 and 807.00 of the Tariff Code.[64] In all, electronics is, in the words of one observer, an "industry on the wing."

If the above factors describe why the electronics industry was a good candidate for the internationalization of its productive base, they do not tell us why, in fact, it actually became internationalized. The product life cycle approach posits that international investments are essentially defensive reactions to foreign competitors who, by producing behind their own tariff walls, can escape the shipping costs and tariffs U.S. firms face and can thereby undercut the prices of U.S. firms. By examining competition and technology in the industry, we will find that the rationale behind international investment was different. Internationalization became a primary method by which U.S. firms, in fierce price competition with each other, sought to lower their own costs in order to capture a larger part of rapidly expanding markets.

Competition and technology in a new industry. Even though some branches of the electronics industry are highly concentrated, intense competition is the rule among all the branches. More than 6,000 firms compete in electronics, nearly half of these firms produce component parts for other branches of the industry.[65] Slightly more than half of these firms have fewer than 100 workers each, and nearly 70 percent

63. *New York Times*, Jan. 18, 1978.

64. See Organization for Economic Cooperation and Development (OECD), *Gaps in Technology: Electronic Components* (Paris, 1968), pp. 29ff; and John E. Tilton, *International Diffusion of Technology: The Case of Semiconductors* (Washington, D.C., 1971).

65. National Credit Office, *Electronic Marketing Directory, June 1976* (New York, 1976).

have yearly sales amounting to less than $5 million.[66] By contrast, only six companies account for more than 92 percent of sales of all mainframe computers, a $7 billion industry in 1975. And one firm alone, IBM, dominated the field with a 65.5 percent market share.[67] The trend toward centralization is equally pronounced in the field of many consumer products. In 1950 more than 140 firms assembled and sold TV receivers in the United States; at present there are only 7 U.S. television producers.[68]

Though many branches of the industry are becoming more centralized, all continue to be characterized by fierce competition, which usually takes the form of price slashing. The strategy most often used by electronics producers is known as the "accumulated experience" strategy. Simple put, producers seek to rapidly expand their volume of production in order to cut their unit costs as rapidly as possible and thereby gain a foothold in the market.[69]

There is a close relation between the development of technology, the expansion of markets, and price slashing in the electronics industry. A newly developed component, for example, is most often extremely expensive when first developed. It represents a large outlay of funds for research and development and for the construction of the first prototype. As such, buyers for the new component will be few and far between. In fact, there is usually only one potential buyer in this market, the U.S. government. When integrated circuits first came on the market, they averaged $50 each and the government (through the Department of Defense and other agencies) bought 100 percent of production.

As firms gain experience and begin to mass produce, the price starts to fall and industrial markets open up. The process continues until the component's price has fallen sufficiently to allow it access to the consumer market. The same integrated circuit that the government purchased for $50 in 1960 cost less than $2.35 six years later and has generated a new range of consumer products—digital watches, calculators, CB radios. The rapidly expanding markets have given smaller firms the possibility of competing with larger ones, since the nature of markets is not as defined as in the steel industry, for example.

66. U.S. Bureau of the Census, Census of Manufactures, 1972, *Industry Series: Office, Computing and Accounting Machines, MC72 (2)–35F* (Washington, D.C., 1975).
67. *Business Week*, Apr. 26, 1976.
68. *New York Times*, Apr. 3, 1977.
69. See Rose, and Y. S. Chang, *The Transfer of Technology: Economics of Offshore Assembly* (New York, 1971), pp. 8–11.

Nevertheless, though technology has often been used to create a better product, it has less frequently been used to improve the way the product is manufactured. In fact, the nature of competition in electronics has made for a relatively low level of automation in the means of production employed. Competition demands that firms constantly innovate. The large investments necessary for machinery would inevitably tie a company to a specific technology. This technology could quickly become obsolete, wedding the firm to an expensive, and now unprofitable, machine. In addition, as mentioned before, firms often produce goods without an assured market, hoping they can create a market with the product in hand. Here, as well, competition dictates maximum flexibility and a minimum investment in costly machinery. David Packard, chairman of Hewlett-Packard, summed up this perspective when he remarked: "My own company will bring out over 100 new products this year. The life of some of these products is not very long because competition is keen and somebody else will have to keep moving ahead. Under these conditions, a big investment in automated equipment to do a particular job isn't feasible, and I don't see automation as a possible solution." [70]

For many work tasks, then, it is not technical difficulties that have limited the spread of automation, but rather costs within the capitalist framework. As long as technology changes so rapidly, and as long as labor power is cheaper to employ than machines, capitalists have no incentive to automate. As Mae-fun, a Hong Kong assembly worker, put it, "We girls are cheaper than machines because a machine costs over $2,000 and would only replace two of us; in addition a machine tender, whose wages are $120 a month, would have to be hired." [71]

Research and development of new products, however, still takes "a pile of dollars," as *Forbes* has put it. If this is the case, though, why have the largest firms not been able to monopolize the development of new techniques and therefore dominate the industry? In fact, there has been a considerable concentration of technological development. Very few companies had a hand in the major innovations in the semiconductor industry between the late 1940's and the 1960's. Three firms in particular dominated the field: Bell Labs (the testing and laboratory arm

70. U.S. House of Representatives, Committee on Ways and Means, Subcommittee on Trade, *Special Duty Treatment on Repeal of Articles Assembled or Fabricated Abroad*, Hearings before 94th Congress, 2d Session, Mar. 24–25, 1976 (Washington, D.C., 1976), p. 33.
71. Janet Salaff, " 'Modern Times' in Hong Kong," *Bulletin of Concerned Asian Scholars*, 6, no. 1 (Jan.–Mar. 1974), p. 3.

of AT&T), Texas Instruments, and Fairchild Camera and Instrument. General Electric, Westinghouse, RCA, and IBM played lesser, but still important, roles.[72]

Government research and development contracts and purchase orders helped insure that technological developments would be concentrated among the largest firms. The Army Signal Corps, for example, financed pilot production lines for transistors and related devices at five sites operated by Western Electric (the manufacturing arm of AT&T), GE, Raytheon, RCA, and Sylvania.[73] And government research and development funds, 25 percent of total R&D funds in the semiconductor industry in 1958, went largely to the major firms.

Nevertheless, technological advances did not become concentrated in a few large firms, since according to most observers it is hard to keep a secret in the industry. Because competent semiconductor firms can duplicate a new device within six to twelve months of its appearance, and because scientists are free to move from firm to firm (which they do frequently, lured by higher salaries or the dream of getting in at the ground floor of an up-and-coming corporation), technology has diffused rapidly in the industry, and electronic patents are worth little.[74] Scientists and engineers from Bell Labs had a hand, ultimately, in creating no fewer than 15 other semiconductor firms between 1952 and 1967. The industry has even developed a name for the common practice of copying another firm's products—"second sourcing" which, according to *Fortune*, "more often than not [is] done without the original manufacturer's permission or cooperation." This practice, together with the prospects of long legal battles with uncertain outcomes, has led to a rapid diffusion of technology within the United States.

Nevertheless, this technology did not spread to foreign firms for many years. Profiting from the destruction of Japanese and German industry in the Second World War, and fueled by huge amounts of government research and development funds, the U.S. semiconductor industry established a dominant technological grip on the field. U.S. firms were awarded over 5,000 semiconductor patents between 1952 and 1968, while Japanese firms received only 83.[75] U.S. firms were responsible for 12 of 13 major product innovations in the semiconductor industry between 1951 and 1963. Of the 10 major process innovations in the industry between 1950 and 1964, U.S. firms developed 9. Compare this

72. Tilton, p. 16; and OECD, *Gaps* . . . , p. 44.
73. Tilton, p. 71.
74. *Economist*, Dec. 31, 1977.
75. Tilton, pp. 57, 141; and OECD, *Gaps* . . . .

with the steel industry, where not a single major steelmaking innovation has been developed in the United States.

Nevertheless, it should be noted that U.S. firms do not maintain a technological lead in all branches of electronics. Japanese firms have surpassed U.S. technology in many branchs of consumer electronics—particularly in the areas of color televisions, radios, and CBs. *Electronic News*, the industry's trade journal, recently noted that Toshiba, which was planning to move some of its operations to the United States, refused to buy Admiral's U.S. television plant on the grounds that the equipment was too dated and technologically backward.[76]

Though Japanese semiconductor firms are driving hard to catch up with their U.S. counterparts, particularly in the development of the next generation of semiconductors, U.S. firms at present maintain an important technological lead. Even as U.S. producers are urging the government to raise tariffs on imported Japanese semiconductors, it nonetheless remains a fact that in 1976 Japan controlled 1.6 percent of the U.S. market whereas U.S. producers controlled 13.4 percent of the Japanese market.[77] U.S. semiconductor firms have also been able to drive some Japanese firms out of their markets. For example, Texas Instruments went to Japan to produce semiconductors in order to prevent Japanese manufacturers from dominating their own markets. Unable to produce in sufficient volume to lower unit costs as rapidly as they otherwise might have, the Japanese competitors have been weakened.[78] It is also important to note that research and development spending by U.S. semiconductor firms is almost twice that of Japanese firms.

The shift to overseas production. U.S. firms began moving their production facilities abroad years before foreign firms possessed the technology to be actual (or even potential) competitors. Most U.S. electronics firms began the search for foreign sites in the 1960's. Fairchild Camera & Instrument opened a plant in Hong Kong in 1961, the same year that assembly production began on the Mexican border. General Instrument in 1964 became the first electronics firm from the United States to enter Taiwan, National Semiconductor moved to Singapore in 1968 and Malaysia in 1972, and Intersil opened the first U.S. semiconductor facility in India in 1974.

The shift of U.S. production to overseas locations is graphically illustrated by the increasing use manufacturers made of Tariff Items 806.30

76. *Electronic News*, Dec. 19, 1977.
77. *New York Times*, Jan. 18, 1978.
78. Rose, p. 60.

and 807.00.[79] These regulations permit U.S. manufacturers to export parts for assembly abroad and to pay duty only on the value added by labor when the items are re-imported. Seventy percent of all imports of electronics components entered the United States under Items 806.30 and 807.00 in 1975.[80] In that same year, all branches of the electronics industry imported over $1.2 billion worth of goods into the United States under these tariff items. This represented more than a tenfold increase in terms of value since 1966. In other words, during the same period in which factory sales of electronics in the United States almost doubled, overseas production increased by a factor of ten.

The major impetus behind the move overseas is the prospect of low wages for labor-intensive industries. Although labor costs typically represent between 20 percent and 45 percent of the total costs in electronics production, fixed capital and materials costs are essentially the same for all manufacturers. With price competition severe at home, and technological advances open to most in the industry, the companies turn to trimming labor costs as a way to get an edge on their competitors.

Wages in the Far East tend to be the lowest. As of 1976 they ranged from 17¢ per hour in Indonesia to 62¢ per hour in Singapore. Wages in Latin America were only slightly higher, on average. (See Table 5.)

Although wages in the United States for most assembly workers in electronics are not high—the average pay of a worker in components in 1976 was $4.13 an hour—the wage differential for a firm is nonetheless tremendous. For example, in 1976 General Instrument, a large U.S. electronics firm, paid its workers an average of $28 a day at its Jerrold's subsidiary in Chicopee, Massachusetts. The wage at Jerrold's plant in Nogales, Mexico, averaged $7.20 a day. And at General Instrument's Taipei factory workers earned an average of $1.93 a day.[81]

Furthermore, productivity rates abroad seem at least comparable to U.S. rates. CTS, a components producer, reported equal productivity rates at its Illinois plant and its Taiwan facility.[82] And Imec, a division

---

79. Item 806.30 covers any metal product returned to the United States for further processing. Item 807.00 requires only that a product's parts originated in the United States. Items entering under this section of the tariff code do not have to be further processed upon return to the United States. It was adopted into the Tariff Schedules in 1963, helping to pave the way for the boom in overseas production in the late 1960s. See "Electronics: The Global Industry," *NACLA's Latin America & Empire Report*, 11, no. 4 (Apr. 1977), p. 13; and Y. S. Chang, pp. 19–20.

80. U.S. Department of Commerce, *U.S. Industrial Outlook, 1977 with Projections to 1985*, (Washington, D.C., 1977), p. 234.

81. "Electronics: The Global Industry," p. 15.

82. *Electronic News*, Nov. 8, 1976.

TABLE 5

Average Hourly Wages, Selected Countries in Asia and Latin America
(*1976 U.S. dollars*)

Country	Hourly wage	Country	Hourly wage
ASIA		LATIN AMERICA	
Indonesia	17¢	Guatemala	36¢[a]
Thailand	26¢	Colombia	37¢
Philippines	32¢	El Salvador	44¢[a]
India	37¢	Brazil	47¢
Taiwan	37¢	Nicaragua	57¢
Malaysia	41¢	Dom. Republic	68¢[a]
S. Korea	52¢	Mexico	78¢
Hong Kong	55¢	Panama	94¢[a]
Singapore	62¢		

SOURCES: *Asia:* Wages given are for unskilled workers, an average of monthly high and low rates calculated at a standard 46-hour week, 1976; *Business Asia*, Apr. 30, 1976. *Latin America:* Wages given are average of wage rates in three labor-intensive, export-oriented industries (apparel, textile mill, and leather and leather goods), 1976 or 1974; Bureau of Labor Statistics, Office of Productivity and Technology, "Estimated Average Hourly Earnings and Total Compensation per Hour Worked of Production Workers in Manufacturing, 12 Latin American Countries, 1974–76," Unpublished Data, Aug. 1977.
    [a] 1974.

of the Republic Corporation with numerous assembly operations in Mexico, found productivity in its Mexican plant 10-15 percent higher than in the United States. *Business Asia* constructed an index of "relative productivity" designed to take wages as well as output into consideration. The business journal ranked the United States twelfth of 15 countries (13 Asian countries, the United States, and West Germany) in terms of "relative productivity." It was followed only by Pakistan, India, and Japan.[83]

How foreign is foreign competition? Most electronics producers have voiced their opposition to legislation that would revoke Tariff Items 806.30 and 807.00, the major portals through which foreign-assembled U.S. products reenter the United States. Their opposition serves as a good reflection of the highly internationalized character of the entire industry. On the other hand, the industry has never agreed on whether the United States should seek import quotas or tariffs on certain items

83. *Business Asia*, Nov. 5, 1976.

entering from particular "competitor" countries——Japan, for example.[84] The importation of color televisions is a case in point. In 1976, 2.8 million color TVs entered the United States from Japan, approximately 40 percent of domestic sales that year. The flood of imports occasioned a heated response by some—but not all—U.S. producers, who sought to stem the tide by appealing to the International Trade Commission. Some of the largest firms, General Electric and RCA, for example, did not join in these moves.

The semiconductor industry is even more united in its *opposition* to protectionist measures in the industry. It has flatly rejected import quotas on semiconductor devices, as well as import quotas in general (although here, too, there is no unanimity of opinion).[85]

Underlying divided industry opinion on tariffs and quotas is a structure of production that has united U.S. and foreign capital. General Electric, for example, holds the largest single block of shares of Toshiba, one of Japan's major electric/electronics producers. It has also recently announced the formation of a joint TV venture with Hitachi. Westinghouse is an important shareholder in Mitsubishi, the other Japanese electrical giant. And Zenith, that "all-American" TV producer—which recently announced the transfer of large parts of its assembly line to Taiwan and Mexico—has shown an interest in working out a joint venture with Sony regarding its Betamax video recorder.

U.S. dominance of semiconductor technology forced open Japanese doors to U.S. capital investments in Japanese semiconductor firms in the 1950's and 1960's. The following are some examples of the results:

—Texas Instruments set up a 50-50 venture with Sony for the manufacture of semiconductor and control devices. In late 1971, TI bought out Sony's semiconductor operations and now owns 100 percent of Texas Instruments Japan, Ltd.[86]

—Fairchild Camera and Instrument Corporation obtained 100 percent control of a joint venture it had previously shared with TDK Electronics Co.[87]

—ITT holds 3.8 percent of the shares of Nippon Electric and 6.7 percent of those of Sumitomo Electric Industries.

84. See, for example, "Statement of V. J. Adduci, President, Electronics Industry Association," in *Hearings on Special Duty Treatment or Repeal of Articles*, pp. 171–90.

85. U.S. Congress, House of Representatives, Committee on Ways and Means, *Tariff and Trade Proposals*, Hearings before the 91st Congress, 2d Session, Part 10 (June 5 and 8, 1970), (Washington, D.C., 1970), p. 2989.

86. *Pacific Basin Reports*, Aug. 1973, p. 162.

87. *Electronic News*, Dec. 26, 1977.

—Honeywell controls 50 percent of the shares of Yamatake-Honeywell Co.

Aside from stock ownership, a web of licensing agreements ties U.S. and Japanese electronics producers together. Special Trade Representative Robert S. Strauss noted this recently when he remarked that most Japanese television tubes are licensed by U.S. companies.[88] Westinghouse signed its first licensing agreement with Mitsubishi in 1923. General Electric has no fewer than 24 licensing agreements with Toshiba.[89] Texas Instruments has technology-transfer agreements with Nippon Electric, Hitachi, Mitsubishi, Toshiba, and Sony. The issue of placing quotas or tariffs on electronics goods produced abroad thus poses a thorny problem for U.S. firms that assemble abroad or are integrated with foreign firms in the same industry.

Technology and the division of labor. Much as the development of manufacturing in the nineteenth century represented an advance in the forces of production over craft production (in terms of both the technical and the social relations of production), so too the growth of globally integrated manufacturing systems in the mid-twentieth century reflects a further stage in the spread of capitalist relations of production, the socialization of the forces of production, and the international division of labor. Capitalism's ability to survive as a system is bound to capital's ability to carry out accumulation on an expanded scale. To accomplish this and overcome a tendency for the rate of profit to fall, capital must continue to revolutionize the means of production and further develop the present division of labor.

We have examined this process in the electronics industry. Unlike steel, which is facing increased competition from abroad because it has not renewed its technical base, electronics is an industry marked by a constant renovation of technology. Those branches of the electronics industry that have not maintained a technological lead—such as the television and other consumer products industries—are suffering a fate similar to that of the steel industry. Yet it is precisely the revolution in the technical relations of production in advanced branches of electronics such as semiconductors that has given rise to a new division of labor in the work force and created a crisis for U.S. workers—the export of jobs. With a de-skilling of the labor force arising from technological

88. Press Conference of Robert S. Strauss, Special Representative for Trade Negotiations, The White House, May 20, 1977.

89. Steve Babson, "The Multinational Corporation and Labor," *URPE Review*, 5, no. 1 (Spring 1973), pp. 23–24.

developments in the industry, high-skill labor inputs can be separated—
technically and geographically—from low-skill labor inputs. Workers
in Taiwan, Indonesia, and Haiti assemble the "bits and pieces," workers
in the Silicon Valley of California test and develop the software.

With each recession in the semiconductor industry, a number of
analysts predict that, at long last, the overseas producers will again return home, that this trend will be reversed. They call attention to the
"rising cost of labor at the offshore sites. . . , increased freight hikes and
the threat of tougher import regulations" as reasons why electronics
producers are pulling in their horns.[90]

Increasingly, however, it appears that overseas producers are not
planning to return to the United States. The clearest indication of this
is the new capital investments electronics producers are making in some
of their overseas plants. Though it is still true that capital-intensive
production will generally remain in the United States and labor-intensive
production abroad, nevertheless firms are beginning to ship expensive
machinery to the Far East and Latin America.

Nat Snyderman, *Electronic News*'s specialist on trends in overseas
production, wrote: "The rate of shipments, the installation of automatic
equipment and the heavy plant expenditures have put to rest all but a
few lingering expectations that assembly operations will be returned to
the United States in the foreseeable future, barring major political upheavals."[91] At the same time, the industry journal was reporting that
National Semiconductor had been spending about $300,000 a day for
six weeks on capital equipment for its facilities in Malaysia, Bangkok,
and Jakarta, and that Texas Instruments had been shipping "impressive
numbers" of automated machinery to its facilities in Taiwan and El
Salvador. Similarly, Analog Devices was planning the firm's largest
single capital investment in Limerick, Ireland, and General Instrument was pushing ahead with a million-dollar expansion of its Glen-
rothes, Scotland, microcircuit assembly facility.[92]

Higher tariff rates, countervailing duties, or other protectionist measures will not bring back jobs that have been exported in the electronics
industry. Neither will they by themselves revolutionize technology in
the steel industry or in consumer electronics. In the next section we will
examine how industry and government are addressing the growing uncompetitiveness of these two U.S. industries.

90. *Electronic News*, Mar. 31, 1975.
91. *Electronic News*, May 31, 1976.
92. See *Electronic News*, Mar. 29, 1976, May 31, 1976, and Sep. 27, 1976.

TOWARD THE RESTRUCTURING OF U.S. INDUSTRY

As different branches of the domestic U.S. industry grow uncompetitive in world markets because of either lack of technological innovation, high labor costs, or, simply, lessened demand for U.S. goods
given an increase of production on a world scale, the government faces
the complex task of guiding a process of industrial restructuring in the
United States. Rather than protect any one sector of capital through
the adoption of restrictive trade measures—and risk that such measures
might touch off a destructive trade war—the government is increasingly
likely to act in concert with industry to ensure, essentially, that the
weakest sectors of capital are sacrificed in the interests of the strongest.
The state, in a sense, determines the *pace* of industrial restructuring
through its numerous commercial, aid, fiscal, and monetary policies, but
competition within the industry itself will determine the outcome. Industrial restructuring is of particular importance in those industries,
such as steel and consumer electronics, that have lost their technological
advantage over competitors. In this section we will examine the inter-
twining of industrial and government policies designed to restore a level
of competitiveness to U.S. industry.

Restructuring Steel

Just as the U.S. steel crisis originates in the technological weakness
of the industry, so only a major infusion of new technology can provide
an answer for the steelmakers. Yet a vast amount of capital is needed
for this. David Roderick of U.S. Steel recently estimated that the industry would have to spend more than $5 billion a year "just to keep
pace with foreign competition."[93] Where will steel get its capital? At
present, much of the industry's income is divided between replacing essential facilities, installing pollution control equipment, and maintaining profits.[94] The industry can always raise its prices—which it has done
with regularity for decades—but the government has tended to look
with disfavor on price increases when they are felt to be too inflationary.
Furthermore, without high tariff barriers to keep out imported steel,
higher prices would only further weaken U.S. steel's hold on domestic
markets.

The industry is left with four roads out of the crisis. First, the entire

93. *New York Times*, Jan. 8, 1978.
94. Edmund Faltermayer, "How Made-in-America Steel Can Survive," *Fortune,*
Feb. 13, 1978, p. 128.

industry can be restructured through the closing of the smaller firms and the further concentration of the larger ones. Second, the industry can rebuild itself through a massive infusion of government aid, thereby shoring up its profits at the taxpayers' expense. Third, within the steel-mills, productivity can again be increased by labor speedup (as well as by the introduction of new technology). And fourth, steel can raise its needed capital by diversifying out of steel or by investing in more prof-itable mills in foreign countries. Here we will examine the restructuring of steel and the role of government aid. In a later section we will turn. to the issue of the intensification of labor. Diversification and foreign investments, broad topics in themselves, remain outside the scope of this paper.[95]

The first step toward the restructuring of steel has already been taken. The companies are lopping off the least productive mills that have weakened output for years, those mills that they have let run down and that they now see as too costly to restore. Each steelmaker has begun to trim inefficient productive capacity. According to William Roesch, former chief executive at Kaiser Steel and now with U.S. Steel, approximately 10 percent of total U.S. capacity will be shut down by the middle of 1978.[96]

Timing is a critical factor in this process of restructuring. As the *Economist* noted, "the time is needed to allow the obsolete plants of established steel industries, notably in the United States and Western Europe, to be run down at a socially acceptable pace."[97] The most recent contract between the United Steelworkers and the steelmakers, however, has upset this timing. According to the 1977 USWA contract in basic steel, only those workers still employed after January 1, 1978, are eligible for the higher severance pay called for in the contract. Thus, though the steel companies blamed foreign imports as the cause of the layoffs that swept the industry in late 1977, they actually arose when steel producers rushed to trim down before the January 1, 1978, deadline.

95. The two most diversified steel companies, U.S. Steel and Armco, are also the most profitable. In 1975 more than 50 per cent of U.S. Steel's profits came from non-steel-producing activities including chemicals, agrichemicals, railroads, ocean transport, cement, natural gas, pipeline and oil-field-drilling equipment, coal, and iron ore. *New York Times*, Feb. 29, 1976. Sixty percent of Armco's net income is generated by non-steel activities. Shearman, Ralston, Inc., "February Market Let-ter," Jan. 26, 1978, p. 3. For a full discussion of this, see Helen Shapiro and Steven Volk, "Steelyard Blues: New Structures in Steel," *NACLA Report on the Americas*, 13, no. 1 (Jan.–Feb. 1979).

96. Faltermayer, p. 124.

97. *Economist*, Dec. 31, 1977.

TABLE 6

Distribution of Crude Steelmaking Capacity by Size of Firm,
United States and Japan, Mid-1950's and Late 1960's

Capacity range (Millions of tons)	Mid-1950's		Late 1960's	
	Japan	U.S.	Japan	U.S.
Below 0.5	28.2%	6.4%	3.0%	3.4%
0.5 – 0.9	14.4	5.6	2.9	2.4
1.0 – 1.9	36.3	8.8	1.6	8.3
2.0 – 4.9	21.1	23.9	7.2	11.8
Above 5.0	–	55.2	85.2	74.2
TOTAL	100.0%	100.0%	100.0%	100.0%

SOURCE: Anthony Cockerill, *The Steel Industry: International Comparisons of Industrial Structure and Performance* (London, 1974), pp. 58, 65.

The second step in restructuring the industry will involve a new period of concentration and centralization in steel. Throughout the history of capitalist production, the concentration and centralization of productive units has served as a spur to increased production. This process can give rise to a more comprehensive organization of the work process and to a revolution in the technical composition of capital that will allow for greater productivity.[98]

One of the most striking, if overlooked, features of the Japanese steel industry is the rapidity with which the concentration-centralization process took place, particularly in relation to the U.S. steel industry. (See Table 6.) In the mid-1950's, no single firm, and no individual plant, had the capacity to produce more than 5 million tons of crude steel. A little more than a decade later, 85 percent of Japanese steel was produced by firms with a capacity of 5 million tons or over, and 35 percent of all steel was produced in plants with that capacity. Concentration and centralization of the Japanese steel industry provided the fuel for its rapid growth.

More than three years of crisis in U.S. steel has generated an important reorganization in an industry that is already highly monopolized. In 1970, 80 percent of the industry's production was centered in only 11 companies. Nevertheless, according to William Roesch, the economy

98. Marx, *Capital*, vol. 1, pp. 582–89.

TABLE 7

Distribution of Crude Steelmaking Capacity by Size of Plant,
United States and Japan, Mid-1950's and Late 1960's

Capacity range (Millions of tons)	Mid-1950's		Late 1960's	
	Japan	U.S.	Japan	U.S.
Below 0.5	46.2%	9.8%	5.2%	4.6%
0.5 – 0.9	32.7	11.4	4.6	4.3
1.0 – 1.9	–	32.8	11.6	13.1
2.0 – 4.9	21.1	35.3	43.4	41.5
Above 5.0	–	10.4	35.2	36.5
TOTAL	100.0%	100.0%	100.0%	100.0%

SOURCE: Anthony Cockerill, *The Steel Industry: International Comparisons of Industrial Structure and Performance* (London, 1974), pp. 58, 65.

cannot support "more than five integrated producers" in the steel industry. "The more capital-intensive an industry is, the fewer companies there should be," he remarked.[99]

In October 1977 the Alan Wood Steel Company in Conshohocken, Pennsylvania, shut down production, throwing more than 3,000 workers on the unemployment rolls. Alan Wood was not among the top ten steelmakers, but its closing represented the largest bankruptcy of a steelmill ever to occur in the United States. The workers at Alan Wood had tried to forestall the plant's demise by voting to give up bonuses accorded them in their contract and by accepting a temporary 10 percent hourly wage reduction, but the firm closed anyway.[100]

As the weakest firms dropped out of the picture, others began to talk of mergers. Attention focused on a proposed merger between the steel subsidiaries of two large conglomerates, LTV's Jones & Laughlin Steel (ranked seventh among steelmakers) and Lykes's Youngstown Sheet & Tube (ranked eighth). The merger plan required the approval of the Justice Department and, as such, was an important indicator of the Carter Administration's stand on domestic steel.

In June 1978 Attorney General Griffin Bell personally approved the merger—overruling a recommendation from his antitrust staff—as "the only viable means for maintaining the Lykes steel producing facilities

99. Quoted in *The Guardian*, Nov. 30, 1977.
100. *Steel Labor*, Dec. 1977.

and for saving the jobs of those concerned."[101] Although the two conglomerates together will assume more than $600 million in debt (exclusive of mortgage debt), the merger instantly created the third-largest steel firm in the country, with combined sales of $3.8 billion in 1977.

The plan, which is expected to set a trend of Justice Department approval for "failing company mergers," recalls the last large-scale merger in steel. In August 1971 fourth-ranked National Steel proposed a merger with eleventh-ranked Granite City Steel Co. The highly unorthodox merger—in obvious violation of the Celler-Kefauver amendment to the Clayton Act barring substantial competitors from merging—was approved by the Nixon-Mitchell Justice Department. It moved National into the third-ranking spot in the nation.[102]

The Role of the Government

Aside from favorable rulings on mergers, the government can play a major role in supporting those firms that remain in the market. If what is necessary is to run down obsolete plant and equipment at a "socially acceptable pace," then the government determines and guides this pace where possible, stepping in to prevent severe disruptions that could adversely affect the entire economy and guaranteeing the profits of the remaining firms. The Carter Administration has already proposed a comprehensive welfare program for steel. This includes legislation to accelerate depreciation allowances for aging equipment, tax breaks for firms investing in antipollution equipment and equipment mandated by OSHA, $550 million in low-cost government loans to domestic mills, freight rate changes designed to lower the cost of steel shipped by rail, and the guaranteeing of private bank loans to steel companies. Such proposals have led some steelmen to conclude that "sometimes crises produce good results. . . . For the first time we are getting some understanding from the Administration on the breadth of our problems."[103]

Government aid plans designed to bolster the profits of the largest

101. *Wall Street Journal*, Jun. 22, 1978.
102. *The New Republic*, Feb. 2, 1974, pp. 12–14. U.S. firms are not alone in this process of restructuring. The Japanese, who face recession after fifteen years of unparalled expansion, speak of performing "surgical operations" on their economy. In particular, some 70 small to medium-sized steel companies will soon come under the knife. (*Business Week*. Jan. 30, 1978.) The Swedish government recently announced plans to merge the country's largest producers into a single company, Svensk Staal AB. And the three largest Mexican steel firms have just been merged.
103. Interview with Lewis W. Foy, quoted in *U.S. News & World Report*, Nov. 21, 1977.

firms have been met with skepticism by the workers. As John Barbero, vice president of a steelworker local said, "Edgar Speer [chairman of U.S. Steel] wants massive government money with no strings. In any other country, such massive aid would mean government control or ownership. Edgar Speer intends for U.S. Steel to survive to the next century with taxpayers' money, but he also intends to be fully independent. He probably will have his wishes."[104]

The government also has acted to shore up the stronger steel companies by establishing a "reference" or "trigger" price for imported steel. If imported steel is sold below this price, the Treasury Department can quickly initiate an antidumping investigation. If it determines that products are being sold at "less than fair value," it can require the importers to post bonds equal to the difference between the sale price and a "fair" price. Finally, if the International Trade Commission determines that imports have harmed the U.S. industry, then duties can be imposed. Once Treasury announced the reference price system, concern in the steel industry shifted to the level at which prices would be set. If they were set sufficiently high—$360 a ton, recommended David Roderick of U.S. Steel—then U.S. companies could raise their prices and still undersell imports. If they were set too low, U.S. firms would be forced to shape up. The price finally selected—$330 a ton on average, including duty—was approximately 5.7 percent below East Coast prices.[105] Trigger prices for the critical areas of hot- and cold-rolled sheet and plate were below U.S. domestic prices.

At this moment, no one is clear about the final effects of the trigger price system. Most analysts agree that the West Coast will still receive a large quantity of imported steel. Since trigger prices are pegged to Japanese shipping and production costs, the trigger price will be lowest in the West.

When the Treasury Department boosted the "trigger" levels in May 1978, thereby narrowing the spread between foreign and domestic prices, most U.S. companies disregarded this opportunity to improve sales by raising their prices at the same time.[106] If such a pattern persists, the trigger price system will only ensure an inflationary trend in steel, since the price of imported steel will continually be forced higher. But unless the U.S. steel industry is willing to sacrifice profits to greater volume, the trigger price system will not solve the crisis of U.S. steel

104. Paula L. Cizmar, "Steelyard Blues," *Mother Jones*, Apr. 1978, p. 38.
105. *Business Week*, Jan. 16, 1978.
106. *Wall Street Journal*, May 8, 1978.

since it provides no guarantees that additional capital will be put into their mills.

The Pace of Adjustment

In those sectors of consumer electronics that have been surpassed by Japanese producers, particularly the television industry, the Carter Administration has tried to limit the challenge, not stop it. As C. Fred Bergsten, Assistant Secretary of the Treasury for International Affairs, noted: "I think the real issue is the pace of adjustment to imports. The Government may have to enter the picture and restrain imports to make sure that the pace of adjustment is not so rapid that it violently disrupts particular industries, communities or groups of workers."[107]

The Carter Administration has used "orderly marketing agreements" (OMAs) to guide the pace of adjustment. OMAs are designed not to protect inefficient import-sensitive domestic industries, according to Frank A. Weil, Assistant Secretary of Commerce for Industry and Trade, but rather to give these industries time to restructure, increase efficiency, or shift into new lines of production.[108]

In May 1977 the White House announced that it had reached an agreement with Japan to limit the imports of color TVs to approximately 1.75 million units per year for three years beginning July 1, 1977.[109] This represented a 40 percent decline in imports from the level set in 1976. Though the pact may provide some solace for U.S. color TV producers in the short run, the OMA will not protect inefficient U.S. producers. First, although imports from Japan are going down, there has been a surge in imports from Taiwan and Korea. Many sources are speculating that at least some of these sets are being diverted from Japan to these countries before export to the United States. Second, nearly every major Japanese television producer has established production facilities in the United States within the last year. Sony is operating in San Diego; Toshiba is building a plant in Tennessee; Matsushita has recently expanded its Chicago plant; Sanyo Electric Co. has entered a joint venture with Sears, Roebuck and Co.; and General Electric and Hitachi have formed General Television of America. In all, Japanese production of TVs in the United States increased from 750,000 sets in 1976 to 1.2 million a year later.[110]

107. Quoted in *U.S. News & World Report*, Aug. 8, 1977.
108. *New York Times*, Jan. 1, 1978.
109. Press Briefing and Statement of White House Press Secretary, May 20, 1977.
110. *Business Week*, May 8, 1978, and *New York Times*, Dec. 8, 1977.

Offshore Production and U.S. Defense Costs

The government neither has taken nor plans to take any steps designed to halt the flow of labor-intensive industries to low-wage areas abroad. In fact, its foreign aid program seems designed to ensure that this trend will continue.

The major locations of U.S. overseas production in the Far East and Latin America are almost all characterized by low wages, poor working conditions, and the repression of organized labor. The Philippines, South Korea, Thailand, Singapore, Indonesia, Malaysia, and Taiwan have all been sharply criticized by international agencies for their antiworker policies. And yet, as a group, these countries have received more military aid from the United States than any other region between 1946 and 1975—$16.3 billion.[111] If we add to this the $13.6 billion that the United States has given these countries (plus Hong Kong) in economic aid from 1946 to 1973, we find that the United States has poured about $30 billion into these eight countries since the end of the Second World War. A continuation of these aid programs, as well as the maintenance of Tariff Items 806.30 and 807.00 encourages more labor-intensive manufacturing firms to leave the United States rather than the opposite.

U.S. WORKERS IN THE NEW ECONOMY

The situation in steel and electronics characterizes that in many other manufacturing industries in the United States. Technologically weak or unable to compete with the low wages paid in the less developed countries, these industries have seen manufacturing jobs stream out of the United States, shifting the entire structure of the U.S. economy in the process. Between 1950 and 1976 more than 34 million jobs were added to the nation's payroll, but only 1.1 million of these were for production workers in manufacturing industries.[112] In this section we will examine the quantitative and qualitative effects of these structural changes on employment, job structures, wages, productivity, collective bargaining, and working conditions in the United States.

Employment and Job Structures

In the last decade, U.S. factory workers as a whole have lost an estimated two million jobs in the United States as manufacturing firms

111. *NACLA's Latin America & Empire Report*, 10, no. 1 (Jan. 1976), pp. 24–27.
112. Bureau of Labor Statistics, *Employment and Earnings*.

have either moved abroad or closed down. The average yearly employment level of production workers in basic steel between 1967 and 1976, for example, stood at 476,000 jobs, approximately 110,000 fewer than existed in 1950.[113] In 1977 at least 20,000 additional jobs in steel were lost through cutbacks and closings at Youngstown Sheet & Tube, Jones & Laughlin, Bethlehem, U.S. Steel, and others.

Other manufacturing sectors mirrored steel's losses. According to David Fitzmaurice, president of the International Union of Electrical, Radio and Machine Workers (IUE), employment in industries where IUE members work dropped by 306,400 from 1973 to 1976;[114] almost 70,000 jobs alone were lost in radio and TV and in the components sectors of electronics.[115] In the last 10 years, employment in shoe production dropped by 70,000 as nearly 40 percent of all U.S. shoe factories shut their doors.[116] Since 1973 an estimated 200,000 workers in textiles and apparel have lost their jobs.[117] In sum, at least half a million workers in steel, electronics, textiles, apparel, and shoe manufacture have been laid off in the course of the last decade, the bulk in the last four years.

Besides these purely quantitative effects, the shift of manufacturing jobs is having a marked qualitative effect on the structure of the U.S. labor force. The proportion of manufacturing jobs to service and clerical jobs is shifting significantly. By 1985, according to a recent government report, white collar employment will account for slightly more than half of all jobs in this country for the first time.[118]

Wages

The shifting of manufacturing jobs to non-unionized sections of the United States and to foreign countries also adversely affects wage rates of U.S. workers. "When employers succeed in moving from an organized plant," according to the Director of Organization for the United Electrical, Radio, and Machine Workers of America (UE), "wages in many cases are set back to where they were ten to twenty years ago."[119] This was confirmed by a visit to a western Massachusetts electronics plant last year. The firm moved from Philadelphia in the early 1970's

113. *Ibid.*
114. *IUE News*, Apr. 1977, p. 9.
115. Bureau of Labor Statistics, *Employment and Earnings*.
116. Sidney Margolius, "A Consumer Alert on Imports," *American Federationist*, Aug. 1977, p. 9.
117. *Forbes*, Apr. 1, 1977.
118. *U.S. News & World Report*, Dec. 27, 1976/Jan. 3, 1977; and Bureau of Labor Statistics, *The Structure of the U.S. Economy in 1980 and 1985, Bulletin 1831.*
119. *UE News.* Dec. 19, 1977.

to escape an active union and a "high" wage rate. Part of the plant's production (assembly work on consumer items) was moved to Mexico; the remainder (assembly and testing of more sophisticated products) was relocated in western Massachusetts. Workers in the Massachusetts plant *now* earn what the Philadelphia workers were making six years ago: $3.50 an hour, on average.[120] Given inflation, the current wage is still below the Philadelphia wage of 1970.

So much is clear about "runaway" plants: they serve as an anchor weighing down the wage rate. As important as an actual runaway, however, is a potential runaway. The fact of capital's mobility vis-à-vis labor is used as an element by employers in disciplining workers. In other words, the threat of moving becomes just as effective as the actual move, as the following case illustrates.

In late 1971, Local 801 of the IUE in Dayton, Ohio, entered into negotiations on a new contract with the Frigidaire Company. Frigidaire—a division of General Motors—had recently laid off half its local work force and now threatened to move out of Dayton or dump its appliance business altogether if the workers did not accept an average wage cut of approximately one dollar an hour.[121] The union finally backed down under the threat, agreeing to forgo wage increases that had been promised them for the next four years and to cut the wage rates of new workers. "What good is it if you got a couple thousand workers making, say, $5 a hour when you've also got 10,000 others walking the street unemployed?" asked Local 801 president Luther Holt.[122]

The new contract created a furor within the IUE, but it won the admiration of Frigidaire, Dayton's business community, and even President Nixon, who remarked that "in taking this splendid action, Local 801 is contributing opportunities for workers in the Dayton area . . . which will allow more of our fellow citizens to share in the new prosperity." [123] Thus the *threat* of moving production was in itself sufficient to depress the workers' wages at Frigidaire.

The story did not end there, however. Within two weeks, the demand for wage cuts spread like wildfire throughout Dayton and other Ohio communities. Chrysler Airtemp, citing the Frigidaire settlement, asked workers "to reconsider wage and benefit provisions of their union con-

---

120. "Electronics: The Global Industry," p. 8.
121. *Dayton Daily News*, Nov. 21, 1971.
122. *Akron Beacon-Journal*, Dec. 6, 1971.
123. *Dayton Daily News*, Dec. 3, 1971.

tract to make the firm more competitive in the marketplace."[124] Dayton's city workers were asked to accept a wage cut on December 21. On January 10, 1972, rubber workers at B. F. Goodrich in Akron began to negotiate a wage cut.[125]

Tax Structures and Social Services

The threat of runaways reflects back on the working class in ways that go beyond wages. Municipalities often slash corporate tax rates as an incentive to attract or hold onto businesses. City after city in the central industrial belt and the Northeast has resorted to this measure. "WE'D RATHER LOSE TAXES THAN BUSINESS," boomed a full page advertisement placed in the *New York Times* by New York State. Ohio begged its businesses to "Look at Ohio's New Tax Incentive Programs for Industry . . . PROFIT IS NOT A DIRTY WORD IN OHIO!"

The impact of such tax-slashing measures has already been felt in the numerous fiscal crises that swept the towns of Ohio and other states in 1977 and 1978. In late 1977 schools throughout Ohio were faced with an immediate shutdown unless the public approved a new school tax. Funds for schools are raised through property taxes and state appropriations. In recent years, however, cities have cut their property taxes on businesses when they have threatened to leave town. The small homeowner, then, is faced with assuming the burden of taxes. In one Ohio city only a 500 percent increase in local property tax rates kept schools open after a plant that had employed 1,200 moved away.

Although many municipalities and states have used tax incentives as a lure for businesses, a survey of the available literature on the subject reveals, with few exceptions, that no significant plant locations or expansions were based on interstate business tax breaks. In other words, communities are rewriting their tax structures to attract and keep businesses despite little indication that their actions are having the desired effect. Often plants will collect impressive tax write-offs for years before finally moving away. Such is the case at an Allen-Bradley plant in Wisconsin. In 1976 and 1977, the company received $3 million in tax rebates from the state. Now it is planning to shift 1,300 jobs to Texas and Mexico.[126]

124. *Journal Herald* (Dayton), Dec. 22, 1971.
125. *Wall Street Journal*, Jan. 10, 1972.
126. *UE News*, Jan. 8, 1978.

Consumer Prices

One could argue that, at the very least, workers as consumers would benefit from the internationalization of productive capital since it would give them access to goods produced at lower cost. To the extent that foreign imports discourage U.S. firms from raising their prices blindly, this may be true (although the price of imports is obviously tied to a large number of general economic factors). Studies of the radio, TV, and apparel industries have demonstrated, however, that imports "do not result in any price benefit to the consumer." [127] In the apparel industry, retailers raise the price of imported products by taking a larger markup than on domestically produced items. In the television industry as well, lower production costs of sets assembled abroad are translated more often into a higher rate of profit rather than into lower consumer prices. [128]

Productivity, Working Conditions, and Collective Bargaining

The struggle over productivity and the actual form the work process assumes has increasingly become a focus of conflict between owners and workers. To an important extent, the work process has come to replace even wages as the major bone of contention between capital and labor. The *Wall Street Journal* recently intimated that employers, "emboldened by recent declines in the membership and public standing of labor unions," would try to press home their advantage by forcing changes in union work rules in order to increase productivity rather than by going after wages. [129]

The struggle over the work process itself has two main facets. The

127. U.S. Congress, Subcommittee on Trade of the Committee on Ways and Means, U.S. House of Representatives, *Library of Congress Study on Imports and Consumer Prices* (Washington, D.C., 1977).

128. Nathaniel Goldfinger, "An American Trade Union View of International Trade and Investments," in Kujawa, p. 39.

129. *Wall Street Journal*, Jan. 27, 1978. The theoretical basis for such a shift in advanced capitalist economies is provided by capital's need to counteract a tendency for the rate of profit to fall. Production of relative surplus value (loosely, productivity increases that arise from a renovation of the technical basis of production) permits capitalists to increase the use values (commodities) received by the working class while increasing surplus value at a faster rate. A simple wage increase with no other change would redistribute surplus between workers and owners. For more on this, see Patrick Clawson, "Some Thoughts on How Does Capitalism Get Out of a Crisis," unpublished manuscript presented at URPE conference, New York, Dec. 28, 1977.

first is the intensification of work with no change in the number of workers, plant, or equipment—speedup, in other words. The second is the introduction of new technology that allows workers to produce the same amount in fewer hours (or to produce more in the same number of hours). Whereas speedups are always a source of conflict on the shop floor, the introduction of new technology is much more under the control of the employer, since the capitalist owns the machinery.

We have seen that the crisis of the steelmakers originated not in the so-called "illegal" trading practices of the steelmaking nations but rather in the relative cost inefficiency of U.S. production. One cause of this inefficiency is surely the weak world demand for steel, which has forced steelmakers to run their plants at inefficient levels of capacity (in the 75–85 percent range over the last three years). But the other cause is that U.S. steelmakers have not improved the technology of their plants at the same pace as other producers, notably the Japanese. For U.S. steelmakers to again become efficient producers on a world scale, they must increase the productivity levels of their mills. In the prior section we noted government and industry plans to reorganize the steel industry, infusing it with capital for new plant and equipment and closing down the least productive mills. Here we will discuss the speedup in steel, the second method of boosting productivity, by briefly sketching a history of productivity clauses in the steelworkers' contracts.

Labor-capital relations in the steel industry can be divided into two main phases since the Second World War. The first, from 1949 to 1960, may be called the strike period. During this time the United Steelworkers (USWA) called at least one major work stoppage every year, including five nationwide strikes and the massive 116-day strike of 1959. The second period, from 1960 until the present, has been a no-strike period marked by the total absence of national strikes and only two local work stoppages of importance.[130]

During the first period, strikes in the industry led many to step up their purchases of imported steel. Still, the USWA resisted company pressures to put productivity clauses into their contracts as a means of counteracting growing steel imports. In a joint letter "To the Members and Families of the United Steelworkers of America," dated June 20, 1959, David McDonald, Howard Hague, and I. W. Abel (USWA president, vice president, and secretary-treasurer, respectively) denounced "the 'inflation' monster and the 'foreign competition' hoax," which they

130. See Gordan and Persky, and Seidl.

saw as standing behind the productivity clause. "While your attention and the eyes of the public have been fixed on the alleged effect of 'inflation' and 'foreign competition,'" they argued, "the steel corporations mapped their plan to atomize and completely undermine your job rights."[131]

Slightly more than a decade later, however, productivity clauses and even no-strike agreements were accepted by the national USWA leadership as a primary means of countering imports of steel. In 1973, the USWA leadership pushed through its "Experimental Negotiating Agreement" (ENA). The ENA established joint advisory productivity committees in every steel mill to allow U.S. producers "to meet the challenge posed by principal foreign competitors in recent years."[132] According to the pact, "the function of the Committee shall be to advise with plant management concerning ways and means of improving productivity and developing recommendations for stimulating its growth so as to promote . . . orderly and peaceful relations with the employees, to achieve uninterrupted operations in the plants, to promote the use of domestic steel, and to achieve the desired prosperity and progress of the company and its employees."

The ENA also included a controversial no-strike agreement. The USWA promised to turn over all unresolved grievances on a national level (including the determination of a national contract between the USWA and the ten major steel producers) to binding arbitration rather than press the issue on the picket line. To no less an extent than the productivity clause, the no-strike agreement was generated out of a concern for imports. It was designed to persuade hedge-buyers of steel that they had nothing to fear, that their supplies of steel would not be threatened by a strike.

The joint USWA–steel corporation push for greater productivity has already increased the hazards faced by workers by encouraging crew reduction and work outside a laborer's training and job description. According to the Bureau of Labor Statistics, the injury rate per million hours worked in basic steel went up throughout the 1960's, reaching a high point in the boom years of 1973–74. A worker at Youngstown Sheet & Tube put it this way: "During the period of the productivity emphasis we had four deaths in our company. One of the men killed was a boy that worked there seven days and another man

131. Quoted in Staughton Lynd, "History of United Steelworkers of America," part 5, *The Guardian*, Apr. 25, 1973, p. 8.
132. *Agreement between United States Steel Corporation and the United Steelworkers of America*, Aug. 1, 1974, p. 203.

was one that worked there 30-some years on the same job. I think it was because of 'Hurry up, get the job done' in unsafe conditions for the sake of production."[133]

CONCLUSION: WORKERS IN THE NEW INTERNATIONAL ORDER

As the essential structures of the U.S. manufacturing economy change, many sectors of organized labor have become increasingly unable to protect their workers' economic rights. Unions are on the defensive. In the last two years, membership in labor unions has declined by 767,000, or four percent, largely as a result of the recession, the shift of jobs to the non-union South and abroad, and industry's assault on progressive labor legislation. By late 1977, only 20.1 percent of the U.S. work force was organized, as against nearly 35 percent some 20 years ago. Despite the omnipotent image of "Big Labor" conjured up in the press, four of five workers in the United States are not in a union. In the past few years, nearly every major piece of prolabor legislation, from tax reform and common situs picketing to labor law reform legislation, has either been defeated or blocked in Congress.

Nor has organized labor distinguished itself in this period. The AFL-CIO has few plans to recapture any organizing initiative it may once have had. According to a recent report in the *New York Times*, labor leaders have "no plans or strategy for a new organizing drive" should Congress pass important pending labor law reforms.[134] Instead, organized labor seems to be fighting a rearguard action designed to protect industries rather than workers. The major concern of the labor federation is import competition. "Free trade is a joke and a myth," stormed George Meany at a recent AFL-CIO national convention. "And a Government trade policy predicated on old ideas of free trade is worse than a joke—it is a prescription for disaster. The answer is fair trade, do unto others as they do to us—barrier for barrier—closed door for closed door."[135]

Leaders of the USWA have espoused a similar line, seeing the source of their problem in the "unfair" trade practices of the Japanese, not the inefficiency of the industry: "We have not lost our markets to foreign producers who can sell in the American market at lower costs than American producers. Rather, we are losing our markets to steel dumped

133. Interview with Ed Mann, secretary-treasurer of the Rank and File Team, a group of insurgent steelworkers, *Michigan Free Press*, Jan. 27, 1974, p. 6.
134. *New York Times*, Feb. 24, 1978.
135. *New York Times*, Dec. 9, 1977.

in the U.S. at prices far below what it costs to produce that steel in foreign mills."[136]

Such an interpretation has led many unions to link forces with the very sources who have created unemployment in the industry either by refusing to turn profits into modern plant and equipment or by shifting the bases of their production abroad. COMPACT (the Committee to Preserve American Color Television) is one example of an industry-union committee designed to lobby for the protection of industry from "unfair" foreign competition. Formed in 1976 by four corporations and eleven unions, COMPACT's first act was to petition the International Trade Commission on the grounds that color TV imports were "destroying, or threatening to destroy, business and jobs" in the United States.[137] On the corporate side, COMPACT members include two producers of glass envelopes for TV tubes, Corning Glass Works and Owens-Illinois, and two electronics firms, Sprague Electric Co. and Wells-Gardner Electronics Corporation. Two of the three major electrical/electronics unions also joined COMPACT, the IUE and the International Brotherhood of Electrical Workers (IBEW). The third major union, the UE, refused to join.

Though COMPACT members encouraged the government to reduce imports of Japanese televisions into the United States, they did not address the major factors that have led to job loss in the industry: the low technological level of U.S. TV producers and the export of jobs in all branches of electronics to low wage areas in the Far East and Latin America. Some COMPACT members had been cutting back their U.S. work force for years. Sprague Electric, a Massachusetts-based firm, began to move its assembly operations overseas in the late 1960's. As of 1976 it operated in 16 countries including Hong Kong, Malaysia, Taiwan, Mexico, the Virgin Islands, Spain, and Scotland. It also held a minority share in a Japanese semiconductor firm. Corning Glass, another COMPACT member, had facilities in Taiwan, South Korea, Thailand, India, Pakistan, Mexico, Bermuda, and throughout Europe and South America. It held a 49.8 percent interest in a Japanese glass company.

Joint committees in steel suffer from this same contradiction. The USWA–steel corporation productivity committees were established to counter imports of steel. But the roots of the crisis in the steel industry

136. From a "Policy Statement" adopted by USWA delegates, *Steel Labor*, Jan. 1978.
137. *IUE News*, Mar. 1977.

originate in the steelmakers' neglect of their plant and equipment. Imported steel can now undersell U.S. steel because it is cheaper than domestic steel. If joint productivity committees are to turn this situation around, they can only do so at the expense of the workers, by intensifying the labor process.

It may be attractive for union leaders in the AFL-CIO to pose the problem as one of "illegal" trade, for the solution flows easily from such a definition: impose trade protection. On the other hand, if "illegal" trade is not the problem, we can hardly expect protectionist measures to be the answer. In fact, when one grapples with the full extent of the problem, it becomes clear that U.S. workers are faced with a serious challenge posed by the changing structures of the U.S. economy and its integration into the world capitalist economy.

The question of how workers can defend their economic and political rights in the coming period of economic restructuring is a difficult one with no easy solution. As we have noted, the attempt by U.S. business to regain a level of competitiveness in some manufacturing industries will strike workers particularly hard, in terms of both wages and working conditions. Many industries—shoes, for example—will most likely never regain their former importance and will become marginal or specialty industries in the United States. Others, such as steel, may be able to restructure to increase efficiency, but thousands of steelworkers will lose their jobs in the process.

The difficulty of the workers' position was highlighted by an organizer for the United Electrical Workers who recently spoke to a group of machinists at a small New England plant whose owner was threatening to move to Mexico unless the workers accepted a wage cut. The organizer told the workers that they had before them a variety of choices. They could accept the wage cut, though this did not guarantee that the company would not move the plant the following week, month, or year; besides, their wages were not keeping up with inflation as it was. They could fight the wage cut, though that most certainly would lead the company to shift production to Mexico. Or they could occupy the plant and run it themselves, without the employer. This would work, he paused, for a day or two, until the owner called in the police to haul everyone to jail. That may be the best choice, but it is no easy solution. His conclusion was broad and general, rather than specific: workers will not find a solution to the problems that beset them in any one plant or even through any one union; only long-term political action by the workers can give them the answers they so desperately seek.

Exporting Repression: U.S. Support
for Authoritarianism in Latin America

MICHAEL T. KLARE AND CYNTHIA ARNSON

President Carter has gone to great lengths to persuade the American
people and others of his "undeviating commitment" to the advancement
of human rights abroad. In his first major address to the United Nations
on March 17, 1977, he affirmed Washington's obligation to "work with
potential adversaries as well as our close friends to advance the cause
of human rights." No member of the UN, he declared, "can avoid its
responsibilities to speak when torture or unwarranted deprivation occurs in any part of the world."[1] Subsequently, on April 14, he told the
Permanent Council of the Organization of American States (OAS) that
"our values . . . require us to combat abuses of individual freedom, including those caused by political, social and economic injustice."[2] Over
a year later, in June 1978, the President reaffirmed these principles, declaring before the General Assembly of the OAS that "my government
will not be deterred from our open and enthusiastic policy of promoting human rights—including economic and social rights—in whatever
ways we can."[3]

Though there is much to applaud in Carter's position on human rights,
there are also some glaring inconsistencies in his and the Administration's approach to the problem. All of the U.S. pronouncements in the
first year and a half of the Carter presidency have suggested that instances of human rights violations and repression abroad are the product
of local malfeasance, and that the correct U.S. response is to condemn
such villainy and, where appropriate, to punish the transgressor through

Michael T. Klare and Cynthia Arnson work with the Militarism and Disarmament Project of the Institute for Policy Studies in Washington, D.C. Mr. Klare is
the author of *War Without End: U.S. Planning for the Next Vietnams*. The authors
would like to extend special thanks to Richard Fagen and Ann Craig for their in-
valuable suggestions, encouragement, and careful editing.

1. Transcript of President Carter's speech, *The New York Times*, Mar. 18, 1977.
2. *Ibid.*, Apr. 15, 1977.
3. "Remarks of the President at the Opening of the Eighth General Assembly of
the Organization of American States," Jun. 21, 1978.

cutbacks in military or economic assistance. This rhetorical and at times juridical approach was manifested in the President's statement of February 23, 1977, to the effect that the Helsinki Agreement invested us with "a responsibility and a legal right to express our disapproval of violations of human rights."[4] Carter carried this approach a step further on the following day when he ordered reductions in military aid to Argentina, Uruguay, and Ethiopia as a penalty for human rights violations in those countries.

U.S. INVOLVEMENT IN FOREIGN REPRESSION:
THE HISTORICAL ROOTS OF THE LATIN AMERICAN CASE

The problem with the President's stance is that it implies that the United States is somehow detached or disconnected from the epidemic of repression abroad—whereas the evidence suggests that U.S. firms and government agencies are deeply involved in supplying the technology and techniques of repression to many of the world's most authoritarian regimes. A brief look at the past will be instructive in illuminating the Latin American case.

The United States has supplied the military juntas that have taken over country after country in Latin America with a steady stream of arms and military aid. Between 1973 and 1978, for example, the United States provided Latin American governments $30.0 million worth of grants of arms and equipment under the Military Assistance Program (MAP), $574.1 million worth of credits under the Foreign Military Sales (FMS) program, $42.8 million worth of "surplus" U.S. arms under the Excess Defense Articles (EDA) program, and $49.5 million worth of training under the International Military Education and Training (IMET) program, for a grand total of $696.4 million in direct military aid (see Table 1). In the same period, the United States sold these governments under the FMS cash sales program and the Commercial Sales program $380 million worth of arms over and above the FMS credits, bringing total military deliveries over this six-year period to a staggering $1.1 billion.[5] This is one-and-a-half times the total for the preceding six years. And as we can see from Tables 1 and 2, the great bulk of these deliveries have been going to nations ruled by military juntas.

4. Press Conference text in *The New York Times*, Feb. 24, 1977.
5. Fiscal 1973–77 data are from U.S. Department of Defense, *Foreign Military Sales and Military Assistance Facts* (Washington, D.C., 1977); Fiscal 1978 data are from U.S. Department of Defense, *Security Assistance Program, Congressional Presentation, Fiscal Year 1979* (Washington, D.C., 1978).

TABLE I

U.S. Military Aid to Latin America, Fiscal 1973–78
(Thousands of U.S. dollars)

Country	MAP	FMS Credits	EDA	IMET	Total
Argentina	128	97,901	—	2,245	100,274
Bolivia	9,939	31,000	25,881	3,974	70,794
Brazil	2,397	164,262	—	2,962	169,621
Chile	754	27,400	—	2,667	30,821
Colombia	438	60,600	—	4,632	65,670
Costa Rica	—	5,000	—	—	5,000
Dominican					
Republic	2,210	3,500	287	3,440	9,437
Ecuador	—	35,000	—	1,777	36,777
El Salvador	772	3,364	1,515	2,772	8,423
Guatemala	3,594	6,400	1,866	2,364	14,224
Haiti	—	1,000	—	488	1,488
Honduras	759	10,500	128	3,871	15,258
Jamaica	—	—	—	—	—
Mexico	—	—	—	619	619
Nicaragua	1,910	10,500	3,383	3,088	18,881
Panama	1,562	4,000	657	2,318	8,537
Paraguay	2,876	1,500	4,443	2,076	10,895
Peru	—	75,500	—	5,392	80,892
Uruguay	2,623	12,000	4,621	1,574	20,818
Venezuela	—	24,712	—	3,256	27,968
TOTAL	29,962	574,139	42,781	49,515	696,397

SOURCES: 1973–77 data: Dep't of Defense, Foreign Military Sales and Military Assistance Facts (Dec. 1977); 1978 data: Dep't of Defense, Security Assistance Program Presentation to Congress for Fiscal Year 1979.
NOTE: MAP = Military Assistance Program; FMS = Foreign Military Sales Program; EDA = Excess Defense Articles Program; and IMET = International Military Education and Training Program.

U.S. support for authoritarianism in Latin America is not, moreover, a peripheral or accidental aspect of U.S. foreign policy; on the contrary, it is a logical consequence of a consistent strategy. U.S. complicity in human rights violations abroad extends beyond the simple matter of supplying arms and training to the central issue of the economic and political goals the United States has pursued in the Third World over the past three decades. Far from being an unintended by-product of other more idealistic objectives in Latin America—such as economic

TABLE 2

U.S. Military Sales to Latin America, Fiscal 1973–78
(*Thousands of U.S. dollars*)

Country	FMS Agreements	Commercial Exports	Total
Argentina	81,767	29,221	110,988
Bolivia	5,105	1,686	6,791
Brazil	149,642	63,551	213,193
Chile	150,742	4,362	155,104
Colombia	21,561	7,652	29,213
Costa Rica	345	593	938
Dominican Republic	731	2,030	2,761
Ecuador	57,075	5,090	62,165
El Salvador	2,162	1,238	3,400
Guatemala	14,852	2,552	17,404
Haiti	1,514	1,626	3,140
Honduras	8,395	900	9,295
Jamaica	127	487	614
Mexico	3,979	4,488	8,467
Nicaragua	3,525	3,734	7,259
Panama	5,926	8,762	14,688
Paraguay	496	1,610	2,106
Peru	147,008	13,988	160,996
Uruguay	13,729	1,231	14,960
Venezuela	98,349	30,933	129,282
TOTAL	767,030	185,734	952,764

SOURCES: 1973–77 data: Dep't of Defense, *Foreign Military Sales and Military Assistance Facts* (Dec. 1977); 1978 data: Dep't of Defense, *Security Assistance Program Presentation to Congress for Fiscal Year 1979.*
NOTE: FMS = Foreign Military Sales Program.

development, or the "defense of democracy"—supplying repression has been a necessary correlate of U.S. efforts to contain revolutionary upheavals in the Third World. Latin America, because of its proximity to the United States and its poverty, which has been seen as a natural impetus to revolution, has been of particular concern to U.S. policymakers.

Few events so shook the foundations of U.S. thinking about underdeveloped nations as the Cuban revolution. The victory of Fidel Castro and his followers in the first days of 1959 illustrated that a small guerrilla army, with the support of masses of people in the countryside and cities, could—under certain conditions—defeat conventional forces equipped and trained by the United States. U.S. strategists drew two related conclusions from this fact that shaped U.S.–Latin American relations over the next decade: first, that conditions of poverty and economic underdevelopment contained the seeds of revolution and thus deserved immediate remedial attention; and second, that the threat of "Communist subversion" emanated not only from the Soviet Union but also from indigenous insurrectionary movements.[6] Thus President Kennedy declared in a 1962 speech at West Point:

Subversive insurgency is another type of war, new in its intentions, ancient in its origins—war by guerrillas, subversives, insurgents, assassins; war by ambush instead of by combat, by infiltration instead of aggression; seeking victory by eroding and exhausting the enemy instead of engaging him. . . . It requires in those situations where we must consider it . . . a whole new kind of strategy, a wholly different kind of force, and therefore a new and wholly different kind of training.[7]

The first set of concerns—that poverty bred revolution—gave rise to the Alliance for Progress, an overinflated program for the internal reform of Latin American economies and extensive U.S. support in the name of modernization and capitalist development. Underlying the Alliance's prescriptions for land and tax reforms, export-oriented industrialization, and increased foreign investment was the notion that rapid capitalist development (with eventual significant benefits for the masses) was the best hedge against future Cubas and the surest guarantor of democracy. According to the conventional wisdom, democratic politics would be strengthened by economic development: benefits would trickle down to peasants and *marginales* (answering the worst of their grievances), and industrialization would contribute to the expansion of a middle class (thought to be a bastion of liberal values and democratic ideals).[8] Launching the Alliance for Progress in 1961, President Kennedy stated:

Our hemisphere's mission is not yet completed. For our unfulfilled task is to demonstrate to the entire world that man's unsatisfied aspiration for economic progress and social justice can best be achieved by free men working within

6. See U.S. House of Representatives, Committee on Appropriations, Subcommittee, *Department of Defense Appropriations for 1963, Hearings*, 87th Congress 2d session (Washington, D.C., 1962).

7. Cited in Roger Hilsman, *To Move a Nation* (Garden City, N.Y., 1967), p. 415.

8. See Jerome Levinson and Juan de Onis, *The Alliance That Lost Its Way* (Chicago, 1970).

a framework of democratic institutions. If we can do this in our own hemisphere, and for our own people, we may yet realize the prophecy of the great Mexican patriot, Benito Juárez, that "democracy is the destiny of future humanity."[9]

Without discussing the economic failures of the Alliance, or the flawed assumptions on which it was based,[10] one can note that evolving alongside it was a set of military and security policies for creating and maintaining the environment in which development could take place. Indeed, military strategies—centered on the doctrine of internal security —were an integral part of the Alliance formula. U.S. programs designed to strengthen conventional Latin American military and police forces were aimed specifically at providing the stable environment in which a process of gradual reform could take place. The role of internal security forces in controlling that process, i.e. in preventing modest changes from feeding revolutionary appetites, was seen as crucial. As General Robert W. Porter, Jr., Commander in Chief of the U.S. Southern Command, told a Congressional committee:

No program of social and economic development will flourish in a climate of political turmoil and internal instability. Thus, if we are to foster the dynamic evolution of the forces which encourage social and economic development, we must assist in the establishment of that degree of internal security and political stability necessary to provide the Alliance for Progress with an environment in which to germinate.[11]

The new military programs designed to fulfill the "need" for internal security represented a departure from past U.S. involvement in the hemisphere, and ultimately served to subvert the very democratic processes to be strengthened under the Alliance.

Before the Cuban revolution, the emphasis in U.S. military aid policies to Latin America was on developing conventional forces capable of withstanding an external military threat, particularly a submarine and naval threat in the South Atlantic.[12] In 1947, at the onset of the Cold War, the United States and the Latin American nations signed the Rio

9. Address by John F. Kennedy at a White House reception for members of Congress and for the diplomatic corps of the Latin American republics, Mar. 13, 1961, quoted in Levinson and de Onis, p. 334.
10. On these points see *ibid.*, esp. pp. 307–31.
11. Statement before the U.S. House of Representatives Foreign Affairs Committee during hearings on the Fiscal 1968 Military Assistance Program, Apr. 25, 1967.
12. See Willard F. Barber and C. Neale Ronning, *Internal Security and Military Power* (Columbus, Ohio, 1966), and Edwin Lieuwen, *The United States and the Challenge to Security in Latin America* (Columbus, Ohio, 1966).

Pact, designed essentially to guarantee hemispheric cooperation and security against Soviet attack. Several years later, in 1951, Congress passed the Mutual Security Act, reaffirming common strategic objectives and setting the stage for a military assistance program aimed at modernizing the armed forces of Latin America. Between 1951 and 1960, Latin American countries received nearly half a billion dollars worth of U.S. patrol ships, reconnaissance aircraft, and similar equipment aimed at providing a strong naval defense for the Southern Hemisphere.[13]

Castro's triumph in 1959 illustrated forcefully that military aid programs emphasizing defense against external attack did not necessarily afford protection from internal guerrilla movements. The emphasis in military strategy shifted abruptly under the Kennedy Administration to one of counterinsurgency,[14] which, according to the Pentagon's definition, included "those military, paramilitary, political, economic, psychological, and civic actions taken by a government to defeat subversive insurgency."[15] Insurgency was defined as "a condition resulting from a revolt or insurrection against a constituted government which falls short of civil war. In the current context, subversive insurgency is primarily communist inspired, supported, or exploited."[16] Aid under the MAP began to focus on training, equipping, and indoctrinating Latin armies for their new mission of counterinsurgency.

In practice, counterinsurgency involved the development not only of special counterguerrilla forces—such as the Green Berets—organized for combat in remote and inaccessible terrain, but also of "civic action" programs designed to generate popular support for the established military. New technologies—remote sensing, night vision scopes, personnel detection gear—were developed to locate and track isolated guerrilla groups in rugged areas. In general, however, the emphasis was on developing indigenous military, paramilitary, and police forces capable of suppressing any internal challenge to the prevailing order.

The implementation of counterinsurgency not only came to include the repression of civilian groups, but also led the military to unprecedented levels of penetration into civilian life.[17] Problems of internal

13. Michael T. Klare, *War Without End: American Planning for the Next Vietnams* (New York, 1972), p. 278.

14. According to Edwin Lieuwen in U.S. Senate, Committee on Foreign Relations, *Survey of the Alliance for Progress* (Washington, D.C., 1969).

15. U.S. Department of Defense, Joints Chiefs of Staff, *Dictionary of Military and Associated Terms* (Washington, D.C.).

16. *Ibid.*

17. Alfred Stepan, "The New Professionalism of Internal War and Military Role

security included identifying and remedying potential threats to stability and order; this necessitated a greater concern for the political, social, and economic roots of radicalism. "Counterinsurgency," declared a faculty member of the U.S. Army War College, "is by definition geared to military, political, economic, and civic action. . . . The major problem before us is to learn to orchestrate the magnificent counterinsurgency resources we have into a single symphony."[18] Whereas the previous focus on external warfare had led Latin American military personnel to acquire distinctively military skills as opposed to civilian ones, the military's new mission required that it become more deeply involved in inherently political and economic questions of national development.[19] That this coincided with a U.S. belief in the military as one of the few "modern" institutions capable of carrying out national projects of economic development only strengthened the hand of those seeking to rationalize U.S. military assistance.[20]

The justifications for counterinsurgency programs, then, grew out of two mutually reinforcing propositions: first, that economic development and the integration of Latin American economies into the international capitalist system required a high level of domestic order and stability; and second, that radical movements—whether directed by Moscow or not—weakened the West's position in the global East-West struggle, thus directly threatening the security of the United States. Counterinsurgency was thus not only a strategy for accomplishing the goals of the Alliance, but also an inevitable by-product of prevailing Cold War attitudes.

On the basis of this counterinsurgency doctrine, the United States began in 1962 to provide the necessary training, techniques, and matériel to combat insurgent movements. Because radical groups were seen as intrinsically undemocratic (i.e., having as their goal the establishment of a totalitarian state à la Cuba and the Soviet Union), U.S. policy had

---

Expansion," in Abraham Lowenthal, ed., *Armies and Politics in Latin America* (New York, 1976), pp. 244–60.

18. Quoted in Alfred Stepan, *The Military in Politics: Changing Patterns in Brazil* (Princeton, N.J., 1971), p. 127.

19. Stepan, "The New Professionalism," p. 247.

20. Thus in a 1961 essay on "Armies in the Process of Political Modernization," Lucian Pye of M.I.T. wrote that "In comparison to the efforts that have been expended in developing, say, civil administration and political parties, it still seems that modern armies are somewhat easier to create in transitional societies than most other forms of modern social structures. The most significant fact for our consideration is that the armies created by colonial administration and by the newly emergent societies have consistently been among the most modernized institutions in their society." (*European Journal of Sociology*, vol. 2 (1961), p. 84.)

as its ultimate legitimation the "defense of democracy" through the elimination of guerrilla and other left-wing movements. Once the essential framework of counterinsurgency had been accepted, however, the United States had no choice but to engage in inherently undemocratic practices; moreover, the defense of U.S. interests broadly defined meant increased reliance on the United States' Latin American military allies.

Assumptions that the military could mobilize the forces for development, provide for internal security, and remain apolitical were inherently contradictory, however. Having defined the enemy—"Castroite Communist subversion"[21]—as well as a national security mission encompassing all aspects of civil and political life,[22] the United States set the stage for the expansion of militarism on the South American continent. Where events threatened to get out of hand, the United States intervened directly with troops or indirectly through the Central Intelligence Agency.[23] More systematic, however, was the U.S. effort to provide Latin American militaries with the ability to "go it alone." In the name of combating subversion—for whatever reason, be it development or democracy—the United States equipped, trained, coordinated, expanded, and actually helped create the forces of repression in Latin America.

COUNTERINSURGENCY PROGRAMS AND ARMS TRANSFERS

The coordination of counterinsurgency in the early 1960's took place in the Kennedy Administration within the Special Group for Counterinsurgency, an interagency committee charged with developing strategies and recommending programs for antiguerrilla warfare. Under the direction of General Maxwell Taylor, later U.S. Ambassador to South Vietnam, the group included such high-ranking officials as the Director of the CIA, the Chairman of the Joint Chiefs of Staff, the Deputy Secretaries of State and Defense, the Foreign Aid Adminstrator, and the

21. See Richard Fagen, "Death in Uruguay," *New York Times Book Review*, Jun. 25, 1978, p. 12.
22. For a discussion of the evolution of U.S. policy and the Latin American trends reinforcing those developments, see Jorge Tapia, "The National Security Doctrine and the Rise of Military Fascism in Latin America," unpub., Yale University, 1976; and Stepan, "The New Professionalism," pp. 249–55.
23. On Brazil, see Jan Knippers Black, *United States Penetration in Brazil* (Philadelphia, Pa., 1976); on Chile, see U.S. Senate Select Committee to Study Governmental Operations with Respect to Intelligence Activities, *Covert Action in Chile 1963–1973* (Washington, D.C., 1975); on the Dominican Republic, see John Bartlow Martin, *Overtaken by Events* (Garden City, N.J., 1966).

Director of the U.S. Information Agency. The emerging counterinsurgency formula had several prominent features in addition to those already mentioned: (1) rapid deployment, to provide the capacity for the rapid transport of U.S. troops and equipment to the scene of insurgency; (2) U.S. training of Latin American military officers and enlisted men, to "foster interservice ties" and provide the ideology and techniques for counterinsurgency; (3) police training, to establish the "first line of defense" against urban guerrillas and "maintain metropolitan order"; (4) improved intelligence, involving not only the expansion of CIA activities but also the employment of social scientists in analyzing all aspects of civilian life,[24] to identify latent sources of unrest and provide specific prescriptions for counterrevolution; and (5) intervention, to wipe out radical guerrilla movements, as in the case of the CIA-directed campaign against Che Guevara in Bolivia in 1967.[25]

Throughout the 1960's public funds provided under the Military Assistance Program were the primary vehicle allowing counterinsurgency programs to flourish. By Fiscal 1968, a full 76 percent of this grant aid ($34.7 million out of $45.5 million) was for equipment or training relating to counterinsurgency.[26] As Secretary of Defense Robert McNamara said at the time: "The grant program will provide no tanks, artillery, fighter aircraft, or combat ships. The emphasis is on vehicles and helicopters for internal mobility, communications equipment for better coordination of in-country security efforts, and spare parts for maintenance of existing inventories."[27] Jeeps, trucks, transport planes, river and coastal patrol boats, observation helicopters, and small arms became the new counterinsurgency arsenal.

It was in this context of counterinsurgency doctrine and the Alliance that the old emphasis on conventional military sales and aid to Latin America began to shift. Throughout the 1960's the Defense Department and Congress discouraged Latin American purchases of advanced weapons systems under the Foreign Military Sales program.[28] The Johnson Administration, for example, turned down in 1965 Peru's request to buy

24. See John Saxe-Fernandez, "From Counterinsurgency to Counter-Intelligence," in Julio Cotler and Richard Fagen, eds., *Latin America and the United States: The Changing Political Realities* (Stanford, Calif., 1974), pp. 347–60.

25. Klare, *War Without End*, pp. 38–55.

26. U.S. House of Representatives, Committee on Foreign Affairs, Foreign Assistance Act of 1967, *Hearings*, 90th Congress, 1st session (Washington, D.C., 1967), p. 117.

27. *Ibid.*, p. 118.

28. For a discussion of U.S. arms sales policy toward Latin America, see Michael T. Klare, "Arms and Power," in North American Congress in Latin America (NACLA), *Latin America and Empire Report*, Mar. 1975.

F-5 A jet fighters on the grounds that such a purchase would be "a prime example of wasteful military expenditures for unnecessarily sophisticated equipment at a time when generous U.S. credits were being extended for economic development."[29] This view reflected the liberal consensus in Congress; conservatives joined in by maintaining that such diversions of revenue were ultimately dangerous to national security. Officials in the Pentagon merely continued to stress counterinsurgency capabilities.

With these constraints placed on their access to weapons (including U.S. legislation in 1967 placing a ceiling of $75 million per year on all arms grants and sales to the region), Latin American nations turned to European suppliers for advanced systems;[30] by 1968, a full 87 percent of the major weapons systems purchased by Latin American countries came from outside the United States.[31]

In response to pressure generated by U.S. arms producers, however, the White House and Congress gradually eased the restrictions on military sales to Latin America. In 1973, President Nixon authorized sales of the F-5 A jet fighter to several of the more advanced Latin American nations, and as a result U.S. producers regained some of the ground lost to the Europeans in the late 1960's. The data on patterns and levels of conventional arms sales and transfers can, in any case, be highly misleading. Even when U.S. sales declined, the primary webs of influence and "cooperation in combating subversion" continued to be woven between the United States and Latin America.

Although U.S. assistance rarely exceeded 5 percent of any country's total defense budget, such aid often represented a large share of the funds devoted by those countries to the acquisition of new weaponry and thus allowed U.S. advisers to help shape the structure of Latin American armed forces. As Joseph Novitski noted in *The New York Times* in a 1971 analysis of U.S. arms programs: "Most South American armed forces bore the stamp of United States influence. Military missions aided in training, organizing, and purchasing to the point where the tactical doctrine, weapons, vehicles and often even the uniforms of any South American infantry outfit would have been familiar to a United States veteran of World War II or Korea."[32] As the principal

29. Quoted in Luigi Einaudi et al., *Arms Transfers to Latin America: Towards a Policy of Mutual Respect* (Santa Monica, Calif., 1973), p. 2.
30. *Ibid.*, pp. 7–21.
31. Sol M. Linowitz, Chairman, *A Report of the Commission on U.S.-Latin American Relations*, in Kalman Silvert, *The Americas in a Changing World* (New York, 1975), p. 35.
32. *The New York Times*, May 4, 1971.

supplier of arms and, more important, tactical doctrine to Latin American armies in the 1960's, the United States was able to convert these forces into sophisticated instruments for counterinsurgency. The U.S. role in creating these specialized internal security forces—many of which later played an active part in the institutionalization of military rule—has been perhaps the most significant and durable U.S. contribution to authoritarianism in Latin America.

One of the principal channels used for transmitting U.S. policies and doctrines to Latin American armies has been the military training program. In testimony before the House Appropriations Committee in 1962, for example, Secretary of Defense Robert S. McNamara noted:

Probably the greatest return on our military assistance investment comes from the training of selected officers and key specialists at our military schools and training centers in the United States and overseas. These students are handpicked by their countries to become instructors when they return home. They are the coming leaders, the men who will have the know-how and impart it to their forces. I need not dwell upon the value of having in positions of leadership men who have first-hand knowledge of how Americans do things and how they think. It is beyond price to us to make such friends of such men.[33]

Between the years 1959 and 1969, the United States trained an average of 3,475 Latin American military personnel per year;[34] 22,059 men were trained in the 1964–68 period alone. Moreover, an additional 21,315 have been trained between 1973 and 1978.[35] Latin American officers at the U.S. Army School of the Americas in the Panama Canal Zone and at the Inter-American Defense College in Washington, D.C., were instructed in such areas as "jungle operations," "urban counterinsurgency," "civic action," and "military intelligence interrogation." (See Table 3.) A total of 142 schools operated by the U.S. Army, Navy, and Air Force provided Latin American enlisted men with the same brand of anticommunist ideology and tactical training as their superiors.[36]

33. U.S. House of Representatives, Committee on Appropriations, Subcommittee on Foreign Operations, *Hearings on Appropriations for Fiscal Year 1963*, 87th Congress, 2d Session (Washington, D.C., 1962), p. 359.
34. Geoffrey Kemp, *Some Relationships Between U.S. Military Training in Latin America and Weapons Acquisition Patterns: 1959–1969* (Cambridge, Mass., 1970), p. 4.
35. U.S. Department of Defense, Office of the Assistant Secretary of Defense for International Security Affairs, *Foreign Military Sales and Military Assistance Facts* (Washington, D.C., 1970 and 1977); and U.S. Department of Defense, *Security Assistance Program, Congressional Presentation, Fiscal Year 1979* (Washington, D.C., 1978).
36. Klare, *War Without End*, p. 304.

TABLE 3

Training of Foreign Military Personnel at the U.S. Army School of the Americas, Panama Canal Zone, Fiscal 1970–75

(Selected courses)

Country	Combat Arms Officer	Command & General Staff	Internal Development Civic Action	Counterinsurgency Operations	Urban Counterinsurgency	Milit. Police Officer	Milit. Intelligence Officer	Basic Infantry Officer	Basic Officer Orientation
Argentina		4		11	7	3	7	2	
Bolivia		9	10		10	2	3		
Brazil					2		8		
Chile		7		8	43		1		1,128
Colombia	1	21		11	14	1	8		
Dominican R.	10	24	7	31	31	10	11		8
Ecuador	2			4	14				
El Salvador	14	4	7		9	1	14		
Guatemala	13	11		5	10	3	8		
Honduras	57	23		16	13	6	4	150	
Mexico	2	3		9	3	1	2		
Nicaragua	14	10		16	9	22	12		
Panama	23	3	2	46	9	3	18	20	
Paraguay	4	4			4	1	7	1	1
Peru	2	5			6	1	7		
Uruguay		3		14	19	13	10		
Venezuela	11	42	1		9	14	25		
TOTAL	153	173	27	171	212	81	145	173	1,137

TABLE 3 (*continued*)

Training of Foreign Military Personnel at the U.S. Army School of the Americas, Panama Canal Zone, Fiscal 1970–75 (*Selected courses*)

Country	Urban Counterinsurgency Operations	Jungle Operations	Milit. Explosives & Detonators	Basic Officer Qualification	Basic Officer Preparation	Basic Combat & Counterinsurgency	Internal Security Operations (Cadets)	Milit. Police Noncom. Officer	Milit. Intelligence Interrogator	Milit. Intelligence Noncom. Officer
Argentina	5	13							6	5
Bolivia			4		436			1	4	6
Brazil	7	3							5	5
Chile										8
Colombia		2							2	
Dominican R.	28	2		87				9	6	4
Ecuador		10								
El Salvador	8		2		124	108		1		6
Guatemala			4		71	32				4
Honduras	5	15		134					12	14
Mexico	2									
Nicaragua	4	27	5	148				5	22	9
Panama	16	282	4					6	14	42
Paraguay	2								2	3
Peru	1	50	2	88		278	631	16	7	10
Uruguay	1			29			197	5	7	10
Venezuela		6						4	14	20
TOTAL	79	410	21	486	631	418	828	47	101	146

SOURCE: Reprinted from Michael T. Klare, *Supplying Repression*, Institute for Policy Studies, Washington, D.C., 1977. Data are from documents obtained by the author under the Freedom of Information Act.

As for the role of such training in creating modern, "apolitical" armies, Professor Edwin Lieuwen noted in a 1967 Senate Foreign Relations Committee report that "most of the Latin American military leaders who conducted the nine coups between 1962 and 1966 had been recipients of U.S. training."[37]

Consistent with the emphasis on internal security was President Kennedy's expansion and reorientation in 1962 of the Office of Public Safety (OPS) within the Agency for International Development. On the premise that "orderly social, economic, and political development of emerging nations" could only take place in "an environment of law and order," and that the police constituted the "first line of defense against insurgency,"[38] the United States spent $324 million between 1962 and 1973 to upgrade Third World police capabilities (the OPS program was terminated by Congress in 1974). Of this amount, some $56.6 million was channeled to Latin American police forces.[39] Though these expenditures appear insignificant compared to MAP grants, they were used to modernize critical police operations—intelligence, communications, mobility—and thus contributed significantly to police counterinsurgency capabilities. Thus, with regard to the Public Safety program in the Dominican Republic, an AID report noted that though the $720,000 budgeted for fiscal 1967 represented only 5 percent of the national police budget, "for U.S. objectives it provides the necessary leverage."[40]

Whereas the Military Assistance Program concentrated on the development of a rural counterinsurgency capability within the military, the Public Safety program was aimed at strengthening the ability of the police to overcome urban guerrilla movements. Public Safety funds were used to assist Latin American police forces in three ways. The first involved training top police officials at the International Police Academy (IPA) in Washington, D.C., and at other specialized police schools in the United States. Some 3,800 Latin Americans were trained under this program,[41] including 113 who attended a CIA course on the manufacture of bombs and assassination devices at the U.S. Border Patrol Academy in

37. Lieuwen, *The United States and the Challenge to Security*, p. 121–22.

38. John A. Hannah, Administrator, Agency for International Development, "In Support of Orderly Change," address at the graduation exercises of the International Police Academy, Washington, D.C., Jul. 11, 1969.

39. U.S. Agency for International Development, *USAID Operations Report* (Washington, D.C. 1973).

40. NACLA *Newsletter*, "How U.S. Aid Shapes the Dominican Police," Apr. 1971, p. 20.

41. U.S. Agency for International Development, *USAID Operations Report*.

Los Fresnos, Texas.[42] The second involved assigning U.S. "Public Safety Advisers" to the headquarters of foreign police forces. These advisers, usually ex-CIA, ex-FBI, or military-police officers, provided "in-country" training to rank-and-file policemen and advised the country's top police officials on counterinsurgency tactics and strategy. This program became particularly controversial when, in the wake of the assassination of Public Safety Adviser Dan Mitrione in Uruguay in 1970, critics charged that U.S. personnel had assisted—or at least condoned—the use of torture to obtain information from suspected insurgents.[43] The third involved making direct grants of specialized police equipment to foreign police forces. Such deliveries, typically including riot gear, communications equipment, jeeps, and computers, were designed to upgrade indigenous capacities for urban counterinsurgency operations.

Given the fact that many Latin American police forces were ill-trained and ill-equipped prior to U.S. involvement through the Public Safety program, it is hardly surprising that U.S. aid had a profound impact on police capabilities of target countries. Before 1960, for instance, Brazil had no centralized police force, and the separate police commands in each of 22 states often refused to cooperate with one another in such critical areas as the sharing of intelligence data. Under U.S. tutelage, and with U.S. funding, Brazil established a national police command in Brasilia and created a National Police Academy, a National Telecommunication Center, and the National Institutes of Criminalistics and of Identification. As police operations became more centralized, it followed that the influence of U.S. Public Safety Advisers over Brazilian internal security policies increased accordingly.[44]

In the middle and late 1960's, in the midst of a protracted war in Viet-

---

42. This final program was officially known as the "Technical Investigation Course." According to OPS documents acquired by Senator James Abourezk in October 1973, the course included lectures and demonstrations on such topics as Introduction to Bombs and Explosives, Incendiaries, and Assassination Weapons. Ostensibly this course was designed to aid foreign police forces in protecting VIP's against terrorist attacks, but the training was so technical that it could just as easily be used by the police for terrorist attacks of their own. (Indeed, the Defense Department considered the subject matter so inherently sensitive that it refused to provide instructors for the course.) At least 196 foreign police officers attended this "bomb school" between 1969 and 1973. (Jack Anderson, *The Washington Post*, Oct. 8, 1973.) For statistics on training and expenditures, see U.S. Agency for International Development, *USAID Operations Report*. OPS training programs are described in U.S. Office of Public Safety, *Program Guide: Public Safety Training* (Washington, 1968).

43. See A. J. Langguth, *Hidden Terrors* (New York, 1978).

44. See U.S. Senate, Committee on Foreign Relations, *United States Policies and Programs in Brazil*, Hearings, 92d Congress, 1st Session, 1971.

nam, senior policymakers began to reappraise U.S. military strategy—especially as it related to combating insurgent movements in the Third World. As domestic opposition to Vietnam intervention grew, U.S. strategists sought a formula that would permit a reduction in *direct* U.S. involvement in future counterinsurgency operations, but that would nevertheless provide Washington with reliable instruments for combating revolutionary guerrilla movements.

The search for new strategies led to the adoption in 1969 of the Nixon Doctrine. In essence, the new policy called for a greater self-defense effort on the part of U.S. allies, backed up by increased aid and technical support from the United States. As introduced by the President himself, the Doctrine's operative clause held that ". . . in cases of [non-nuclear] aggression, we shall furnish military and economic assistance when requested, but we shall look to the nation directly threatened to assume the primary responsibility of providing the manpower for its defense."[45]

The adoption of the Nixon Doctrine also coincided with a reappraisal of counterinsurgency doctrine. A new consensus emerged that the United States was too late in Vietnam, that once a national liberation movement gained the support of the masses it could not be stopped short of massive intervention, which in itself could not even assure victory. As a natural corollary, the new wisdom held that the surest way to prevent a major intervention later was to wipe out insurgency at its very earliest appearance, before it developed a wide popular base. In 1965, former Chairman of the Joint Chiefs of Staff General Maxwell Taylor explained to the graduating class at the International Police Academy: "The outstanding lesson of the Indochina conflict is that we should never let a Vietnam-type situation arise again. We were too late in recognizing the extent of the subversive threat. We appreciate now that every young, emerging country must be constantly on the alert, watching for those symptoms which, if allowed to develop unrestrained, may eventually grow into a disastrous situation such as that in South Vietnam."[46]

This new approach to counterinsurgency also placed much greater emphasis on urban warfare than had earlier ones, which had generally stressed rural operations. This shift reflected a belief that rural guerrilla

45. Richard M. Nixon, *U.S. Foreign Policy in the 1970's, Report to the Congress* (Washington, D.C., 1970), pp. 55–56.
46. Maxwell D. Taylor, address at graduation exercises, International Police Academy, Washington, D.C., Dec. 17, 1965.

movements often start out as urban political movements, and that therefore prompt action in stamping out dissident groups could make elaborate military operations unnecessary. At the same time, the emphasis on
urban warfare reflected a new strategic reality, namely that with the
growing proficiency of rural counterinsurgency forces, guerrilla leaders
were increasingly turning the city into a revolutionary battlefield. This
was particularly true in Latin America, where the guerrilla tactics employed by Che Guevara in Bolivia gave way to the unconventional ex-
ploits of Carlos Marighela in Brazil and of the Tupamaros in Uruguay
following Che's death in 1967.

U.S. concern over the growing threat represented by urban guerrilla
movements was compounded by a sense that Latin American cities had
become more vulnerable to revolutionary action. By the late 1960's
U.S. policymakers and academics had come to see that economic development without redistribution of the benefits of growth was a potentially destabilizing influence in Third World countries. Rapid industrialization and urbanization, along with "green revolutions" and
other changes in the countryside that displaced peasants in favor of
capitalized agriculture, sent shock waves through traditional societies.
What modernization required, according to the emerging view, was not
only economic development but also political structures capable of ab-
sorbing and channeling the newly created strains.[47]

Although early Alliance for Progress thinking held that economic
development would strengthen democratic institutions, theoreticians in
the middle and late 1960's began to question the ability of liberal democracies to keep pace with the disorder of growth. New catchwords
("political order," "efficiency," and "control") penetrated the dialogue,[48] and stability was sought not, as in the early 1960's, as the basis
for creating a climate in which development could take place, but now
as an end in itself. Controlling mobilized masses while preserving the
status quo led inevitably to an acceptance of—and indeed a preference
for—authoritarian solutions to the turbulence of change.

Nelson Rockefeller's famous 1969 report to President Nixon on *The
Quality of Life in the Americas* gave eloquent testimony to such concerns. Although the governor did not persuade Nixon to adopt many
of his recommendations, his observations reflected, in somewhat more

---

47. See Samuel P. Huntington, *Political Order in Changing Societies* (New
Haven, Conn., 1968).
48. See Richard Fagen, "Studying Latin American Politics: Some Implications of
A *Dependencia* Approach," *Latin American Research Review*, 12, no. 2 (1977).

rhetorical form, the prevailing views of those charged with "combating subversion" in Latin America. Warning that "the seeds of nihilism and anarchy are spreading throughout the hemisphere"[49] he noted that "With urbanization in the Western Hemisphere have come crowded living conditions and a loss of living space. The urban man tends to become both depersonalized and fragmented in his human relationships. Unemployment is high, especially among the young. . . . These sprawling urban areas of the hemisphere spawn restlessness and anger which are readily exploited by the varying forces that thrive on trouble."[50] Under these circumstances, according to widespread fears, any rupture in the prevailing equilibrium could result in a massive popular uprising, leading to basic socioeconomic changes, the loss of U.S. hegemony, and the establishment of regimes inimical to U.S. economic and political interests. U.S. doctrine thus came to emphasize to an even greater extent than before the development of internal security forces strong enough to defend the urban-centered society against domestic threats.

Clearly, however, maintenance of the status quo in urban areas required a different kind of strategy from the one developed for combating isolated guerrillas in the countryside. Whereas the original counterinsurgency doctrine called for the development of elite, highly mobile counterguerrilla forces capable of outfighting insurgent groups in remote areas, the new counterinsurgents had to contain entire communities on the very doorstep of the metropolis. Given the likelihood that punitive actions by regular military troops would involve excessive force and could, in such densely populated areas, trigger uncontrollable public disorders, U.S. strategists began to recognize the risks involved in overreliance on conventional military forces. As an alternative to the earlier formula, U.S. counterinsurgency doctrine thus increasingly called for the stepped-up development of highly trained police and paramilitary forces that with the aid of a deeply entrenched intelligence apparatus, could be dispersed throughout the population to identify and neutralize dissidents without creating major disturbances.[51]

49. Nelson A. Rockefeller, *Quality of Life in the Americas: Report of a U.S. Presidential Mission for the Western Hemisphere* (reprinted by the Agency for International Development 1969), p. 9.

50. *Ibid.*, p. 14.

51. In testimony before the Senate Subcommittee on American Republics Affairs, for instance, Professor David Burks of Indiana University testified in 1969: "I think we have to face a reality. The reality is that when insurgents appear, the governments will call upon the army to eliminate the insurgents. And, in most cases that I have examined, this was not too difficult to do. But . . . there can come a point

This doctrine held that the surest way of protecting an incumbent regime was to exterminate the nuclei of nascent opposition at the earliest possible moment. The best way to accomplish this, in the U.S. view, was to develop a strong police force with undercover agents in every classroom, factory, and neighborhood. As Under Secretary of State U. Alexis Johnson explained in 1971: "Effective policing is like 'preventive medicine.' The police can deal with threats to internal order in their formative states. Should they not be prepared to do this, 'major surgery' would be needed to redress these threats. This action is painful and expensive and disruptive in itself."[52]

And whereas Rockefeller had urged that "we should equate police with security, not political action and repression,"[53] the implementation of the new counterinsurgency doctrine of "preventive medicine" inevitably spawned ever more repressive practices. "Neutralizing" the threat in an "incipient subversive situation" involved such tactics as the prolonged incarceration or outright assassination of key political activists, and interrogation techniques sanctioning torture of the most brutal sort. Moreover, effective "prevention" relied on the creation of a climate of fear, in which citizens were discouraged from associating themselves with political activities and organizations that were, in some sense, against the status quo. Arbitrary arrest, routine torture, assassination, and "disappearance," carried out by established police and such paramilitary groups as Brazil's notorious Death Squads, became the new instruments of prevention, precluding—it was thought—the need for more elaborate and costly actions later.

"Preventive medicine," by extension, led not only to an expansion of what was defined as subversive, but also to the growth of intelligence and police networks capable of identifying—and destroying—threats to "national security." In Latin America, this meant a decisive increase in

---

when the army cannot handle this kind of situation simply because the military establishment tends to use too much force, tends to use the wrong techniques and tends, therefore, to polarize the population and gradually force the majority of those who are politically active to support the revolutionary or insurgent force. . . . Whereas a civil police force . . . is with the people all the time carrying on the normal functions of control of or apprehension of ordinary or common criminals and can, therefore, move very quickly whenever an insurgent problem develops." U.S. Congress, Senate Foreign Relations Committee, Subcommittee on American Republics Affairs, *Survey of the Alliance for Progress*, Compilation of Studies and Hearings, 91st Congress, 1st Session, 1969, p. 414.

52. U. Alexis Johnson, "The Role of Police Forces in a Changing World," *Department of State Bulletin*, Sep. 13, 1971, p. 282.

53. Rockefeller, *Quality of Life*, p. 51.

repression, as in Brazil in the late 1960's, where the subversive label was extended to all critics of the military government, including elected officials, clergymen, trade unionists, university professors and students, journalists, and many ordinary citizens.[54]

This shift to a reliance on police and intelligence services naturally affected a much larger proportion of the population than did conventional counterguerrilla operations, and when geared to preemptive strikes against individuals or groups whose dissidence may have been marginal or only potential inevitably resulted in widespread violations of human and political rights. What has followed, then, has been the almost universal subversion of civil society and the institutionalization of authoritarian rule. Thus, U.S. complicity in supporting repression and human rights violations precedes the delivery of any repression hardware, and must be traced back to changing perceptions of the threats to security and the implementation of strategic prescriptions for their solution.

From the U.S. end, "preventive medicine" rationalized the CIA's covert intervention to ensure international security as defined by the United States. Rather than allow an elected Marxist government in the hemisphere, the CIA spent millions of dollars in Chile first to forestall the election of Salvador Allende, and then, after he assumed the presidency, to topple his government. This is only the tip of an iceberg. In fact, U.S. covert action and the proliferation of U.S.-trained and -equipped intelligence agencies throughout the Third World are responsible for many of the most shocking abuses of human rights now so loudly condemned by the Carter Administration.

U.S. RESPONSIBILITIES: THE CONTINUING PROBLEM

It would be overly mechanical to claim that the United States is wholly responsible for the wave of repression now sweeping Latin America. To do so would be to underestimate historical conditions, class structures, and the traditions and tendencies of Latin societies. To partially disassociate the United States from causality, however, is not to lessen U.S. responsibility for what it intended and undertook in the hemisphere. U.S. doctrine throughout the 1960's and early 1970's saw Latin America not only as a staging ground in an epic and global East-West

---

54. See U.S. House of Representatives, Committee on International Relations, *Torture and Repression in Brazil*, Hearing, 93d Congress, 2d Session, 1974.

conflict, but also as a place where U.S. economic interests dictated that radicalism be contained, i.e. eliminated. The policy implications were direct: aid programs were designed not only to imbue Latin American soldiers and police with the mission of anticommunism and national security, but also to provide them with the necessary infrastructure, techniques, and equipment to carry out that mission. The question of a U.S. role in repression in Latin America is thus not only a matter of degree but also a matter of conscious design and ongoing policies.

Seen in this light, the Carter Administration's human rights campaign is both ironic and ahistorical. But it is not without its logic. Essentially, it has three sources. First, the Administration's moral exhortations should be understood more as a campaign to reestablish public support for U.S. foreign policy in the wake of Vietnam and to regain a measure of world leadership than as an effort to reorient the fundamental principles of U.S. conduct abroad. Although the moral tone may reflect true revulsion, especially in Latin America, for the brutality of certain regimes, the implementation of the human rights policy is more notable for its inconsistencies and continuation of past patterns than for its departure from recent practices.

Second, underlying U.S. human rights rhetoric is a continuing emphasis on political stability. To the extent that massive violations of human rights threaten the domestic and international legitimacy of a regime, cosmetic improvements in human rights practices may reduce widespread public opposition, thus enhancing political stability. In Latin America and elsewhere, instability has long been viewed as inimical to U.S. economic and political interests. Whereas past threats to stability were seen as coming from the Left, today's are in part the result of the excesses of the Right. Human rights pressures are thus a mechanism for reestablishing a political equilibrium that serves long-run U.S. policy goals.

Third, a significant proportion of the human rights critique does originate in the legislative branch, a situation seen as threatening by the White House and characterized as excessive public and Congressional intervention in foreign policy. The Harkin and Fraser amendments to the Foreign Assistance Act,[55] passed several years before Carter took

55. See *Legislation on Foreign Relations Through 1977*, U.S. House of Representatives Committee on International Relations, and U.S. Senate Committee on Foreign Relations, Foreign Assistance Act of 1961, as amended, Section 502(b) (the Fraser amendment) and Section 116 (the Harkin amendment) (Washington, D.C., 1977).

office, require that human rights be a key criterion in the disbursement of foreign aid; and arms embargoes to Chile, Argentina, and Uruguay have been decried in the Pentagon as depriving it of necessary "leverage." In fact, all of these human rights initiatives have been opposed by the Ford and Carter Administrations as infringements on executive "flexibility" in the conduct of foreign policy.

Thus although President Carter has been forced by public and Congressional pressure, and the inescapable logic of his own rhetoric, to reduce or ban aid to some of the more pronounced violators of human rights, there is still little evidence that the Administration questions the fundamental assumptions upon which U.S. aid policy is built. In fact, Presidential Directive No. 18, the basic Carter Administration policy paper on U.S. national security, actually reaffirms the Nixon Doctrine of relying on "friendly" Third World powers, regardless of their human rights record, to maintain regional stability in crticial areas. Hence, when Carter announced aid cutbacks to Argentina, Uruguay, and Ethiopia, he also indicated that aid to South Korea, the Philippines, and other strategically located countries would not be cut, despite their equally unacceptable records on human rights.

Ultimately there remains the irony that Latin America has been the target of a disproportionately large share of Congressional and executive human rights sanctions precisely because U.S. security interests in the hemisphere are now seen as less critical. Indeed, the 1974 report of the "Linowitz Commission" on U.S.–Latin American relations concluded that "there are no hemispheric or internal security threats to warrant the continuation of military assistance programs,"[56] and recommended that the "U.S. should not associate itself, through military programs, with the security forces whose repressive activities are inconsistent with the U.S. commitment to human rights."[57] In retrospect, the very lack of threats to internal security in Latin America may be seen as the ultimate triumph of U.S. policy.

Whatever the motives, rhetoric, and reality of the human rights policy, however, the fact remains that both directly and indirectly the United States continues to provide many of the materials and much of the climate reinforcing repression in Latin America. Supplying repression takes a different form today than it did in the 1960's and the first half of the 1970's, but it is no less a feature of U.S. activities in the

56. Linowitz, *Report . . . on U.S.-Latin American Relations*, p. 33.
57. *Ibid.*, p. 35.

hemisphere. We may identify five basic trends that, taken together, suggest the new modalities of U.S.–Latin American linkages in this area.

The Arms Pipeline and the Commercialization of Transfers

Although public opposition and fiscal constraints have caused some of the publicly financed military aid programs to be discontinued, there is little evidence that U.S. policymakers intend for the pipeline of repressive technology and training to fall into disuse. Much of the responsibility for supplying repressive equipment to foreign governments has been assumed in recent years by private U.S. corporations, which conduct a brisk trade in police and security equipment through the Foreign Military Sales and Commercial Sales programs. The financial burden of such sales has thus been shifted to the recipients themselves.

Ostensibly, most of the weaponry provided under the FMS and Commercial Sales programs is intended to help countries defend themselves against external attack. An examination of U.S. export data reveals, however, that a substantial portion is intended for internal use, to deter and suppress popular dissent. Recent deliveries to Latin America, for example, include such internal security equipment as *Commando* armored cars, counterinsurgency planes, and substantial quantities of riot-control devices. One of the most notable cases is Nicaragua, where virtually all equipment in the National Guard's arsenal is of U.S. origin.[58]

Other statistics suggest the scope of commercial sales: between 1973 and 1976, for example, U.S. private firms sold Latin American police forces some 24,402 pistols and revolvers, 21,715 tear gas grenades, 3,002 gas guns, and 3,027 canisters of MACE. In addition, unknown quantities of computers, surveillance and eavesdropping devices, truncheons, and electric shock batons were supplied under the Commercial Sales program and through Commerce Department channels (see Table 4). Customers for these items have included the DINA of Chile, the military police of Brazil, and the Palace Guard of Haiti.[59] Although future reforms in the Arms Export Control Act (the basic legislation governing

58. See also testimony of Rep. Thomas Downey, U.S. House of Representatives Committee on International Relations, Subcommittee on International Security and Scientific Affairs, Hearings, Mar. 8, 1978.

59. From licenses issued by the U.S. Office of Munitions Control for the export of Munitions List items to foreign police agencies (copies acquired by Michael Klare under the Freedom of Information Act); see also Cynthia J. Arnson, "The Exporting of Torture by America," *Los Angeles Times*, Apr. 26, 1978.

U.S. military exports) may succeed in placing tighter controls on the export of this equipment to human rights violators, one might expect that private companies will be seeking to maintain and expand the market for such weapons.

TABLE 4
U.S. Arms Sales to Latin American Police Forces, 1973–1976

Country	Revolvers & pistols	Sub-machine guns & rifles	Ammo. (K=1000 rounds)	Tear gas grenades	Gas guns	MACE	V-150 armored cars
Argentina	186	3	1 K				
Bermuda		6	16 K	78			
Bolivia	17			48		12	
Brazil	20	30	11 K		658	1,326	
Chile	22		500 K				
Colombia	333	100		3,500	235		
Costa Rica			6 K			24	
Dominican R.	200		50 K				
Ecuador	10,000			6,500	2,000	950	
Guatemala	1,120						
Haiti							6
Honduras	469						
Jamaica				446			5
Mexico	1,850		20 K	24		300	
Neth. Antilles			58 K	635	1	35	
Nicaragua	1,713		40 K	200	12		
Panama				4,500	10		
Paraguay	731						
Peru	1			2,760			
Trinidad				524	64		
Uruguay	1,134		2 K				
Venezuela	6,606	7	10 K	2,500	22	380	
TOTAL	24,402	146	730 K	21,715	3,002	3,027	11

SOURCE: Reprinted from Michael T. Klare, *Supplying Repression*, Institute for Policy Studies, Washington, D.C., 1977. Data are from documents obtained by the author under the Freedom of Information Act.
NOTE: Includes direct sales and sales via export firms by Smith & Wesson (handguns, MACE, tear gas), Colt Industries (handguns, M-16 rifles), Cadillac-Gage (V-150 armored cars), and Federal Laboratories (chemical weapons); includes sales via export firms only by High Standard (rifles, shotguns), Remington Arms (rifles), Winchester International (rifles), and Federal Cartridge (ammunition). The export firms in question are Polak, Winters & Co., Fargo International, and Jonas Aircraft & Arms Co. This information comes from export licenses issued by the U.S. Office of Munitions Control.

New Instrumentalities of U.S. Government Support

Rather than let the publicly financed pipeline of repressive technology fall into disuse, U.S. policymakers have developed new channels of supply in unlikely places. The International Narcotics Control program conducted through the State Department, for example, closely resembles the now-outlawed Office of Public Safety in that it aids local police forces, ostensibly for the purpose of stemming drug traffic. Like OPS, the INC provides funds for police training and grants for the purchase of small arms and equipment, and it places U.S. advisers in key posts abroad.[60] Between fiscal 1973 and fiscal 1978, the INC granted $85.3 million to Latin American police agencies.[61] Although these funds were intended for professional drug units exclusively, a 1976 General Accounting Office report to Congress revealed that support often went to multipurpose police units that engaged in political as well as narcotics raids.[62] In launching an INC-funded program in Argentina, for instance, Minister of Social Welfare José Lopez Rega announced that "guerrillas are the main users of drugs. Therefore, the antidrug campaign will automatically be an antiguerrilla campaign as well."[63]

Movement Toward Latin American "Self-Sufficiency"— With a Little Help[64]

Cutbacks in military assistance on the basis of human rights performance have encouraged the drive for self-sufficiency in arms manufacturing in Latin America. Such a capability is sought not only for reasons of technological-industrial development, but also for reasons of nationalism. Said a Brazilian Marine commander, "a nation is independent when it manufactures its own arms."[65]

---

60. Under Section 481 of the Foreign Assistance Act (as amended in 1971), "Notwithstanding any other provision of law, the President is authorized to furnish assistance to any country or international organization, on such terms and conditions as he may determine, for the control of the production of, processing of, smuggling of, and traffic in, narcotic and psychotropic drugs."

61. U.S. Department of State, International Narcotics Control, *Congressional Presentation Fiscal Year 1978* (Washington, D.C., 1977).

62. Comptroller of the United States, *Stopping U.S. Assistance to Foreign Police and Prisons*, Report to the Congress (Washington, D.C., 1976), pp. 22–25.

63. Quoted in Carlos Wilson, "The American Connection," *Seven Days*, Apr. 19, 1976, p. 16.

64. This section, on the development of indigenous repressive capabilities in Latin America, is based on a study prepared for the authors by Ann Laurent and Horacio D. Lofredo of the Argentine Commission on Human Rights, Washington, D.C.

65. Quoted in Center for International Policy, *Human Rights and the U.S. For-*

Two countries, Argentina and Brazil, have made particularly significant progress in their efforts to develop an indigenous industrial capacity
for arms manufacture. Both countries fulfill their military and police
requirements for small arms and ammunition with domestically produced hardware, and both produce such ancillary equipment as grenades, machine guns, light artillery, and tear gas canisters.[66] Argentina
and Brazil have also each developed state-owned aircraft industries,
which produce light trainer and attack planes and counterinsurgency
aircraft for domestic use and for export.[67] Embraer, Brazil's nationalized
aircraft firm, has recently sold transport and reconnaissance planes to
Chile and Uruguay; Inbel (Industria Belico do Brasil), the state-owned
corporation coordinating all munitions production in Brazil, has exported indigenously designed armored vehicles to Libya and Qatar.[68]
In addition, both Brazil and Argentina produce under co-production
licensing arrangements with American, British, German, and Italian
companies a wide range of aircraft and components (including helicopters), ships, and missiles.[69]

Although the more advanced Latin American countries will gradually
be able to reduce their dependence on the United States for repressive
technology, it is important to note that this is not a linear process. A
careful examination of Argentina's and Brazil's domestic arms program
reveals, for instance, that in a majority of cases critical components and
know-how are supplied from abroad. Thus, Brazil's "Xavante" counterinsurgency plane is based on Italian technology and is powered by a
British engine, and Argentina's indigenously designed counterinsurgency plane, the "Pucara," is powered by a French engine and uses
American avionics equipment.[70] The same holds true for Embraer's
popular "Bandeirante" plane, which uses Pratt and Whitney engines
and U.S. radar.[71] Even the small arms produced by Argentina and Brazil
are based on foreign designs. Though these countries will gradually
become more independent in producing simpler arms, they will remain
dependent on foreign sources of technology and components as long as

eign Assistance Program, Fiscal Year 1978, Part I: Latin America (Washington,
D.C., 1977), p. 29.
66. See Denis H. R. Archer, ed., Jane's Infantry Weapons 1977 (New York, 1976).
67. See John W. R. Taylor, ed., Jane's All the World's Aircraft 1976–77 (New
York, 1976).
68. The Washington Post, Dec. 18 and 19, 1977.
69. Stockholm International Peace Research Institute, SIPRI Yearbook, 1978
(London, 1978).
70. Taylor, Jane's . . . Aircraft, pp. 3–4, 13–14.
71. Cynthia Arnson and Michael Klare, "Law or No Law, The Arms Flow," The
Nation, Apr. 29, 1978.

they lack the broad-based research and development establishments maintained by the advanced countries.

Although most Latin American efforts at arms independence have been confined to industrial enterprises, they have included such other undertakings as the establishment of specialized schools and transnational data-sharing operations. Chile, Argentina, Uruguay, and Brazil have developed sophisticated computer systems for storing data on political activists—using equipment supplied by U.S. firms but employing indigenous "software" (i.e., programming and processing techniques).[72]

The New Face of Inter-American Cooperation

Transnational cooperation between security agencies in locating and abducting political dissidents has increased in the mid-1970's as country after country in Latin America has fallen under military rule. According to exiles from Latin America now in the United States, computer systems are connected in such a way as to enable intelligence agencies in one country to "pull" information stored in the data-bank of another. One such operation, code-named *Plan Mercurio*, involved the arrest and execution of Uruguayan activists who had fled to Argentina following the installation of a military-dominated government in Uruguay.[73] Likewise, a memo from the head of the Chilean secret police Manuel Contreras to General Pinochet, which was obtained by Chilean exiles living in Mexico, requested funds "for our supporters in the Peruvian Navy."[74] These intelligence activities are facilitated by U.S. firms; an IBM computer, for example, sold to the Technical University of Santiago, Chile, is linked to a computer network that includes the company serving Chile's secret police and other government agencies.[75]

In addition, some Latin countries are providing training to other nations in the hemisphere. The same "leaked" memo to Pinochet requested "funds for the officials of the Directorate who attend courses in preparation for antiguerrilla groups in the city of Manaus, Brazil." The National Police Academy in Brazil, set up with U.S. grants, has long been training officers from all over the continent.[76]

72. See Laurie Nadel and Hesh Weiner, "Would You Sell a Computer to Hitler?" *Computer Decisions*, Feb. 1977, pp. 22–25.

73. See Amnesty International, *The Amnesty International Report, 1975–76* (London, 1976), pp. 87–88.

74. See Marlise Simons, "Chile Allegedly Asked Funds to Neutralize Foes," *Washington Post*, Feb. 4, 1977.

75. Nadel and Weiner, "Would You Sell a Computer," p. 23.

76. Nancy Stein, "Command and Control: U.S. Police Operations in Latin America," NACLA's *Latin America and Empire Report*, Jan. 1972.

Over the long run, then, it appears that the world is heading toward increasing interdependence in the repression trade. The United States, along with other industrial powers, will continue to supply a large portion of the arms and equipment used by Latin American and other Third World police and security agencies. However, the more advanced Third World countries will produce increasing shares of their basic arms requirements, while continuing to rely on advanced countries for sophisticated weapons and production technology. These "middle level" producers will also begin to export some unsophisticated arms and equipment to other less-developed neighbors.[77]

Larger Interests and the Expendability of Human Rights

U.S. support for repression in Latin America is bound to persist as long as human rights take second, third, or fourth place behind other foreign and economic policy objectives. American efforts to limit nuclear proliferation, for example, necessitate Brazilian cooperation; thus as of mid-1978, State Department officials were busy renegotiating the military cooperation treaty abrogated by Brazil the preceding year. As a gesture of good will, moreover, and in disregard of any human rights implications, U.S. officials approved the sale of a very sophisticated computer to the Brazilian police for the purpose of establishing a national identification system.[78] Such transactions, including sales of major weapons systems, are likely to increase as the U.S. recognizes the need to treat Latin nations as "equal partners" in new arenas of international security.[79]

77. At the same time, there is likely to be a growing reverse flow of repression as countersubversive techniques developed for the Third World find application in advanced countries. In the early 1960s, for example, the CIA trained Cuban exiles for the thwarted Bay of Pigs invasion to topple Castro's government. Imbued with a powerful anticommunist ideology, these exiles have become a semiautonomous terrorist group operating throughout the world. Acting as agents of Chile's secret police, they were charged, along with high-ranking Chilean officials, with carrying out the assassination in Washington, D.C. of former Chilean ambassador Orlando Letelier and an American citizen, Ronni Moffitt. Additionally, we have witnessed the incursion of foreign intelligence agencies into American institutions—the Korean CIA operates in Congress and SAVAK, the Iranian secret police, conducted its activities on American soil, against Iranian students. These developments should hardly come as a surprise to U.S. officials who have tolerated, encouraged, and helped set up ruthless intelligence agencies throughout the world.

78. Cynthia Arnson and Michael Klare, "Human Rights: Here Is the Noble Theory . . . But Is This the Practice, at Least in Brazil?," *Los Angeles Times*, Jul. 2, 1978.

79. See David Ronfeldt, "The Future of U.S. Security Assistance in the Latin American Context," in Kalman Silvert, ed., *The Americas in a Changing World*;

Moreover, just as during the Alliance for Progress the United States overlooked the contradictory goals of military aid and democratic development, the United States in the 1970's continues to pretend that human rights and economic prescriptions for the Third World are complementary.[80] Having financed industrialization by heavy borrowing from advanced capitalist countries, Third World nations are now faced with enormous debts and debt service payments. Meeting these obligations requires the extension of still more credit and the implementation of austerity programs. New loans from U.S. banks or from such multilateral lending institutions as the International Monetary Fund are often contingent on the recipient's acceptance of economic "stabilization" measures designed to "put the economy back in order." Austerity measures developed by the IMF for reducing inflation call for, among other things, the reduction of government social expenditures, the freezing of wages, and the lifting of price controls—all of which have a severe and negative impact on workers and the poor.[81] Containing popular protest over such belt-tightening measures greatly increases the need for and likelihood of repression. In Peru, for example,[82] an IMF stabilization program touched off riots and strikes in 1978. The military government responded by declaring martial law, postponing scheduled elections, and suspending the constitutional guarantees of free speech.[83] The advancement of human rights is thus in part undermined by the very economic policies pursued by the United States or U.S.-dominated institutions.

Supplying repression is thus likely to continue as both a deliberate feature and an unintended by-product of U.S. policy toward Latin America. Dissociating the United States from human rights violations will require much more than the token suspension of aid or rhetorical criticism at a diplomatic level. True advancement of human rights would involve not only restraining those corporations and banks that profit from repression, but also reevaluating strategic objectives and accompanying notions of a just economic world order. But because

---

and David Ronfeldt and Caesar Sereseres, *U.S. Arms Transfers, Diplomacy, and Security in Latin America and Beyond* (Santa Monica, Calif., 1977).

80. Patricia Weiss Fagen, "The Links Between Human Rights and Basic Needs," *Background*, Center for International Policy, Washington, D.C., Spring 1978.

81. Howard Wachtel, *The New Gnomes: Multinational Banks in the Third World* (Washington, D.C., 1977).

82. See Barbara Stallings's essay in this volume.

83. Judith Miller, "Peru Crisis: A Dilemma," *The New York Times*, May 24, 1978.

U.S. moral overtures in Latin America have never been accompanied by a sacrifice of some greater political or economic interest, the United States will continue to be allied with some of the hemisphere's most brutal dictators.[84]

Ultimately, however, governments that rule by terror and violence do not last. Repression has the effect of alienating all but the most privileged classes, creating broad-based opposition to the incumbent regime, as recent events in Greece, Spain, Portugal, and Iran have demonstrated. Herein lies the importance of the work of U.S. activists, who, by challenging the overt manifestations of U.S. complicity in repression, and by questioning the underlying assumptions on which they are built, lend support to popular struggles against authoritarianism in Latin America.

84. See Noam Chomsky and Edward Herman, "U.S. vs. Human Rights in the Third World," *Monthly Review*, vol. 29, Jul.–Aug. 1977, pp. 22–45.

Part Two
Cases in Transnational Relations Between Center and Periphery

The "Stabilization Programs" of the International Monetary Fund and Their Internal Impacts

ROBERTO FRENKEL AND GUILLERMO O'DONNELL

INTRODUCTION

This study is the product of our broad interest in the interactions between politics and economics during the periods that precede and follow the establishment of what we have called the "bureaucratic-authoritarian" states (from here on, BA) in contemporary Latin America. In this work we address ourselves to one of the topics within that particular set of problems: the standby agreements established with the International Monetary Fund shortly after the coups d'etat that abruptly terminated processes experienced by numerous sectors (including, very prominently, the internal ruling classes and their foreign supporters) as deep political and economic crises. Argentina, Chile, and Uruguay are particularly appropriate examples of this phenomenon.

Therefore it is necessary to start by summarizing what we understand to be the purpose of the orientation and intervention of the IMF. We will then proceed to show how their intervention, regardless of the prevailing political arrangements, has an effect that hardly accords with their orientation. These effects are also very different from the effects that similar policies tend to produce in more homogeneous productive structures. This will allow us to see how state policies designed to implement agreements with the IMF generate effects that are highly slanted toward the benefit of a small group of economic participants— basically toward the sectors involved in the production of primary products and in finance capital.

Roberto Frenkel and Guillermo O'Donnell are, respectively, an economist and a political scientist. Both are associated with the Center for Studies of State and Society (CEDES) in Buenos Aires, Argentina.
1. See especially Guillermo O'Donnell, "Reflexiones sobre las tendencias generales de cambio en el estado burocratico-autoritario," Document CEDES/G.E. CLACSO no. 1, Buenos Aires, 1976.
2. This overview is supplemented by some notes on the origin of these orientations, included in the Appendix.

At that point we will discuss some of the specific results of the shaking of the productive structure and the sociopolitical system of domination that the implantation of the BA state seeks to "solve," as well as the results of the subsequent efforts to reestablish a particular order in society. The policies agreed upon with the IMF converge with these processes. These policies are the new state's main instrument for undertaking one of the great tasks arising out of its preceding crisis: the achievement of a no less peculiar "normalization" of the economy. It is in the context of this dynamic overlapping of politics and economics that we will take up again some of the questions that will emerge in the next two sections; they are related to the reasons behind the adoption and continuation of certain policies, as well as to the influence that the agreements with the IMF might have on these policies.

Unfortunately our answers, for a number of reasons, are bound to be of a tentative nature. Although they are based on our research on various aspects of the general set of problems outlined above, this study is focused on one country only, Argentina. In addition to the difficulties inherent in any effort to generalize from a single-case study, an adequate understanding of a single-case requires cross-time longitudinal comparisons of the various "normalization" attempts undertaken in Latin America during the last two decades; such research is just now beginning.[3] However, there is a wide area of ignorance on our part, largely because of factors out of our control: we can only contribute to this subject on the basis of the information available in the "recipient country," which receives the premises, orientations, and attentions of the IMF (and in general of public and private transnational finance capital) in a manner already determined by the centers of world capitalism. We are surprised at how little information is available (at least in Argentina) on the IMF and other public and private transnational financial institutions, specifically on the IMF's internal power system, the main criteria and processes used in decision making, and the ways the IMF relates to other sectors of finance capital and to the governments of the member countries. What we need above all are studies that approach the IMF as an important participant in the world's political economy, inserted in the cluster of social relations, thus allowing us to understand the direction and main repercussions of its premises, actions, and omissions. The

3. A joint project of CIEPLAN (Chile), CEBRAP (Brazil), and CEDES (Argentina) will use such a comparative perspective to study the respective "programs of economic normalization" in force since the present BA states were established. Roberto Frenkel is doing research on how these programs were enacted in Argentina under various political regimes, from a longitudinal perspective.

blanket of confidentiality with which finance capital covers its operations is undoubtedly a severe obstacle for conducting the type of empirical work that has been done, say, on the U.S. Congress.[4] We suspect, nevertheless, that another reason for the lack of research on this subject is that the place where the studies have to be undertaken happens to be the very center of world capitalism—precisely where the effects of the IMF's actions are least visible.

It is for these reasons that this study can only be a reflection (and an incomplete one at that) of a part of the problem, namely, certain impacts and interactions in one peripheral case. Our objective is to open up a discussion that may lead us to overcome these deficiencies, and thus lessen the risk of seeing the IMF and its criteria either as the univocal expression of economic rationality or as the embodiment of an omniscient conspiracy.

HOW THE IMF WORKS

The IMF formally established its "tranches policy" in the mid-1950's, in response to the new problems involved in financing peripheral economies.[5] This policy rules that hard currency requests are to be handled according to their ratio to the quota contributed to the IMF by the member country in question. Applications within the gold tranche (leaving the IMF with no more than 100 percent of the applying country's currency) are approved almost automatically; within the first tranche (between 100 and 125 percent of the quota), applications are usually handled with a "liberal" attitude; beyond that limit, applications need a "substantial justification" to be approved. The precise meaning of this phrase was established in 1958; applications beyond the first tranche would receive favorable treatment if the funds were to be used for "supporting an effective program for establishing or keeping the

4. An interesting exception is Cheryl Payer, *The Debt Trap: The International Monetary Fund and the Third World* (New York, 1974).

5. Emphasizing the short-term nature of the credits, a number of changes in the rates to be charged were approved in late 1951; in the same resolution the duration of the credits was reduced. The so-called Rooth Plan was approved shortly afterward; it included a number of rules foreshadowing the future standby agreements. Among other things, it established that the normal repurchasing period would be three years (with five as the maximum) and changed the "tranches policy," making a distinction between applications within the gold tranche and the rest. See J. Keith Horsefield and Gertrud Lovasy, "Evolution of the Fund's Policy on Drawings," in *The International Monetary Fund 1945–1965* (Washington, D.C., 1966), vol. 2, chapter 18.

stability of the currency of the member country at a realistic exchange rate."[6]

This tying of currency withdrawals to the presentation and approval of stabilization programs came to be the main activity of the IMF, especially through the standby agreements, the importance of which increased substantially over the years. A large number of credits has now been approved. There is no reference to the standby agreements in the founding documents of the IMF, since they were not conceived of until later. Technically, the implication is that the member country may purchase hard currency up to a fixed limit during a given period, without having to rediscuss its general situation and policies. Originally this was envisioned as a line of credit that would be open for a certain period of time, during which the country could withdraw funds with no limitations other than those set by the general rules of the IMF. Later, however, it developed into the main instrument for making the availability of IMF resources conditional on the internal adoption of certain policies, once the application has exceeded the first tranche. Approval of the standby agreement requires the signing of a "letter of intention," in which the member country, after discussing the subject with IMF representatives, sets forth its policies and agrees to implement them. The standby agreement is a resolution by the IMF setting forth the terms under which the member country can purchase hard currency; it includes certain goals the economy must reach and the policy procedures to be used, as well as the criteria to be observed in order for the IMF not to suspend withdrawal rights. The letter of intention includes indicators of the economy's behavior and of economic policy; the limits established by these indicators cannot be exceeded for the duration of the agreement. The violation of these clauses may lead to the suspension of the agreement; in this regard there are generally clauses establishing the need to consult the IMF before certain policy decisions are made, as well as renegotiation clauses in case one of the objectives is not met.

By virtue of these standby agreements, the IMF has tended to become an autonomous and interventionist institution in its relations with the economically less powerful countries. The standby-agreement clauses have been under constant revision to "protect the resources of the Fund from undue use."[7] Legally, access to resources can be interrupted on the basis of the IMF's contractual right to decide unilaterally that non-

6. IMF Annual Report 1959, in Horsefield and Lovasy, "Evolution of the Fund's Policy," p. 404.

7. Joseph Gold, "Use of the Fund's Resources," in *The IMF 1945–1965*, vol. 2, chapter 23, p. 534.

attainment of certain goals of the program may mean improper use of its funds. However, the IMF's role as the "technical secretariat" of the central economies' finance capital is even more important in increasing the institution's leverage. The IMF's decision to enter into a standby agreement with a member country is considered by other international financial sources a sign of approval for the stabilization program set forth in the letter of intention. The consultation and evaluation clauses in the agreement allow the IMF to exercise a permanent auditing function, so to speak, over the national economy of the country that is party to it, a task of great interest not only to the IMF itself, but also to finance capital. The unwritten rules of international finance have led both private and public financiers to wait for a decision by the IMF regarding a standby credit before negotiating their own agreements, which often involve access to considerably higher amounts of hard currency than those provided by the standby credit itself. In relation to the country in need of external funds, transnational finance capital thus acts as a giant monopolist, imposing conditions that are made explicit by the IMF. It would be difficult to find any better indication of the convergence between the interests of finance capital regarding the evolution of the debtor country on the one hand, and the policy and evaluation criteria of the IMF on the other. We will return to this point after examining these criteria.

The criteria and quantitative goals that have to be met by the recipient country's economic policy, according to the standby agreement, constitute a program based on the IMF's principles of how the problems of external disequilibrium and inflation should be approached. These phenomena are approached in many peripheral countries with programs that—although not identical with each other—are based on a common body of ideas, which constitute what we might call the "outlook" of the IMF. This outlook includes not only a diagnosis of the situation, but also standards that specify the most desirable state of the economy in any given country and the conduct of international economic relations. These notions are expressed in the form of seemingly unquestionable "technical" criteria, expressions of an apparently axiomatic economic rationality. The IMF thus attributes universality and objectivity to a particular view of the functioning of the world economy and of what ought to be the "best" situation of the national economies.

Focusing our attention on the behavior of the IMF in various Latin American countries, especially in Argentina and Chile during the last two decades, we will now attempt to make a synthesis of this outlook. The IMF considers external disequilibrium and inflation to be problems generated by "distortions" in the economic-development process. As countries try to expand public services and accelerate economic growth, they often generate a tendency to overspend, thus creating considerable pressure on the balance of payments and on prices. Excessive expansion of credit to finance consumption or private investment is often responsible for this pressure, but more commonly it is considered to be a result of large government deficits financed through bank credits. Excessive public spending is caused by subsidies to producers or consumers (for example, in the form of an inflated public payroll), operational deficits of public enterprises (determined largely by their pricing policy), and excessive public investment. Inflation and balance-of-payments deficits are manifestations of disequilibria caused by an excess of demand in relation to available supply. This demand is attributed to excessive money supply, in turn generated basically by the government deficit and by pumping too much credit into the economy. On the other hand, the existence of these disequilibria in various markets implies a distortion of the price system—both internally and in relation to international prices. This distortion is caused by state-imposed obstacles that do not allow the free working of the price system in those markets. In the IMF's view, distorting state actions stand in the way of an automatic correction of these disequilibria. Excessive demand for available resources derives largely from the claims of various social sectors to increase their share of a limited national income. Bad economic leadership or political incompetence are responsible for supporting relatively distorted prices, partly as a response to the pressures of these social sectors.

The IMF's outlook can be summarized in the following propositions: there is a price system operating in commodities, wages, exchange rates, and interest rates. This price system equilibrates markets and provides stability to the economy. If inflation and external-payments difficulties arise, it is because of a distortion of the price system through excessive money supply as well as because of obstacles to the free play of market forces. This ideal equilibrium system is optimal, in the sense that it makes full use of resources and provides the best indicators for their allocation. The more it reflects the international price system, the better it will guide investment and production according to the advantages of the country in international trade. This outlook provides the basis for stabilization programs whose substance is relatively simple: the idea is to lead markets and prices to their points of equilibrium, thus allowing a broad action of market forces and eliminating excessive money supply. As far as balance-of-payments difficulties are concerned, the main objective is to adjust disparities among internal and international prices. This generally implies a significant devaluation.[8]

To eliminate excessive money supply, the IMF establishes programs that include general limits to its expansion, as well as more specific limits to the expansion of private and public credit and government financing. In the latter case, control clauses may include specific numeric references to the government deficit and to limits to public spending, as well as to public saving goals. In general, the financial objectives of the public sector demand a strong increase in the prices of goods and services produced by it.

The exchange measures and financial policies that form the basis of the program are often complemented by direct action on prices and salaries. In this respect, stabilization programs show a remarkable asymmetry in the way they treat commodities and labor markets. Whenever price controls and regulations are in force, the program tends to demand their elimination; conversely, when the IMF considers that the government has sufficient power to establish ceilings on salary increases, they are imposed by the program. This incongruence goes considerably beyond the criteria based on the theoretical outlook and implies a socially biased pragmatism whose political significance is demonstrated most clearly under authoritarian regimes.

We cannot undertake an exhaustive analysis of this outlook here, but we must refer to two lines of criticism. They have emerged largely from the debate brought about by the repeated experiences of dependent countries with these programs. The first refers to the presumed optimality, in terms of general welfare and economic-development criteria, of the objectives of the stabilization policies—objectives that the program sets for itself, assuming that its measures would effectively lead the economy to a stable equilibrium position.

The origins of the criticism of the IMF's outlook in this regard can be traced back to the first postwar writings on development and inter-

---

8. If it is considered that the devaluation needed for these purposes is too high, the IMF allows for the possibility of "gradualist" policies to raise the exchange rate in several stages. In case of very high inflation, the exchange policy includes regular adjustments of the exchange rate, according to the evolution of internal prices. In this case, the stabilization program is aimed at a gradual lessening of the inflation rate; however, as long as inflation goes on, successive devaluations are needed to achieve a change in relative prices. In these cases, control clauses include specific references to the relationship that has to exist between the evolution of the exchange rate and certain price indicators, in addition to the budgetary and balance-of-payments controls that are usually included.

national trade in Latin America.[9] Since then it has repeatedly been argued that the trade- and capital-accumulation patterns resulting from an unregulated international market tend to favor a persistent deterioration in the relative position of the peripheral economies. More recently, economists have emphasized the basic inequality existing between the center and the periphery in matters of international trade.[10] Initially, the notions that inspired the IMF clearly reflected the purpose of rebuilding the type of world order in existence before 1929. In that type of international order, however, the peripheral economies' role was reduced to that of producers of raw materials and consumers of manufactured products. The persistence of these notions—and the consequent perpetuation of the old division of labor they assume—has obvious normative implications. They indicate that the IMF embodies the specific financial and commercial interests of the centers of world capitalism, which join forces in partial but decisive manner in the IMF to impose certain economic guidelines on the peripheral countries.

The substance of these guidelines becomes apparent once we take up the second criticism of the IMF's outlook. It deals with the theory that is used to explain inflation and balance-of-payments deficits and provides the basis for the stabilization program's policies. Starting with the work of the "structuralists,"[11] Latin American economists have long been concerned with refuting the IMF's arguments on this matter. There is no need to go into the whole debate here; suffice it to say that this body of work made it possible to start building a theory of inflation and foreign trade that would allow for the structural specificities of the Latin American economies. In marked contrast with these efforts, the IMF's outlook is abstract and ahistorical; its diagnosis and policies are considered valid and are in fact recommended under almost any circumstances, regardless of time and place. Its notions are part of the neoclassical and monetarist perspective that became very influential in academia from the 1950's onwards. These intellectual currents "guarantee" the scientific accuracy of the IMF's outlook, which thus seems to

9. See Paul Prebisch, *The Economic Development of Latin America and Its Problems* (New York, 1950).

10. See Arghiri Emmanuel, *L'échange inégal* (Paris, 1969), and Samir Amin, *L'accumulation à l'échelle mondiale* (Paris, 1971).

11. Juan F. Noyola, "El Desarrollo Económico y la Inflación en México y otros Países Latinoamericanos," *Investigacion Economica*, vol. 16, no. 1, 1956; Osvaldo Sunkel, "La Inflacion Chilena: Un Enfoque Heterodoxo," *Trimestre Economico*, vol. 25, no. 4, 1958; and Julio G. Olivera, "La Inflación Estructural y el Estructuralismo Latinoamericano," in *Inflación y Estructura Económica* (Buenos Aires, 1967).

enjoy a monopoly on technical rigor. However, this is no longer a mere academic issue; the IMF's perspective has become the official doctrine of several Latin American governments, and it has long been the official language of most international financing institutions. This perspective thus performs an important function: it provides a logical, elegant, simple basis for stabilization policies whose social impact has been profound and painful. It is from this notion of the IMF's outlook as an ideological support system for certain policies that we can move toward examining the stabilization program's impacts and the type of international interests that seem to be embodied in the IMF.

Both the rapid growth and the absolute levels reached in the 1970's by the medium- and long-term foreign debt of the peripheral countries have raised worrisome questions in the world's financial centers. Foreign debt has risen from 36 billion dollars in 1967 to approximately 200 billion by the end of 1976. Even more important than its accelerated growth is the fact that during this period multilateral financial institutions and the governments of the central countries were largely replaced by international private banks as main lending sources. Using World Bank figures, one study has concluded that out of 200 billion dollars owed by peripheral countries by late 1976, 120 billion (60 percent) was owed to private financial sources.[12] It seems logical that the zeal of these financial centers has been exacerbated by these developments; the balance-of-payments problems of some peripheral countries are so severe that not only the position of their creditors but also the stability of the international financial system as a whole may be endangered. Under these conditions, international creditors are bound to promote strongly the type of economic policies that, by improving the balance-of-payments positions of these countries, allow them to pay their debts. The Latin American experience in this regard shows that the stabilization programs of the IMF perform this function rather well, although at a high internal cost in terms of economic growth and income distribution.

The increasing influence of the IMF and its notions is thus not totally unrelated to the processes through which the international financial system has been going lately. In sum, the IMF's outlook and its growing influence correspond to the new and important role private finance capital has come to play in the peripheral economies. Increasing demands on the peripheral economies, generated by the spectacular growth

12. Miguel S. Wionczek, "La Deuda Externa de los Países de Menor Desarrollo y los Euromercados: Un Pasado Impresionante, un Futuro Incierto," *Comercio Exterior*, vol. 27, no. 11, 1977.

of foreign debt, have led to stabilization programs geared fundamentally toward guaranteeing the external financial solvency of the debtor countries. The IMF, officiating as the "technical secretariat" of transnational finance capital, provides not only the programs but also the logical foundation to make them coherent, plus the type of "auditing" services needed to ensure that the debtor country will comply with the agreement.

IMPACTS OF THE STABILIZATION PROGRAMS

The objective of this section is to illustrate the recessive and redistributive impacts of the stabilization programs oriented by the IMF's outlook. With that purpose in mind we will examine some aspects of the recent Argentine experience.

It is evident that the structural socioeconomic conditions of Argentina, as well as the specific features of its economic policy cannot be generalized *sine die*. Our purpose, nonetheless, is to point out the marked incongruence between the effects the program was supposed to have achieved and those it has in fact achieved, on the one hand, and the remarkable distortion of the distribution of benefits and losses, on the other. Accordingly, we will look especially closely at those aspects of economic policy directly related to the assumptions and objectives of the stabilization plans. With this purpose in mind, we will first present a simplified model of the Argentine economy;[13] this model will then be used to describe, on a comparative basis, some of the most important aspects of the stabilization plan. We will show that the mechanisms employed to confront the critical balance-of-payments situation demand a high price in terms of economic growth and income distribution.

13. This model is developed in A. Canitrot, J. L. Machinea, and R. Frenkel, *Cambio Estructural e Inestabilidad en la Economía Argentina*, mimeograph (CEDES, Buenos Aires, 1977), and A. Canitrot, "La Experiencia Populista de Redistribución de Ingresos," *Desarrollo Económico*, vol. 15, no. 59, 1975. Several authors have described the Argentine economy in similar terms: Carlos Diaz-Alejandro, *Ensayos sobre la Historia de la Economía Argentina* (Buenos Aires, 1973); Aldo Ferrer, "Devaluación, Redistribución de Ingresos, y el Proceso de Desarticulación Industrial en la Argentina," in *Los Planes de Estabilización en la Argentina* (Buenos Aires, 1969); R. Mallon y J. Sourrouille, *La Política Económica en una Sociedad Conflictiva. El caso Argentino* (Buenos Aires, 1973); E. Eshag, and R. Thorpe, "Las Consecuencias Económicas y Sociales de las Políticas Económicas Ortodoxas aplicadas en la República Argentina durante los Años de Postguerra," *Desarrollo Económico*, vol. 5, no. 16, 1965; and O. Braun and J. L. Joy, "A Model of Economic Stagnation. A Case Study of the Argentine Economy," *The Economic Journal*, vol. 78, no. 312, 1968.

Second, we will examine in greater detail the adjustment processes of macroeconomic variables, trying to underline the short-term dynamics generated by the policy being implemented; particular attention will be paid here to the evolution of prices.

The recessive and regressive character of the stabilization plan is paralleled by two features of the Argentine economy that are largely ignored by the IMF's outlook. The first is of a structural nature and addresses itself to the character of the principal consumer goods among exportable products, on the one hand, and to the weight of consumer demand among wage earners relative to total demand, on the other. The second is of a dynamic nature, and addresses itself to the adjustment process of the economy once a reduction of effective demand takes place. Both features and the consequences flowing from them can be analyzed if one views the Argentine economy as the product of two different sectors, one producing goods for export and the other for internal consumption. The exportable goods are mainly agricultural products, which in turn are the main consumption items of wage earners. Given the low relative weight of Argentine production in world markets, we can safely assume that the international demand for exportable Argentine goods is perfectly elastic at current international prices. Accordingly, employment in the sector producing exportable goods will stay full regardless of the state of the rest of the economy. The number of wage earners in the export sector is low, and its demand for imported goods practically zero. On the other hand, the sector oriented toward the internal market is made up of industrial and service activities; its exports are limited, and it has a high demand for imported raw materials and capital goods. This sector is also the main source of employment in the Argentine economy. Consumer demand by wage earners and nonactive members of the population represents approximately two-thirds of the total consumer demand. Wage earners do not save, for all practical purposes; accordingly, their level of spending is directly determined by the wage level. Given that they are essential consumer goods, the demand for agricultural products is inelastic; if there is a price increase, the total amount of goods demanded goes down, but spending per unit goes up. Since total spending stays at a certain level, there is a decrease in the effective demand for industrial products.

How are prices determined in each of these sectors? The price of exportable goods (including subsidies and taxes) is determined by its price in the international market and by the exchange rate fixed by the government. The same mechanism determines the prices of goods imported by the internal-market sector. Prime costs in the internal market depend, in the short term, on the nominal wage level and on the price of intermediate goods that have either been imported or bought from the export sector; given international prices, those costs will depend on the wage level and the rate of exchange. The relationship between prices and prime costs of the internal-market sector—which would be the markup of that sector—is a crucial variable in the economy's short-term behavior. For the moment, we shall assume that this markup does not change in the short run; the prices of the internal-market sector are thus determined by the nominal wage level and the exchange rate. Accordingly, if international prices are given, the exchange policy and the level of the nominal wage will define the relative price system, including the real wage level.

If we assume that in the short term the levels of private and public investment, government consumption, and consumer demand by non-wage earners are fixed, the level of activity in the internal-market sector will depend on wage-earner demand; the latter in turn will be determined by the level of real wages.[14] Given the nonwage components of spending, this implies that the exchange rate and nominal wages determine—through a multiplier effect—the level of activity and employment of the internal-market sector, and consequently of the whole economy. Close attention has to be paid to the ways in which the levels of activity and employment depend directly on the level of real wages. Consumption by non-wage earners does not depend on current benefits; in addition, we can assume that public spending in investment and consumption operates, in the short term, without regard to the price system. Private investment is determined by long-term expectations; the latter can depend on current benefits and on the level of activity, but it is difficult to imagine that the form of this relationship is such that increased investment will correspond exactly to the decrease in wage-earner consumption within total effective demand.[15] Accordingly, effective demand for industrial goods depends on wage-earner spending, which in turn depends on the level of real wages.

Since a relatively low number of wage earners are to be found in the export sector, we can distinguish among three income-receiving groups: two types of capitalists—those from the export sector and those oriented

---

14. This is a provisional assumption made to simplify the description of the recessive and redistributive impacts of the stabilization programs. We shall return to this point and its implications for setting prices in the internal market.

15. On the contrary, the Argentine experience seems to show that there is a positive correlation between wage-earner consumption and private investment in the internal-market sector.

toward the internal market—and the wage earners of the latter sector. Income distribution among these groups is determined by the ratio between exchange rate and wages. The larger the ratio between the price of foreign exchange and the wage level, the lower the real wage is bound to be, and the higher will be the proportion of income accruing to the export sector. An increase in the exchange rate is translated into a proportional increase in the prices of exportable goods. If the level of wages remains fixed or grows at a lower rate, the costs of the internal-market sector will increase less rapidly than the prices of exportable goods. Any income variation among internal-market entrepreneurs will thus depend on the markup on prime costs and on the magnitude of the downturn in their activity.

The trade balance is also regulated by the ratio between the price of foreign exchange and the price of labor. Any increase in the exchange rate has positive effects on exports in two ways: directly, on the production of the export sector; and indirectly, through a reduction of its internal demand and consequent increase in the amount of goods available for export. On the import side of the equation, the recessive impact on the internal-market sector brings about a consequent reduction in the demand for imported intermediate goods.

These simplified features of the Argentine economy allow us to show the basic effects of the IMF's stabilization program. Devaluation brings about an increase in agricultural prices and a lowering of real wages. This leads to a recession in the internal-market sector. The recessive impact of a drop in effective consumer demand is not offset by a sufficiently strong expansion of export activities; as a consequence, the gross national product falls.[16] Imports are reduced, and the amount of goods available for export increases. Devaluation alleviates the balance-of-payments situation largely through its recessive effects and its impact on the income and consumption of wage earners. The magnitude of the recession depends on the size of the devaluation and on the evolution of prices in the internal-market sector. On the other hand, the reduction in public spending and tightening of credit that goes along with these changes in relative prices intensifies the effects of the recession. The larger the reduction in effective demand induced by the devaluation—and backed

---

16. This is not a consequence ingrained in the logic of the model, but something that occurs in practice. Theoretically, at least, the level of export expansion needed to offset the recessive impact of the drop in wages could be determined; in practice this is difficult to accomplish owing to the relatively low weight of exports (and investment) in total demand, and to the lower multiplier effects of this spending in relation to wage-earner spending. As we shall see below, the Argentine case we are analyzing is a good illustration of this phenomenon.

up by fiscal and monetary policy—the larger the recessive impact of the stabilization program will be. Another important effect of the program is regressive income redistribution. Wage earners are confronted with a drastic reduction of their income, whereas the income of those in the export sectors, especially the rents of the Pampa Húmeda (wet pampa) landowners, is increased substantially.

The stabilization program we are concerned with began in March 1976, as the official economic policy of the new military authorities.[17] At that time the economy was clearly undergoing a crisis: there were serious difficulties in meeting foreign payments, and since mid-1975 the inflation rate had accelerated, reaching peaks of 30 percent a month. This was largely the result of a frustrated attempt by the previous government to enact a somewhat similar stabilization program, but in a situation where the trade unions had strong bargaining power to defend wage levels. Accordingly, there was an intense struggle for the appropriation of income, in which the state found itself arbitrating an increasing number of recurrent conflicts. Nonetheless, during the first quarter of 1976 the devaluations of the Peronista government increased the ratio between the value of foreign exchange and wages by more than 70 percent,[18] whereas real wages fell during the same period by 22 percent.

17. The new authorities were faced with urgent external-payments problems. They immediately obtained 300 million dollars in 6-month maturity loans from commercial banks; creditors also allowed them to roll over to the fourth quarter an additional 350 million dollars owed by the public sector in the second quarter of 1976. The economic program was presented for the first time to international financiers at the annual meeting of governors of the Inter-American Development Bank at the beginning of May. On May 27, delegations from the IMF and the World Bank arrived in Buenos Aires. The Argentine Government applied for a number of long-term credits to the World Bank, and the latter released a public report highly favorable to the program. By mid-June, Minister of Economics Martínez de Hoz traveled to the United States, where he made all the necessary arrangements with the IMF to obtain the first tranche immediately and two-thirds of the second tranche by April of 1977, depending on the Argentine government's presentation of a program for the first half of 1977. On August 6 the agreement with the IMF was signed, and 180 million dollars were drawn, which correspond to 160 million in Special Drawing Rights. Simultaneously, a standby agreement with international private banks had been sought. A consortium of U.S., European and Japanese banks, headed by Chase Manhattan, extended a line of credit for slightly over a billion dollars, with a four-year maturity rate and at an interest rate 1⅞ higher than LIBOR. Dealings with the IMF culminated in April 1977, when it approved the economic program for the first half of 1977 and made the 100-million-dollar balance of the agreement available to the Argentine Government. See *Boletín Semanal del Ministerio de Economía*, various numbers, 1976 and 1977, and *Mercado*, various numbers, 1976.

18. During the first quarter of 1976 the exchange rate for traditional export products went up by 137.6 percent.

This meant that some of the main elements of the stabilization program were being implemented when the new government started to develop its policy. In this regard, the most significant elements of the new stabilization program—besides the increase in the exchange rate—can be seen to be the virtual elimination of price controls in the internal market and the freezing of nominal wages.

Let us examine some of the methods of implementation and effects of the stabilization policy, starting with relative prices. During the second quarter of 1976 (when the program was first implemented), the initial wage freeze and subsequent prohibition of any raises beyond a certain ceiling led to a drop in real wages of 37 percent. Wages at the end of this quarter had about 60 percent of the buying power they had had in late 1975 and a little over 67 percent of what they had had in 1960.

Table 1 shows the evolution of an industrial worker's minimum wage, as set by collective agreements; its average value for 1960 is taken as a starting point. This series gives us an idea of the evolution of income in the groups with less bargaining power; however, during the second half of 1976, and to a greater extent during 1977 and 1978, wages in fact reached higher levels than those registered in the index. Although there

TABLE 1
Basic Real-Wage Index
(Industrial Worker)
(Base: 1960=100)

Month	1976	1977
January	125.7	64.4
February	107.3	59.3
March	97.8	69.0
April	72.6	65.1
May	64.2	61.1
June	71.8	56.8
July	68.8	61.4
August	66.0	55.2
September	66.8	51.9
October	62.0	47.6
November	66.5	43.7
December	58.0	40.8

SOURCE: Instituto Nacional de Estadísticas y Censos, *Boletín Estadístico Trimestral*, various numbers.

TABLE 2
Sectorial Price Indexes

	March 1976	September 1976	March 1977	March 1978
Wholesale agricultural	100	210.7	309.0	725.0
Wholesale nonagricultural	100	161.5	244.9	617.1

SOURCE: Instituto Nacional de Estadísticas y Censos, *Boletín Estadístico Trimestral*, various numbers.

is no reliable information on this subject,[19] an estimate using the evolution of family allowances and a sliding adjustment of 40 percent—which was the ceiling set by the government—enables us to conclude that real wages during the first quarter of 1978 were equivalent to those of the third quarter of 1976.[20] In two years then, the impact of the stabilization program was to cut wages by about 30 to 40 percent in relation to their already deteriorated level of March 1976.

During the initial implementation period of the program, prices in the export- and internal-market sectors behaved according to explicit policy objectives.[21] As Table 2 shows, at the end of the first half of the period agricultural prices went up by 30 percent in relation to industrial prices. This new price ratio tended to persist during the first year of the program, despite the inflationary upsurge, which we will discuss below. Nonetheless, the new relative price structure was altered by a drop in the international price of exportable goods, the exchange policy, and the price behavior in the internal-market sector.

19. During the second half of 1976 workers with greater bargaining power probably obtained greater wage increases than those registered in these tables. The so-called wage-flexibility policy later allowed business to provide higher increases than those that had been set by the official "ceiling."

20. Computed by the Instituto de Economía y Finanzas, Faculty of Economics, National University of Córdoba, *Comentarios Económicos*, Córdoba, April, 1978.

21. Although between March and December of 1976 nonagricultural wholesale prices went up by 100 percent, during that same period the real exchange rate for wheat exports was increased by 360 percent, and for corn and sorghum by 330 percent. Data obtained from the Central Bank, and FIEL, *Indicadores de Coyuntura*, various numbers.

In this comparison, as in other tables, we take as base figures those of March 1976. This corresponds to our objective of comparing the impacts of the program with the conditions prevailing at the moment it was initiated; it does not by any means imply that the base figures are considered normal.

TABLE 3
Total Demand
(Variation rates compared with the same period of the preceding year)

	1976 yearly total	1977 yearly total	1977 quarterly totals				1978 quarterly total
			I	II	III	IV	I
Total demand	−4.6	5.3	1.8	7.2	9.4	2.9	−6.2
Total consumption	−8.1	−4.1	−10.3	−5.7	−0.9	0.5	−2.4
Investment:							
durable							
equipment	−0.4	26.6	31.3	39.5	33.0	5.4	−30.0
building	−12.7	9.8	3.2	8.1	16.2	11.6	8.1
Exports	40.7	51.4	87.3	76.7	51.8	7.9	−9.4

SOURCE: Central Bank, Republic of Argentina, provisional figures.

These changes in relative prices had a foreseeable and strong impact on demand. In spite of a 40.7 percent growth in exports during 1976, total demand fell by 4.6 percent, reflecting a 8.1 percent drop in consumption and a 6.2 percent drop in gross internal investment.[22] Taken as a whole, the first two years of the stabilization program resulted in a strong cut in demand. During 1977, however, especially during the second and third quarters, investment demand and the growth of exports led to increased expansion, and as a result, for 1977 as a whole total demand went up by 5.3 percent. Nonetheless, this expansion was ephemeral; total demand dropped badly during the fourth quarter, and 1978 started under very recessive conditions. This development illustrates an important aspect of the stabilization program's impact on the Argentine economy. In spite of the strong increase in investment and export demand, both fail to exercise a multiplier effect on consumption. Consumer demand fell during 1977 by 4.1 percent, thus showing how much it depends on the level of real wages. In addition, the growth figures for exports and investment were exceptionally high;[23] in relation to them the intensity and duration of the expansion effect was rather low and short-lived. The recessive nature of the stabilization program is confirmed by this experience; even if investments and exports react favorably, this reaction is not sufficient to offset the effects of the drop in wages.

22. 1975 was a year marked by recessive tendencies; the gross internal product fell by 1.3 percent.
23. See Table 3.

Economic-activity indicators follow the tendency determined by the evolution of effective demand. The gross internal product fell by 2.9 percent during 1976; it went up by 4.4 percent during 1977; this expansion took place mainly during the second and third quarters; recessive tendencies manifested themselves again during the fourth quarter. Table 4 shows the evolution of the gross internal product on a quarterly basis; in it we can see the different effects of the stabilization program on the export- and import-market sectors. Although the agricultural sector sustained its expansive tendency until the fourth quarter of 1977, the industrial sector was seriously affected by the recession. In the fourth quarter of 1976, nine months after the program started, the level of industrial production was, on average, 11 percent lower than that of the fourth quarter of 1974. A brief expansionary period during 1977 led industrial activity to a high point during the third quarter of 1977 (reaching a level similar to that of 1974). However, recessionary tendencies subsequently reasserted themselves. During the first quarter of 1978 industrial production fell by 11.5 percent in relation to the first quarter of 1977; its level corresponds to 83 percent of the first quarter of 1974.

Though the industrial sector as a whole was affected by the recession, the reduction of demand in those industries producing goods consumed primarily by wage earners was particularly strong. Table 5 shows the gross industrial product divided by subsectors. It demonstrates the impact of decreasing demand on the production of food and beverages, textiles and clothing, and woods and furniture; in these cases, we would have to go back in our statistics to the early 1970's or even to the late 1960's to find levels of activity similar to those of the last quarter of 1977 or the first quarter of 1978.

The balance of payments reacted as predicted by the program. During 1976 exports went up by more than 30 percent, reaching almost 4 billion dollars; imports were cut by 23 percent, reaching almost 3 billion dollars. This 900 million dollars surplus on the trade account, together with 600 million dollars of net capital inflow made it possible to meet payments for financial services and increase foreign exchange reserves by about 1 billion dollars. During 1977 import levels stayed low; in nominal terms they were equivalent to those of 1975; exports, on the other hand, mainly owing to an exceptionally good harvest during 1976–77, reached a value of over 5 billion dollars. In this regard, the evolution of Argentina's international trade can be seen in Table 6.

By late 1976 the objectives of the stabilization policy in the external sector had been achieved. Foreign exchange reserves had reached a

TABLE 4

Gross Internal Product

(Variation rates compared with the same period of the preceding year)

Sector	1976					1977					1978
		Quarters					Quarters				Quarter
	Year	I	II	III	IV	Year	I	II	III	IV	I
Gross internal product	−2.9	−4.4	−5.2	−1.7	0.2	4.4	0.9	4.9	9.1	2.5	−7.2
Agriculture, hunting, and fishing	3.5	7.9	−0.1	0.8	5.9	7.1	5.1	14.3	9.7	−2.1	−7.0
Mining	0.8	−6.0	−2.5	3.3	8.3	8.8	9.0	12.0	11.0	3.4	−1.6
Manufacturing	−4.5	−6.7	−6.3	−2.9	−2.0	3.8	0.3	2.1	11.5	2.6	−11.5
Building	−14.1	−26.7	−15.0	−10.7	−0.8	13.3	−6.3	10.5	19.7	16.7	9.2
Electricity, gas, and water	3.4	4.2	1.6	4.8	3.4	5.0	4.3	4.3	5.4	5.9	−0.7
Commerce, hotels, and restaurants	−5.9	−9.8	−9.2	−2.4	−2.1	5.5	1.1	6.7	10.0	3.8	−6.0
Transportation and communications	−4.3	−5.3	−10.2	−2.0	0.5	5.8	3.6	8.0	9.7	2.1	−4.6
Finance and real estate	3.5	6.7	3.5	2.0	2.1	0.2	−1.8	−0.7	1.2	2.1	1.5
Community services, social, and personal	−0.2	1.1	−0.1	−0.1	−0.1	−0.4	−4.0	−1.0	4.0	−0.5	−6.9

SOURCE: Central Bank, Republic of Argentina, provisional figures.

TABLE 5

Gross Industrial Product

(Variation rates compared with the same period of the preceding year)

Sector	1976					1977					1978
	Year	Quarters				Year	Quarters				Quarter
		I	II	III	IV		I	II	III	IV	I
Food, beverages, and tobacco	0.3	−1.2	5.6	−1.1	−2.1	−3.5	−4.5	−6.7	−1.0	−1.6	−8.1
Textiles, clothing, and leather	−4.6	2.7	−5.4	−6.1	−2.5	−6.0	−11.5	−5.9	−1.2	−5.7	−22.0
Woods and furniture	−27.8	−26.3	−35.5	−26.0	−21.0	−11.5	−24.9	−19.0	−3.0	−0.6	−22.0
Paper, printing, and publishing	−7.3	−10.5	−7.5	−2.9	−8.2	−4.8	−1.5	−4.6	−10.8	−4.2	−2.7
Chemicals and petrochemicals	−0.7	−1.3	−0.4	0.0	−0.4	4.1	1.2	2.5	7.3	5.2	−4.5
Nonmetallic minerals	−4.5	−3.4	−8.9	−3.3	−2.3	−0.6	−3.7	−1.5	3.9	−1.3	−1.6
Basic metal industries	−24.1	−25.4	−30.2	−19.7	−19.1	15.1	0.5	7.3	25.0	28.0	−5.2
Machinery and equipment	−3.8	−12.1	−8.1	−0.6	4.1	10.4	7.3	9.0	21.6	3.7	−17.8
Other industries	−3.4	−0.9	−4.9	−7.4	0.0	2.4	3.3	2.0	6.6	−1.6	−7.6

SOURCE: Central Bank, Republic of Argentina, provisional figures.

TABLE 6

Argentina's International Trade

(Millions of U.S. dollars)

Year	Exports	Imports	Balance
1974	3,930.7	3,634.9	+ 295.8
1975	2,961.3	3,946.5	− 985.2
1976	3,916.3	3,033.0	+ 883.3
1977	5,610.0	4,100.0	+1,510.0

SOURCE: Instituto Nacional de Estadísticas y Censos, *Comercio Exterior*, various numbers; Central Bank, Republic of Argentina, provisional figures.

level of 1,812.3 million dollars (almost two-thirds of the total import bill for that year). However, the fact that the policy remained unchanged, combined with its success in the external sector, put the Argentine economy in a paradoxical situation. During 1977, in addition to the 1.5-billion-dollar surplus on the trade account, there was a net capital inflow of 1.5 billion dollars, partly as the result of differences between internal and external interest rates. This led to a level of foreign exchange reserves of 4,038.8 million dollars,[24] which was equal to the value of all imports during 1977. The paradox lay in the simultaneous occurrence of this exceptional external liquidity and an increased foreign debt on the one hand, and a strong recession, which left an important proportion of the industrial capacity unused, on the other—in a country where the external sector had traditionally been an obstacle to growth.

Another point that merits attention is the impact of the stabilization program on the inflationary process. We have deemed it necessary to treat this issue separately because the program's failure to achieve its manifest objectives in this regard has underlined the magnitude of the drop in real wages, the consequent income redistribution and the seriousness of the recession. The simultaneous occurrence of high inflation rates and a strong drop in effective demand produces an unusual economic situation. It can only be compared with the results of another stabilization program developed according to the IMF's philosophy—the post-1973 Chilean experience.

To analyze the impact of the stabilization program on the inflationary process, it is useful to reexamine the model of the Argentine econ-

24. Fundación de Investigaciones Económicas Latinoamericanas, *Indicadores de Coyuntura*, Buenos Aires, March, 1978. Computed on the basis of information provided by the Central Bank.

omy described above. According to the model's hypothesis, the initial impact of the program is always inflationary: the prices of exportable goods go up in the same ratio as the price of foreign exchange; the same happens with the prices of the imports of the internal-market sector. For this reason, even though wages may stay constant, prime costs in the internal-market sector will go up, although at a lower rate than the prices of exportable goods. The proportion in which prices rise in this sector will thus depend on the markup.

If enterprises tend to keep their markup constant—this was the provisional assumption we made above for descriptive purposes—prices in the internal-market sector will grow at the same rate as their prime costs; accordingly, average-price indicators of the economy will go up at a slower rate than the devaluation rate. Under depressed demand conditions a low markup in this sector is to be expected as prime costs go up; the tendency is to keep the markup constant or reduce it at least partly. One consequence of this would be that, after the initial inflationary impact, the inflation rate would tend to go down, even though successive devaluations would keep the relative price structure desired by the stabilization program. If the economy behaved in such a fashion, the program would lead to a cost inflation characterized by gradually receding rates.

The hypothesis that the markup rate will be constant in the internal-market sector implies a Keynesian assumption about the existence of an adjustment mechanism in commodity markets that operates on the basis of quantity; faced with a reduction in effective demand, enterprises would tend to keep prices constant, reducing the amount of goods sold and the level of activity. Under inflationary conditions, reduction in demand occurs simultaneously with an increase in prime costs. The Argentine experience before the enactment of this stabilization program largely tends to confirm the accuracy of this assumption.

It is nevertheless clear that the stabilization program inaugurated in 1976 has led to new price behavior in the internal-market sector. The first measures of the program—particularly the elimination of subsidies, regulation, and direct controls—brought about a drastic rise in prices. After this initial impact, during the first months of the program the monthly inflation rate went down steadily—from 35 percent in April to less than 5 percent in June and July of 1976. During this initial period, price behavior seemed to follow the historical pattern, in a manner that accorded with the level of wages and the exchange rate. However, six months into the program, prices in the internal-market sector started to go up rapidly again; during the following six months the cost of living

TABLE 7

Evolution of Prices

(Monthly variation rates)

Month	1976		1977		1978	
	Retail	Wholesale	Retail	Wholesale	Retail	Wholesale
January	8.9%	19.5%	8.0%	13.8%	13.4%	10.1%
February	19.0	28.6	8.3	7.0	6.2	5.3
March	37.6	54.1	7.5	3.9	9.5	9.0
April	33.9	26.3	6.0	5.7		
May	12.1	4.8	6.5	6.3		
June	2.7	4.7	7.6	6.6		
July	4.2	6.1	7.4	5.7		
August	5.5	8.0	11.3	12.6		
September	10.6	8.8	8.3	7.3		
October	8.5	4.4	12.5	13.6		
November	8.0	6.8	9.0	7.9		
December	14.3	6.5	7.3	4.2		

SOURCE: Instituto Nacional de Estadísticas y Censos, Boletín Estadístico Trimestral, various numbers.

went up at an average rate of 8.2 percent a month, and the industrial-price index (wholesale, nonagricultural prices) at a rate of 7 percent a month. During the following twelve-month-period—from March 1977 to March 1978—there was a new burst of inflation which reached rates of 8 to 12 percent a month.

The course of inflation has had important effects on income distribution; these effects may be of an even deeper and more permanent nature because of the long-term tendencies generated by the stabilization program. The seriousness of the internal-market shrinkage induced by this policy is directly related to these inflationary tendencies. The persistence of a "monetarist" diagnosis of inflation justifies the renewed application of contracting measures; if we add the reinforcing effect of a policy designed to "open" the internal market for foreign industrial products, the effects are twofold (as the recent Chilean experience shows all too clearly[25]), namely a dismantling of a significant part of the industrial sector, and a drop in real wages that takes income-distribution patterns back to what they were several decades ago.

To examine the impact of the programs guided by the IMF's outlook

25. An important contribution on the hyperinflationary Chilean process can be found in Joseph Ramos, The Economics of Persistent Inflation and Hyperstagflation. Lessons from Inflation and Stabilization in Chile (Santiago, 1977).

under conditions of this new phenomenon of hyperstagflation, we have to point out some elements lying at the root of this process. Hyperstagflation seems to result from the combination of some elements of the stabilization program and the special circumstances under which the economy finds itself at the moment the program is enacted.

The balance-of-payments crisis that the program was trying to confront was accompanied by an acceleration of the inflation rate from mid-1975 onwards; at its highest points, inflation had reached more than 30 percent a month. Government price controls were increasingly ineffective, and black markets had become standard; the economy was beginning to resemble more and more a collection of highly speculative markets. One of the characteristics of this situation is the significant impairment of the ability of the economic participants to make medium- and long-term predictions. Accordingly, investment that depends on such prediction goes down. Another characteristic is the importance assumed by short-term expectations; a high value is thus placed on all information that facilitates their formulation. With such high rates of inflation, short-term expectations have to be related not only to future demand but also to the future price of inputs and of the enterprises' assets. The key to this process seems to be the relationship between the amount of time required for producing and selling a given product and the rate at which the prices of these goods change. In the short term, the amount of time needed for production and sales is less than the time needed to collect information about significant variations in the prices of inputs and assets.[26] Sales prices thus have to include estimates of the future prices of these goods. Mistakes in predicting these future prices can be very costly, eating into the capital of those businesses that underestimate them. On the one hand, these characteristics of the market give rise to a pressing demand for information to formulate short-term expectations. On the other hand, a risk-avoiding policy by those who set prices will probably tend to overestimate future prices, thus leading to an increase in the expected inflation rate and to a consequent rise in the markup.[27]

The stabilization program's policy measures respond to the demand for information; however, far from dampening inflation as they are intended to, they have exactly the opposite effect. In the first place, the disappearance of government price controls (announced as a critical step to allow the free play of the "invisible hand") in fact increases the

26. Variations that affect expected returns, and on some occasions capital itself.
27. In addition to its self-accelerating effect on inflation, this has effects on the level of sales and general economic activity, as well as on income distribution.

high level of uncertainty in the economy. It eliminates one of the main sources of information for short-term expectations, diminishing the visibility of those who set prices, but it also stimulates even more the need for information. In this context of reduced visibility and increased sensitivity, information provided by agricultural prices, prices, tariffs in the public sector, and the interest rate—determined directly or indirectly by the program's policies—boost expectations, accelerating the inflationary pace in the internal-market sector.

In effect, both the evolution of prices and tariffs in the public sector and the level of the interest rate are dependent on the control and restriction of the monetary supply set by the counter-inflationary program. As far as public enterprises are concerned, the plan to reduce the government deficit involves a price policy that tries to get ahead of inflation by means of periodic price increases; this then becomes an expansive factor in the formation of expectations.

In Argentina, the goal of controlling monetary variables led to a transformation of the financial sector and the way it operates. Policies in this area have brought into being a financial market with a great diversity of very short-term assets; given high rates of inflation, this market operates under highly speculative conditions. To raise the interest rate was part of the counter-inflationary program; this objective was pursued by direct and indirect means. Intensive use of private credit for overcoming the public deficit was strongly encouraged; federal support for provincial governments and institutions, public enterprises, and municipalities was curtailed, and these bodies were asked to finance their deficits through price increases, taxation, or loans from the financial market. Passive and active real interest rates went up, with the latter reaching in some periods a monthly rate of 8 percent. Table 8 shows the evolution of interest rates during the second half of 1977 and first months of 1978. The real monthly interest rate shows variations of up to seven points in certain periods.

The inflationary "push" of high interest rates is probably not limited to shaping short-term expectations but also exercises pressure on prices through an increase in the financial costs of the internal-market sector. During the severe recession that took place in late 1977 and early 1978, coinciding with a boom in interest rates, interest rates reached a real rate of approximately 30 percent per four-month period, in relation to the prices of that sector. Some indication of this can be seen in Table 9, where the active, thirty-day interest rate has been adjusted by the monthly rate at which some wholesale prices rose, accumulating in the resulting rate for the last quarter of 1977.

TABLE 8

Interest Rates for 30 Days

	1977			1978		
	Passive	Active	Rise in wholesale prices	Passive	Active	Rise in wholesale prices
January				10.3%	13.5%	10.1%
February				8.1	11.2	5.3
March				7.0	9.2	9.0
April				6.8	8.3	9.5
•••						
June	6.1%	7.4%	6.6%			
July	6.6	7.2	5.7			
August	7.3	8.2	12.6			
September	8.0	9.2	7.3			
October	9.4	12.2	13.6			
November	10.3	13.7	7.8			
December	10.6	13.6	4.2			

SOURCE: Interest rates, Fundación de Investigaciones Económicas Latinoamericanas, *Informe Financiero Mensual*, various numbers. Prices, Instituto Nacional de Estadísticas y Censos, *Boletín Estadístico Trimestral*, various numbers.

A summary of the main effects of the stabilization program outlined so far can thus only conclude that of all its explicit short-term objectives the only one that has been achieved is a definite easing in the international payments situation. Inflation goes on unabated at a high and fluctuating level; the "freedom-of-prices" policy, apparently imposed as a counter-inflationary measure, has merely meant that the state has lost its capacity to regulate and control. Something similar has happened in capital markets, where, with the participation of foreign finance capital, heavy speculation takes place;[28] this has resulted in an unstable financial situation that reduces the options available to the state in this regard. There has been a drop in productive investment, and the conditions created by the program do not seem to have attracted direct investment by transnational enterprises. Long term confidence on the part of the local bourgeoisie and transnational investors has not been

28. During the last quarter of 1977 and the first of 1978, there was an inflow of over one billion dollars of private finance capital into the country. Data from the Central Bank, Republic of Argentina.

TABLE 9

Ratio Between the Active Short-Term Interest Rate and the Growth Rate of Some Wholesale Prices

(September–December 1977)

Sector	Ratio	Sector	Ratio
Food and beverages	25.7%	Oil	34.5%
Tobacco	10.6	Rubber	−0.2
Textiles	25.8	Leather	38.2
Clothing	17.0	Stone	−1.5
Wood	30.4	Metals	6.1
Paper	16.2	Vehicles	7.5
Chemicals	16.8	Machines and tools	6.3

SOURCE: Table 8 and Instituto Nacional de Estadísticas y Censos, *Boletín Estadístico Trimestral*, various numbers.

restored.[29] Present internal-market tendencies and inflation make it unlikely that confidence will be restored in the near future. The country is thus faced with a strong recession, a drastic reduction in real wages, and a regressive redistribution of income that is unique in Argentine history.

It is by no means easy to identify the beneficiaries of this economic policy in the industrial sector.[30] Even though, as in all recessionary processes, there has been an expansion of some groups to the detriment of others, the contraction of the internal market has affected industrial activity to such a degree that, in some sectors, one would have to go back ten years to find production levels similar to the ones of 1978. The direct beneficiaries of this economic policy should be those in the traditional export sectors that are identified by the program as the axis on which the economy will be rebuilt. However, inflation and the more

29. The total amount of foreign direct investment during 1977 was only 52 million dollars. Data from the Central Bank, Republic of Argentina.

30. This evaluation refers to enterprises considered sectorial activities and encompasses only the short term. There is no doubt that industrial entrepreneurs have made immense profits through commercial and financial speculation in this period. On the other hand, it is not our purpose to refer here to the long-term accumulation strategy that might be implicit in the short-term measures of the stabilization program. In this regard, our evaluation in this paper is limited to the framework of the objectives that have been explicitly acknowledged by the authorities. A good sample of these objectives can be found in the memorandum that provides the technical foundation for the agreement with the IMF for the first half of 1977: *Boletín Semanal del Ministerio de Economía*, no. 179, May 2, 1977.

recent exchange policy has reduced considerably the benefits they originally received from the program. The most direct beneficiaries are unquestionably those sectors related to financial speculation, an activity that has attracted a significant part of business profits.

If it is difficult to find direct beneficiaries of the stabilization program among internal social participants, this is not the case once we move to the international scene. The critical balance-of-payments situation was quickly solved by the program; this made it possible for the country to pay 1,100 million dollars as foreign-debt service during 1976 and 1977.[31] In this respect, the success story of the Argentine stabilization program can be best told by international creditors. Not only have they been paid punctually, but they have also been offered, as a warranty, a foreign-currency-reserve stock equal to a fifteen-month import bill.[32] International creditors could hardly be happier regarding the success of the IMF's recommendations.

We will now turn our attention to the internal political processes of those countries where the stabilization programs agreed upon with the IMF are enacted through the imposition of a BA state.

POLITICS AND ECONOMICS

Robert Campos, Otávio Bulhoes, Jorge Cauas, Guillermo Vegh Villegas, Adalbert Krieger Vasena and José Martínez de Hoz—champions of the stabilization programs undertaken by the Latin American BA states—all have one thing in common. Before becoming cabinet ministers they all belonged to the group that, in their own countries, had extensive personal relations with private and public international financial circles. In fact, they were all part of the local "chapter" of those circles. This was one of the reasons they were appointed to their positions in the first place. The abrupt implantation of BA states, starting with the Brazilian coup of 1964,[33] was an effort to put an end to a situation perceived by many as a deep political and economic crisis. A high inflation rate and an acute balance-of-payments crisis were some of its elements.

31. Data from the Central Bank, Republic of Argentina.
32. As of March 31, 1978. Considering the level of reserves as of December 31, 1977, and 1977 imports, Argentina ranked first in a world ranking of external liquidity coefficients (reserves/annual imports). The Argentine coefficient duplicates that of the country occupying second place in the ranking. Data from IMF, *International Financial Statistics*, March, 1977.
33. On the Brazilian BA state, see Guillermo O'Donnell, "Reflexiones sobre las tendencias generales," and "Tensiones en el Estado Burocrático—Autoritario y la Cuestión de la Democracia," CEDES/GE. CLACSO no. 11, Buenos Aires, 1978.

To overcome this situation it seemed imperative to reach an agreement with the "international financial community"—starting with the IMF—on a set of policies that would make available the resources needed to alleviate the crisis. Nobody could do a better job in going north with these programs, it was thought, than these cabinet ministers. They already enjoyed considerable prestige in such circles, and they were convinced, too, that the objectives and policy measures embodied in those programs were the expressions of an economic rationality without which it would be impossible to rescue these countries from their respective crises. We will elaborate further on this topic below, but it is important to emphasize at the outset that we are dealing with an issue involving complex causality. It is simplistic to believe that "somebody" imposed these programs from abroad. But is also simplistic (or diplomatic) to assert that a given government "freely" elected a certain program that was "later" approved by the IMF. What we are really facing is a convergence of determinations, or better still, a case of overdetermination. Even without the need for the IMF's blessings, the stabilization program of these cabinet ministers would have been similar to the one they agreed on with the IMF. On the other hand, even if the respective economic teams did not believe that these policies would succeed, the need to formulate a program to satisfy the IMF and the international financial community would also have determined a policy package similar to the one actually approved. This convergence is one of the issues we are interested in exploring here.

It would be superfluous to again go into the various analytical points we have made in other studies quoted above. We shall limit ourselves then to setting out a few crucial aspects of the establishment of the BA state, which is generally founded as a fearful response to what many consider a deep economic crisis. Politically, society seems to be characterized by great disorder; the state shows a decreasing capacity to guarantee the current system of domination; the threat that society might collapse is seen as a very real one. This threatening feeling leads the bourgeoisie to rally around its basic interest—the ability to reproduce itself as a class. This provides the support for the coup undertaken by the Armed Forces, in turn permeated by the doctrine of national security, which acts as a reinforcing factor. The middle sectors, incensed by disorder and the "insolence" of formerly passive sectors of society and by the economic uncertainty they are going through, also throw their support behind the coup.

This predetermines the two great tasks that the emerging government sets for itself. The first of them is to reintroduce order. This involves dismantling any threatening popular political activities, eliminating their political self-expression, and putting trade unions under strict control. This, with the suspension of all institutions of political democracy, results in the political exclusion of the popular sectors and their allies. The second great task is to "normalize" the economy; that is, to stabilize some crucial variables, and supposedly in the long term to again begin economic growth on the basis of a more efficient and healthy productive structure. There are, however, serious obstacles in the path of these objectives.

First, the political and economic uncertainties of the previous period have led almost everyone—including the bourgeoisie—to speculative behavior that in turn deepens the crisis. This has resulted in a lack of investment, the flight of capital, and a dislocation of the capital accumulation circuit. Second, especially in the cases of Chile, 1973, and Argentina, 1976, the situation has expressed itself in an extremely high and fluctuating rate of inflation. On the other hand, the growth rate of the economy as a whole has slowed down; the balance-of-payments situation has reached a point where the country might be unable to meet its foreign obligations.

It is in this context that the stabilization programs insert themselves. Their objective is to redress the economic situation, approaching first of all the problem that is both the most urgent and the easiest to handle —the balance-of-payments situation. To overcome its foreign-payments problem the country needs three things: new credit lines; a comprehensive renegotiation of its foreign debt, since the burden of the debt has been made even more unbearable by the previous crisis;[34] and a consequent easing of conditions for other commercial and financial international transactions. As long as one of the immediate manifestations of the crisis is in the balance-of-payments situation and its alleviation requires some sort of solution in that sphere, the problem "naturally" comes under the IMF's jurisdiction. Policies that are required to obtain the IMF's and the international financial community's support then emerge.

This implies a crucial task for the new governments and their internal supporters—the restoration of international confidence in the country. This is by no means easy; to begin with, the image of a previous situation that generated deep pessimism about the future has to be overcome. This was an evaluation not only of a certain government, but also of

34. Undoubtedly helped by the hostility towards the internal situation showed by governments and private creditors.

a country that had the explosive potential to reach such a situation in the first place. Nevertheless, in spite of the efforts to restore order, the renewal of trust in the future of the economy also demands a guarantee that order will be maintained at least for the period of time considered sufficient by potential investors. The political exclusion of the popular sectors and their allies is the main component of that guarantee. But this implies also that the popular sectors—especially the working class and the public employees—lose the capacity to participate in determining their income. This leads to additional measures to put the trade unions under control; the right to strike is eliminated, and wage levels are set by the government in a manner that leads to a severe, regressive redistribution of income. As a consequence, the popular sectors are also excluded economically. Again, there is an understanding that these controls (an aspect of the class dimension of the imposed order) will continue for the time span set by those who are evaluating the new economic situation. After all, the history of these countries has shown recurrent attempts to impose strong governments, and, with or without them, to enact stabilization programs that were aborted because of political activism and the ability of the popular sector and its allies to formulate economic demands. For that reason, to be able to obtain trust and confidence neither a new strong government, nor a "correct" economic program, nor prestigious cabinet ministers are enough. All these are necessary but not sufficient conditions; the important point is to convince the international financial community that "this time" these arrangements will last.[35]

Paradoxically, the very deepness of the previous crisis lends credence to such an assertion. The deeper the crisis, the greater the effort and cost needed to impose order; accordingly, it seems more and more probable that to return to the demagogic past is out of the question. But this is not enough. The top positions in the state are held by members of the Armed Forces. Yet, institutionally this is the segment of the state and the social group that is in principle least compatible with the stabilization policies to be undertaken and with their executors. Is it possible to make the socialization of the Armed Forces (reinforced by national-security doctrines centered on the potentialities of the nation) compatible with the basic approach and consequences of a policy that in so many ways

---

35. The previous bureaucratic-authoritarian experiment in Argentina (1966–70) shows this very clearly. After the success of its relatively unorthodox stabilization program (in turn related to a significantly less serious preceding crisis), the great social upheavals of 1969 led to a rapid evaporation of confidence and an aggravated resurgence of the crisis the 1966 coup had apparently eliminated.

implies precisely the opposite? The internationalization of the productive structure, the predominance of "efficiency" criteria over those of national origin and control and the dismantling of a significant portion of industry (precisely that sector under unquestionable national control) are only some of the consequences of the stabilization programs. They appear to be, prima facie, deeply opposed to the very heart of the belief system the Armed Forces are supposed to have. This puzzle cannot be solved by analyzing the discourse of those involved, and this is not the place to attempt to do so. Suffice it to say that for the period dealt with in this study (the adoption and initial implementation of the stabilization programs), there is one factor providing a common bond between the members of the Armed Forces and the economic "technicians"—a belief that the deepness of the previous crisis demands unhesitating, drastic action. The Armed Forces view the nation as a sick body needing surgery, even terrible surgery, to be saved. The technicians view the situation as the ideal occasion to use another sort of scalpel, namely their belief in an economy saved from "demagogic temptations" through the suppression of "politics" and the elimination of the pressures that for many years prevented then from putting their policies into practice in the "right manner" (i.e. using drastic measures that last as long as necessary to obtain the desired effects). Since both groups tend to see a similar "illness," they can communicate on the similarities of the hard tasks—order and normalization—that both are taking up with their respective tools.

The second important problem of these policies is that they not only punish many by excluding them, but that they also bring severe hardship to many supporters of the coup. It is evident that only a small group in those sectors that back the establishment of a BA state benefit from these programs. The need to cut the government deficit leads to a drastic drop in income among public employees, as well as to numerous dismissals that highlight the uncertainty of even those meager salaries. On the other hand, the recession, credit, and cash shortages, and the increased concentration on the productive structure tend to harm a broad spectrum of people, from small merchants (lumping together, in its typical fate, most of the petty bourgeoisie that had been so active against disorder) to a significant portion of the industrial and commercial bourgeoisie. And we are not referring here merely to a drop in income or to an increase in the number of bankruptcies; the basic problem arises from the lack of protection of various bourgeois factions from the actions both of oligopolistic sectors and of the more internationalized segments of the bourgeoisie itself. Many enterprises find that they cannot any longer rely on the state—which may have been demagogic but was also nationalist and protective—and that this change has occurred precisely at the moment when, owing to the recession, their economic space is shrinking.[36]

The question, then, becomes more complex than simply one of guaranteeing the continuity of these policies against the opposition of the excluded. Continuity has to be preserved despite the grumblings of those who were part of the coalition backing the BA state. Some of these bourgeois sectors are difficult to repress, and they can hardly be accused of having supported the previous, threatening process. In addition, the middle sectors and the local bourgeoisie can voice an argument that is bound to be much more amenable to the Armed Forces' outlook than the rationale of the technicians. How is it possible to think about the potentialities of the nation if the long-term result of these policies is a productive structure dismantled for cold "efficiency" reasons, with an extremely meager local bourgeoisie and with a state apparatus that has also been dismantled (at least in terms of the technicians' statements, not in observed results)? On the other hand, how can these objectives be reconciled with a process favoring the export sector and finance capital to the detriment of productive activities of an industrial and commercial nature? And a strong argument for those worried about subversive activities—how will such an economic arrangement provide employment to the masses, who presumably will not remain silent indefinitely?

Nonetheless, with the exception of Argentina during the previous bureaucratic-authoritarian experience, the technicians of the stabilization program and their policies have stayed in office for a much longer period than any examination of public pressure on the program's main allies in the state apparatus would allow us to predict. What are the reasons for this situation? Despite the opposition of the excluded, the complaints and grumblings of so many who were originally allies, and the ambivalence of a significant portion of the Armed Forces, this challenge to the law of gravity can be explained by two reasons. The first of them (only apparently paradoxical) is that these policies are failing even within the framework of their own premises. The second is that

36. For an initial approach to these topics, see Guillermo O'Donnell, "Notas para el estudio de la burguesía industrial local en sus relaciones con el capital internacional y el aparato estatal," CEDES no. 12, Buenos Aires, 1978, and Instituto Latinoamericano de Estudios Transnacionales (ILET).

the convergence or overdetermination whose presence we postulated at the moment these policies were adopted is still operative. Let us examine these issues.

ACCOMPLISHMENTS AND FAILURES OF STABILIZATION

Earlier we showed how these stabilization policies tend to favor those sectors related to the export of primary products and finance capital.[37] We also examined the manner in which these policies alleviate the tight balance-of-payments situation and concluded that they were significantly less successful in their efforts to curb inflation. On the other hand, we saw that those policies tend to deepen the recession and penalize wage earners heavily through regressive income redistribution. All this leads to an economy that, officials speeches notwithstanding, moves basically around financial speculation. As a consequence, there continues to be little space for productive investment, not even for transnational capital. The economy is thus ruled fundamentally by financial speculation. In sum our argument is the following: (1) the adoption and implementation of policies that are considered reasonable by the IMF and the international financial community is a necessary condition for alleviating the balance-of-payments situation once the BA state has been implanted; (2) the deeper the preceding crisis, the more urgent that alleviation is bound to be, and the more strict and orthodox the design and implementation of policy measures have to be to "merit" international support; (3) a speculative economy is thus recreated, not only excluding the popular sectors but also suffocating the internal productive structure; although (4) the consequent improvement in the ability to meet foreign obligations is perfectly congruent with the interests of transnational finance capital.

The standby agreements and the subsequent opening of new credit lines are not the only indications of international approval for stabilizations policies and their stubborn implementation; there is also an inflow of external capital, on a short-term basis. Nonetheless, the limits of the confidence these programs may develop is shown by their incapacity

---

37. One of the effects we do not deal with here—basically because it manifests itself more in the long term—is that the higher sectors of the industrial and commercial bourgeoisie, although often suffering the consequences of this drastic market shrinkage, are frequently able to make strong progress in their degree of market control, owing to the recession and the consequent increase in the mortality rate of weaker enterprises. This helps to consolidate even more the highly concentrated nature of the urban productive structure.

to attract important amounts of transnational capital for direct investment purposes to economies that find themselves in a recession and plagued by numerous uncertainties.

The only relative success of these stabilization policies (which in fact do not promote stability at all) is in improving the balance-of-payments situation.[38] However, to maintain the improvement it is necessary to obey the codes of presumed economic rationality permeating the IMF's outlook and embodied in these agreements. The reason for this state of affairs is not difficult to ascertain: the loss of the short-term confidence placed on the stabilization program would lay bare, even for its own supporters, the failure of policies that have already involved such a high cost in many respects. Consequently, what is to be done? Assuming that there has not been any significant change in the correlation of forces,[39] the only alternative—unfortunately for many—seems to be to engage in more of the same. That is, to persist a little longer in those policies, hoping that this tenacity will finally attract foreign capital on a long-term basis; as the efficiency levels of the productive structure are improved (basically a euphemism for its dismantling) it is hoped that the economy will start to grow again, through the appearance of forces stronger and more dynamic than those provided by an oversized financial sector and the export sector.[40]

This may allow us to explain the continuity of policies (like those implemented in Chile since 1973 and in Argentina since 1976) that lack

38. This statement assumes the existence of some interest in the protection and eventual expansion of the internal productive structure. In terms of the IMF's and the international creditors' standpoint—basically interested, as we have already argued, in a "solid" balance-of-payments position and in free international movement of capital—these internal troubles are much less important than the achievements obtained in the latter fields.

39. For a number of reasons, including those mentioned in this study, we do not consider it plausible for any such change to occur through the internal dynamics of this state; change will have to come from outside the state; any such tendencies are, of course, under severe control, especially during the initial stage we are examining.

40. In this study we are focusing on the short-term period immediately after the BA state has been implanted and the stabilization program has started. It is therefore not possible to enter here into the subject of the "model" and the long-term tendencies within which these developments take place; that issue, however, constitutes a central aspect of the collective project mentioned above. Any analysis of those tendencies will demand careful comparative work that will pay attention to the specific features of the economic and social structures of the countries of the Southern Cone, as well as to the severity and characteristics of the preceding crisis. Nonetheless, the short-term stabilization programs deserve specific attention; their impacts contribute decisively to rearticulate society as a whole to the benefit of a small—but obviously powerful—group of economic participants.

almost any social support and hurt many sectors that originally backed the BA state. It is not true that these policies lack any social support whatsoever, or that nobody benefits from them; the point rather is that the supporters and beneficiaries are an extraordinarily small group, which imposes on the economy a particularly perverse manner of reproduction that hurts not only its opponents but also a significant portion of the bourgeoisie itself.

This is one of the points where the overlap between economics and politics appears clearly. In Latin America there have been numerous stabilization programs during more or less democratic periods. Their implementation, however, broke down earlier than in the cases we are analyzing now, not only because the capacity, now suppressed, of the popular sectors to fight for their wages was then effective, but also because of the influence of the bourgeois factions hurt by those policies.[41] It is only since the establishment of the BA state that governments have been able to stick obstinately to these programs. It is perfectly obvious that the mission of imposing order is incompatible with the demands of the popular sectors; however, it is also evident that in today's Argentina, Chile, and Uruguay the complaints of important bourgeois sectors have fallen on deaf ears.

What are the reasons for this? The answer to this question is a fairly complex one, and we can here only provide a partial approximation to it. The roots of the explanation lie in the seriousness of the preceding crisis; the deeper the crisis has been, the greater the dislocation of the economy, and, more important, the greater the feeling that capitalist society was coming to an end. This fear is remembered by the bourgeoisie during the following period; the BA state, despite its enactment of policies hurting the economic interests of various bourgeois sectors, is thus considered the savior of the bourgeoisie as a class. This in turn limits in the short- and medium-run, the possibility of alliances with the popular sectors (who are seen as the bearer of the threat) and increases the harshness of the imposed order. The bourgeoisie's grumblings are thus translated merely into bureaucratic infighting within the state apparatus—trying, on a piecemeal basis, to minimize the cost of these policies—but unable to develop any alternatives to them. In other words, the opacity, bureaucratism, and lack of overall perspective of the defensive maneuvers undertaken by most bourgeois sectors (fractions, groups, and even individual enterprises) make it impossible for their efforts to

41. On this point, see Guillermo O'Donnell, "Estado y Alianzas en la Argentina, 1956–1976," CEDES/GE CLACSO no. 5, Buenos Aires, 1977, and *Desarrollo Económico*, vol. 16, no. 64.

appear as a credible defense of the general interest. The only argument that qualifies at least partially in this regard is the one embodied in vague references to a sort of nationalism without the people (whom the BA state, with its "order" mission excludes). The bourgeoisie as a whole is grateful that the BA state has saved it as a class; consequently, it limits itself to grumblings when, in the first stages, the normalization technicians crucify a not insignificant part of the bourgeoisie as a tribute to an efficient and internationalized capitalism. At that point, these sectors discover that in previous periods conditions for their reproduction existed but that they have now been eliminated by the BA state; despite their demagogic character, these conditions (which had almost been overrun at the end of the preceding period) provided important protection. At the same time, in a context that presupposes the exclusion of the popular sectors—their possible allies—these groups discover their inability to promote an alternative within the BA state's cabinet politics. The threat of the popular sector is still too recent, the coercive power of the state is focused too heavily on it, and its past threat to capitalist society is still on the bourgeois mind. For that reason, the most that can be expected are pious appeals to the effects that the drop in real wages has had on the recession, showing thus once again how divided and petty the bourgeoisie's schizophrenic attitude towards the BA state is. In any case, all this does not go beyond complaints and rumors that are locked into the dynamic imposed by the order and normalization tasks of the BA state; it cannot, for the moment, become a serious alternative to the ongoing economic program.

Grumblings and complaints can also be heard within the Armed Forces; as time goes by, and the costs to be paid as well as the failure of these policies become evident, the dismantling of the productive structure in its most genuinely national sectors (which is by no means a coincidence in these dependent capitalist economies) is increasingly apparent. In addition, the efforts of the local bourgeoisie to minimize the costs of these policies and to explore the possibility of a less burdensome alternative are directed precisely toward the Armed Forces. Since little information is available in the mass media, a tremendous variety of rumors results. There is talk about this or that group within the services being opposed to the economic policies, and intrabureaucratic struggles revolve around the continuity of the policies in which the interests of bourgeois forces are reflected. Nonetheless, despite casual algebraic operations regarding the correlation of forces—according to which the stabilization program is about to be scrapped—the continuity of the program is reaffirmed over and over again. To understand this phenomenon we have to take into account an important element within the Armed Forces. The initial authorities of the BA state, pressed by the need to obtain quickly the IMF's and the internationational financial community's blessings, commit themselves deeply to the economic program as well as to the technicians embodying it. This commitment of the top military authorities is one of the basic conditions (aside from implanting order) for developing the confidence needed to obtain balance-of-payments relief. The international financial community has had too many experiences with "acceptable" programs that could not be implemented owing to a lack of political and military support. The authorities of the BA state thus do not have many alternatives to sticking with the program no matter what; amidst the doubts and dissident opinions of their own colleagues, they can only hope that perseverance will ultimately bear fruit and bring about the goals of a lower inflation rate, a moderate expansion, and an efficient economy. After having announced *urbe et orbi* that the stabilization program, accepted as the essence of economic rationality, is the program of the Armed Forces, who will therefore support it along the harsh road of its implementation, the supreme authorities of the BA state are tied to it. The program gives rise to dissent and opposition, but any real alternative to it—a change in the course of the economy with a concomitant realignment of alliances —is extremely dangerous for the permanence in office of the authorities. The obvious leaders of any new period would be the military officers who have been arguing all along against the stabilization program, and have been developing links with those bourgeois sectors who share their notion of a BA state that is more benign economically, although no less concerned with keeping order.

In addition, the Armed Forces have seen, together with the bourgeoisie, the dangers of the previous period; they have also assumed the responsibility of imposing order. They tend to share, therefore, the fear of developments that might be taking place behind the wall of silence imposed on a large part of society.[42] Therefore, decisions on any policy alternative—and primarily on any new economic policy—must include a credible guarantee that they will not lead to a reactivation of the threats whose suppression was so demanding.

Another factor provides additional support to the stabilization pro-

---

42. This is one of the reasons for the search for mediation and "participation" mechanisms; it can also account for the emergence of certain democratic postulates within this state, which would otherwise be a surreal phenomenon. For a development of this topic, see Guillermo O'Donnell, "Tensiones en el Estado Buro-crático-Autoritario," CEDES/GE CLACSO no. 11, Buenos Aires, 1978.

gram; expressions of international support for the program and its executors—conveniently publicized throughout the world—play an important role in this regard. They are generally combined with explicit warnings that any abandonment of the program would mean the loss of international confidence, and therefore the wasting of all costly efforts already made. These warnings and the implications of losing the internal and international support already achieved by the program become an important element in the internal political struggle in the BA state. It is there that the external support comes in to back the economic teams and the policy directives provided by them. Other alternatives either cannot be articulated by the excluded sectors, or appear to be, as reflected in the complaints of numerous bourgeois factions and groups within the Armed Forces, understandable but premature concerns. They might be dealt with "at the appropriate moment," once the economic program has finally borne the fruits it is supposed to.

In sum, there is nothing inevitable about the continuity of policies that have failed in so many ways and can show only one accomplishment (in the balance-of-payments area). However, once the BA state is implanted, and the need arises to ask the IMF for urgent relief, it is a necessary condition that the economic apparatus within the BA state be controlled by personnel whose outlook agrees with the IMF's, and that the Armed Forces' leadership be deeply committed to support this program. From that moment on there is no going back, and the program has to be continued for a much longer period than one would expect, given the grumblings of its important allies and its evident failures. Undoubtedly, an additional element in this situation is provided by the very nature of the game in question—largely cabinet and bureaucratic politics, to which, by definition, those sectors excluded by the BA state have no access. In this context, the misfortunes of the weaker and more nationally oriented factions of the bourgeoisie can only lead to small battles over minor issues.

This combination of factors explains why policies that harm a vast majority of the population continue to be implemented even after it is evident that their many failures cannot be matched by any comparable list of achievements. The background to these developments is provided by bureaucratic politics, since the popular sectors have been excluded and all representation channels that would make it possible to transmit general-interest arguments have been eliminated. Thus the phenomenon of this markedly capitalist state's harsh punishment of factions of its own bourgeoisie and total deafness to their hesitant complaints becomes intelligible. The resulting rumor-filled vacuum creates the conditions for the perseverance of an economic program harmful to the interests of society as a whole; its policies are perceived to be the only way to avoid the threatening dangers of the recent past.

VARIATIONS

If we move to a case that is in some ways exactly the opposite of that of contemporary Chile, Argentina, and Uruguay—the normalization program that started in March 1967 during the preceding bureaucratic-authoritarian experiment in Argentina—our argument may become clearer. That program achieved some significant results (it did more than merely ease the balance-of-payments situation), but until now it has also been the only one to be interrupted, owing to a chain of circumstances started by the May 1969 events (the Cordobazo) and their sequels. This combination of success and abrupt end was not a mere coincidence.

The 1967 program was launched under much more favorable conditions than the ones existing in the 1970's. The level of political threat was lower and the economic crisis had by no means the seriousness it later had in Chile, Uruguay, and Argentina. Largely in response to this, the standby agreement with the IMF as well as the ensuing loans from transnational banking consortia and the U.S. Government set up less stringent conditions. The agreement in fact admitted that inflation was determined mainly by costs and the expectations of economic participants and not by demand. This allowed for an expansive monetary policy and easier credit (which is not possible if demand is seen as the main cause of inflation). On the other hand, orthodoxy reasserted itself by requiring the elimination of the government deficit, although this was clearly incompatible with the diagnosis of inflation that had been made. However, this problem was solved by the government's heavy taxing of the *pampa*'s bourgeoisie. Their high income made it possible for the government to appropriate part of it through manipulation of export prices. Although the tax obviously antagonized this sector of the bourgeoisie, it had the fundamental advantage of reducing the government deficit and launching an important program of public investment. The dynamic impulse of such a tax has not been available in Argentina, Chile, or Uruguay in the 1970's.[43]

43. In the case of Argentina this fraction of the bourgeoisie has had to be incorporated into the ruling coalition (at the cost of not taxing it); this development, showing that the question can by no means be reduced to an economic problem, has led the government to lose that source of income.

As a direct consequence of the tax, by 1968 inflation had gone down considerably, and the economy had started to grow again. Although the process was characterized by the increasing concentration and internationalization of capital as well as by a regressive redistribution of income (although less markedly than in the other cases), the program had been quite successful.

And this was the problem. In effect, why should the country go on enduring the costs and the denationalization process implied in the program if its achievements made it possible to go back to policies supporting the more national sectors of the bourgeoisie? Wasn't it possible now, thanks to the improved balance-of-payments situation, to reactivate the internal market through wage increases? These questions allowed the industrial and commercial local bourgeoisie to find in the state apparatus (mainly in the Armed Forces) allies willing to promote what appeared to be a viable, fair, and national alternative of capitalist development. In addition, the lower level of threat apparently posed by the popular sectors (which had not articulated any socialist goals) had led to less severe controls over them; they could thus be presented as an ally that would not awake any fears. All this paved the way for the crucial political event that has not been possible on other occasions— the formation of a winning combination of these various sectors that agrees on the need to replace the economic program.

The main point is that the contemporary cases, starting from a far deeper crisis and level of threat, have been less successful in their explicit premises and goals than Argentina in 1967–69. It is not *in spite* but *because* of this that these programs are kept alive; their very failure seems to preclude any other alternative. Any substantial drop in inflation and resurgence of growth in the economy would politically undermine the continuity of these programs. This is not only because of the opposition of the popular sectors but also because many original supporters of the BA state may visualize the possibility of reorienting economic policies towards goals that are more compatible with their immediate interests.

Grumblings and rumors notwithstanding, there is no better guarantee for the continuity of the stabilization programs and the permanence in office of the technicians implementing them, than their own failure. Their failure is at the same time their success, as well as the fundamental root of significant support by the IMF and the international financial community. There is no greater risk for the program, aside from challenges that might come from outside the imposed power system, than its own success in curbing inflation and achieving economic growth. On the other hand, nothing is so helpful in subordinating these capitalist economies and an important part of their own ruling classes than the disruptions imposed by financial speculation. Also, few things exemplify as well the political importance of apparently having saved capitalism in those countries, even at such a cost.

It must be evident by now that this study is of a highly tentative and partial nature. There is still much to be done, from the perspective both of the center and of the periphery, to increase our understanding of institutions, processes, and effects involving more than complex economic issues. At least we hope to have shown the intrinsic overlap between economics and politics in this area of our concern. Among other things, these economic programs are supported by a narrow (albeit powerful) social segment, and the congruence of these postulates with the free play of market forces is contradicted by rigid governmental wage controls. These programs thus cannot be implemented without a state that is sufficiently authoritarian to suppress the opposition rising against their high social cost. The technocratic argument about the neutrality of this or any other economic policy is of course fallacious. However—going a bit beyond this obvious point—in these cases it seems to be clear that only such an authoritarian state can take upon itself the harsh implementation of such programs. There is thus a contradiction between recent efforts arising in countries of the center to safeguard certain values and the fact that their institutions, directly or through the IMF, uphold policies demanding a very particular type of state. Whether this support results from explicit decisions or—as is probably more frequent—from the belief that in certain situations there is only one type of economic rationality, the IMF's outlook, is relatively unimportant in terms of the immediate impacts of those programs. However, on a long-term basis, the impetus of what is apparently obvious and of beliefs reinforced by the authority of "the" science points to an ideological field that has been largely abandoned by those who might formulate the type of critical questions we have been concerned with.

Some Notes on the Origins of the Orientations and Functions of the IMF

The IMF was born as one of the institutions intended to reconstruct world economic order after the Second World War—an issue that came up among the Allies around the middle of the war. The idea was not so much to revitalize the old, destroyed system, as to find a new arrangement for international economic relations, since the international economic order had been in a deep crisis long before the war. Until the twenties, the principles of laissez-faire had more or less intermittently dominated international economic relations. This notion provided the basis for a relatively simple international policy, inspired by the desideratum of free trade, and the consequent removal of all obstacles in the path of the "invisible hand" in international and national markets. The gold standard was the monetary system designed to allow the functioning of these relations through a self-correcting mechanism of balance-of-payments disequilibrium and through monetary movements that would affect the level of prices, investment, and economic activity in general.

In practice the gold standard imposed a painful adjustment process on the national economies with external disequilibria. This adjustment was not always accepted with good grace; on various occasions, the observance of the free-trade principles was violated to safeguard national interests. The coup de grace to these principles, however, was given by the crisis that started in 1929 and later became the Great Depression. During the crisis, the measures that were taken to protect internal income implied an active intervention of the state in the protection of certain activities and the level of employment. In addition, these measures pushed international relations toward bilateralism, the inconvertibility of currencies, and unilateral decision making in foreign economic policy. Once the crisis showed itself to be of a deep and lasting nature, the automatic transmission of the deflationary impacts imposed by the gold-standard mechanism came to be an unforgettable experience, even for the hardheaded defenders of its principles in international trade and internal policy.

Traditional monetary theory was thus in poor standing by the early 1940's. Government practices, impelled more by the political need to overcome the crisis internally than by doctrine, had ventured along new paths. The ideological climate of the postwar period was permeated both by the New Deal experience and Keynes' ideas. Among the Allies, a favorable attitude toward intervention and control of international economic relations was to be found.

According to these opinions, any new international order ought to leave space for the benefits to be reaped from wide international trade without renouncing the national objective of full employment. Clearly, the simultaneous search for both goals required new public institutions, both at the national and international level.

These ideas, of course, were not entirely new. They still adhered to the basic principles and assumptions of free trade, although they included now the theoretical and practical developments of the previous decade. Regulation of economic activity by the state was considered as important as the advantages of free trade. The point was to organize the world in such a manner as to make free trade compatible with full employment. Multilateralism would substitute for laissez-faire, the gold standard would have to give way to some other sort of monetary system, and procedures would have to be agreed on for correcting external financial disequilibria, since the self-correcting mechanisms of the previous system had shown many insufficiencies.

It was clear that the old economic order had come to an end. It had worked as long as Britain kept her primacy in trade and international capital movements, and as long as capitalism was not faced with a crisis as serious as that of the 1930's. The interwar period witnessed the decline of Britain's leadership, and a concomitant strengthening of the United States. The destruction of productive equipment and the deterioration of economic relations brought about by the Second World War was only the culmination of a process that had started long before 1939. Toward the end of the war, multilateralism appeared to be an appropriate doctrine for a power such as the United States, whose clear economic preeminence required free access to markets and raw materials, but to whom experience had shown the disadvantages of too open and indiscriminating a system. The war came to facilitate the bargaining conditions under which a new economic system would be established. Its origins were marked by the international power relations of the postwar period as well as by the ideological climate of the era.[44]

The creation of the IMF was the result of intense negotiations principally between the United States and Great Britain. The actual functioning of the IMF often does not correspond to the original Bretton Woods design; nevertheless, we can find in the functions, characteristics, and premises that were assigned to it from the beginning some of the basic features of its impacts and future performance. Two main projects, one sponsored by Britain, the other by the United States, converged during the negotiations; there were important similarities but also significant differences between them. These

---

44. An analysis of the ideological climate and the projects that converged to create the new monetary system is provided by Richard Gardner, *Sterling-Dollar Diplomacy. Anglo American Collaboration in the Reconstruction of Multilateral Trade* (New York, 1956). The text of the original projects can be found in *The International Monetary Fund, 1945–1965*, vol. 3, part 1 (Washington, D.C., IMF, 1966).

discrepancies and differences in emphasis were not unrelated to the distinct needs and national objectives of both countries at that time. Whereas the United States was trying to institutionalize its role as the center of world capitalism by assuming an active role in its direction and control, Britain gave the highest priority to its urgent need for resources to rebuild its economy. The projects agreed, however, on the basic philosophy that ought to inspire the IMF. In the first place, they incorporated the ideas on international trade flows that predominated in the countries located at the center of the world economy. Free-trade principles would provide the basis for international economic relations; the interwar experience was evaluated as an eminently negative one, insofar as it witnessed the rise of obstacles to the free play of supply and demand in international markets, thus not permitting specialization and resource allocation according to prices and comparative advantages. Under certain circumstances, both projects admitted trade restrictions as inevitable to attain certain national goals. Nonetheless, they agreed on the general convertibility of currencies and fixed exchange rates as an ideal objective that would provide the basis for a multilateral trade system, which ought to be as inclusive as possible. To attain that objective the IMF would be instrumental in replacing the self-correcting mechanism of the previous period; both projects apparently tried to make free trade compatible with the achievement of full employment and economic development; however, they perceived foreign-trade policies as responses to short-term, immediate problems, and were mainly oriented toward counterdeflationary objectives.

Second, both projects assumed a natural tendency towards equilibrium in international transactions. According to this view, the problem was thus reduced to the provision of resources for solving transitory external disequilibria; needs arising out of structural disequilibria or more long-term causes were simply not taken into account. This lack of attention to long-range factors led to the setting up of several institutions to deal with the need to rebuild the European economies, and to ignore the specific necessities of the peripheral countries. The system envisioned in both projects was thus focused strictly on short-term problems; once this was translated into the IMF's practice, it developed into a particularly inadequate approach for the periphery's financial needs.

The peripheral countries were considered to be nothing more than sources of raw materials and markets for manufactured products. This was the role they had performed in the world economy at the beginning of the century.[45] However, neither the Ricardian paradigm of international trade, nor the multilateral approach that replaced laissez-faire, nor the notion of state regulation of foreign trade as something transitory and undesirable corresponded

45. Important bargaining took place regarding control over the peripheral economies. The United States, for example, strongly opposed preferential trade agreements. U.S. exporters were eager to enter into Britain's markets.

to the future demands and needs of the industrializing process in the peripheral economies. In several Latin American nations, counterdeflationary measures had already evolved into a policy of active protection and promotion of the internal market. As the colonial empires started to break apart, the number of new nations that needed to implement policies aimed at controlling and directing their foreign trade grew very rapidly. The basic principles of the monetary system created in Bretton Woods and expressed institutionally in the IMF were bound to conflict with those needs; this conflict would come up again and again in different forms during the following decades.

A new element in this system was the functions assigned to the IMF; they would play an important role in the relationship between the institution and the peripheral countries. Two basic issues are vital in this regard: the type of adjustment required from a member country faced with external disequilibria and the conditions required for gaining access to support-funds.[46] These matters define the nature and the degree of the IMF's intervention in national economic policy, and although there were important differences between the British and the U.S. plans,[47] we must not forget that the Bretton Woods agreements were only a partial reflection of those original projections. Many discrepancies remained unsolved and were incorporated into the treaties in the form of deliberate ambiguities; they would be confronted only later, as the IMF started to discharge its functions. In any case, the United States gained the upper hand in the negotiations, and it was thus able to impose conditions regarding both the availability and repayment terms of credits, and the economic policy of the countries requesting loans.

As far as the IMF's relationship with the peripheral economies was concerned, this implied that its basic principles were embodied in the very real power to impose conditions and control policy. The standby operations and the ensuing stabilization programs became especially important in this regard.

46. The objective of the new multilateral monetary system was to facilitate the redressing of imbalances in external accounts without having to modify the exchange rate or resort to exchange controls. These regulatory mechanisms were thus excluded *a priori*. Consequently, the main instrument for stabilizing the balance of payments was the adjustment of prices and internal income to the conditions imposed by foreign trade. This is the "adjustment mechanism" that the gold standard supposedly provided automatically through monetary movements. As a substitute for those self-adjusting mechanisms, governments now had to adopt internal economic policy measures to obtain stabilizing adjustments of their external transactions.

47. The differences between the British and the U.S. plans were related to the conditions to be imposed for selling hard currency. The U.S. plan favored the establishment of some conditions for approving British requests, whereas the British stood for unconditional withdrawal rights within fixed limits. The powers that the IMF would have over member countries gave rise to heated arguments. On this, see Gardner, *Sterling-Dollar Diplomacy*, and J. Keith Horsefield, *The International Monetary Fund 1945–1965*, vol. 1, part 1 (Washington, D.C.: IMF, 1966).

Peru and the U.S. Banks: Privatization of Financial Relations

BARBARA STALLINGS

INTRODUCTION

The dominant trend in U.S.–Latin American financial relations during the 1970's has been "privatization." After 40 years of hovering in the wings, while bilateral and multilateral agencies took center stage, the private bankers have once again assumed the dominant role in providing funds to the governments of Latin America (and other Third World nations as well). These governments have borrowed large sums from the private capital market, and they have also begun to float bond issues in Europe and New York. At the same time, multilateral aid has risen only slowly, and U.S. bilateral aid has fallen off, so that private bank funding now constitutes over 50 percent of total development finance, more than twice as much as it did a decade ago. In addition, bilateral and multilateral funding agencies are bringing the private banks into their loan arrangements, so that public sector loans themselves are being privatized.

This trend toward privatization in Latin American finance has been characterized by three main features. First, privatization has enabled the banks to maintain and even bolster their profits during the most serious global recession since the 1930's; this has occurred in spite of the so-called "country risk" problem. The banks are taking whatever steps

Barbara Stallings is Assistant Professor of Political Science at the University of Wisconsin (Madison) and a Ph.D. candidate in Economics at the University of Cambridge in England. She has published a book and various articles on the political economy of Latin America and is currently working on a study of private bank loans to Third World countries. She wishes to thank the following people for comments on earlier versions of this paper: Jonathan Aronson, Julio Cotler, Jessica Einhorn, Richard Fagen, Stuart Fagen, Richard Feinberg, E. V. K. Fitzgerald, Harry Magdoff, Cheryl Payer, Clark Reynolds, Janet Shenk, and especially Tom Seidl.

they deem necessary in order to protect and extend these profits, including reliance on public institutions. Second, privatization, while certainly not eliminating public-sector loan activity, has produced a shift in its emphasis. Thus U.S. government agencies, the World Bank, the International Monetary Fund (IMF), and similar institutions now place more stress on supporting the private sector than on taking the lead in providing funds. When necessary, this includes support for the stability of the international financial system as a whole. Third, privatization, far from benefiting Latin American countries, has squeezed them—and especially their working classes—even more than before. Terms on the new private loans are more stringent than on loans from public institutions, and private lenders are less patient about repayment. The hope (or fear) present a few years ago—that governments would gain new leverage as a result of their indebtedness—is being proved a myth.

Of all Latin American countries, Peru exhibits these trends most clearly. There, in 1976, a consortium of six U.S. banks imposed conditions for the management of the economy and undertook to monitor their implementation. In return, the banks extended a $200 million loan to tide the beleaguered Peruvian government over a growing balance-of-payments crisis. The following year, in response to widespread criticism, the banks retreated from such direct intervention and called in their ally, the International Monetary Fund. The policies the banks and the IMF imposed have left the Peruvian working class with only a fraction of its former purchasing power as the two sets of lenders—with the help of the Peruvian government itself—strive to make sure that Peru pays its debts.

Before turning to the Peruvian case, I want to present a more general historical analysis of the changing role of private banks in U.S.–Latin American financial relations. Once this is done, I will describe the economic policies of the current military regime in Peru, showing the buildup of the crisis that faced the country in mid-1976. The agreement with the banks will then be discussed, together with the effects of the banks' measures on Peru. One of those effects was the entry of the IMF into Peruvian policy-making in 1977, when the banks imposed this as a requirement for refinancing their loans. I will attempt to explain the bankers' decisions—why they moved in to monitor the Peruvian economy in 1976 and, equally important, why they then stepped back and called in the IMF in 1977. The final section offers some tentative conclusions on the meaning of the growing role of the private banks in Latin American finance—for the countries and for the banks themselves.

THE ROLE OF PRIVATE BANKS IN U.S.–LATIN
AMERICAN FINANCIAL RELATIONS

It is useful to think of the history of U.S.–Latin American financial relations as divided into three periods: 1898–1945, 1945–70, and 1970 to the present. The 1898–1945 period was characterized by the dominant role of private U.S. bankers and the U.S. government, often acting in concert. In the postwar period, by contrast, the panorama became more complex as the financial actors multiplied. The private bankers mainly retired from the field, to be replaced by the International Monetary Fund, the World Bank, the Inter-American Development Bank, the Export-Import Bank, and U.S. aid agencies. A division of labor between the various institutions was gradually worked out, as we will see below. In the 1970's, this division of labor has begun to break down as the private banks have again assumed a more important position. Although in some ways the new situation appears to be a throwback to that in the period before the Second World War, in reality it is quite different— as befits the much more complex international context.

The 1898–1945 Period

Before the twentieth century, financial activities in Latin America were predominantly the affair of European banks, especially those of England. The United States was a net importer of capital, mainly concerned with developing its own territory. The turning point was the Cuban War of Independence (the so-called Spanish-American War). With U.S. acquisition of control over Cuba in 1898, and with the further maneuvers to secure territory for building an interocean canal in 1903, the attention of banks in the United States began to be directed toward the south.

The main activity during the 1898–1945 period was the floating of bonds for Latin American governments by major U.S. banking houses.[1] Between 1898 and 1914, Latin American securities sold in the United States amounted to $236 million; the outstanding value as of December 31, 1914, was approximately $156 million. Between 1915 and 1935, such sales increased more than tenfold to $2,672 million—$674 million in

1. Other banking activities included the beginning of U.S. branch banking in Latin America after the change in U.S. legislation in 1914. By 1925, there were around 50 branches in Latin America, most of them involved in financing U.S. trade. See Clyde Phelps, *The Expansion of American Banks* (New York, 1927), esp. pp. 131–66.

short-term and $1,998 million in long-term securities. Outstanding value as of December 31, 1935, was $1,622 million.[2] Lending was slow until the First World War, but afterwards the pace picked up rapidly as New York became the world's principal financial center. By the mid-1920's, agents for major U.S. banks were out scouring the world for prospective customers, often convincing foreign governments to take loans in excess of their needs and funding borrowers who were poor risks. At one point, for example, there were 29 representatives of U.S. banks in Colombia alone trying to negotiate loans with public and private entities.[3] This led the commercial attaché in Bogotá to write to the Department of Commerce: "I think Colombia is going wild on borrowing. She has started too many railroads and too many highways, and she has not any idea where she is going to get all the money, except that the money is coming in so readily now that she just thinks she can borrow ad infinitum."[4] By the early 1930's, however, the bubble had burst in Latin America as in the rest of the world. Bolivia defaulted on her loans in December 1930, and she was followed by Peru, Chile, and Brazil in 1931, and by Uruguay, Colombia, and various Central American countries in 1932. By the end of 1933, almost every Latin American country was in default except Argentina and Haiti. Thus ended Latin America's access to private capital markets for almost four decades.

It is necessary to look at the stories behind these loans to understand the nature of the relationship between bankers and client governments and also the relationship between the banks and the U.S. government. Apart from the last half of the 1920's, when a borrower's market existed, conditions imposed were harsh—frequently to the point of impinging on the sovereignty of the borrowing countries. The collaboration between banks and the U.S. government was often a key factor in these operations.

One example was the Dominican Republic.[5] In 1907, the U.S. Senate approved a treaty between the two countries that provided (1) for the issuance of $20 million in bonds to pay the Dominican Republic's public debt (the loan was handled by Kuhn, Loeb & Co.), and (2) for the collection of the Dominican Republic's customs revenues by a U.S. government appointee in order to insure the servicing and repayment of the

2. Cleona Lewis, *America's Stake in International Investments* (Washington, D.C., 1938), pp. 347, 628–29.
3. *Ibid.*, p. 377.
4. *Ibid.*, p. 381.
5. Scott Nearing and Joseph Freeman, *Dollar Diplomacy* (New York, 1927), pp. 122–33. Their sources are principally U.S. government documents.

loan. Following up on these financial manipulations by President Roosevelt, his successors (Taft and Wilson) ordered direct military intervention to protect American financial and "security" interests. In 1911, Taft sent two special commissioners and 750 marines to investigate the assassination of the Dominican president and the establishment of a provisional government. At the "suggestion" of the commissioners, the provisional president resigned. This intervention by the United States led to further revolutionary outbursts over the next five years and further U.S. gunboat diplomacy. Finally, in 1916, the marines landed and established a military dictatorship. The Dominican Congress was dissolved, Dominican officials were ousted, and a rear admiral of the U.S. Navy became military governor.

Repression was the order of the day in political terms, while the military government floated bonds through U.S. bankers in the name of the Dominican Republic. In 1921, Speyer & Co. and Equitable Trust Co. of New York handled a $2.5 million bond issue; in 1922, Lee, Higginson & Co. handled one for $6.7 million. A circular issued in connection with the former said that the bonds would contain the following clause:

With the consent of the United States there is secured the acceptance of and validation of this bond issue by any government of the Dominican Republic as a legal, binding, and irrevocable obligation of the Dominican Republic, and the duties of the General Receiver of Dominican Customs as provided in American-Dominican Convention of 1907, are extended to this bond issue. . . . Until all these bonds shall have been redeemed, the Dominican Republic agrees not to increase its debt, nor to modify its customs duties, without the previous consent of the United States Government; and its customs revenues shall continue to be collected by a General Receiver of Customs appointed by and responsible to the President of the United States.[6]

The military dictatorship ended in 1924, when the Dominicans agreed to ratify a treaty providing for U.S. control of customs, treasury, army, and police. Similar events occurred in other Central American republics.

Another example shows that the bankers did not always need government help to impose harsh conditions on desperate Latin American governments.[7] In 1921, the Bolivian government was in serious need of money to refund its foreign debt and develop its railway system. Therefore it took a six-month $1,000,000 loan from a St. Louis banking house called Stifel-Nicolaus. Rather than pay a stiff $90,000 commission, the

6. *Ibid.*, p. 131.
7. Margaret Marsh, *The Bankers in Bolivia* (New York, 1928), pp. 90–121.

government agreed to give Stifel-Nicolaus a preferential option on any external loans taken over the next three years. Because of the option, Bolivia was unable to seek the best terms for a longer-term refunding loan in 1922; instead, Stifel-Nicolaus provided a $33 million loan—far in excess of the government's desires. The security for the bonds covered over half the national income in 1922 and almost two-thirds of it by 1925. Included were the entire customs receipts and certain indirect taxes (on alcohol and tobacco) and direct taxes (on net profits of mining and of corporations, and on net income of banks). In addition, the government's (majority) shares in the National Bank and in an as-yet-unconstructed railroad were mortgaged. To insure the collection of taxes, and thus the servicing of the debt, the loan terms stated that a three-member Permanent Fiscal Commission must be appointed (two members nominated by the bankers) to be in charge of tax collection over the 25-year period of the loan. The Commission had the power to supervise tax collection on both the national and the departmental levels and to revise the national accounts. One of the bankers' representatives was named chairman of the Commission, Inspector-General of Banks and Monopolies, and a director of the Bolivian National Bank. The other banker member was made Director-General of Customs.

Virtually no new Latin American bonds were floated in the United States between 1930 and the 1960's, and the nominal value of externally held government debt was substantially reduced in many countries. Already by 1945, a large portion of Latin American bonds had been repurchased by individuals and Latin American governments. Further reduction came from normal amortization and from the direct scaling down of the nominal value of foreign-held bonds, especially by Brazil and Mexico. In Brazil, the principal of many bonds was reduced by 20 to 50 percent; in Mexico a debt resettlement plan lowered the nominal value of debt by 80 percent.[8]

The banks' experience with Latin American debt was reflected in regulations imposed by the United States and many European countries on the further purchase of Latin American bonds. Barriers to entry were of four main kinds: (1) regulations relating to the balance of payments; (2) the necessity of obtaining permission from national authorities (especially in Europe and Japan); (3) information-disclosure requests that increased costs; and (4) restrictions on the buying institutions (in many U.S. states and in almost all European countries, banks, insurance companies, and pension funds are prohibited from or strictly

8. United Nations, Department of Economic and Social Affairs, *Foreign Capital in Latin America* (New York, 1955), pp. 10–12.

limited in buying Third World issues). In the United States, many of these barriers are informal, involving the complex regulatory apparatus of the Securities and Exchange Commission and the individual states, which make the securities market too costly for most Latin American issues. Such regulations are as effective as the more stringent legal limitations in European countries, substantially if not entirely closing the U.S. market to Third World securities, whether debt or equity.[9]

The 1945–70 Period

As the private banks and other purchasers of Latin American securities retired from the financial arena, their place was taken by international institutions and U.S. government agencies. The immediate aftermath of the Second World War saw the creation of the Bretton Woods twins—the International Monetary Fund and the World Bank. The purpose of these institutions was mainly to revive international trade among the developed nations, and specifically to rehabilitate Western Europe. It was only later that the Latin American countries began to participate in this international network.

In Latin America, the IMF has become the kingpin around which other multilateral, and even bilateral, economic agencies function.[10] The Fund itself gives short-term (three- to five-year) loans for the specific purpose of alleviating balance-of-payments difficulties. The size of the loans is directly related to a country's quota in the Fund. The first 25 percent of the quota—the so-called gold tranche—can be drawn almost automatically. Succeeding tranches carry greater restrictions, in the sense that the Fund can and does prescribe policy changes (embodied in a Letter of Intent) that must be made before a tranche is released. The nature of the prescriptions tends to be highly deflationary: wage cuts, budget cuts, and devaluations usually form the heart of the recommendations. In addition, the IMF "seal of approval" is usually required by other agencies before they will consider giving loans to the country concerned. It is in this sense that the Fund constitutes the center of financial operations.

9. Carlos Díaz-Alejandro, "The Post-1971 International Financial System and the Less-Developed Countries," in G. K. Helleiner, ed., *A World Divided* (Cambridge, Eng., 1976), p. 195.
10. The IMF's own version of its activities can be found in J. Keith Horsefield, ed., *The International Monetary Fund 1945–65: Twenty Years of International Monetary Cooperation* (3 vols.; Washington, D.C., 1969), and Margaret Garristen de Vries, *International Montary Fund, 1966–71* (2 vols.; Washington, D.C., 1978). For a critical analysis of the IMF in Third World countries, see Cheryl Payer, *The Debt Trap* (New York, 1974).

The World Bank is composed of several parts, the most important of which are the International Bank for Reconstruction and Development (IBRD) and the International Development Association (IDA).[11] The IBRD, which was formed at the same time as the IMF, makes long-term loans (15–25 years) at commercial rates (6.5 percent in the late 1960's, now about 8 percent). Most loans are for specific projects, especially economic infrastructure, although about 10 percent of World Bank loans through 1970 were more general program loans. In 1962, the IDA was formed to make development loans on soft terms. IDA loans are for 50 years and carry a 0.75 percent service charge. Both types of World Bank loans are for similar uses, with the decision on whether a loan should come from the IBRD or the IDA based on a country's ability to service debts. This has meant that the vast majority of IDA money has gone to Africa and Asia, and that little has been left for Latin America. Total World Bank loans to Latin America through 1970 were $4,495 million, with $4,352 million from the IBRD and only $143 million from the IDA (see Table 1).

The Inter-American Development Bank (IDB) began operations in 1961.[12] Its structure is quite similar to that of the World Bank, giving hard and soft loans, both long-term. Originally the sectoral distribution of loans in the two banks was different, with the IBRD concentrating on infrastructure and the IDB more involved in the productive sectors, especially agriculture; but both have now developed a more even spread of loans across sectors. Remaining differences are that about one quarter of IDB loans are to the private sector whereas IBRD/IDA loans are to governments or government agencies, and that the Latin American countries have a majority of votes in the IDB. Structural changes in the IDB, however, as well as the operation of the "soft loan window," need a two-thirds majority, thus giving the United States a veto.[13] Total IDB loans through 1970 were $4,069 million (see Table 1).

11. For an authoritative account of The World Bank, see Edward S. Mason and Robert E. Asher, *The World Bank Since Bretton Woods* (Washington, D.C., 1973). A critical account can be found in Teresa Hayter, *Aid as Imperialism* (Harmondsworth, Eng., 1971).

12. Sources on the Inter-American Development Bank include Sydney Dell, *The Inter-American Development Bank* (New York, 1972), and John A. White, *Regional Development Banks* (London, 1970).

13. The federal watchdog agency (GAO) criticized the United States for adopting a "soft-line approach" in its dealings with the IDB, allowing the Latin American members to "generally shape policies and dictate terms." The GAO report notes that the United States has never voted against a loan proposal—which, of course, misses the point, since a loan strongly opposed by the United States would never be formally proposed. (See *New York Times*, Aug. 28, 1972.)

TABLE I

Flow of Bilateral and Multilateral Financial Capital to Latin America, 1945–77
(*Millions of U.S. dollars*)

Source of capital	1945–60	1961–70	1971–77
World Bank	1,053	3,442	7,941
IBRD	1,053	3,299	7,698
IDA	—	143	243
Inter-American Development Bank	—	4,069	7,942
Export-Import Bank[a]	2,925	1,695	3,150
Agency for International Development	1,829	8,754	4,044
Private capital			37,363
Bond issues	n.a.	1,284	4,293
Euroloans	—	n.a.	33,070

SOURCES: *World Bank*: World Bank, *Annual Reports*; *Inter-American Development Bank*: Inter-American Development Bank, *Annual Reports*; *Export-Import Bank and Agency for International Development*: AID, *U.S. Overseas Loans and Grants*; *Bond Issues*: U.N., *External Financing of Economic Development, International Flow of Long-term Capital, 1962–66* and World Bank, *Annual Reports*; *Euroloans*: World Bank, *Borrowing in International Capital Markets.*

[a] Credits only, excludes insurance and guarantees.

The other main participants in Latin American financial relations in the 1945–70 period were two sets of U.S. government agencies: the Export-Import Bank and various aid agencies. The Eximbank was formally created in 1934, but it did very little business in Latin America until after the war.[14] Although often considered part of the U.S. aid apparatus, the Eximbank is actually designed to increase the export business of U.S. firms by providing lines of credit and insurance for U.S. exporters. Several kinds of assistance are available: (1) credits (especially long-term) provided to the buyers of U.S. goods so that they can make purchases; (2) insurance (especially short-term) provided to U.S. exporters to cover commercial and/or political risks; and (3) guarantees provided to private banks to insure goods being shipped by U.S. exporters. Total Eximbank authorizations affecting Latin America in all

14. On the Export-Import Bank, see Richard Feinberg, "The Export-Import Bank in the U.S. Economy," Ph.D. dissertation, Stanford University, 1978.

forms through 1970 amounted to $10,429 million; this was divided into credits of $7,052 million, insurance of $2,299 million, and guarantees of $1,078 million.[15]

The final actor that played an important role in providing financial capital to Latin America was the U.S. aid agencies.[16] The aid office was reorganized—and renamed— at various times during the postwar period, with the designation Agency for International Development being adopted in 1961. During the 1960's, AID was the most overtly political of the agencies we have discussed. It openly discussed its attempts to influence the overall economic policies of Latin American countries, and a large portion of its funds were distributed because the U.S. government had decided to support a given country, regardless of specific projects presented for AID loans. In addition to project loans, AID established several program loans in Latin America during the 1960's (to Brazil, Chile, and Colombia); these loans had general macroeconomic conditions that were similar to those stipulated by the IMF and that were also spelled out in a Letter of Intent. Because of AID's openly political criteria, it worked fairly independently of the other aid agencies—though general lines of agreement were maintained. Loans—generally long-term and with low interest rates—were often tied to purchases of U.S. goods, so that in this sense AID was similar to the Eximbank in providing business for U.S. exporters. AID (and its predecessor agencies) made loans and grants to Latin America totaling $10,583 million through 1970 (see Table 1).

During the 1960's, private bankers again began to play a role, though not a very large one. As mentioned previously, both formal and informal restrictions in the United States and other major capital markets prevented most Latin American countries from floating bonds. Nevertheless, certain nations managed to overcome these difficulties. Mexico, especially, was a heavy borrower in the U.S. bond market during the entire decade of the 1960's, floating $383 million worth of bonds. Argentina was second with $107 million, all borrowed between 1966 and 1970. Other Latin American countries that floated securities in New York during the 1960's included Panama ($52 million), Venezuela ($35 million), Peru ($15 million), Colombia ($5 million), Nicaragua $(2.5

15. Export-Import Bank, *Annual Report*, 1970.
16. A general study of U.S. foreign aid, written for the Council on Foreign Relations, is Paul G. Clark, *American Aid for Development* (New York, 1972). A book focusing on U.S. aid to Latin America is Jerome Levinson and Juan de Onis, *The Alliance That Lost Its Way* (Chicago, 1970). A critical account is Lynn Richards, "The Context of Foreign Aid: Modern Imperialism," *Review of Radical Political Economics*, 9. no. 4 (Winter 1977), pp. 43–75.

million), Brazil ($800,000), and the Dominican Republic ($200,000).[17]

During the latter half of the decade there was a strong switch away from New York toward the newly developed Eurobond market, where restrictions were minimal. Thus between 1966 and 1970, only 37 percent of all bonds floated by Latin American countries were in New York. The total amount of bonds floated in New York during the decade was $603 million, whereas the total in Europe for 1966–70 alone was $646 million.[18] In addition to floating bonds, Latin American countries also began to take advantage of short-term loans in the Eurodollar market, though the amounts involved are unclear since systematic statistics date only from the 1970's.

Thus in theory there were a variety of different institutions involved in providing financial resources to Latin America during the 25 years after the Second World War, with each performing a different function in the process. The World Bank provided long-term development loans for specific development projects, with the IBRD lending at close to commercial conditions and the IDA lending on concessional terms. The IDB played a role similar to that of the World Bank, with both commercial and concessional loans. The Eximbank provided trade credits to highly solvent clients, and AID and its predecessor agencies provided soft loans and some grants to a broad range of countries, rich and poor, mainly selected on political criteria. The private sector provided long-term financing through bonds and short-term loans to highly reputable clients. The IMF, meanwhile, provided short-term balance-of-payments financing as well as the general seal of approval required before many other organizations would lend. In practice, of course, this clear-cut picture became much fuzzier as various institutions began to assume functions that had originally been "assigned" to others. Nevertheless, some semblance of a division of labor could be observed.

The 1970's

The last half of the 1960's began to foreshadow new trends in U.S.–Latin American financial relations; privatization began with the re-emergence of the private banks, mainly working through the Euromarket. The Euromarket consists of two sectors—the Eurocurrency market and the Eurobond market. It is these private markets that have

17. Calculated from World Bank, *Annual Report*, various numbers, and United Nations, *External Financing of Economic Development, International Flow of Long-term Capital, 1962–66* (New York, 1968).

18. *Ibid.*

dominated the current decade, while bilateral and multilateral forms of assistance have diminished in relative importance.

The Eurocurrency market consists of a group of banks operating in London and other financial centers that takes deposits and makes loans in currencies other than those of the local economy. Most deposits and loans are denominated in dollars—hence the shorthand term "Eurodollars." The dominance of U.S. currency is paralleled by the dominance of U.S. banks. The market originated in the late 1950's, although the exact cause is a subject of debate.[19] Whatever its origins, however, it has flourished because it has been able to pay higher rates for deposits and charge lower rates for loans than its domestic competitors in Europe and the United States.

Smaller margins exist for various reasons. First, because the Euromarket is a wholesale market, with the minimum size of transactions generally $1 million, economies of scale mean lower unit costs. Second, there is greater competition in the Euromarket than there is among domestic banks, which tend to be oligopolists. Third, restrictions that curb the domestic banks are lacking in the Euromarket. On the supply side, the lack of reserve requirements means that Euromarket banks can lend out a greater percentage of their deposits than can domestic banks. In addition, regulations in domestic markets—the best-known of which is U.S. Regulation Q, which places a ceiling on the interest rates U.S. banks can pay on time deposits—have led them to have a smaller supply of money available to be lent out. Similarly, U.S. banks cannot pay interest on deposits of less than 30 days' maturity. On the demand side, U.S. regulations have also helped the growth of the Euromarket: for example, the Interest Equalization Tax, which existed from 1963 to 1974, effectively closed the New York market to foreign borrowers. Moreover, the Voluntary Foreign Credit Restraint program (1965–68) and the mandatory controls on capital export (1968–74) meant that U.S. corporations wanting to invest abroad had to secure capital outside the United States.

In their early phase (i.e., in the 1960's), Eurodollar loans were almost exclusively short-term credits, primarily working capital for U.S. and European multinationals. The risk on this type of loan was minute. During the 1970's, however, the pattern changed substantially. Comparisons

19. For a discussion of the origins of the Euromarket, as well as one of the better accounts of its functioning, see Geoffrey Bell, *The Eurodollar Market and the International Financial System* (London, 1974). A useful book dealing with Third World participation in the Euromarket is Phil Wellons, *Borrowing by Developing Countries on the Eurocurrency Market* (Paris, 1977).

are difficult because of the lack of data before 1971, but in that year 24 percent of publicized Eurocurrency loans went to Third World countries; such loans increased to 36 percent in 1972 and 1973. In 1974 there was a dip as advanced countries took out huge loans to finance balance-of-payments deficits caused by the increase in oil prices, but by 1975 a majority of all loans were going to Third World countries. Loans to Latin America as a percentage of all Third World loans ranged from 34 percent in 1971 to 47 percent in 1975.[20]

Other changes accompanied the new geographical distribution of loans. Third World countries wanted credits for financing development projects, so these had to be medium- or long-term loans rather than short-term ones. More recently, Third World countries have been borrowing to meet balance-of-payments deficits and to refinance old loans. The net result has been that commercial loans, which were typically for one year or less in the 1960's have often been made for 8–10 years in the 1970's. Every six months, however, the interest rate can be revised.

Interest rates are calculated as a percentage above the London Inter-Bank Offer Rate (LIBOR), with this spread varying according to the availability of money, the competition between banks, and the creditworthiness of the borrower. Thus in times of abundant liquidity a highly creditworthy borrower can get a loan at 0.5 percent above LIBOR, whereas in tighter periods a less creditworthy borrower may have to pay 2.5 percent. Management fees are in addition to interest rates.

The other sector of the Euromarket—the Eurobond market—is of more recent origin than the Eurocurrency market, having been an important force in supplying funds only since about 1968. Only during the last three years have bonds begun to match loans in amounts of money provided. For Third World countries, however, bonds are still of minor importance as a source of capital. During the 1975–77 period, funds raised in the Eurobond market as a whole were 48 percent of total funds, whereas for Third World countries the figure was only seven percent.[21] The main difference between Euroloans and bonds, in terms of the mechanics involved, is that the latter are long-term debt instruments with fixed interest rates in contrast to the former, which are medium-term, floating rate credits.

20. Most of the data on Euroloans are compiled from "tombstones" (bank advertisements). Since placing tombstones is not obligatory, it is estimated that this source underestimates loans by 20 percent. More accurate, but still incomplete, information is published by the World Bank, based on its access to country data. See the Bank's quarterly publication *Borrowing in International Capital Markets*.

21. Calculated from Morgan Guaranty Trust, *World Financial Markets*, March 1978.

Why the sudden importance of Third World countries to the Euromarket? In part, the demand for loans increased, but more important was the impetus from the supply side. Loan demand in the United States and Europe fell off in the early 1970's, meaning that the banks had excess liquidity. This problem was greatly exacerbated after the 1973 oil price hike as (1) recession hit the advanced capitalist world, further dampening loan demand (after a spurt in 1974 to finance transitory balance-of-payments deficits), and (2) the OPEC countries deposited the majority of their new revenues in U.S. banks.

Faced with a potential falling rate of profit if they could not loan out this money at an adequate interest rate, the banks turned to a new set of clients: a small group of Third World countries whose export possibilities were considered sufficiently good that obtaining foreign exchange to repay the loans was not felt to be a major problem. (In practice, of course, this did not always turn out to be true.) The narrow range of the group is indicated by the fact that Brazil and Mexico account for almost half of all Euroloans to the non-OPEC Third World. Fewer than a dozen other countries make up the bulk of the remaining half: Argentina, Chile, Hong Kong, the Ivory Coast, Malaysia, Morocco, Peru, Panama, the Philippines, South Korea, and Taiwan.

The desire for profits also led to another important characteristic of the Euromarkets. Politics is less of a deterrent to obtaining money there than is the case with the bilateral and multilateral agencies. Thus Cuba and the socialist countries of Eastern Europe have borrowed considerable sums on the Euromarket in recent years; Vietnam and North Korea obtained smaller amounts; and Peru resorted to the Euromarket when the United States imposed a credit blockade in 1968–74. In addition, the private bankers have placed fewer restrictions on the use of their loans than have official agencies.

The result of this splurge of borrowing has been that the countries involved have piled up huge debts that they may not be able to handle. For the non-oil-exporters among those Third World countries that have borrowed heavily on the Euromarket, debt service ratios (interest plus amortization payments divided by exports) for public-sector debt alone often approach 20 percent or more.[22] Special problems may occur at the very end of the 1970's since repayments are bunched in this period. Bankers deny that they are overextended in terms of Third World loans, but it is clear that many would like help from public-sector institutions in managing problem loans.

22. World Bank, *Annual Report*, various numbers.

One form of public-private cooperation is the introduction of "co-financing." Co-financing refers to loans jointly arranged by a bilateral or multilateral agency and one or more private banks. In effect, the official agency assumes the risk of the loan in return for greater participation of private funds in Third World financing. Co-financing was first introduced by the Export-Import Bank in 1970. Thus the Eximbank often no longer provides 100 percent of the credit for export financing, but divides the package between itself and the private banks. In addition, for a small fee the Eximbank provides a financial guarantee that covers all commercial and political risks and that assures full repayment of principal plus most interest payments.

In 1976, co-financing was extended to the World Bank. The first such arrangement involved a $150 million loan to a Brazilian steel company arranged by the Bank of America and involving a syndicate of 16 commercial banks. According to the *New York Times*, "The World Bank will be the channel for the payments on the loan, and a default to the private creditor will be considered a default on the Bank, one of the best possible guarantees for the private loan."[23] More recently, calls have also been made from various sources for co-financing operations between the International Monetary Fund and the private banks.[24]

Thus it is obvious that the private banks have been expanding into the various activities formerly considered the "turf" of other institutions. They have moved into medium-term project loans, formerly handled by the IBRD and the IDB. They have joined the Eximbank in financing large U.S. export deals. And they have been giving balance-of-payments loans, an area that used to be the IMF's exclusive domain. The climax of this trend was the 1976 Peruvian loan, when the banks took over the IMF's other traditional role of setting macroeconomic conditions for a loan and monitoring the economy to assure compliance. It is to this case that we now turn.

THE U.S. BANKS IN PERU

Background: 1968–75

In October 1968, General Juan Velasco Alvarado led a coup that overthrew the civilian government of Fernando Belaúnde Terry. The

---

23. *The New York Times*, Jan. 15, 1976.
24. See, for example, Arthur Burns, "The Need for Order in International Finance," (speech at the Annual Dinner of the Columbia University Graduate School of Business, New York, April 12, 1977).

subsequent military government broke with the tradition of military governments in Latin America in that it did not support the established socioeconomic structure, but rather proposed to radically restructure Peruvian society.

Under an ideology that promised a "third way" between capitalism and communism, the new government undertook (1) an extensive agrarian reform centering on the creation of cooperatives, (2) an industrial and mining reform introducing worker participation and profit-sharing (the *comunidades industriales* and *mineras*), and (3) the nationalization of some key foreign firms, including branches of Standard Oil, ITT, W. R. Grace, Cerro, and Chase Manhattan. The government was not opposed to foreign capital, but it did want to change the nature of foreign investment. On the one hand, it wanted to decide what types of investment were desirable; on the other hand, since it planned to have the state itself become the principal investor, it was interested in attracting foreign loans more than direct investment.

Despite the redistributive rhetoric, the reforms actually benefited only a small part of the population: recipients of land, workers in those production units where the *comunidades* were actually introduced, and elements of a domestic industrial bourgeoisie that was fostered by the military as another part of its strategy. Even these groups did not wholeheartedly support the military government, which was thus unable to consolidate a strong political base. The government's program remained very much a "revolution from above," or more accurately an attempt at modernization from above.[25]

During the regime's first five years, despite the changes going on and the lack of political support, the Velasco government managed to maintain a "healthy" economy in terms of traditional economic indicators. Growth in Gross Domestic Product between 1969 and 1973 averaged 5.5 percent, while that in industry averaged 7.1 percent. Unemployment fell from 5.9 percent in 1969 to 4.2 percent in 1973. Real wages and salaries both increased by an average of 6.6 percent, while inflation was held to an average of 7.2 percent. The trade balance was positive, and the service balance, though it generally dragged the current account into deficit, did not create any serious problems with financing. Net reserves, in

25. For background information on Peru and the military government, see Abraham Lowenthal, ed., *The Peruvian Experiment* (Princeton, N.J., 1975); E. V. K. Fitzgerald, *The State and Economic Development, Peru since 1968*, (Cambridge, Eng., 1976); Aníbal Quijano, *Nationalism and Capitalism in Peru* (New York, 1971); and *Latin American Perspectives* 4, no. 3 (1977) (issue on Peru). The most complete political-economic history of recent Peru is E. V. K. Fitzgerald, *The Political Economy of Peru, 1956–77* (Cambridge, Eng., forthcoming).

fact, increased from almost $131 million in 1968 to almost $411 million in 1973.[26]

Under this prosperous surface, however, potential problems lurked. On the one hand, the threat of accelerating inflation existed. Real wages, which were increasing faster than the food supply, were one warning signal. So was the budget deficit, which averaged between 15 and 20 percent of total central government expeditures between 1971 and 1973. Such a deficit was not surprising, of course, for a government taking a greater role in the economy. Expenditures increase, but taxes cannot be increased enough to offset them, owing to the political resistance of the local landowners and bourgeoisie. Rising inflation rates, in addition to making economic planning more difficult, tend to cut real wages, thus creating political unrest as well as human suffering.

More serious from the government's point of view were potential problems with the balance of payments. The outlook *appeared* to be favorable, but this was because of very optimistic forecasts about mineral exports. Although few went as far as the state oil company spokesman who declared when Petroperú struck oil in 1971 that Peru's economic future was assured, Peruvian and foreign analysts alike put an increasing emphasis on oil. Great stress was also placed on the expectation of major volume increases that would raise the value of copper exports. The volatility of prices for primary exports—traditionally one of the key problems for Third World countries—was seemingly forgotten.

At the same time, plans were being laid for an industrial development strategy that would rely heavily on capital-intensive technology. Such a strategy would not only reduce the job-creating potential of industrialization but also would necessitate large imports of capital goods and intermediate inputs. Meanwhile, the Peruvian military was importing large amounts of expensive military equipment from the Soviet Union and various Western countries, and these imports, together with the debt service payments to be discussed below, had the potential of locking Peru into a balance-of-payments crisis if the export boom failed to materialize.

At the same time, the question arose of how to finance the industrialization program and the equipment necessary to produce the additional exports. The United States and its allies in the multilateral agencies refused to supply funds, since the Velasco government had incurred their wrath by nationalizing Standard Oil's subsidiary (the International Pe-

26. All figures are from tables in Barbara Stallings, "Peru and the U.S. Banks: Privatization of Financial Relations," Working Paper no. 16, Woodrow Wilson Center, Washington, D.C., 1978.

troleum Company), defending the 200-mile fishing limit, establishing close relations with the socialist countries, and generally denouncing capitalism. In concrete terms, this meant that foreign investment dried up and Peru received almost no loans from AID or the Export-Import Bank between 1969 and March 1974 (although the Hickenlooper amendment was never formally invoked).[27] Loans from multilateral agencies were also conspicuously few. Between 1968 and late 1973, Peru received only one loan from the World Bank. Getting credits was slightly easier from the Inter-American Development Bank, but a significant portion of the IDB loans were in response to a serious earthquake in Peru in 1970.[28]

There appeared to be only one source to which the government could turn to finance its investment projects—the international capital market. Realizing that Peru was going to need good relations with the private bankers, the government took early steps to prepare the ground. When it took control of the domestic banking sector in 1970 (including Chase Manhattan's Banco Continental), it sought favor with Chase—and presumably the rest of the financial community—by buying its shares for five and a half times their stock market value and three times their book value.[29] Thus, Peru was able to escape the official credit blockade by raising $147 million on the Eurocurrency market in 1972 and $734 million there in 1973. In the latter year, Peru was the third-largest borrower among Third World nations.[30]

Despite its leftist rhetoric, Peru seemed to the banks a good credit risk because of its copper and oil. Since Peru's need for money coincided with the banks' excess liquidity, what appeared to be mutually advantageous deals were possible. However, these loans added to Peru's debt burden, which almost doubled between 1968 and 1973, and which nearly tripled between 1968 and 1974. Debt service (interest plus amortization) surpassed 20 percent of export earnings by 1973 (see Table 2). Neither borrower nor lenders were concerned, though, since it was presumed that Peru's mineral wealth would provide repayment.

By 1974, the potential problems outlined above began to appear. Although growth rates continued high and unemployment low, the in-

27. For an analysis of relations between Peru and the United States during this period, see Jessica Einhorn, *Expropriation Politics* (Lexington, Mass., 1974).
28. See annual reports of all four organizations (AID, Eximbank, World Bank, and IDB) over this period.
29. Shane Hunt, "Direct Foreign Investment in Peru," in Lowenthal, ed. Two years later, Chase returned the favor by agreeing to head an international syndicate to find funds for the Cuajone copper mine—a key project whose financing had been stalled for two years.
30. OECD, *Development Cooperation*, 1976.

TABLE 2

Peruvian Debt and Debt Service, 1968–78

(Millions of U.S. dollars)

Year	Public debt[a]	Service payments[b]	Service ratio[c]
1968	1,100	146	14.6%
1969	1,132	126	11.8
1970	1,196	168	13.7
1971	1,309	209	19.6
1972	1,606	213	18.5
1973	2,155	434	32.2[d]
1974	3,008	449	24.4[d]
1975	3,466	402	23.0
1976	4,383	505	29.0
1977	n.a.	811	45.9
1978	4,800	1,000	55.0

SOURCE: World Bank, "Peru: Informe Socioeconómico," Jan. 1978 (1968–77); television speeches by the president and finance minister (1978).
 [a] Disbursed and undisbursed public and publicly guaranteed debt.
 [b] Interest plus amortization.
 [c] Service payments ÷ exports.
 [d] Includes prepayments without which ratios would be 23.6 percent (1973) and 18.1 percent (1974).

flation rate shot up to 17 percent, causing real wages to fall. Moreover, for the first time since the military took power, the trade balance showed a deficit: while exports increased 35 percent between 1973 and 1974, imports almost doubled. In percentage terms, the main culprit was the oil price increase, which made the cost of Peru's fuel and lubricant imports nearly triple. Of greater significance in absolute terms, however, were volume and price increases of inputs and capital equipment for industry. The former was accounted for mainly by increases in international prices, and the latter by big increases in the government investment program.

Between 1969 and 1973, capital formation by the public sector (central government and public enterprises) had increased by an average of 15.6 percent per year; in 1974, this figure jumped to 56.5 percent. Major increases included central government investment in agriculture (44 percent) and public enterprise investment in Petroperú (88 percent),

Mineroperú (139 percent), Sideroperú (1016 percent), and Pescaperú (which increased from nothing to $32 million).[31] Most of the equipment involved in this investment spurt was produced abroad—hence the increase in imports. This marked a qualitative change in the government program. The "cheap" phase of the reforms (expropriation of agriculture and some industrial enterprises) was over; the "expensive" phase (creating new heavy industry) was beginning. Like the trade deficit, the deficit in services also increased, such that the current account deficit in 1974 totaled $725 million (up from $174 million in 1973).

This deficit was financed by going to the Euromarket for another $366 million in medium-term loans and a large amount of short-term money. In addition, AID, the Export-Import Bank, and the international agencies also poured in large sums when the credit blockade was lifted after the signing of the so-called Greene Agreement in February of 1974.[32]

In 1975, both the inflation and the balance-of-payments problems became more acute. In addition, the budget deficit doubled. The situation was so serious that emergency measures were introduced at the end of June. The most important of these was an average 20-to-30 percent increase in prices of basic consumer items as many subsidies were lowered in an attempt to cut the budget deficit and thus eventually the inflation rate. Trying to forestall opposition from workers and to partially offset the fall in demand, the government announced a general wage increase. The minimum wage, however, was increased by only 20 percent, and the poorest groups (the unemployed and the "informal" sector) did not benefit.[33] As a result of the June measures, the growth rate faltered as demand fell; unemployment also rose.

The growing economic crisis provided justification for the August 1975 "coup within a coup." General Francisco Morales Bermúdez, Velasco's prime minister, took over as president. Although Morales Bermúdez characterized his regime as a continuation of his predecessor's, it was obvious that the change meant a move to the right. Repression

31. Calculated from Banco Central de Reserva, *Memoria Anual*, 1975.
32. The Greene Agreement was an agreement between the United States and Peru, negotiated by James Greene, former official of Manufacturers Hanover. In a feat of economic diplomacy, it resolved the long-standing disagreement between the two countries over compensation for Standard Oil's subsidiary International Petroleum Company. A lump sum was agreed on as compensation for *all* companies nationalized by Peru, with separate lists of recipients presented by the United States and Peru. See discussion in *Latin America Economic Report*, 2, no. 9 (Mar. 1, 1974).
33. See accounts in *Latin America Economic Report*, 3, no. 27 (Jul. 11, 1975).

increased, leftist military officers were forced to retire, and more ortho-dox economic policies were introduced. Balance-of-payments problems nevertheless remained, despite $433 million in loans from the Euro-market and the World Bank, and net reserves fell from $693 million to only $116 million by the end of 1975.

A further round of austerity was introduced in January 1976, when the new finance minister, Luis Barúa Casteñeda, announced a series of changes similar to those of the previous June. More price increases on basic consumer items were introduced, and wage increases were again authorized to try to limit opposition and maintain demand. A second set of measures—tax increases and budget cuts—was designed to reduce the government deficit. Attempts were made to lower imports by a system of licensing, and a set of production incentives was promised.

The aims of the measures were threefold: to increase production, to control inflation, and to keep the balance-of-payments deficit from getting out of hand. If the economy could manage to limp through the year, the government hoped that the balance of payments would im-prove through an increase in copper and oil exports and that other dif-ficulties would thus be mitigated.[34] Meanwhile, further international credit would be needed to cover the deficit.

The Bankers Intervene: 1976

By early 1976, then, the Peruvian economy faced a serious crunch, owing to a combination of bad luck, bad planning, and the inevitable dilemmas of dependent capitalist development. The bad luck had to do with the failure of the expected oil bonanza, the disappearance of the anchovy schools that had provided a major Peruvian export, and the fall of copper prices. Bad planning reinforced these problems through over-fishing and borrowing money to build a billion-dollar pipeline before the extent of the oil reserves was known.[35] As mentioned previously, how-ever, export revenues always exert a disproportionate influence on the economies of small dependent countries that specialize in primary exports.

The key problem from the government's point of view was the balance of payments, which could not be brought into equilibrium in the short run because exports could not be increased and imports could

34. *Andean Report*, January 1977.
35. Another interpretation of the pipeline decision, however, says that it was made not on economic but on military grounds. That is, for reasons of national defense, the military decided to build the pipeline rather than use the cheaper means of shipping the oil by way of Brazil.

not be cut without bringing the economy to a standstill. The only possible flexibility seemed to center on manipulating debt service payments (which were about $500 million compared with the trade deficit of $740 million). Outright suspension of payments would end access to the international capital market, so refinancing was necessary.

The traditional way to solve a balance-of-payments crisis would have been for Peru to go to the IMF and sign a Letter of Intent. This would have given Peru access to certain IMF funds. More important, it would have opened further doors to bilateral, multilateral, and private banking sources that wanted an IMF "seal of approval" before lending. The problem was that the IMF would demand a drastic stabilization program that even the Morales officials could not and would not accept. They realized that the results would alienate workers (through wage and employment cuts), industrialists (through a fall in demand, and thus profits), and the military (through curbs on the purchase of arms). Given the regime's relative lack of support, the potential was too explosive: the government might be brought down.

The Peruvians therefore approached the major U.S. banks in March 1976 and asked for a large balance-of-payments loan *without* having signed a prior agreement with the IMF. The bankers ultimately accepted the Peruvian position, reasoning that if a crunch were to come, General Jorge Fernández Maldonado and the left-wing faction of the government might come out on top and lead Peru back toward a radical nationalist position. It seemed safer to support the Morales government, with its new rightist tendencies, than to risk such a leftist outcome. One New York banker involved in the negotiations put the point very clearly. He said the "main reason" for the loan was "to perpetuate Morales Bermúdez in power," since the banks considered this the best bet for getting their money back.[36]

Having accepted the Peruvian position vis-à-vis the IMF, the banks then faced a dilemma. On the one hand, they wanted to refinance the Peruvian loans for several reasons beyond just keeping Morales Bermúdez afloat. First, Peru was important both in itself and in symbolic terms. Its debt—$3.7 billion at that point—was one of the largest in the Third World. Half of it was owed to private banks, including $1.5 billion to U.S. banks alone. Second, a Peruvian default might trigger a chain reaction among other Third World countries in trouble with their foreign debts. Third, default would create animosity among the smaller U.S. banks and the international banks that had been involved in the syndi-

36. *Washington Post*, Mar. 14, 1978.

cates for Peruvian loans arranged by major U.S. institutions in the past. These smaller banks might then refuse to participate in future Third World loan syndications, having been badly burned in Peru. On the other hand, the banks had no intention of making it easy for the Peruvians. For one thing, they had to save face and to keep from getting the reputation of being a "soft touch." Thus they needed to construct a set of requirements that would provide their pound of flesh. This was especially the case since Peruvian officials had paraded around the world denouncing imperialism and capitalism for the last seven years. Also, some formula had to be devised to mollify the banks' clients, who were at that very minute being threatened by the Peruvian government. These included Marcona Mining Company (still negotiating compensation for the nationalization of its iron mines in mid-1975), and Southern Peru Copper Corporation (which faced problems over depreciation allowances and tax delinquency). Finally, a way had to be found to make sure Peru generated sufficient foreign exchange to be able to pay the service on its past loans without resorting to further international credits for this purpose in the future.

The resulting deal between Peru and the banks was a three-part program that dealt with all of the banks' problems. It included (1) an orthodox stabilization program, though of a milder sort than the IMF would have imposed, involving a 44 percent devaluation, price increases, and minor budget cuts; (2) more favorable treatment of foreign investment, including reopening the jungle and coastline to private oil companies, agreeing with Marcona on a price to be paid for its iron mine, and agreeing with Southern Peru on payments due; (3) partial withdrawal of the state in favor of local private entreprise, which began with the sale of Pescaperú's anchovy fleet to private interests and changes in labor legislation to attract more private investment.[37]

All of the loan conditions, of course, were described by the bankers as essential for guaranteeing Peru's economic future. They argued, for example, that Southern Peru's immediate repayment of the $50 million in back taxes, depreciation allowances, and penalties would have meant postponement of completion of the Cuajone mine—and thus Peru's loss of an estimated yearly output of $250 million of copper, a key foreign-exchange earner. In the Marcona case, they rationalized that if the com-

37. Accounts of the package can be found in various places. See, among others, *The Andean Report*, August 1976; *Latin America Economic Report*, 4, no. 30 (Jul. 30, 1976); *New York Times*, Jul. 24, 1976, and Aug. 4, 1976; *Financial Times*, Jul. 27, 1976; and Nancy Belliveau, "What the Peruvian Experiment Means," *Institutional Investor*, October 1976.

pany were not compensated, the Hickenlooper amendment could be invoked, cutting off essential U.S. aid and other funds. Finally, the bankers expected more favorable treatment of the private sector to increase private investment so that the government would not have to run up huge deficits and borrow abroad to finance its projects.[38]

The most controversial aspect of the program, however, was the provision that the banks were to monitor the Peruvian economy to make sure that the agreed-upon inflation, budget, and other targets were met. Not since the 1920's had private banks become so involved in the domestic affairs of a Latin American government. The loan was divided into two equal tranches; the first was released immediately, the second was withheld for several months. Authorization to draw the second tranche was to be contingent on agreement of 75 percent of the lenders (by dollar participation) that Peru was making satisfactory economic progress. Even the bankers admitted the weakness of this arrangement in comparison to the more detailed IMF monitoring. As one stated: "We won't be seeing any major changes. This second drawdown is just something to keep *some* sort of control."[39]

The package was put together by Citibank, with the participation of Bank of America, Chase Manhattan, Manufacturers Hanover, Morgan Guaranty, and Wells Fargo. These six banks composed the "steering committee" for the loan, since no bank was willing to take total responsibility as lead manager. Bankers Trust and Continental Illinois were also invited to join but refused because they disagreed with the notion of banks assuming the monitoring function.

The steering committee banks agreed to provide $200 million, contingent on a further $200 million to be raised from private banks in Western Europe, Canada, and Japan. The steering committee banks would themselves place half of their share with smaller U.S. banks, with the aim of spreading Peru's debt and their risks as widely as possible. Above and beyond the special conditions described above, the terms of the loan were quite stiff. The interest rate was 2.25 percent above LIBOR (London Inter-Bank Offer Rate), and the maturity was only five years. Completing the negotiations proved difficult. The original announcement was made on July 26, but the final signing did not take place until nearly the end of the year. The European and Japanese shares were not arranged until the first half of 1977.[40]

38. Belliveau, p. 35.
39. *Ibid.*, p. 34.
40. One of the complications was the disclosure in mid-August that the Peruvians had bought a large number of Soviet aircraft worth approximately the same amount

The effects of these policies on the Peruvian economy were dramatic and negative, but determining who was responsible for them becomes complicated. The banks imposed a set of conditions, but Morales and his top economic officials wanted to move in this direction in any case. They definitely favored private enterprise and foreign capital more than the Velasco regime had. Furthermore, they had announced stabilization measures before the loan negotiations were even begun (in January 1976), and it must be remembered that Morales was *de facto* head of government when the first such measures were introduced in June 1975. Thus it seems likely that many of the changes would have been made with or without the banks' intervention, although the latter was certainly useful in helping overcome internal opposition to austerity measures. Some of the blame could be shifted to the bankers, who also provided access to extra funds that somewhat softened the austerity program.[41]

One result of the banks' policies was a drop in production. This drop had already begun in 1975, in part owing to extremely poor performance in the fishing and mining sectors. There were also important declines in industry and services as a result of the 1975 emergency measures. Thus the GDP growth rate fell from an average of 6.3 percent in 1972–74 to only 3.5 percent in 1975. The bank measures further depressed the economy, pushing growth down to 2.8 percent in 1976, despite a strong recovery in fishing, mining, and agriculture (sectors essentially unrelated to government demand policy). Sharp declines in 1976 occurred in those sectors most susceptible to changes in internal demand—industry, construction, and services.

The employment situation also suffered reverses. In a pattern similar to that of production, open unemployment had already increased in 1975, going up from an average of 4.1 percent during 1972–74 to 5.2 percent in 1975. This figure increased only very slightly to 5.3 percent in 1976. On the other hand, underemployment increased from 41 percent to 45 percent between 1975 and 1976.

The biggest effect of the 1976 measures was on wages and salaries. According to an OAS study, real wages and salaries for the Lima area

---

as the U.S. loans. Rumors that the loans would therefore be canceled proved groundless, but the bankers were not pleased. See *Financial Times*, Aug. 1, 1976.

41. The relationship between the banks and the Peruvian government was similar to that which often exists between the IMF and governments seeking loans. Like the banks, the Fund has its views of how an economy should be run, and these often concide with the views of one faction of the government. This faction, however, may not have sufficient power to impose its policies without outside help.

reached a peak in 1973, 33 percent above their 1968 level. They then fell in 1974 and remained at the same level in 1975. During 1976, the drop was so serious that average remunerations were back to about their 1968 level. The World Bank, for instance, calls attention to mid-1976 as a watershed in incomes policies. Before that point, the policy had been "to maintain and even increase real wages"; afterwards a drop was accepted.[42]

In addition to these negative effects in terms of growth, employment, and remuneration, structural changes also resulted from the banks' conditions. Specifically, private enterprise in general, and foreign capital in particular, began to regain much of the economic and political power it had lost during the Velasco years.

Enter the IMF: 1977–78

The Peruvian drama repeated itself in 1977, but with an important change in the cast of characters. Though the balance of payments was expected to improve, a huge trade deficit still threatened, and service payments on the debt remained oppressive. Thus Peru had to look for foreign financing once more. This time, however, the banks refused to negotiate without IMF participation. Why did the bankers change their minds? The reasons for their switch are easier to understand than the explanation for their original decision to monitor the situation themselves. Many factors were at work, yet all pushed in the same direction.

The first set of factors was negative from the banks' point of view and concerned problems arising from the direct intervention. Most important was the opposition to the new monitoring role. Opposition from the left had been expected, both within Peru and internationally. A typical example was the commentary by the editors of *Monthly Review*, one of the leading leftist journals in the United States. Calling the new agreement "an intensification of the debt peonage of [Peru]," the editors then went on to say:

To a significant degree this development is hardly new, but it does bring into the open what is usually hidden in the relations between bankers and weak borrowers: influence over the affairs of client states by tacit agreement, secret covenants, or "financial discipline" imposed by a supposedly disinterested international agency such as the IMF. What is new in the Peruvian case is the unabashed announcement of direct and overt control by private bankers in an era that is supposed to be characterized by growing sensitivity to the devices of imperialism and by a strengthening of the nationalist spirit among

42. World Bank, "Peru: Informe Socioeconómico" (Jan. 1978), p. 13.

ruling classes in under-developed countries. While we might speculate on what the various explanatory factors might be, this new wrinkle at the very least reflects a deepening of dependency on the financial centers of imperialism by many Third World countries.[43]

The banks, however, were probably unprepared for the opposition from within their own ranks. As mentioned earlier, both Bankers Trust and Continental Illinois, two major U.S. institutions with heavy involvements in Peru, refused to join the steering committee or to participate in the new loans, objecting to the damage to the banks' image that might result. As Alfred Miossi, Executive Vice President of Continental Illinois, put it: "For a private bank to police the actions of a sovereign government puts it into a difficult position. International agencies have a more neutral role and are better suited for this."[44] Another banker, whose own institution was a steering committee member, said, "I don't think the banks can play the role of appearing to intervene in the affairs of a country. Whether they like it or not, it could be considered Wall Street imperialism."[45] European bankers expressed similar concerns, speaking of the "politicization" of the deal. They pointed out that banks identified with the stabilization program ran the risk of becoming scapegoats for the unpleasant results.[46]

Bankers also expressed doubt that they would have as much clout as the IMF because of their commercial ties to Peru. As one critic suggested, "The banks have a vested interest in Peru, and they've got to think of their commercial lending relations in the country. What are the Peruvians going to think if they start snooping around and delving into the books?" Considering the problem of checking on the figures Peru would provide, another banker argued that the last thing the banks wanted to do was to send their Lima branch managers over to the Peruvian Central Bank to verify the data.[47] Presumably G. A. Costanzo, Citicorp's vice-chairman, spoke for the other banks when he said: "The reaction to this loan was a signal to me that I want *no* part in deals with this kind of discipline in the future."[48]

The second set of factors explaining the banks' decision focused on the advantages of working more closely with the IMF. First, bringing

43. "The Editors' Comment," *Monthly Review*, Sept. 1976, p. 20.
44. Belliveau, p. 34.
45. Harvey D. Shapiro, "Monitoring: Are the Banks Biting Off More than They Can Chew?," *Institutional Investor*, Oct. 1976, p. 2.
46. Belliveau, p. 34.
47. *Ibid.*
48. *Ibid.*

in the Fund would end the criticisms leveled at the steering committee banks and would reunify the banking community, since those bankers who had opposed the 1976 operation had all advocated closer relations with the IMF. It would provide a more "neutral" façade for imposing conditions on Peru—although appearances were not the only advantage. The banks would also be able to profit from the Fund's experience in dealing with Third World governments, from its access to data on Third World economies, and from its capacity to set up and implement a monitoring procedure.

Closer cooperation with the IMF would also square with the wishes of the Federal Reserve, the U.S. government agency charged with regulating the banks' overseas operations. Arthur Burns, then chairman of the Federal Reserve, had been advocating such increased cooperation for some time, pressuring the banks to stop acting independently with respect to the debt problem. In a February 1977 speech he made this position public, declaring "We need to develop the rule of law in this field, and the only instrument for this is the IMF. Unless we have the rule of law, we will have chaos."[49] The exact nature and extent of bank-IMF cooperation was undetermined. Proposals varied from greater sharing of information to joint loans.

The third factor behind the reversal of the banks' position was what *enabled* them to work more closely with the Fund. They knew that the IMF economists would demand more stringent conditions than they themselves had imposed the previous year, but such conditions now seemed more viable. In 1976, the banks had been fearful of forcing the government to the wall; now intervening events had made them more confident that the outcome would produce a shift to the right rather than the left. The most important confirmation of this belief was the July 1976 ouster of the leftist-leaning cabinet ministers—Jorge Fernández Maldonado, Miguel Angel de la Flor, and Enrique Gallegos. No public protest resulted. In addition, the government's ability to disperse the demonstrations and break the strikes protesting the mid-1976 stabilization measures was comforting to the bankers. They drew the conclusion (soon to be severely challenged) that the Peruvian political climate was not as explosive as they had believed it to be the previous year.

Given the banks' insistence on involving the IMF, the Peruvian government acquiesced and a Fund mission arrived in Lima in March 1977. The mission decided that Peru should hold its 1977 inflation rate to 15 percent, should reduce its budget deficit to no more than 20 billion

49. *Business Week*, Mar. 21, 1977.

soles,[50] and should achieve equilibrium in its balance of payments with no new loans. In a typical set of demands, the IMF "suggested" that Peru (1) cut all subsidies to public enterprises, leaving them to acquire necessary financial resources through price increases; (2) raise gasoline and other fuel prices enough to both eliminate the Petroperú deficit (16 billion soles) and provide a surplus for the central government; (3) cut another 10–20 billion soles from the deficit by eliminating the purchase of capital goods for public sector investment and selling off firms to the private sector; (4) tighten up the tax system by eliminating all tax exemptions (including those on traditional exports), creating an emergency "wealth tax," and indexing tax payments; (5) eliminate noneconomic restrictions on imports (e.g. quotas); (6) devalue the sol by 30 percent (i.e. to 90 soles/dollar); and (7) limit wage and salary increases to 10–15 percent.[51]

The political implications of this program were intolerable even to Peru's conservative financial officials. Central Bank President Carlos Santistevan and several Central Bank directors sent a letter to Finance Minister Barúa, threatening to resign if the IMF program were accepted. The letter stated that the Fund was "seeking to balance the economy in an extremely short term, and its measures would have excessive and unnecessarily depressive effects which can, and should, be avoided."[52]

Santistevan and the Central Bank countered the IMF with a more flexible set of proposals, but at the same time other members of the government (especially Industry Minister General Gastón Ibáñez) proposed measures to *expand* the economy by increasing government spending, pegging the exchange rate, reinstating food subsidies, and cutting the price of gasoline. Caught between these opposing pressures, Morales Bermúdez made no decision, and in May, Finance Minister Luis Barúa resigned in frustration.

The new minister, Walter Piazza, was the first private businessman appointed to a cabinet post by the military government. His proposals resembled those of the IMF, the main differences being a higher budget deficit and a higher expected inflation rate. On the basis of this program, Piazza managed to negotiate a deal with the Fund, but it was rejected by the cabinet and he too resigned.[53] Nevertheless, certain elements of

50. The sol in 1976 was valued at 65 per dollar.
51. Details are presented in the Lima weekly *Caretas*, Apr. 5, 1977, pp. 11–15.
52. *Latin America Economic Report*, 5, no. 15 (Apr. 22, 1977).
53. For a more extensive account of the contradictory sequence of events surrounding the IMF negotiations, see Nicholas Asheshov, "Peru's Flirtation with Disaster," *Institutional Investor*, Oct. 1977.

his program—mainly price rises—were put into effect and aroused strong popular opposition, including the first general strike since 1919. The government response was two-edged. On the one hand, it imposed a curfew and sent in police and army troops. Hundreds of workers were arrested, and at least nine people were killed. Laws were subsequently suspended to allow factory owners to fire strike participants, and some 6,000 workers lost their jobs. On the other hand, the government also tried to mollify the strikers by raising wages and salaries. The increases, however, were not enough to cover increases in food and transportation costs.[54]

Three months later, the Peruvian government signed an agreement with the IMF that was very similar to the Piazza proposals. According to the agreement, the real crunch would come in 1978, when the government was to cut the budget deficit to a third the 1977 total and inflation by half. This implied a further increase in unemployment and a further reduction in the purchasing power of wage earners. In return, Peru was to receive $100 million, to be disbursed in bimonthly installments over two years.

The first installment of the IMF loan was released in December, but in February the Fund's mission returned to Lima and declared Peru in massive violation of the agreement. In refusing the second and all further drawdowns, it focused special attention on the budget deficit (reportedly already over the yearly total agreed upon), the pegging of the sol at 130 to the dollar, and some dubious accounting procedures designed to help cover up the shortfalls.[55] When the banks heard the report, they called off a $260 million loan then under negotiation; the U.S. government also refused further assistance. This meant that Peru's only debt relief still on line was the Soviet Union's agreement to postpone 80 percent ($100 million per year) of the payments for arms purchases between 1978 and 1980.

The dilemma of the Morales Bermúdez government at this point was dramatic. The Peruvian public sector foreign debt was $4.8 billion (private debt added another $3.4 billion), and Peru was scheduled to pay over $1 billion in interest and amortization during 1978 alone. This sum would constitute some 55 percent of export revenues, a figure the government estimated could rise to 70 percent by 1980 (see Table 2). The Central Bank had virtually no foreign exchange, and lines of credit

54. Bill Bollinger, "Workers' Militancy Grows in Peru," The Guardian, Apr. 26, 1978.
55. Latin American Economic Report, 6, no. 10 (Mar. 10, 1978).

were shut off.[56] In practical terms, this meant that without quick action Peru's imports would have to be cut drastically, throwing tens of thousands of people out of work and cutting the food supply.

The banks and the IMF nevertheless insisted on further austerity measures as the *sine qua non* to extending any relief. Some officials in the Carter Administration were slightly more hesitant (although they did nothing), because they recognized the obvious contradiction between the need for repression implied in further austerity measures and the Morales Bermúdez plan to return the government to civilian control. Although some people in Peru—including members of the local bourgeoisie as well as the left—suggested a moratorium on debt payments rather than further austerity, there is no indication that Morales Bermúdez or any of his top economic officials seriously entertained this idea. Their own inclinations, and the overwhelming financial power of the banks and the Fund, pushed in the same direction. Thus on May 15, prices were doubled on fuel, public transportation, and basic foodstuffs as government subsidies were eliminated in order to cut the budget deficit.

Coming after workers had already lost a fourth of their purchasing power to inflation in the first quarter of the year, the measures quickly produced clashes in the streets of Lima and strikes in provincial cities. After more than a dozen persons were killed, the government placed the country under martial law, jailed hundreds of leftist labor leaders, and announced a two-week postponement of elections to choose a Constituent Assembly. This did not stop a two-day general strike on May 22–23. The strike was almost total in many parts of the country, but the power of the workers was simply not sufficient to outweigh that of the financial community.[57] This was especially true since the government was at most mildly against the austerity measures and possibly wholeheartedly in favor of them.

What did Morales Bermúdez gain from the price increases besides the heightened enmity of the vast majority of the population? Apparently he gained the support of the IMF, the banks, and the U.S. government in his search for debt relief. Within days of the new austerity measures,

---

56. Information comes from television speeches speeches by Morales Bermúdez and Finance Minister Javier Silva Ruete. See *Wall Street Journal*, May 22, 1978, for the former, and *Latin America Economic Report*, 6, no. 24 (Jun. 23, 1978), for the latter.

57. Bill Bollinger, "Peruvian Workers Stage General Strike," *The Guardian*, May 31, 1978.

and with the sound of strikes and rioting still echoing in the streets, the international banks tentatively agreed to roll over some $200 million in amortization owed them during the rest of 1978. Interest was still to be paid, however, and the deal was tied to the signing of a new agreement with the IMF by September.[58] The IMF agreement was actually completed in August, and it paved the way for a complete rescheduling of the foreign debt, as the Peruvians requested. Governmental lenders, meeting in the so-called Club of Paris, agreed to put off 90 percent of the interest and amortization payments owed them by Peru in 1979 and 1980. These were turned into seven-year loans with three-year grace periods. Similar arrangements were made with the private banks.[59]

But the relief is only temporary and partial; the basic question still remains. Can the Morales Bermúdez government implement an austerity program that calls for further cuts in workers' incomes, plus a drop in military imports and in inputs for local industry? The task may be even more difficult this time around, since opposition has been institutionalized in the Constituent Assembly elected in 1978 to prepare for Peru's return to civilian rule. The left won 28 percent of the 100 seats, and even the right-wing Popular Christian Party (27 percent of seats) has said it will oppose the military government.[60] Thus the only way an austerity program is likely to be implemented is by greatly stepping up the existing level of repression and probably closing the Assembly. The process will provide an exceptionally clear test of the Carter human rights policy. Are human rights in Peru more important than support for the IMF?

CONCLUSION

The Peruvian case is important in itself, but it also sheds light on a number of more general problems of private bank financing in Latin America and the rest of the Third World. These problems can best be seen by returning to the three characteristics of the privatization of finance mentioned at the beginning of the paper.

58. *Financial Times*, Jun. 1, 1978, and *New York Times*, Jun. 10, 1978. The one major bank holding out on this latest agreement was Chase Manhattan, lead bank for the huge Cuajone copper project. Chase sent a telex to the Peruvian government demanding that a law be approved immediately guaranteeing continuation of the current practice of setting aside money from copper sales to service the Cuajone loans. Retaliation, in the form of interfering with new loans, was threatened if such a law were not forthcoming. (See *Financial Times*, May 24 and Jun. 1, 1978.)

59. *Journal of Commerce*, Nov. 2, 1978, and *New York Times*, Nov. 6, 1978.

60. *Latin America Political Report*, 12, no. 24 (Jun. 23, 1978).

We will recall that the first characteristic was the role of privatization in helping to sustain the growth of bank profits. In the early 1970's, the banks' U.S. and European loan demand began to falter; in response, the banks began to look upon a group of Third World countries as desirable clients. Although adequate published data are lacking to verify the importance of these new Third World loans, it is suggestive that the international share of the profits of the top dozen U.S. banks rose from 17 percent in 1970 to 49 percent in 1977. In the case of Citibank, South American profits went from less than two percent of total profits in 1971 to 27 percent of total profits in 1977—with Brazil alone accounting for 20 percent. Brazil similarly accounted for 13 percent of Chase's profits in 1977.[61]

Peru was an early participant in the new loan market, entering in 1972. A year later, it represented eight percent of all loans to Third World countries, surpassed only by Mexico and Algeria.[62] The importance the banks attributed to the Peruvian loans can be deduced from the fact that they broke the informal blockade the U.S. government and the multilateral agencies had established against the Velasco government to make them. The prospect of profits—both immediate and long-term—outweighed political factors. In fact, descriptions of the situation in Peru in the early 1970's are reminiscent of Latin America in the 1920's. One top officer in a big private Lima bank (who opposes the military government) said: "The foreign bankers came down here lending money as if there were no tomorrow. Of course the government took their money. How would it refuse? Why should it?"[63]

When problems arose with the Peruvian loans, the banks initially intervened directly; but the strong negative reaction has probably eliminated direct intervention as a future option. The criticism that arose—especially inside the financial world—was decisive. The banks do not want the publicity and controversy that come with setting macroeconomic conditions for loans and monitoring their implementation. They are still inexperienced in dealing with countries as clients. Not only do such clients differ from individuals and private corporations in size, source of income, and political considerations, but the setting is different as well. Rather than behind-the-scenes negotiations where no outsiders know the details, the new-style negotiations become front-page news when the press and political opponents dig for information.

61. Information is from the annual reports of the banks.
62. OECD, *Development Cooperation*, 1976.
63. Asheshov, p. 38. See similar comments in *Business Week*, Sept. 5, 1977, pp. 31–34.

After the Peruvian experience, it seems clear that in the future some official agency will have to be brought in from the outset; the IMF remains the obvious candidate.

The second characteristic of the privatization process of the 1970's was precisely that it led to a new role for the public institutions. Rather than being the key actors themselves, as they had been during the 1950's and 1960's, they began to put more emphasis on supporting the private banks. An especially close collaboration developed between the banks and the IMF—although they have not always been in agreement, and the simplistic view that the latter is the "tool" of the former is incorrect. The Fund has its own ideas about how an economy should be run and does not need any coaching from the banks. In fact, one of the continuing disagreements between the two seems to center on the banks' view that the Fund is *too* rigid in its prescriptions.[64] The new supportive relationship is also evidenced by co-financing of loans by the Export-Import Bank, the World Bank, or the Inter-American Development Bank.

In general, opinion within the U.S. government also favors privatization. Thus the Eximbank went into co-financing, and AID funds fell dramatically in favor of private finance. Treasury officials also support this trend. As C. Fred Bergsten (now Assistant Secretary of the Treasury for International Affairs) said at the time of the banks' Peru operation: "I think it is better in international political terms that a Morgan Guaranty—or hopefully a consortium of international banks—makes the loan. It's better for them to put tight controls on than to have a national government have to do that. It can then be portrayed as coming through market pressures, and judgments on the economic merit of the country's position, rather than being laden with political overtones."[65] On the other hand, some members of Congress are intent on imposing controls to prevent the government from "bailing out the banks." In the Peruvian case, the government gave less help than the banks and Peruvian officials advocated. Both the State Department and the Treasury stressed, however, that if the situation became critical they would reevaluate.[66]

Support for the private banks also implies support for the international financial system as a whole. One of the key issues raised by the subject

64. For an analysis of differences of opinion between the banks and the Fund, see Cary Reich, "Why the IMF Shuns a 'Super' Role," *Institutional Investor*, September 1977.

65. Shapiro, p. 27.

66. Interviews with State Department, Treasury Department, and private bank officials.

of private loans to Third World countries has revolved around the question of stability, with some arguing that sooner or later an important country will default on its debts, and that others may then follow (a new version of the domino theory). But even if the dominoes do not fall, a single default may bankrupt some of the weaker banks and trigger a chain reaction throughout the banking system. In historical terms, the analogy goes back to the heavy Latin American borrowing during the 1920's and fears of defaults similar to those of the 1930's.

Short of a recession much more serious than that of 1974–75, however, such a scenario does not seem likely. First, the institutional changes brought about partially because of the upheaval of the 1930's—the creation of the IMF and the World Bank, as well as the greatly increased economic role of capitalist governments—militate against a repeat of the chain defaults. Second, the bankers themselves are aware of the potential problems and are taking steps to avoid them. Specifically, they refuse to accept a default. Rescheduling has replaced default as the worst possible scenario from the banks' point of view, with both banks and governments (for different reasons, to be sure) wanting to avoid even rescheduling in order to maintain the countries' creditworthiness. Refinancing loans provides one alternative.[67] Another alternative is increased assistance from the U.S. government, and this is where the foreign policy implications of the debt problem arise. Will the U.S. government sit by and watch some of the major U.S. banks endanger themselves—and thus the system as a whole—because of repayment problems on loans? Or will it come to their rescue, either positively (by making public loans to Third World governments so they can repay their private loans) or negatively (by forcing the governments to pay, through a credit blockade or other means)?

The third characteristic of the privatization process has had to do with the price paid by Third World countries. The most concrete change has involved the worsening terms on the money they have borrowed. Even leaving aside grants and soft loans, there has been deterioration of two kinds. Hard loans from multilateral agencies usually matured in about 20 years, whereas the new Euroloans average 8–10 years. Also,

---

67. The difference between rescheduling and refinancing has both economic and psychological aspects—although both mean that a country cannot pay its debts. A rescheduling involves a lengthening of the period during which the country will repay its loans, and usually a grace period as well. Refinancing, on the other hand, means that a new loan is given to enable the old one(s) to be repaid. Because interest may be increased and commissions will be earned by the banks under this method, it is the preferred one from the banks' point of view. In psychological terms, a rescheduling is considered more damaging to a country's creditworthiness.

the new loans carry floating interest rates that create planning problems and probably make overall payments more costly than they were under the old fixed-rate system. In addition, the profit-making character of the banks makes them less patient with repayment problems than were AID, the World Bank, and the IDB.

Ultimately, both public and private loans have tended to lead to IMF austerity programs. Just as the IMF "seal of approval" was the lynchpin of the system of public development finance in the 1950's and 1960's, so it has come to be under the privatized system of the 1970's. In both cases, the political and economic costs imposed on the beleaguered countries are tremendous, as the Peruvian case illustrates very well.

In economic terms, stabilization programs wreak utter havoc on domestic economies. A few groups profit—those connected with the banking and primary-export sectors—while the vast majority suffers the consequences. Those who suffer most are workers, who see their wages cut or lose their jobs. In Peru, even official statistics admit that average incomes in real terms are now only 60 percent of their 1973 level and that less than half the work force has "adequate employment."[68] In structural terms, the industrial sector as a whole seems to be in danger. On the one hand, credit and demand have fallen as a result of the stabilization measures. On the other hand, if imports are cut to provide foreign exchange to service the debt, those cuts must fall heavily on capital goods and inputs for domestic industry. In any case, growth will have to be much slower than in the past, as increasing proportions of export earnings go for debt service.

The political consequences of stabilization programs are equally dramatic. Such programs have proved impossible to implement in Third World countries without highly authoritarian regimes. The growing repression in Peru since 1976—curfews, arrests, deportations, deaths, suppression of strikes and demonstrations, dissolution of workers' organizations—is not mere coincidence. It is an integral part of stabilization, as workers refuse to passively accept the burden of maintaining the banks' profits. Under these circumstances, many doubt that Morales Bermúdez's plan to return Peru to democratic rule by 1980 will prove feasible.

A couple of years ago, some hoped and others feared that private loans would give Third World governments increased leverage in dealing with the banks because the threat of default could be used to gain concessions. Peru provides dramatic evidence of the naïveté of such a

68. Television speech of Finance Minister Javier Silva Ruete. See *Latin America Economic Report*, 6, no. 24 (Jun. 23, 1978).

notion: the government has now accepted all of the IMF-bank demands. Available evidence indicates that new leverage exists only under certain very specific conditions. First, of course, the government must be united against the stabilization policies—which the Morales Bermúdez government certainly was not, with some factions opposed to austerity and the President and his top officials not. Second, leverage exists only if the country in question is of key importance in political and economic terms *and* is under clear and immediate danger from a credible leftist force.

In the Latin American context, there are probably only two countries of sufficient economic importance to threaten the banks—Brazil and Mexico. In neither case, however, is there any immediate leftist threat or any apparent desire on the part of the governments to use their potential power, so the question remains moot. Looking farther afield, two European cases are instructive. In Italy, the IMF and the banks failed to gain any major concessions in terms of economic policies because of Italy's importance to the EEC and NATO, and because the Communist Party has a real chance to take control of the government. In Britain, on the other hand, the IMF did manage to wring major concessions, despite the UK's international importance, because the government was divided and no serious threat existed.[69]

In summary, the Peruvian case (and other more general evidence) indicates that the banks have been the primary beneficiaries of the privatization of development finance in the 1970's. In direct terms, they have protected and expanded their profits, and in indirect terms, they have obtained increased suport from public sector institutions. The Third World countries—and especially their working classes—have borne the brunt of the banks' successes, as living standards have decreased and repression increased so that available resources can go to service the foreign debt. Those of us who find such a situation unacceptable must turn our attention to looking for alternative solutions, not just for the immediate crises but for the long run as well. Many of us doubt that such a solution can be found within a capitalist framework, but this is the subject of another paper.

69. On the Italian and British experiences with the IMF, see Barbara Stallings, "The IMF in Europe: Inflation Fighting In Britain, Italy, Portugal, and Spain," in Leon Lindberg, ed., *Inflation and Political Change* (New York, forthcoming).

The Difficult Path to Socialism in the English-Speaking Caribbean

ANTHONY P. MAINGOT

There was a time when the American fleet was the dominant instrument of American diplomacy and policy in the area Alfred T. Mahan used to call "our Western Hemisphere Mediterranean." No other area of the world had been as accessible and malleable to the expansionist ideologies of Mahan, a Henry Cabot Lodge, a Theodore Roosevelt—all believers in the efficacy of foreign remedies for domestic ailments. In fact, American "insular imperialism" had its beginning in the Caribbean. Islands, Frederick Merk noted, were believed to be "restoratives of youth and preventatives of premature old age."[1]

There are Mexicans and Cubans who can still remember today the time when American battlewagons kept a permanent patrol before the Mexican ports of Tampico and Veracruz and the Cuban port of Havana. As United States Secretary of State Knox was apt to explain, those ships were meant to keep the Mexicans "in salutory equilibrium, between a dangerous and exaggerated apprehension and a proper degree of wholesome fear."[2] That was the military approach to keeping the Caribbean an American *mare nostrum*.

But the United States was not the only imperial power in the Caribbean; Spain, Great Britain, France, the Netherlands, and even Denmark all had territorial interests there. U.S. concern (except for the purchase of the Virgin Islands from the Danes in 1917) was always with the independent Caribbean and Central American nations. The Monroe Doctrine coexisted very nicely with the remaining European presence in the area. Thus at a time when Nicaraguans and Mexicans had already fought the U.S. Marines and made that struggle part of their ideology of liberation, Barbadians were celebrating their 350th anniversary of un-

Anthony P. Maingot, a citizen of Trinidad and Tobago, is a Professor in the Department of Sociology and Anthropology at Florida International University in Miami. He has taught at Yale and at the University of the West Indies, Trinidad.
1. Frederick Merk, *Manifest Destiny and Mission in American History* (New York, 1963), p. 232.
2. Quoted in H. F. Cline, *The United States and Mexico* (New York, 1963), p. 165.

interrupted rule by Britain and King Sugar. Similarly, the colonial experiences and memories of Guyana, Jamaica, and Trinidad differ from those of Cuba, the Dominican Republic, and Haiti; the image of the United States as an imperial power is dimmer in the former than in the latter. But with the recent and continuing withdrawal of the Europeans from their Caribbean outposts, the United States remains as the dominant power; its conception of the Caribbean as a *mare nostrum* now encompasses these ex-colonies.

Though the United States has not entered into this new situation totally unprepared, it is doubtful whether its experience with the Hispanic Caribbean served as an adequate preparation for or parallel to its new undertaking.[3] Many of the attitudes of diplomats and policymakers have had to change. Policy, however, is not based purely on attitudes. It relates even more fundamentally to interests, short- and long-term. U.S. interests in the Caribbean stem first from the fact that parts of the United States are *in* the Caribbean, if not precisely *of* the Carribbean. Further interests include the $4.5 billion in U.S. investments in the Caribbean (excluding Puerto Rico) and the $2 billion worth of goods exported to the Caribbean in 1977. Then there is the matter of vital trade routes, which have increased in significance with the emergence of Cuba as a socialist state. Some of the 31 "essential" American foreign trade routes are in the Caribbean, and all the busiest of them border Cuba. Trade Route No. 4 (so designed by the Merchants Act of 1936) —"United States Atlantic Ports and Caribbean"—is by far the busiest, making heavy use of the Windward Passage (between Cuba and Haiti) and the Straights of Florida.[4] Obviously, these routes are also vital to the Latin American and Caribbean countries whose main market is the United States. By the early 1970's 55 percent of Caribbean exports and 43 percent of imports were to and from the United States.

To these material interests one must add a human dimension. Between 1820 and 1973 a total of 1,279,768 West Indians emigrated to the United States; the figure continues to grow as the United States replaces Great Britain and Canada as the most probable destination. These West Indians join an additional two million immigrants from other Caribbean

3. In 1941 Franklin D. Roosevelt appointed Charles Taussig as his adviser on Caribbean affairs. Taussig's one notable publication before that appointment was a book entitled *Rum, Romance and Rebellion* (New York, 1928). He later became the American Chairman of the Caribbean Commission. More significant to our understanding of liberal American thinking on the non-Hispanic Caribbean is Paul Blanshard's *Democracy and Empire in the Caribbean* (New York, 1947). Blanshard was a State Department official in the Caribbean from 1942 to 1946.

4. U.S. Dep't of Commerce, Maritime Administration, *Essential United States Foreign Trade Routes* (Washington, D.C., 1975).

islands to form an important minority and a significant point of contact with the Caribbean, especially at a time of heightened ethnic and racial awareness in the United States

Certainly as relevant as these other interests are the dramatic changes brought about by the Cuban Revolution. As the first nation to break away successfully from U.S. hegemony, Cuba demonstrated that such a move was possible, if costly. Its role in Africa, its formal alliance with the socialist bloc, and its efforts to assume leadership of the nonaligned nations have further complicated contemporary international relations among Caribbean nations. Even China feels compelled to compete actively for the attention of these small islands, stressing the mercenary role Cuba is playing for the USSR. At a time when the bipolar Cold War has given way to ideological pluralism and innovation, an often vague Third World identification has taken on specific meaning and importance for the Caribbean, frequently as a means of mediating between the many competing invitations to join this faction or that.

Race, ethnicity, ideology, and a keen sense of the economic and social inequalities that divide the world are all parts of that newly independent non-Hispanic Caribbean with which the United States now has to deal. The three English-speaking nations analyzed here are part of that complex new Caribbean setting. Their differing responses to the challenges facing them and to U.S. reactions to them are part of our story.

One is soon aware in dealing with contemporary U.S. responses to the new ideological pluralism found in the Caribbean that those responses arise from both very definite interests and a complex array of past and present attitudes, policies, and laws—some with unexpected momentums of their own. Similarly, the decisionmakers and politically active populations of the new Caribbean nations bring to their relationships with the United States a history of political and ideological debate and struggle that invariably have an impact on their actions, though the most vital parts of that history unfolded with little or no influence from the United States. With the exception of Guyana, where as we shall see the United States has actively intervened at least since 1953, the political cultures of the British Caribbean colonies had already crystallized by the 1960's, when as new nations they developed significant political contacts with the United States.[5]

It is a fundamental task of those who would understand the contemporary relations between the United States and the English-speaking Carib-

5. Although the U.S. military presence in Trinidad during the Second World War had a profound impact on Trinidadian society in many ways, politics was not one of them.

bean to understand the origins of the ideological pluralism in Guyana, Jamaica, and Trinidad. In fact, it is the central thesis of this paper that the political cultures of all three nations had already crystallized by the time the United States took over as the dominant power from the European nations; these political cultures, moreover, reflected advanced consumer societies more prone to state-directed populism than to people-oriented socialism. These developments have made Washington's policy objectives considerably easier to achieve.

RACE AND SOCIALISM: A HISTORICAL BACKGROUND

The two dominant themes of West Indian politics have been the ideological dependency of the leadership and the tenacity of the race question. Other major issues, such as the growth of the state bureaucracy or the role of the public sector versus that of the private sector, seem always subordinate to these two themes.

Jamaica

The Jamaican case illustrates this point from the beginning of party politics in the late 1930's. The widespread labor unrest of those years had a significant result: the emergence of a true, charismatic trade unionist called Alexander Bustamante (né William Alexander Clarke in 1884), and of his half-cousin, a politically oriented intellectual lawyer, Norman Manley. Politics and labor unionism were tied together from the beginning. The history of Jamaican politics from that time up to the early 1970's has been the history of the counterpoint between Bustamante and Manley, between Bustamante's nonideological populism and Manley's intellectual socialism. "The Bustamante-Manley polarization," notes Rex Nettleford, "is seductive. The rival cousins, each with undoubtedly major talents, have provided an excellent scenario for the nation's political drama."[6] That scenario incorporated a solid two-party system based on a spoils and patronage network and also a propensity to violence.

Whereas both Bustamante and Manley organized on the labor front (the Bustamante Industrial Trade Union [BITU] and the National Workers Union [NWU] respectively), only Manley moved politically, and his People's National Party (PNP) was the first serious Jamaican ef-

6. Rex Nettleford, *Manley and the Politics of Jamaica* (Mona, Jamaica, 1971), p. 70.

fort at a mass-based political party. In 1940, the PNP proclaimed itself a socialist party. To Manley at that time socialism meant "a fundamental change . . . a demand for the complete change of the basic organization of the social and economic conditions under which we live."[7] Manley included in his definition the notion that "all means of production should in one form or the other come to be publicly owned and publicly controlled." Lest he be misunderstood, Manley did add that "you are not being committed to revolution or to godlessness." Not surprisingly, a fundamental characteristic of Manley's socialism was its foreign intellectual origins, which Nettleford tells us included the "exposure of a few bright self-made intellectuals to Fabian socialist thought then current in Britain. Sir Stafford Cripps of the British Labour Party's left and Gollancz's Left Book Club publications were important intellectual and inspirational sources in the Jamaican genesis and adoption of the creed."[8] Though clearly labor unrest played a major role in awakening native leadership, foreign ideological influence was vital in providing that leadership with a perspective.

The sequence is important: ideology followed organization, it was not the basis of it. It is doubtful that at a time of heightened Black awareness the rank-and-file would have chosen Manley's examples of his socialism. Under attack from members of the colonial government, Manley as early as 1940 noted that it was the socialisms of Norway, Sweden, Ireland, Denmark, New Zealand, Australia, and the British Labour Party that were the PNP's ideal. In the mid-1950's Manley wrote that he was a democratic socialist, which was "the essence of British socialism . . . and that is the socialism to which I subscribe."[9] This approach held a wide appeal for the middle class, especially the intellectuals. They joined the PNP, as Wilmot Perkins notes, because it "appropriated not only the country's leading intellectuals and artists, . . . but the very idea of intellectualism in politics." Bustamante's Jamaican Labour Party (JLP), founded in 1943, could never rival the PNP in terms of the glamor of its following; the JLP, Perkins continues, was "repellent to the status-conscious 'brown skinned' intelligentsia."[10]

Manley demonstrated his adherence to democratic parliamentary prin-

7. Quoted in Rex Nettleford, ed., *Manley and the New Jamaica, Selected Speeches and Writings, 1938–1968* (London, 1971), p. 61.
8. Nettleford, *Manley and the Politics of Jamaica*, p. 35.
9. Quoted in Nettleford, ed., *Manley and the New Jamaica*, p. 89.
10. Wilmot Perkins, "The Intellectuals, the PNP and the JLP," *The Sunday Gleaner*, Nov. 27, 1977, p. 7.

ciples and his aversion to "alien" ideologies in 1952, when he expelled some of his most important left allies from the PNP on the grounds that they had formed a Marxist caucus within the party.[11] Yet Manley and the PNP were always vulnerable to opposition attacks on two grounds —the "foreign" origins of the party's philosophy, and race. To the opposition the PNP was a party of socialist, middle class, "brown men." As George Eaton has noted: "Bustamante . . . elected to fight the PNP on the issue on which they were most vulnerable and one which they themselves had interjected, namely, ideology. . . . Socialism was equated with Communism, and Communism meant tyranny and slavery. Besides, as the PNP was also the party of the urban middle classes . . . a PNP victory would mean tyranny and slavery."[12]

With Bustamante's JLP successfully pushing an anticommunist populist line and the radicals within the PNP at bay, the latter party's commitment to socialism weakened over the years. Nonetheless, its ideological dependency did not. Only the focus shifted: to the Puerto Rican model of development through import substitution. Socialism would not be pushed to the forefront again until the electoral victories of Norman's son, Michael Manley, in 1972 and 1976. Despite these impressive electoral victories, the outcome of the new socialist initiatives is far from decided in socialism's favor. The bitter battles within the PNP in 1977 between the so-called "moderates" and the "radicals" are reminiscent of the battles of the early 1950's and center, now as then, around the charges of "ideologies alien to the party."

Trinidad

This link between trade unionism and political party organization was not replicated in Trinidad. The first significant socialist political organizer, Captain Andrew Cipriani, did not come onto the scene until after the First World War. Cipriani became president in 1919 of the moribund Trinidad Workingmen's Association, which within a decade became the largest and best-organized labor-oriented political movement in the British West Indies. He affiliated the Association with the British

---

11. Expelled from the Executive Committee of the PNP were Ken and Frank Hill, Richard Hart, and Arthur Henry—known as the "4 H's." Norman Manley's son, Michael Manley, returned from England to head up a new union to counter these Marxist trade unionists—the National Workers Union (NWU), the main labor base of the PNP up to today.

12. George E. Eaton, *Alexander Bustamante and Modern Jamaica* (Kingston, Jamaica, 1975), pp. 106–7.

Labour Party and the Labour and Socialist International, and he was regularly present at the Biennial Empire Conferences of the British Labour Party, "looking for your help and support."[13]

The next stage in the development of Trinidad's radical movement came in the 1930's, when a considerable rise in labor consciousness led to active trade union organization (trade unions having been legalized in 1932). But the 1932 ordinance made no provision for the right of peaceful picketing and gave unions no immunity against action in tort —both part of Great Britain's union legislation since 1906. The deep-rooted dependency of the Trinidad Left was again evidenced when Cipriani's Association refused to register as a union as a protest—a decision taken on the advice of the International Department of the British Trade Union Congress.[14]

It is interesting to speculate on the consequences of Cipriani's decision not to register as a trade union. The 1930's were the period when the two most significant groups of workers—Blacks in oil and Indians in sugar—were joining two newly registered unions, the Oilfield Workers' Trade Union and the All-Trinidad Sugar Estates and Factory Workers' Trade Union. When in 1937 labor unrest escalated, power seemed to pass from Cipriani's hands into those of men who grabbed the leadership of labor. Such a man was Uriah Butler. Given the colonial structure of the government, Cipriani found that by entering the political arena he had cut off his room to maneuver. Part of Cipriani's problem, aside from his white, middle-class background, was his dependency on British legalistic approaches to labor. Butler had no such restrictions and could fit his methods to local needs, which involved mostly bread-and-butter issues but also racial ones—for instance, the employment of South Africans on the oil companies' staff.[15] Totally lacking in any organizational talents or political ideology, however, Butler was unable to grasp the political opportunity the times presented.

Cipriani's attempt to emulate the British Labour Party's structure did not conform to the island's fast-changing economic scene. By not converting the Trinidad Workingmen's Association into a legal union and making it a branch of his Labour Party, Cipriani paved the way for the

13. Quoted in C. L. R. James, *The Life of Captain Cipriani* (London, 1932), p. 31.
14. See *Trinidad and Tobago Disturbances, 1937. Report of Commission* (G.P.O., Port of Spain, 1938), p. 40.
15. Even though Mr. Cola Rienzi was General President of the OWTU and of the All-Trinidad Sugar Estates and Factory Workers' Trade Union, the colonial authorities regarded Butler as the functional leader of the workers and Rienzi as "without question Butler's accredited emissary." (*Trinidad and Tobago Disturbances, 1937*, p. 58.)

effective separation of trade unionism from parliamentary politics in Trinidad. Labor expected its leaders to deal with bread-and-butter issues—no matter what the ideology of the union leadership. By 1956 this had permitted a totally pragmatic, nonideological politician named Eric Williams to organize and launch a racially based political party, the People's National Movement (PNM) without association with any union structure and leadership. This in turn permitted Williams to exclude from party membership any radicals whose outright loyalty he doubted. Given the Indian-Black division which had already crystallized, and given the relative backwardness of Indian political thought,[16] the Black unions had no alternative but to support the predominantly Black PNM, as did some Marxists (whose grounding in Marxist doctrine was not always a sure thing).[17]

The dramatic consequences of this separation of radical trade union leadership from parliamentary politics can be seen in election results. In the 1956 general elections for the Legislative Council, the Marxist West Indian Independence Party (WIIP) contested only one of a possible 24 seats. Its candidate received 3.8 percent of the vote in that district. In 1961 the WIIP ran no candidate. In the 1966 parliamentary elections the radical groups ran under the banner of the Workers and Farmers Party (WFP) and competed in 35 of the 36 constituencies. This radical left alliance did not elect a single member, in fact, its total vote was 3.46 percent. Table 1 indicates how the most prominent Marxists fared against the Black PNM and the Indian Democratic Labour Party (DLP) in that 1966 election.

All these men had long histories of direct or indirect ties with the labor movement and were a mix of Black, Indian, Colored, and White Trinidadians. They had strong personal ties with different parts of the island. Their defeat in 1966, four years after independence and two

16. As early as 1947 a perceptive American liberal noted that "One reason for the lack of labor unity [in Trinidad] is that thousands of East Indians have become small proprietors, not sympathetic with the proletarian aims of the Negro majority. . . . In plain English, they were afraid of Negro and mulatto control until their high birth rate gave them the majority in the population." (Paul Blanshard, *Democracy and Empire*, p. 114.)

17. See Lennox Pierre and John LaRose, *For More and Better Democracy* (Trinidad, 1956). The authors were encouraged no doubt by the fact that the island's best-known radical, C. L. R. James, had returned to work with the PNM as editor of its newspaper, *The Nation*. See Lennox Pierre, *Quintin O'Conner, A Personal Appreciation* (n.d.)

An English trade unionist recalled hearing the *Communist Manifesto* referred to as by Marx and Lenin by a Trinidadian Marxist. (F. W. Dalley, *General Industrial Conditions and Labour Relations in Trinidad* [Trinidad, 1954], p. 67).

TABLE I

Parliamentary Elections in Trinidad, 1966

WFP candidate / pct. of vote	PNM	DLP
Lennox Pierre, .355%	54.6%	40.9%
Eugene Joseph, .891	88.9	4.5
C. L. R. James, 2.8	53.8	40.8
George Weekes, 4.9	28.06	51.2
Basdeo Panday, 3.5	15.0	65.8
Stephen Maharaj, 5.5	39.2	53.9
John Kelshall, 1.2	49.9	46.2

SOURCE: Report of the Parliamentary General Elections, 1966 (Trinidad, 1967).

decades after universal suffrage, was very clear proof of the fundamental weakness of the radical left movement in Trinidad. Politics had already become a racial matter in which ideology played a minimal role. After two successive PNM governments, the number of declared Marxist-Leninists had been reduced to insignificance.[18] Understanding the racial basis of politics, and in keeping with a "critical support" program followed by other movements in the Caribbean at the time, a "popular front" of labor union–based radicals called the United Labour Force (ULF) competed in the 1975 elections. Led by the charismatic Indian lawyer, Basdeo Panday, the ULF won 10 of 36 seats—all in the predominantly Indian areas formerly contolled by the Indian-based DLP. In early 1977 a group of Marxist-Leninists united in a semisecret organization called NAMOTI (National Movement for the True Independence of Trinago)[19] and carried out an anti-Panday coup within the ULF (hoping to carry the membership of the major trade unions with them).

As with the "moderate-radical" battle in Jamaica in 1977, the long-range outcome of this schism is still to be determined. For the short term, it is evident that the radical left has no mass support and even less unity among themselves. A Maoist/pro-Soviet split has rendered the radical left even less effective than usual. Panday, who in early 1978 recaptured command of the party and who is himself an old ally of the

18. In 1965 they were calculated to number 15. See Report of the Commission of Enquiry into Subversive Activities in Trinidad and Tobago (House Paper No. 2 of 1965), p. 19.

19. This group was led by some well-known radical labor leaders, including Raffique Shah, Lennox Pierre, Clive Nunez, Joe Young, and George Weekes.

left, has now reassessed the political-ideological terrain: "These arm-chair ideologists," he told the press, "have no conception of how our people feel and think. They mislead themselves into believing that the working class care what is happening in China, Cuba, and the Soviet Union or that our people are ready to accept, lock, stock and barrel, these foreign systems."[20]

Guyana

The significance of race and the ideological dependency of socialist organization, central to the political evolution of Jamaica and Trinidad, can also be seen in the case of Guyana (the former British Guiana). For example, the Marxist-Leninist leader Cheddi Jagan, who was educated in the United States, notes in his autobiography that the first thing he became very conscious of in the United States was the question of color —for him an entirely new experience. "I, too, had imbibed the psychology of fear which had gripped the U.S. Negro."[21] In the United States he married a young socialist, Janet Rosenberg, and was exposed to Marxist ideas. Jagan's ideological maturing, however, came from his travels to Trinidad in the 1950's to meet radical labor union and political leaders, of whom he writes "These were some of the 'gods' I then worshiped."

It was not until July 1969 that Jagan announced that his People's Progressive Party (PPP) was being reorganized along the lines of Communist parties of the Soviet bloc. (The month before Jagan had attended the Moscow Conference of World Communist Parties and had formally enrolled the PPP in the Communist movement.) A purge of internal opponents of that open identification immediately began to take place —not the first such purge in the PPP's history.

Since 1946, when a political discussion and action group called the Political Affairs Committee became the forum for nationalists of all types, the two major points of tension within Guyanese politics have been race and ideology, but certainly the former more than the latter.[22]

20. *The Express* (Port of Spain), Aug. 11, 1977, p. 1.
21. Cheddi Jagan, *The West on Trial* (London, 1966), p. 49.
22. R. T. Smith noted that "Neither in the country at large nor in such intellectual circles as existed, was there any informed discussion of either Marxism or of economic development. . . ." (*British Guiana* [Oxford, 1962], p. 169.) Leo A. Despres commented on the communist-noncommunist debate: "The accumulation of verbiage that represents the ideological pronouncements of most Guianese politicians is so devoid of style and inconsistent with their political behavior that it is difficult if not impossible to extract from it any sense of commitment other than . . . to national integration and independence." (*Cultural Pluralism and Nationalist Politics in British Guiana* [Chicago, 1967], p. 179.)

Yet the PPP which contested the 1953 elections, the first to be held
under universal adult suffrage, was a multiracial party largely put together by two young socialists, the Indian Cheddi Jagan and the dynamic young Black lawyer Forbes Burnham. Each brought his own labor
organization: Jagan the largely Indian sugar worker Guiana Industrial
Workers' Union (GIWU), and Burnham the largely Black and urban
British Guiana Labour Union (BGLU). The PPP won 18 of the 24 seats
at stake in the 1953 elections, but this was achieved with only 51 percent
of the votes cast by 37 percent of the electorate.[23] The PPP constitution,
drawn up in 1951, stated specifically that its goal was to "promote the
interests of the subject peoples by transforming British Guiana into a
Socialist country." One of the cofounders of the GIWU and the PPP
put its goals even more succinctly: "We are fighting for national independence which leads to socialism and communism. We will have to do
like the people of Russia." In one of his first speeches before the new
House of Assembly (July 24, 1953), Jagan portrayed a world "to all
intents and purposes . . . divided into two camps—fascism, imperialism
and capitalism on the one hand and socialism and communism on the
other." Clearly this was not the kind of language commonly heard in
this hemisphere; President Arbenz of Guatemala was overthrown a year
later for saying much less than that. And within the PPP there were
those who were uncomfortable with such a position. The Jagans apparently knew that Burnham was one of them. As Leo Despres relates,
soon after the 1953 victory the radical wing of the PPP held a series of
secret meetings at which the vacillating Burnham was one important
topic. They concluded that he must either come to terms with the left
wing or leave the party.[24]

Events soon gave Burnham an out. Following major labor disturbances
and conflicts between the PPP and the British Governor, British troops
landed, suspended the Constitution, and threw the PPP out of office.
This was the overt intervention; the covert intervention was being
sponsored by the United States. Most Guyanese did not realize that
what was unfolding was the first major anticommunist offensive by the
United States in the Caribbean—an offensive in which the United States
had substantial local support. In the early 1950's, a major struggle was
taking place between the Moscow-dominated World Federation of
Trade Unions (WFTU) and the Western-dominated International

23. The Colonial Office took these figures to argue that the PPP in 1953 hardly
had the kind of popular support to warrant the radical changes it was proposing.
(See *Report of the British Guiana Constitutional Commission*, 1954., Cmd. 9274.)
24. Despres, *Cultural Pluralism*, p. 204.

Confederation of Trade Unions (ICTU). In the Western Hemisphere the anticommunist attack was led by the AFL-supported Inter-American Regional Workers Organization (IARWO).[25] In 1952 and 1953 the ICTU and the IARWO scored major victories throughout the West Indies. In Jamaica, the PNP expelled the major left-wing leaders of the Trade Union Congress. Both the BITU and the NWU became members of the ICTU. In Barbados, Grantly Adams, first President of the WFTU-related Caribbean Labour Congress, called for the disbandment of that Congress, saying it was dominated by a Caribbean-wide clique of communists. In Trinidad, the Marxist trade unionists had been isolated even further from the evolving political arena. In Guyana, Burnham's BGLU joined the ICTU in 1952, thus formally associating himself with such "moderate" West Indian politicians as Manley, Bustamante, and Adams—all subjects of virulent attacks as "bourgeois labor unionists" in the PPP's paper *Thunder*.[26]

In 1954, the Royal Commission investigating the causes leading to the 1953 suspension of the Constitution concluded that six of the PPP's most prominent leaders were communists, including the two Jagans. Though "ideologically ambiguous," according to the Commission, three others (including Burnham) were socialists. Burnham was perceived to be Jagan's main rival. The Commission concluded that they had no doubt that the socialists in the PPP were "essentially democrats." They did doubt, however, if the democrats had "the wit to see the essential difference between themselves and their communist colleagues or the ability to avoid being out-maneuvered by them."[27]

Repeatedly, the Commissioners asserted their belief that the more moderate PPP leaders were "hardly a match for the extremists."[28] The Commission underestimated Burnham's political skills; worse, it underestimated how those skills in conjunction with foreign intervention and

25. Later the AFL gave birth to another even more interventionist arm, the American Institute for Free Labor Development, directed by Serafino Romualdi. Specifically created to challenge communist control of Latin American labor unions, it would be deeply involved in Guyana. See Sidney Lens, "American Labor Abroad: Lovestone Diplomacy," *The Nation*, Jul. 5, 1965, pp. 10ff.

26. Much later Cheddi Jagan would write that the events of the early 1950's were "catastrophic for the whole West Indian labour movement. . ." (not the least of which was the development of "a strong right wing within [Jamaica's] P.N.P. . . ."). The one lesson learned was that "While trade unions must have an active political outlook and interest, they must under our multiparty political system jealously guard their independence." (*Trade Unions and National Liberation* [Georgetown, 1977], p. 27.) How he reconciled this with his plans for a Marxist-Leninist state is not revealed.

27. *Report of the British Guiana Constitutional Commission* (1954), p. 37.

28. *Ibid.*, p. 32.

the powerful forces of racial antagonisms could capture power despite an admittedly ambiguous program. Between 1955 and 1958 several major splits occurred within the PPP. In 1956, the year of Khrushchev's attacks on Stalin and of the suppression of the Hungarian uprising, Jagan launched major attacks on "deviationists" of the right and left within the PPP, citing "Comrade Stalin" and "Comrade Mao" as authorities. Three Afro-Guyanese Marxists left the party soon thereafter, and by 1960 the Guyanese political scene reflected nearly perfectly the racial divisions existing in the society. Racial and ethnic loyalties had taken the upper hand, often in stark contrast to ideological rhetoric.[29] Faced with a new opposition, Jagan began to appeal to the Indian capitalist, developing the concept of the "reactionary-progressive"—one who would put his "national" interests above his "class" interests. In fact, it amounted to little more than pitting the Indian capitalists against the white, native, and foreign capitalists during the periods of PPP government. "Because of Jagan's efforts," writes Leo Despres, "the power and influence of the Indian business community increased substantially after 1957."[30]

When Forbes Burnham's People's National Congress (PNC) took office in Guyana after the elections of 1961, and when the nation was given independence in 1966, Burnham's political strength was virtually guaranteed by a number of foreign interventions, not the least of which

29. While Caribbean Marxists had split with international communism on racial grounds before (the 1940 case of George Padmore—first black member of the Comintern—reflects that past), the year 1956 was a significant watershed. Aimé Césaire's break with the French Communist Party in 1956 was not a break with Marxism but with the White French Communist Party and Stalinism. In a way, the neo-Marxist theories of Frantz Fanon can also be interpreted through an understanding of the racial factor. The wide and virtually uncritical acceptance of Fanon's race-based theories is a further indication of the "ideological permeability" of the area. In the Caribbean, socialism will have to come to grips with the impact of slavery and the plantation in the shaping of the contemporary configuration of the black masses. This has been a theme of a vigorous new school of radical West Indian intellectuals who combine an intense concern with race with an intellectual and political commitment to Marxian socialism. See Norman Girvan, *Aspects of the Political Economy of Race in the Caribbean and in the Americas* (Mona, Jamaica, 1975); Trevor Munroe, *The Politics of Constitutional Decolonization* (Mona, Jamaica, 1975); and George Beckford, "Institutionalized Racism in Jamaica," *Socialism*, 4, no. 2 (Jun. 1977), pp. 42–47.

30. Despres, *Cultural Pluralism*, pp. 233–34. Jagan and the PPP have long been criticized as being inconsistent by maintaining a highly profitable import-export agency (GIMPEX), which serves as the commercial arm of the party. Jagan owns 49 percent of the shares, a fellow PPP member, Ramkarran, 46 percent. In 1963 the opposition Trade Union Congress charged that GIMPEX had made a profit of over BWI$68,000 in two weeks in one area of its business alone (*The Freedom Strikers* [Georgetown, 1963], p. 11).

was the unprecedented British act of changing the electoral system from the traditional British first-past-the-post to the continental system of proportional representation.[31] This allowed Burnham to exploit successfully a much expanded system of overseas voting by proxy. As ambiguous as Burnham might have seemed to the vested interests, he was clearly the lesser of two evils. In 1966, during independence celebrations, the *New York Times* reported from Guyana that in the foreign diplomatic and business community the outward attitude was much the same: they believed that the government of Premier Forbes Burnham, supported by Britain and the United States and by business, would "remain stable and continue to be hospitable to foreign investment."[32]

THE PROBLEMS OF INDEPENDENCE

The struggle for political power in parliamentary systems characterized by pluralistic and well-developed parties very often has meant the subordination of programs to the exigencies of electioneering. Such was the case with these three West Indian societies as they passed from colonial to independent status (Jamaica and Trinidad gained independence in 1962), and as they joined the Inter-American system.[33] All had institutionalized the trappings of the Westminster parliamentary model; most had adopted a number of the attitudes that make that model function. Indeed, the parliamentary model suited the urban, "middle-class" background (not the least part of which was an English education) of many of the new elites quite nicely. And in terms of the criteria of Westminster-based systems, these three countries have been successful. It bears stressing that by 1978, Jamaica, Trinidad, and Guyana had had

31. As late as 1954, the Royal Commission empowered to recommend changes in the British Guiana Constitution noted that, "if some system of proportional representation were now introduced it could hardly be represented as other than a device to mitigate the present dominance of the P.P.P. To enshrine in the constitution such a device would in our view be wrong and we, therefore, recommend no change in the present electoral system" (*Report of the British Guiana Constitutional Commission* (1954), p. 30). In all fairness to the British government, however, it must be recognized that the conflicting parties themselves had concluded that there was no prospect of an agreed solution: "In these circumstances, we are agreed to ask the British government to settle on their authority all outstanding constitutional issues, and we undertake to accept their decision." (Letter from Cheddi Jagan, L. F. S. Burnham, and P. S. D'Aguiar, Oct. 25, 1963, in *British Guiana Conference*, 1963, CMND 2203, p. 4.)
32. *New York Times*, May 24, 1966, p. 14.
33. Because of the unsettled territorial dispute with Venezuela, Guyana has not been admitted to the Organization of American States; but it is a member of other Inter-American agencies, including the Inter-American Development Bank.

TABLE 2

Basic Statistics on Jamaica, Guyana, Trinidad & Tobago
(Unless otherwise indicated, figures are for 1975)

	Jamaica	Guyana	Trinidad & Tobago
GNP per capita	J$1,279	G$1,181	TT$3,295
Aggregate population (1976)	2,300,000	800,000	1,200,000
		African 35%	African 43%
		Indian 53%	Indian 40%
		Colored 10%	Colored 15%
		White 2%	White 2%
Birth rate/1000 (1970–75)	33.2	32.4	25.3
Death rate/1000 (1970–75)	7.1	5.9	5.9
Life expectancy at birth (1970–75 average)	70	68	70
Infant mortality/1000 live births	26	40	35
Population density/km² (1972)	175	4	203
Migration balance (1970)	265,000	n.a.	17,370
Urban proportion	40.9%	33.5%	25.1%
Per capita energy consumption (kg. coal equivalent)	1,338	996	3,962
Literacy rate	82%	76%	89%
Private cars	109,628	22,400	88,800
Commercial vehicles	28,609	n.a.	23,052
Average daily circulation of newspapers (no. of papers in brackets)	277,800 [3]	50,000 [3]	155,552 [3]
Number of radios	640,000	150,000	296,000
Number of telephones	100,000	21,074	67,064
Number of television sets	100,000	No T.V.	93,000

more experience with democratic parliamentary politics than most Latin American nations had had in the 160 years since their Wars of Independence.

Yet this model, though admirably suited to managing political and ideological pluralism and conflict, was hardly geared to mediating conflict that had both class and race origins. And race was by far the dominant feature of West Indian political strife. Parties, traditional patronage-distributing mechanisms, became in the cases of Guyana and Trinidad the articulators and aggregators of ethnic interests. In both cases, however, the parties remained in theory "nonracial." In Jamaica political patronage generated a kind of cannibalism among all classes and "racial" groups. And since both parties were fundamentally polyclass in composition, it was difficult to establish a clear-cut racial cleavage in political terms—which did not stop race from being a major part of the ongoing tensions. In many ways these racial conflicts were reflections of the strides in modernization these societies had made.[34] Those strides are illustrated by the statistics in Table 2.

By the 1960's the elites of these societies had overcome the foremost challenge to the system they had opted to rule by: the ideological challenge from the radical left. When in the mid-1970's this left (which had returned to the fold) showed new strength and political aspirations, it encountered even more formidable vested interests than had been the case in the 1950's. A review of these socialist initiatives of the 1970's indicates that the new West Indian left has not been any more successful than its predecessors some two decades earlier.

Guyana

In the early 1970's it was Guyana that took the leadership in many radical reforms. Its nationalization in July 1971 of the Demerara Bauxite Co. (DEMBA), a subsidiary of the Aluminum Company of Canada (ALCAN), contributed to legitimizing the idea of state ownership in the British Caribbean. "In that sense," a noted Caribbean scholar wrote in 1974, "the nationalization signaled the initiation of a new wave of economic nationalism that is now sweeping the region from one end to the other."[35] The DEMBA nationalization was followed by that of the Commonwealth Development Corporation (a wood-processing complex), of the British-owned sugar plantations (Jessel Securities), of the U.S.-owned Reynolds Metals bauxite operations, and, in 1976 of Booker-McConnell, Ltd., a British conglomerate that in 1975 generated fully 25 percent of the Guyanese GNP. Since 1976 the public sector has been increased by nationalizations of newspapers and the drug distribution trade; so many enterprises have been nationalized, in fact, that by the end of 1977 Forbes Burnham governed a country in which the state controlled 80 percent of the economy. While government has been increasing, private consumption as a percentage of the GNP has been steadily decreasing since 1972.

34. An excellent analysis of the attitudinal dimension of these strides is contained in Wendell Bell, "Inequality in Independent Jamaica: A Preliminary Appraisal of Elite Performance," *Revista/Review Interamericana*, 7, no. 2 (1977), pp. 294–308.

35. Norman Girvan, *Corporate Imperialism: Conflict and Expropriation* (White Plains, N.Y., 1976), p. 184.

Burnham's moves, opportunistic though they seemed to the PPP, were dramatic enough to have caught Washington unprepared. Emerging victorious from the last three elections, the PNC has steadily moved to the left, not only in terms of its internal nationalization programs, but, and perhaps especially, in terms of its foreign policy. Guyana's Burnham took the lead in the joint West Indian recognition of Cuba in 1971 and again in emphasizing a Third World, "nonaligned" stance. He was rewarded with visits by Fidel Castro, who heaped praise on his performance, and with invitations to the USSR.

The real opportunity for Burnham, however, came in 1975. In June of that year the Conference of Communist and Workers Parties of Latin America and the Caribbean declared itself in favor of the so-called theory of "non-capitalist development." The Declaration, writes the influential Guyanese Marxist, Clive Y. Thomas, "virtually underwrites all the major propositions of the theory of non-capitalist development" and marks "a definite shift in emphasis in the struggle for decolonization and socialism in the Third World." [36] It accepts the state of "national democracy" as a legitimate phase, both operationally and theoretically, in the transition to socialism and the dictatorship of the proletariat. Broad alliances of "progressive forces" rather than the leadership of "vanguard" parties were now acceptable, since the priorities were no longer the enthroning of socialism but rather the anti-feudal, anti-imperialist, and national democratic struggles.

This theory was precisely what Burnham needed, especially in the year before his move against the powerful Booker interests. In August 1975, Cheddi Jagan and the PPP announced their new stance of "critical support." Though charging that the PNC's electoral victory was "stolen" and that "many evils like the Booker's monopoly, erosion of fundamental rights, absence of democracy, discrimination, corruption, and squandermania still persist," Jagan concluded that the PNC's recent policies had weakened imperialism and that the PPP should put an end to its two-year-old boycott of Parliament. It was now Jagan's turn to shift positions: "The situation now therefore demands a more flexible approach on the part of the PPP . . . Our political line should be changed from non-cooperation and civil resistance to critical support. This can lay the basis for a political solution in our country." [37]

36. Clive Y. Thomas, "The Havana Declaration of June 1975," paper presented to the Conference on Contemporary Trends and Issues in Caribbean International Affairs (Trinidad, May 23–27, 1977), p. 2.

37. "Cheddi Jagan on Critical Support," address to the 25th Anniversary Conference of the PPP, Aug. 3, 1975, p. 12.

It was not the first ideological and strategic shift in young Guyana's political history. But, as in the past, in the zero-sum game of Guyanese racial politics there could only be one winner. Despite considerable Cuban and Soviet pressure on Burnham, Jagan and the PPP were the losers.[38] Burnham rejected the PPP call for a National Front Government and proceeded to make plans for a change in the Constitution that further threatened the PPP politically. Burnham seemed untouchable. Yet the economic performance of the regime was spotty, as Table 3 indicates, especially in 1975–76.

TABLE 3
External Trade 1972–76
(G$ million)

	1972	1973	1974	1975	1976
Exports	292.8	288.3	594.9	837.2	468.2
Imports	299.0	349.2	563.6	806.4	687.2
Balance	−6.2	−60.9	31.3	30.8	−219.0

SOURCE: *The Economist,* Quarterly Economic Review, Annual Supplement, *The West Indies* (1977), p. 47.

By 1976 Guyana had a restless labor movement—even in the formerly loyal bauxite mining areas—agitating for wage increases. Moreover, productivity was declining in virtually every major sector—especially in rice and bauxite. The price of sugar had plummeted in the world market and the price of oil kept rising. It was also clear by 1977 that Guyana's application for admission to Comecon had gotten nowhere.[39]

It seemed time for another shift, now to the only source of the means to salvage the deteriorating economic situation—Washington. Dr. Fred Sukdeo, Economic Adviser to the Government, first raised the signals of a shift in direction:

The dialectics of this period requires a temporary shift to selected capitalist strategies of development. The state sector is not an efficient producer of wealth and is likely to experience complex traditional problems. Foreign private capital should be encouraged to invest with the incentives more

38. An interpretation given me by many informed Guyanese during my visit to Georgetown, Sep. 2–8, 1977, and also reported in *The Latin American Political Reporter* (London), no. 35 (Sep. 9, 1977).
39. Whether this was a result of Burnham's refusal to invite Jagan into the government is a matter of speculation in Guyana and outside.

favorable than similar developing countries. The local capitalists and the petty-bourgeois class should also be provided with opportunities to enhance the developmental process.[40]

By 1977, the PPP and other Marxist-Leninist groups in the British Caribbean had given indications that the "critical support" stance called for from Havana in 1975 was wearing thin. In an April 1977 meeting of these groups, which the PPP called a "turning point in the struggle in the region," the West Indian representatives seemed to interpret events in Vietnam, Angola, Mozambique, Cambodia, and Guinea-Bissau as having changed the "correlation of forces" in the world. They were now in the epoch of transition from capitalism to socialism.[41] Again, as was the case with the nationalization of bauxite in 1971, Guyana seemed to serve as a rallying point for West Indian Marxists. "We come here," noted Jamaica's Trevor Munroe, "under the inspiration, the guidance, the initiative of the PPP. We look to the Communist Movement in Guyana, for the movement of Marxism in Guyana has shown us how to fight."[42] Jagan, it seems, had decided that the time had come to fight. In September of that year the PPP-dominated sugar union, the Guyana Agricultural and General Workers' Union (GAWU), called its workers out on strike. The grievance: workers' "profit share" for 1974, 1975, and 1976 had not been paid. The profit-sharing formula implemented in 1974, when the price of sugar had been soaring and plantations were in private and expatriate hands, seemed quite a different thing in 1977, when the price of sugar had hit rock bottom and the government was now the owner of the estates. The strike lasted a painful six months and was finally broken by the government's use of the army and friendly urban unions as strikebreakers. As the emboldened government overcame the most dramatic challenge the PPP could muster, it moved in mid-1978 to modify the Constitution and succeeded in a referendum boycotted by the PPP. Changes in the "deeply entrenched" clauses of the Constitution will no longer require referendums, only a two-thirds majority in Parliament—something the PNC has achieved with singular regularity and gives no indication of relinquishing. "Rise Up and Fight for Rights" was the headline in the PPP's *Mirror* on April 12, 1978. Calling it "one of the most dramatic moments in the history of the Guyana Parliament" the paper reported Dr. Jagan shouting "We will not be a party to this confounded nonsense!" while sending his parliamentary desk with all its contents flying to the floor.

40. *Guyana Chronicle*, May 26, 1977, p. 1.
41. *The Mirror* (Overseas Edition) Apr. 1977, p. 4.
42. *Ibid.*, p. 3.

With the PNC calling itself a "vanguard party," with Burnham snugly entrenched as a major Third World leader enjoying the friendship of the Soviet Union and Cuba, with 80 percent of the economy in state hands, and with a new and convenient Constitution and no successful challenge to the electoral system that secures Burnham two-thirds majorities without fail, Jagan and the PPP seemed outmaneuvered and outwitted.

By the end of 1977 Forbes Burnham governed a country in which the public sector accounted for 80 percent of the economy. To support this expansion, income taxes were increased 336 percent between 1964 and 1975; during the same period revenues from import and excise duties increased from G$40 million to G$352 million, or by 774 percent. Yet, by the second quarter of 1978 it was calculated that Guyana's foreign exchange reserves were enough to cover less than two weeks' imports.[43] The fact is that the public sector has not been producing. "Management in the Public Sector," noted a University of Guyana economist, "seems to be reduced from a science to a manipulative art with an entrenched crimplene shirt-jac and long and wide sideburn mentality. The functioning of this elite group is not compatible with socialism."[44] The figures in Table 4 indicate that after nearly a decade of "cooperative socialist" schooling, Guyana's youth seem unenthusiastic about government control of their society, despite the fact that 64 percent of them believed that the government was already in full control of "all the power" in the society. Two-thirds of these Guyanese youth hoped to do university studies abroad, and fully 42 percent of those with professional career ambitions wanted to engage in those professions abroad.

In 1978 Guyana was well on its way to state capitalism and even further away from socialism. The years 1976 and 1977 had been crucial, as they were in Jamaica. Many of those who worked hard for the socialist offensive begun in 1971 were now, in Guyana as in Jamaica, falling by the wayside.[45] In 1977 both multilateral and bilateral international deals were successfully completed by the government. As the chargé

---

43. *The Economist, Quarterly Economic Review, The West Indies*, 2d Quarter 1978, p. 20. (Henceforth cited as *Q.E.R.*)

44. Quoted in *The Sunday Chronicle*, Dec. 15, 1976, p. 2.

45. *The Miami Herald* carried the following news item on Mar. 20, 1978 (p. 22). "More than just 'reasons of health' were behind the resignation last month of Foreign Minister Fred Wills of Guyana, United Press International reports. Wills was too heavily identified with the left wing of Prime Minister Forbes Burnham's ruling People's National Congress Party, according to diplomatic observers, and he had to be sacrificed because Guyana seeks new financing from the West for major development projects."

TABLE 4

Student Attitudes Toward Government Control

	Government control of what is grown			Government power & control in a cooperative society			Government control of trade unions		
	D	NS	A	D	NS	A	D	NS	A
Barbados	69	19	13	37	40	23	35	27	38
Guyana	67	12	21	35	32	33	39	19	42
Trinidad	79	10	11	44	37	19	34	26	40

SOURCE: W. W. Anderson and R. W. Grant, "Political Socialisation among Adolescents in Schools—A Comparative Study of Barbados, Guyana and Trinidad," *Social Economic Studies*, 26, no. 2 (Jun. 1977), pp. 225–26.

NOTE: D = Disagree; NS = Not Sure; A = Agree. Barbados is included here for comparative purposes. All figures represent percentages.

d'affaires at the U.S. Embassy put it during ceremonies announcing the completion of negotiations (initiated four years previously) on a loan, "the loan was evidence of the Carter Administration's desire to foster development both here and in other developing countries."[46] Guyana's minister of finance admitted that there had finally been an end to the differences in views that had separated the two nations.

In June 1977, Assistant Secretary of State Terrence Todman told the House Subcommittee on Inter-American Affairs: "Guyana is seeking a different path to social and economic development, one with which we have no quarrel and which we have no reason to fear. Despite its different political philosophy, and our differences in the past, Guyana looks to us for understanding and cooperation."[47]

As in Jamaica, the United States seemed content to sit back and wait for economic conditions and political ambitions to do their work. Also by 1978, race once again assumed its traditional position of center stage in Guyanese politics: "critical support" now seemed like a sellout to the other side.

Jamaica

In the general elections of 1976, Michael Manley and the PNP won 47 out of a possible 60 seats in the Jamaican Parliament. It was the larg-

46. *Guyana Chronicle*, Jul. 16, 1977, p. 1.
47. "U.S. Policy Towards the Caribbean," *Hearings, House Subcommittee on Inter-American Affairs* (Jun. 28, 1977), p. 30. (Henceforth cited as *Hearings, SIAA*.)

est electoral margin since the beginning of universal suffrage. Even though the British-introduced first-past-the-post electoral system allowed such a massive number of seats with only 53 percent of the popular vote, it is clear that Manley had received a mandate to continue the program of "democratic socialism" initiated in 1972. He wasted no time. Within one month the government had introduced a new tax schedule that gave relief to those earning under J$10,000 per year and imposed a surtax of from 70 percent to 80 percent on those earning J$20,000 and over; a proposed permanent ceiling on incomes was also announced. This was hard on the middle class. The private sector feared the encroaching state. Nationalization of foreign banks was announced, as was that of the island's only cement factory, which belonged to the powerful Ashenheim clan. Radio Jamaica was purchased as part of a new "mobilization program" (under a new Ministry of National Mobilization headed by a popular young radical dentist, D. K. Duncan); and, perhaps most worrisome to the private sector, a new State Trading Corporation was announced, "to be the sole importer, through its subsidiary companies, of all imports from the most reliable sources. . . ."[48] Diplomatic relations were established with the Soviet Union, and a Jamaican team met in Havana with Comecon officials at a time when Guyana was requesting formal association with the Comecon. With well-known left-radicals occupying four cabinet positions, it appeared that Jamaica in 1976 was finally catching up with Guyana, if not Cuba. Those who believed so misunderstood the nature of Jamaican political culture and, even more importantly, miscalculated the desperate economic conditions already quite apparent by 1976.

Though no student of Jamaican social structure would eliminate race as a source of ongoing social conflict, there is evidence that it is secondary—across all occupational groups—to material and economic issues. Specifically, Jamaicans are concerned with problems of unemployment and wages; crime; government policies on housing, education, and health; population growth; politics; and, lastly, race and cultural or social discrimination.[49] Clearly, the high correlation between class and race, and the substantial concentration of corporate ownership in the hands of highly visible and long-entrenched ethnic minorities, has created a popularly held view that there exists in Jamaica a widespread hostility

48. *The Jamaican Weekly Gleaner*, Dec. 19, 1977, p. 16. The STC was established in December 1977.
49. See Carl Stone, *Race, Nationalism and Political Community* (Mona, Jamaica, 1973), pp. 14–15.

toward these minorities.[50] Yet, in a 1974 poll, Carl Stone discovered that only 9 percent of a representative class and community sample admitted hostility or anger toward whites,[51] and in a 1978 poll of those Jamaicans who perceived conditions to be "getting worse" (and in April 1978 fully 84 percent in urban Kingston felt that way), 70 percent blamed "the government" first, whereas only 17 percent put the blame on "capitalists and political enemies of the government."[52] In an earlier poll (January 1978) "governmental mismanagement" and "radical talk" consistently outpolled the "private sector" as the main culprits in the opinion of those who see the situation as deteriorating.[53]

There is a danger of assuming that all social conflict takes place along clear class lines and that these divisions are accurately reflected in the composition of the two political parties. In fact, as Table 5 illustrates, both parties show a polyclass composition.

TABLE 5
Cross Tabulation of Social Class and Partisan Preference, 1973

Social class	Percent PNP	Percent Independent	Percent JLP	Percent antiparty
Business	19%	10%	71%	0%
Professional	40	20	37	3
Small business	47	0	43	10
White collar	60	16	16	8
Self-employed artisan	59	13	14	14
Working or blue-collar class	48	12	29	11
Lower class	28	10	41	31

SOURCE: Stone, *Class, Race, and Political Behavior*, p. 43 (figures for "Lower class" total 110 percent in the original).

To understand the nature of political conflict in Jamaica, especially in the 1970's, one must understand the "middle sector" support for both the PNP (especially among "white collar" workers) and the JLP (which divides the "professional sector" nearly equally with the PNP). It is to

50. *Ibid.*, pp. 16–22. Excellent descriptions of the economic power of these ethnic minorities (the so-called "21 families") are in Peter Phillips and Stanley Reid's essays in Carl Stone and Aggrey Brown. eds., *Essays on Power and Change in Jamaica* (Kingston, Jamaica, 1977), pp. 1–44.
51. Carl Stone, *Electoral Behavior and Public Opinion in Jamaica* (Mona, Jamaica, 1974), p. 79.
52. Carl Stone Poll, *The Weekly Gleaner*, Apr. 17, 1978, p. 7.
53. Carl Stone Poll, *The Weekly Gleaner*, Jan. 16, 1978, p. 1.

this middle sector that an active and expanding government (tertiary sector) appeals most. As Peter Phillips notes, "the civil service has continued, along with the political parties, to be one of the main avenues for entry to the political elite open to the formerly low-status, dispossessed and largely powerless black peasant and working class personages."[54]

Michael Manley himself has not ignored this problem of the political pressures for an expanding state machinery in both capitalist and socialist economies. "The astonishing growth of bureaucracies the world over during the last two centuries," says Manley, "does not only represent itself by asexual fission: it demonstrates the unending demand made on the political arm that it experiment with forms of intervention."[55]

And since independence, but especially since 1972, there has been a steady increase in full-time civil servants. Whereas in 1970 public administration accounted for 8.4 percent of the Gross Domestic Product (J$82.0 million), in 1975 the figure was 14.3 percent (J$358.0 million). Wendell Bell reports that the numbers of civil servants increased from 8,570 in 1962–63 to 15,570 in 1975, excluding teachers, police, and judges.[56]

In the face of such an expansion of the state bureaucracy and number of elites, the fundamental question becomes, Has there been an equivalent expansion of the rest of the economy? The answer is a categorical no.

Except for government services, stagnation and decline have characterized the past decade. Not that the increase in government expenditures was unexpected: much of the increases reflect the PNP's fulfillment of its campaign promises and its populist orientation. Expenditures for education rose from J$47,750,000 in 1972–73 to J$209,000,000, as education became free all the way to the bachelor's degree at the University of the West Indies. Similarly, agriculture's share of the budget went from J$17,087,000 in 1972–73 to J$151,134,650, reflecting the land reform program and the extension of the cooperative system.[57]

But it was in the unplanned (because undesirable) areas that the greatest increases have been registered. The most dramatic increase has been for the police and military services—from J$7,220,000 in 1971–72

54. Peter Phillips, "Jamaican Elites: 1938 to Present," in Carl Stone and Aggrey Brown, eds., *Essays on Power and Change in Jamaica*, p. 11.

55. October 1976 speech by Michael Manley quoted in John Hearne, ed., *The Search for Solutions* (Toronto, 1976), p. 191.

56. Wendell Bell and J. William Gibson, Jr., "Independent Jamaica Faces the Outside World," *International Studies Quarterly*, 22 (Mar. 1978), p. 10.

57. *Statistical Yearbook of Jamaica*, 1976, p. 656; *The Weekly Gleaner*, May 29, 1978, p. 1.

to J$86,462,875 in 1978–79,[58] reflecting the ferocious increase in crime and political violence that has been sweeping the island. Not far behind, and even more significant, were the figures for the ministry of finance. The 1978–79 budget totaling J$1.6 billion allocated J$580,257,138 to this ministry, of which J$355,000,000 was earmarked for repayment of loans and interest charges. It is this last datum that illustrates many of the problems in Jamaica's move toward socialism.

When the island's oil import bill jumped from J$50 million in 1973 to J$180 million just one year later, the new PNP government found itself in difficult straits. Though increases in income tax levies yielded J$208 million in 1975–76, as compared to J$65 million in 1969–70, Jamaica still required loan receipts of J$201 million in 1974–75 and J$242 million in 1975–76 to meet its obligations. It was this budgetary crisis as much as any pledge to create a new economic system that led to two of the major initiatives of the Manley government.

The first of these initiatives was welcomed by nearly all Jamaicans: the "Bauxite Offensive" of 1974.[59] A "production levy" was applied on all bauxite, whether exported or processed locally into alumina. The levy was accompanied by a flat royalty of J$0.50 per ton on all production. The result was a government take of approximately J$12 per ton as compared to J$2 per ton prior to 1974. The total payments of the bauxite and alumina companies increased from J$42,966 million in 1971 to J$165.662 million in 1975.

Though one company, Revere Jamaica Alumina, Ltd., closed operations in Jamaica in protest, and another, Reynolds Metal Co., filed a suit against the Jamaican government with the International Center for the Settlement of Investment Disputes, the levy was eventually accepted by the companies that remained, including Reynolds, and became a model for the rest of the members of the newly created International Bauxite Association.[60] By 1977 the government had successfully carried out the next phase of the "Bauxite Offensive"—acquisition of majority

58. Under the PNP the name of the Ministry of Defense was changed to the Ministry of National Security and Justice.

59. The often polyclass support for some measures of economic nationalism is evident in the fact that the chairman and vice-chairman of Jamaica's National Bauxite Commission, which negotiated both the levy and the establishment of the International Bauxite Association, were important members of Jamaica's capitalist class—Mayer Matalon and Patrick Rosseau.

60. Very much the brainchild of Jamaica, where it has been headquartered since its establishment in 1974, the IBA includes Australia, the Dominican Republic, Ghana, Guinea, Haiti, Indonesia, Jamaica, Sierra Leone, Surinam, and Yugoslavia.

ownership of the alumina and bauxite exporting companies—with little or no public opposition from the companies.[61] As in the 51 percent nationalizations of Chile and Zambia in 1969, the Jamaican initiative left the foreign companies in managerial control of the enterprises and all phases of marketing.

The second initiative was more politically explosive: the PNP's attempt to deal with the growth of the government's external public debt. Table 6 indicates the sizeable growth of that external public debt up to 1975, both absolutely as well as a percentage of the GNP and of Export Earnings. The debt grew to even more staggering proportions between 1976 and 1977. As with so many other countries, in 1977 and again in 1978 Jamaica turned to the International Monetary Fund (IMF) and the World Bank as a last resort; and as in the cases of other countries, their assistance was accompanied by demands for devaluation, increased taxation, and a general belt-tightening program with IMF review every six months. In early 1977 any discussions with the IMF were strongly criticized by radical sectors of the society, both within and outside the PNP. More than anything else, the IMF issue crystallized the long-simmering "radical" versus "moderate" division within the PNP. Perhaps typical of the "radical" position was that taken by economist Norman Girvan, at the time Director of the National Planning Agency. Girvan labeled IMF demands a "massive destabilization attempt," and took the line that "It would be demoralizing if a government which used the opportunity of its massive electoral victory [in 1976] to reassert that the principles of its sovereignty were not negotiable for the proverbial mess of pottage, were now to buckle under to the pressure of the imperialist countries exerted through their financial leverage."[62] The nature of the "radical" alternatives were never outlined publicly. To the "moderates" the alternatives to such IMF assistance at a time when economic stagnation was accompanied by a "socialist" expansion of the public sector were, of course, hardly palatable: budget cuts and cutbacks in public programs, deficit financing by the Bank of Jamaica (with its inflationary consequences), increased taxation (with its further dampening of the already sagging spirits of the beleaguered middle sector), and general public discontent. The Jamaican government took the path of economic expediency despite the damage to its ideological pos-

61. See the cordial exchanges between the prime minister and the chairmen of the Kaiser Bauxite Co. and the Reynolds Bauxite Co. *The Weekly Gleaner*, Feb. 8, 1977, p. 1, and Apr. 12, 1977, p. 29.
62. Quoted in *Caribbean Contact* (Jun. 1977), p. 7.

TABLE 6

External Public Debt of Guyana, Jamaica, Trinidad & Tobago
(*Millions of U.S. dollars*)

	1969			1971			1973			1974			1975		
	Debt	Pct. of GNP	Pct. of exports	Debt	Pct. of GNP	Pct. of exports	Debt	Pct. of GNP	Pct. of exports	Debt	Pct. of GNP	Pct. of exports	Debt	Pct. of GNP	Pct. of exports
Guyana	63.9	27.9%	44.4%	144.1	53.6%	88.0%	166.9	55.9%	104.4%	202.4	49.0%	68.7%	237.6	50.6%	61.8%
Jamaica	123.9	11.3	26.6	147.9	10.6	27.2	306.0	16.6	48.4	474.9	19.7	48.9	647.4	22.9	58.3
Trinidad & Tobago	76.0	10.2	12.8	91.3	9.9	25.1	145.1	11.3	25.6	161.1	8.6	14.7	155.5	7.0	11.6

SOURCE: World Bank, *World Debt Tables*, vol. I (1977), pp. 220, 221, 81.

ture: it announced what would be the first IMF loan (US$74 million) in July 1977.[63] And in May 1978 it announced a second loan, which the minister of finance called "a shock to the society." In Parliament Michael Manley confessed that his heart was with those who opposed the IMF terms, since "fundamental questions of sovereignty arise," but that realistically there was no alternative to IMF assistance.[64]

It must have been evident to the Manley regime that his party's "left" wing did not command the kind of support it was originally believed to have. Carl Stone's poll of May 1977 indicted that only 14 percent of those polled opposed seeking aid from Washington.[65] But Stone's polls indicated more than a lack of opposition to foreign assistance and foreign investments. They indicated that a major part of the radical left campaign (the discrediting of those who were migrating to the United States) had little public appeal. Fully 60 percent of those in Stone's sample indicated they would go the United States if the opportunity presented itself. Even on the question of migration to Miami, Florida, which Prime Minister Manley had converted into a hot political issue, 59.1 percent indicated their approval (with the highest approval rate coming from the working classes). Interestingly, the urban working class appeared more eager to migrate to the United States than the much criticized urban middle class—68 percent to 45 percent.

The defeat of the "left" on the issue of the IMF loan was, on the surface, a policy defeat. In reality it reflected a major political battle raging within the ranks of the PNP that led to significant setbacks for the "radicals" in 1977 and 1978.[66] One setback was the "resignation" of Dr. D. K. Duncan from his posts as party secretary and minister of mobilization. Duncan had been the fastest-rising star on the left, and many of his staff resigned with him. Another setback was the disciplining of the party's youth organization, which had been pushing a "scientific socialism" line. In his letter of resignation Duncan claimed that his every action over the past four years had been "an attempt to realize the visions as explained to me on my very first encounter with the Party Leader [Michael Manley]." Duncan then explained that "We are in a new era. In April 1976, the Party Leader met with the Hanover Progressive Movement, an Extra Party Left Group, for discussions on their

63. Negotiations were actually begun in November 1976 but were suspended because of the December 1976 elections. Negotiations resumed in April 1976.

64. *The Weekly Gleaner*, May 22, 1978, p. 7.

65. The Carl Stone Polls were published in the *Daily Gleaner* during the month of June 1977.

66. These interpretations are based in part on interviews conducted in Jamaica Aug. 20–30, 1977.

involvement in elections. In April 1977, my meeting with the Hugh Buchanan Movement in St. Elizabeth, also an Extra Party Left Group, is placed under a microscope for inspection."[67] The tones and overtones surrounding the Duncan resignation show a strong similarity to the arguments surrounding the expulsion of the radicals in 1952.

Manley emerged stronger than ever from this confrontation, not only because he took on the portfolios formerly held by Duncan and the direction of the land reform program, but also because he reasserted the tradition of "one leader." This was the tradition that the PNP masses perceived was being challenged by the radicals, a perception that Duncan, in his repeated vows of loyalty to Manley, attempted to dispel. As "Comrade Leader" Manley was upholding what Archie Singham called the "hero and the crowd" characteristics of Jamaican and West Indian political culture. But what was the nature of this "hero" and this "crowd?"

In November 1974 Manley revealed that the PNP had, since 1972, been involved in a major reevaluation and restudy of the party's basic philosophy and had arrived at a basic partywide consensus on "thirteen principles."[68] Principle 1 reaffirmed the party's dedication to a multiparty democratic system, but the other principles taken together are not so straightforward. Principle 2 says unambiguously "We reaffirm the right of every Jamaican to own private property." Principle 6 reaffirms the PNP commitment to "build a socialist society" through "cooperation." Principle 7 states the party's "belief that Jamaica will flourish best under a mixed economy in which there is a clear and honourable role for responsible private business working in partnership with the public sector of the economy." Principle 12, on the other hand, reaffirms "our rejection of capitalism" as being exploitative and restates its commitment to "building socialism." Principle 13 restates the party's "faith" in "cooperation" as the best method for organizing the society.

The "right to private property," "socialism," "cooperation," and the "mixed economy" all figure as programmatic objectives—not merely pious intentions. This lack of ideological and programmatic clarity, not to mention consistency, is apparent also in the thinking of Michael Manley. Though he got his political start by leading the "moderate" trade union movement during the battles of the early 1950's, he has been any-

67. Dr. Duncan's letter of resignation was published in *The Sunday Gleaner*, Oct. 9, 1977, pp. 7ff.
68. Excerpts from "Democratic Socialism, The Jamaican Model," in Hearne, ed., *The Search for Solutions*, pp. 155–60, 163–69.

thing but predictable politically, either in actions or in thought.[69] In his first book, the autobiographical *A Voice at the Work Place* (1975), Manley describes how his trade union experience transformed his conventional (orthodox) interpretation of socialist doctrine into "a humanist and individualistic focus" concerned with the human equation within society as distinct from a "more general and structural focus" concerned with the ownership of the means of production.[70] It is clear that the unmentioned targets here were those who in the 1970's, like the "4 H's" in the 1950's, maintained that trade unionism could not separate the immediate issues surrounding the workplace from the broader issues of macrosocial and economic organization.

Under pressure from the "radical" wing of the PNP, which showed increased strength in the 1976 elections, Manley began radicalizing his, and his party's, rhetoric. The role of Cuba in that rhetoric was noticeable. As early as on a July 1975 visit to Cuba his speeches had not only a strident pro-Cuban and anticapitalist tone, but also an anti-American one. The USA, Manley told the Cubans, now finds itself "morally isolated."[71] Yet, not two months after his return from Cuba in 1975 Manley lectured the National Executive Council of the PNP on the "vital matter of the difference between communism and socialism," noting that the two ideologies had "totally different" perspectives on a wide range of subjects and that the PNP was decidedly in favor of "democratic socialism."[72] When addressing North American audiences his tone was considerably more conciliatory, especially after mid-1977.[73]

The difficulty of maintaining a high level of rhetoric on "democratic socialism" in a society accustomed to relatively high levels of consumption—yet a society which, as one authoritative source put it, "will have to

69. While there has been a consistent concern with the oppressed and the poor, I disagree with John Hearne's view (in 1976) that while much of what Manley has said and done has been controversial, "It is, however, consistent" (*The Search for Solutions*, p. 178). In 1977, Hearne, one of Jamaica's outstanding novelists, turned against Manley and the PNP on grounds that they had betrayed the ideals of "democratic socialism."

70. This is a view that had formed the basis of his democratic socialist philosophy expounded in *The Politics of Change: A Jamaican Testament* (London, 1974), p. 70.

71. "Excerpts from Address to Cuban Workers, Alamar, 12 July, 1975," in Hearne, ed., *The Search for Solutions*, pp. 205–6. For an example of party rhetoric, see the speech by the minister of foreign affairs, Dudley Thompson, to the Second Socialist International Meeting, Caracas, May 25, 1976.

72. Hearne, ed., *The Search for Solutions*, pp. 169–71.

73. See "Jamaica's Manley," *The Tropic Magazine* (Miami), Apr. 11, 1976, pp. 24ff., and "Michael Manley, Jamaica and the U.S.," *The New York Times*, Jan. 21, 1978.

continue to live from hand to mouth, seeking loans and aid wherever it can find them"[74]—is not lost on anyone. Though the Cuban connection, including state visits by Manley to Cuba and by Castro to Jamaica, has been highly visible and controversial, Manley's regime continues to promote a platform more populist than Marxist. One of the most dramatic illustrations of this populism is provided by the conditions that led to the need for the second IMF loan mentioned above.

Though Jamaica had lived up to nearly all the IMF strictures set for it on the first loan (on public expenditures, public borrowing from the banking system, and the level of foreign exchange earnings), it had failed to meet one condition: it had not kept to a ceiling of J$355 million in domestic bank assets. That ceiling had been exceeded by 2.6 percent. It is clear that the overrun resulted from the high level of withdrawals from the central bank by commercial banks attempting to satisfy the usual heavy demands resulting from Christmas spending. In the midst of a severe economic recession, Jamaican consumers approached Christmas of 1977 as any other (the Jamaican press reported ample supplies of rum, beer, hams, butter, flour, and other traditional luxuries), and the PNP government was unable and/or unwilling to put a damper on things after a year of consistently bad news on the economic front and considerable public unrest. The results were a third devaluation in twelve months—for a total devaluation of 45 percent—a further increase in taxes, and the resignation of the minister of finance, David Coore, one of Manley's closest allies.

In 1974 Carl Stone concluded that "in Jamaica there is neither a will to achieve the socialist alternative nor the necessary political supports to sustain it even if such a will existed."[75] By 1978 Jamaican elites had not defined the nature of the "socialist" system they were striving for. What was clear by 1978, however, was that the majority of people were in no mood for radical left experiments in "scientific socialism," as the data in Table 7 indicate.

Other views in 1978, ran toward the moderate end of the scale. Even among the urban working class, the most radical in the sample, only 19 percent favored government expropriation of land and only 12 percent saw the private sector as "exploiters" (though 48 percent saw it as "selfish").[76] Even more surprising was Carl Stone's finding that fully 63

74. Q.E.R., *The West Indies*, 2d quarter, 1978, p. 10.
75. Carl Stone, *Electoral Behavior and Public Opinion in Jamaica*, p. 96.
76. *The Weekly Gleaner*, Feb. 13, 1978, p. 17; Jan. 30, 1978, p. 8. In 1962 Wendell Bell found that of his elite sample 25 percent were "economic radicals," 17 percent liberals." In 1974 the "economic radicals" numbered 15 percent and the "liberals" 49 percent. (Bell and Gibson, "Independent Jamaica . . . ," p. 26.)

TABLE 7

Social Class and Ideological Position in Jamaica

Social class	Support for ideological principles (Feb. 6, 1978)			Views on increasing gov't ownership (Jan. 30, 1978)	
	Capitalism	Demo. socialism	Communism	Support	Oppose
Kingston middle class	45%	25%	3%	27%	73%
Kingston working class	20	38	14	48	52
Small farmers	4	33	2	21	79

SOURCES: Dr. Carl Stone Poll, *The Weekly Gleaner*, Feb. 6, 1978, p. 1; and Dr. Carl Stone Poll, *The Weekly Gleaner*, Jan. 30, 1978, p. 1.

NOTE: Percentages are of those with views on these ideologies.

percent of the urban working class disliked Trevor Munroe and that 65 percent disliked D. K. Duncan—the two most visible radicals on the Jamaican political scene. Fully 42 percent of the small farmers could not even identify them.[77]

Surely such findings were not lost on the Jamaicans, who, as distinct from the Guyanese, do not vote race and consequently are capable of a different vote in subsequent elections. Again in contrast to Guyana, where both parties claimed to be socialist "vanguard" parties, Jamaicans will have a choice between "democratic socialism" and the "nationalistic *laissez-faire*" of the JLP. That Jamaican parliamentary democracy survived the hectic 1976–77 period is in itself is an accomplishment not to be minimized. It is clear, however, that Jamaicans in 1978 were having second thoughts about any new "socialist offensives."

Trinidad and Tobago

Interestingly, it is precisely in the most developed of the British West Indian islands that the call for socialist-type reform had its most dramatic climax. The "Black Power" revolt of 1970 is a misnomer. Though there certainly were strong American-style Black Power influences, symbolic and personal, the movement was much more than that: it reflected discontent in the Indian sugar-growing areas, tensions between Sandhurst-trained professionals and politically appointed officers in the army, seething anger among the young and unemployed urban Blacks, and the rebellious mood that University of the West Indies students shared with their counterparts around the world. The rebellion of half

77. *The Weekly Gleaner*, Feb. 20, 1978, pp. 8, 7.

the army signaled the culmination of an abortive attempt to overthrow the regime of Dr. Eric Williams. Although both U.S. and Venezuelan naval units were within sight, the rebellion was over without any material assistance from them. This frustrated movement of 1970 was followed by an attempt by university students to create a Cuban-style guerrilla "foco" in the hills of Trinidad. By 1973 these students had been either killed or captured.[78] By 1974 Trinidad was back to politics as usual; Williams was stronger than ever.

Eric Williams, Prime Minister of Trinidad and Tobago, is the most enduring of the West Indian—and Third World—leaders. An Oxford-educated historian whose book *Capitalism and Slavery* (1944) was a methodological model of Marxian analysis of slavery's role in the rise of capitalism, Williams learned early in his career to manipulate charges that he was a dangerous socialist to his advantage. He has never been anything of the sort; both his domestic and his foreign policies have been consistently pragmatic. Since it is the very essence of pragmatism to be flexible and nonaligned, one necessarily will find wide variations in his verbal expressions of policy that should not be confused with structural shifts.

In June 1956 the Peoples National Movement (PNM), through Williams, outlined its program in a long memorandum to the British Secretary of State for the Colonies.[79] Among the points made was that the PNM's economic program "is modelled consciously on the experience and achievements of another Caribbean community, Puerto Rico. . . ." Trinidad was following Jamaica, then, in adopting a program that involved an import-substitution type of industrialization through foreign investments. This program was accelerated after Independence in 1962 and continued unchallenged into the late 1960's. Its flaws, however, were becoming all too evident, the fundamental one being that unemployment seemed to grow with the economy, especially among young urban Blacks. By 1970 between 20 and 25 percent of the work force was unemployed. For the first time in its history the island showed an out-migration trend. In 1970 Williams wrote that the path taken by his

---

78. An attempt was made in 1973 to have amnesty granted to the guerrillas. The model used was the one successfully implemented by the Rafael Caldera regime in Venezuela in 1969. The stark differences between the Latin American political cultures and the West Indian were soon evident. The Latin American concept of political amnesty does not exist in British common law, nor was the idea even conceivable in political practice. Interestingly enough, the idea was attacked as much by the "left" as it was by the right-wing sectors of the society.

79. Eric Williams, *Inward Hunger: The Education of a Prime Minister* (London, 1969), p. 150.

government since Independence was *sui generis*—the "Trinidad Model," he called it.[80] It differed from the two other prominent models in the Caribbean, the Puerto Rican and the Cuban, in that it had not sacrificed national identity for economic growth (as in the case of Puerto Rico) and was not totalitarian (as Cuba was).

Trinidad's domestic program has been a state-directed mixed economy in which the growth of state-created employment opportunities has been balanced with the greatest amount of freedom for the native private sector. Though foreign capital is encouraged, the emphasis is on "localization": eventual local ownership of majority shares in all sectors. Both the domestic and the international dimensions of Williams's political philosophy are described in a 1963 piece in France's *Monde Diplomatique*.

This then is the significance of Trinidad and Tobago as an independent country in the modern world, that it represents a confrontation in the Caribbean of the two dominant points of view that face the world today:

(a) Active partnership between government and investors in Trinidad and Tobago as against the state direction of the economy in Cuba;

(b) A direct democracy superimposed upon a parliamentary tradition in Trinidad and Tobago as against Cuba's one party state dominated by its caudillo;

(c) The vision in Trinidad and Tobago of a Caribbean Economic Community with some sort of independent existence as against the submerging of the Cuban personality in the International behind the Iron Curtain.[81]

Williams has, at least since 1970, engaged in a minimum of ideological rhetoric, either at home or at international forums. Cabinet appointments have been invariably of a technocratic type, and the thrust of government policy in the late 1970's is clearly toward an increase in this direction.[82]

Despite this pragmatism, however, every expansion of the public sector has led to an outcry from the private sector. One newspaper recently

80. Eric Williams, *From Columbus To Castro: The History of the Caribbean* (London, 1970), p. 511.

81. Cited in *Inward Hunger*, p. 302. These views continue to be a valid description of Williams's basic philosophy. The fact that Williams was the first hemispheric head of state to call for the readmission of Cuba to the OAS (in 1970), that he established relations with Cuba in 1972, and that during his visit to Cuba in June 1975 he told students at the University of Havana that "In this mighty effort to achieve greater Caribbean solidarity, Cuba has a great role to play" (*Trinidad Guardian*, Jun. 21, 1975, p. 1) in no way changes this assessment.

82. See, for instance, the plans for educational, cultural, and social policy in the Republic of Trinidad and Tobago, *White Paper on National Institute of Higher Education: Research, Science and Technology* (Oct. 1977).

editorialized about the "octopus-like" approach the government was taking toward the private sector, an approach that was "stifling."[83] An independent senator representing business talked about the government "blindly cutting a path to a dictatorship of the State where there will be no room for private endeavour."[84] Interestingly, neither complaints spoke of a "socialist threat." The newspaper spoke of the Government's "hordes of bureaucrats" for whom jobs had to be found, and the senator twice emphasized that this public sector growth was taking place without the government "ever intending it." Intended or not, the public sector has been growing. The minister of petroleum and mines reported to the senate that, in 1976, twelve Government-owned companies showed losses totaling T$45,595,944 and 14 profits totaling T$378,234,-986.[85] The government's share of the Gross Domestic Product had passed the 50 percent mark by 1975. The largest share of the public sector investments are in oil, in either joint or totally national ventures. By 1978 the government bureaucracy employed some 70 percent of the total labor force.

This entry of government into the petroleum industry is a result of the tremendous increase in oil revenues since the OPEC-induced raises of 1973. Petroleum revenues in 1973 were T$130 million, in 1977, T$1,540 million. The sensational aspect of this development is best understood when we know that 23 percent of the government's revenues of T$474 million in 1973 came from oil, whereas only two years later the government collected T$1,687 million, 70 percent from oil.

Despite this sizable growth of state ownership, the fact remains that the greatest activity exists in the private sector. Direct foreign investment provided no less than 68.4 percent of the total external financing between 1965 and 1975; other sizable amounts came from institutions like the U.S. Export-Import Bank, and were geared toward creating a role for the U.S. private sector. Total external financing for 1965–75 was T$2,435.5 million. Activity in the private sector included a healthy growth of new companies in the native sector, the introduction of a goodly number of foreign companies, and an outflow of capital (as dividends and profits) that exceeded inflow by T$38.5 million over the period 1965–74. Even more dramatic are the developments in the area

83. *The Express*, Dec. 18, 1977, editorial.

84. Senator Tommy Gattcliffe, "The 1976 Budget Debate," in *Report on the Mobility of Dom. Fin. Res.*, vol. 2, p. 46.

85. The minister proceeded to chide the business community by saying that there was an abundance of businessmen on the island but a noticeable lack of entrepreneurship (*The Express*, Dec. 16, 1977, p. 1).

of heavy industry, specifically the plans for the multi-billion-dollar industrial complex known as Point Lisas Estate (described in Table 8).

It is not at all surprising, given the magnitude and the complexity of the plans, that the Trinidadians should regard the mobilization of human and financial resources as "the critical problem that is beginning to take a frightening shape." The need to develop linkages with the oil industry, which by 1978 accounted for nearly half the economy, are obvious. The oil industry presently employs only 2 percent of the work force, and more and more of the exploration activities are taking place offshore, where the labor requirements are even less. It has been calculated that though the economy grew at a rate of 20 percent (of the GDP) for

TABLE 8

Trinidad & Tobago Industrialization Program for Point Lisas Estate

Project	Accumulated capital requirement (T $000,000)	Labor requirement[a]	Cost per job (T $)	Ownership
Tringen ammonia	192	120	160,000	Joint venture: Gov't and W. R. Grace & Co. (U.S.)
Iron-and-steel complex	651	1,000	65,000	Joint venture: Gov't, ESTEL, Kawasaki, and Mitsui
Polyester fibre	85	850	100,000	Unspecified U.S. and European involvement
Furfural[b]	41	213	192,488	Joint venture: Gov't and International Finance Corporation funding
Fertilizer (ammonia)	759	unspecified	n.a.	Joint venture: Gov't and AMOCO
Cement (expansion of existing plant)	70	258	271,318	Gov't (wholly owned)

SOURCE: Ministry of Finance, *Report on the Mobilization of Domestic Financial Resources*, vol. I, pp. 9–17.

NOTE: In addition to a major liquefied natural gas (LNG) plant at Point Lisas (Peoples Gas Co. and TENNECO contracted in November 1977 for the construction of plants and export to the United States), there will be the following infrastructure projects: water development, T$265 million; electricity development (Point Lisas), T$105 million.

a Jobs resulting from creation of these industries.

b Furfural is used in the manufacture of nylon.

the five years 1972–77 unemployment was reduced by only 1 percent.[86]
It is precisely because of this development program's need for foreign,
and largely private, human and financial resources that the Trinidad
economy will long remain dependent on foreign and private sector influence. A role for the private sector is virtually guaranteed by each of
the following aspects of this industrialization program, but especially
by their combined impact. Trinidad receives no special consideration as
a Third World country; it is expected to pay going commercial rates.
Loan repayment is to be in a foreign currency, different thus from the
currency in which the revenues are being generated; the payments,
therefore, will be subject to the vagaries of exchange rate fluctuations.
Since the loans generally only cover the supply of equipment and all
services from a particular country, there necessarily must be supple-
mentary loans from other sources if national projects are to be undertaken. Experts of the leading institutions were demanding drastic modifications in the scope and parameters of plans laid down by Trinidad
experts. Lending organizations were insisting on the incorporation of
expatriate management in projects financed by them. Despite water-
tight provisions on viability and sales contracts, Trinidad and Tobago
government guarantees were being demanded as a prerequisite to any
negotiations. Whatever the government's *attitudes* might be toward
the native business sector, the facts speak louder than words in terms
of the nature of Trinidad and Tobago's economy.

It is, perhaps, this very presence of a booming private sector and an
active role for foreign capital and expertise that puts Trinidad in sharp
contrast to Jamaica and Guyana. In fact, Eric Williams made his feel-
ings known in reviewing the steep decline of the island's non-oil exports
to Jamaica and Guyana:[87] "Socialism," he told a group of schoolteachers,
"is the same as slavery. The only thing missing is the master." Although
the very next day the press reported that the prime minister's words
had been quoted out of context,[88] and that the minister of external affairs had already notified the governments of Guyana and Jamaica of

86. Q.E.R., *The West Indies*, 2d quarter, 1978, pp. 11–13.
87. Trinidad and Tobago's balance in non-petroleum trade with Guyana moved
from being TT$6.8 million favorable in 1974 to a 1976 deficit of TT$5.9 million.
The same thing happened with Jamaica—from a favorable balance of TT$19.4 mil-
lion in 1975 to a TT$13.1 million deficit in 1976. Between January and July 1977,
the unfavorable balance with Jamaica stood at TT$20.3 million. By May 1977, local
businessmen were owed a total of TT$4.2 million by Jamaica.
88. The original report was carried with banner headlines in *The Trinidad
Guardian* (Oct. 28, 1977); the explanation retraction in the same newspaper was
carried on Oct. 29, 1977, on the front page.

Williams's "real" statement, there could be no doubt (regardless of the target) of the growing resentment in Trinidad against the actions and rhetoric coming from Guyana and especially Jamaica.

Addressing a Rotarian luncheon in September 1977, Prime Minister Williams noted that Jamaica and Guyana "come with their balance-of-payments problems; we do what we could to help, only to find we are being cursed." In October 1977, Williams gave his now much-quoted "tit for tat" speech, in which he announced a new "system of selective controls" on imports into the island, fundamentally a retaliatory move against Jamaican and Guyanese reductions in imports from Trinidad. Trinidad had already made loans for balance-of-payment support between 1974 and 1976 to Jamaica (T$264 million), to Guyana (T$50 million), and to Barbados (T$28 million).[89] Certain sectors of Trinidadian society, therefore, felt that Jamaica had added insult to injury when its minister for trade, P. J. Patterson, explained that it was Trinidad's failure to come up with an additional T$100 million line of credit that accounted for the trade imbalance. One newspaper noted that this "looks like political blackmail."[90]

Given the continued dependence of all three societies on imports to sustain both consumer and capital development needs, the international reserves position of each is a critical indicator of economic capability. The following figures for January 1978 tell the story. The figures include the IMF Reserve Position and Foreign Exchange reserves.[91]

Jamaica	US$ 45.2 million
Guyana	US$ 10.0 million
Trinidad and Tobago	US$ 1,462.4 million

In mid-1978, a 13-man mission from the City of London was in Port of Spain exploring the feasibility of a sophisticated stock market on the island, a means of encouraging wider local ownership in the booming economy. In mid-1978, one should recall, both Guyana and Jamaica

89. Government of Trinidad and Tobago, *Accounting for the Petrodollar* (Port of Spain, 1977), pp. 36–37.

90. *Trinidad Guardian*, Oct. 28, 1977, editorial. The anger at Guyana and Jamaica was shared by Barbadian exporters. Noting that both Guyana and Jamaica have major natural resources while Barbadians have only their expertise and enterprising spirits, the president of the Barbados Manufacturers Association took note of the declining exports to both Jamaica and Guyana. "From my observations now, they are attempting to rape the region . . ." (*Trinidad Guardian*, Oct. 27, 1977; *Weekly Gleaner*, Nov. 4, 1977, p. 11).

91. Q.E.R., *The West Indies*, 2d quarter, 1978.

were laboring under what Jamaicans have come to call philosophically "the heavy manners" of the IMF. The stark contrasts between these three West Indian societies explain something of the tensions within the Caribbean Common Market (CARICOM), of which they are the leaders, and the reasons why by 1978 it seemed doubtful that the CARICOM would survive. In fact, the main casualty of the uneven development of the West Indian economies and the tensions resulting from rhetorical ideological battles has been not American security interests but rather the long-elusive hope for greater Caribbean unity.

THE U.S. RESPONSE

Radical and dramatic shifts in the foreign policy of a major nation are rare occurrences. Not only do vital interests not change that readily, but the weight of the past continues to influence contemporary attitudes and predispositions. So it is with the thinking of certain official and unofficial circles of the American foreign policy community about the Caribbean. In these circles the "psychological" dimension of strategic thinking on the Caribbean remains.

Admitting that "Cuba is not vital to the United States as a base," Hanson W. Baldwin, military editor of the *New York Times*, concluded nevertheless that "Its global importance is chiefly positional and political-psychological. . . ."[92] Psychological factors usually are linked to "prestige" and domino theory effects. "Revision of the treaty terms for Guantanamo," Baldwin continued, "will inevitably lead to revisionism elsewhere—in Panama, in Trinidad, globally. . . . United States power and prestige are involved in Gitmo, whether we like it or not."[93] Similarly, Robert D. Crassweller, an influential author on Caribbean affairs, asserts that "The American strategic presence at selected points in the Caribbean regions is itself a psychological and symbolic reality of very high importance."[94] In fact, those who take a psychological approach to strategic interests are usually prepared to defend a more general "sphere of influence" thesis. Crassweller is not shy in defending such a position. The nature of U.S. security interests dictate that no part of the Caribbean can be safely permitted, through conquest, subversion, "*or even through orderly process*," to become a military base hostile to the

92. Hanson W. Baldwin, "A Military Perspective," in the Brookings Institution, *Cuba and The United States* (Washington, D.C., 1967), p. 206.

93. *Ibid.*, p. 211.

94. Robert D. Crassweller, *The Caribbean Community: Changing Societies and U.S. Policy* (New York, 1970), p. 10.

United States.[95] Similar views stressing "psychological," "prestige," and sphere of influence thinking are found in the conclusions of an influential group of foreign policy experts who met at Georgetown University in 1973. The Caribbean, they observe, "has always been associated in the minds of friends and enemies as the *mare nostrum* . . . [and] the erosion of America's position [there] could adversely affect U.S. prestige."[96]

Yet, in the past few years, the United States has returned the Chaguaramas Base to Trinidad, concluded a major treaty with Panama on the return of the Canal, and generally taken a more conciliatory attitude toward Cuba. These changes plus an emphasis on a much lower military profile in the area have characterized the Carter Administration's diplomacy toward the Caribbean.

The broad context of recent American policy clearly indicates a shift in perspective about where vital U.S. interests lie. Though the United States has not abandoned concern with military security (especially in view of Soviet naval activities),[97] it is clear that U.S. policy emphasis is no longer military, as Assistant Secretary of State for Inter-American Affairs Terrence Todman explained:

We no longer see the Caribbean in quite the same stark military security context that we once viewed it. Rather, our security concerns in the Caribbean are increasingly political in nature. The threat is not simply foreign military bases on our doorstep. It is possibly an even more troublesome prospect: proliferation of impoverished Third World states whose economic and political problems blend with our own.[98]

The shift in American foreign policy must be seen in terms of what is virtually axiomatic in political analysis: the powerful will nearly always exercise a degree of influence and force consonant with the effects sought and with the tenacity of opposition present or anticipated. Events in the West Indies indicate that the constraints on further ex-

95. *Ibid.* Emphasis added.
96. The Center for Strategic and International Studies, Georgetown University, *Russia in the Caribbean. Part One: Panelists Findings, Recommendations, and Comments* (Washington, D.C., 1973), p. 5.
97. Satellite monitoring of movements in the Caribbean is very effective. And though Guantanamo is today described as a training base, it also has military capabilities. At any one time there can be "a dozen destroyers, an aircraft carrier, and so forth" in port. "It is my opinion," said the Deputy Director for Intelligence, DIA, in 1972, "from the point of view of having to draw up contingency plans for the Caribbean area that Guantanamo is a good resource." (Soviet Activities in Cuba, *Hearing, Subcommittee on Inter-American Affairs*, Part 3, Sep. 26, 1972, p. 17.)
98. *Hearings, House Subcommittee on Inter-American Affairs*, Jun. 28, 1977, p. 30.

pansions of Marxist-Leninist influence in the British Caribbean stem from problems of development—internal and external—that these nations have experienced in the 1970's. Washington clearly understands those limitations and has trimmed its Caribbean policy accordingly. The growing *entente* with Cuba and that nation's shift of focus from Latin America to Africa have also contributed to the obvious lack of panic or hysteria in Washington's responses to socialist developments in the hemisphere.

The external constraints are illustrated by an analysis of Jamaica's foreign policy under the PNP government. Central to that foreign policy have been passionate appeals for a New International Economic Order, an aggressive Third World stance, and a highly visible new association with socialist Cuba. Yet Jamaican interest in some form of association with Comecon came to nothing, and tangible benefits from its Cuban links have been minimal. Cuba's assistance to Jamaica up to 1977 was in the areas of education (one school), housing (a prefabricated housing plant), health (thirteen doctors), and some other minor projects in sports, agriculture, and fisheries.[99] While minor in material terms, the Cuban projects had high visibility and soon became part of the very volatile political strife on the island. Fidel Castro's six-day visit to Jamaica in October 1977 was an attempt to defuse that strife, and he succeeded marvelously. Castro was the epitome of diplomatic discretion. So reassuring were Castro's repeated vows of noninterference in Jamaican affairs that one seasoned American reporter called his visit "a virtuoso performance."[100]

Castro must have been aware of the dangers of the growing anti-Cuban debate in Jamaica, a completely new phenomenon. It was, in fact, the previous JLP governments that had opened diplomatic relations with Cuba and that had refused to sign any anti-Cuban agreements as a condition for entering the OAS. Today that same JLP was making the Cuban link a major part of its antigovernment campaign. Very much in Castro's mind must have been the parallels with Allende's Chile: Cuba's inability to provide significant aid, yet the contribution its presence made to the climate of unrest. It was not lost on Jamaican political observers that Castro was projecting a moderating image in his visit to Michael Manley, who was preaching "democratic socialism," rather

99. *The Daily Gleaner*, Oct. 18, 1977, p. 18.
100. Don Bohning in *The Miami Herald*, Oct. 23, 1977, p. 14f. This differed radically from the performance just a week before of Mozambique's President, Samora Machel, who told a Jamaican audience that they should begin "killing the bourgeoisie in the egg." This unleashed a storm of controversy.

than siding with Trevor Munroe, leader of the genuine Marxist-Leninist party on the island, the Worker's Liberation League. Castro's visit to Guyana's Forbes Burnham two years before had presented a similar picture, surely a painful one for Cheddi Jagan, an official member of the communist movement. Castro's presence was hardly a call for revolution in either society, and neither visit led to any major economic exchanges.[101]

A further contrast to the visits by Machel and Castro was the June 1978 visit of President Carlos Andres Perez of Venezuela. Perez immediately indicated his support for the New International Economic Order: "Jamaica and Venezuela," he said, "are fused within the Third World in a message of unity."[102] But Perez brought more than speeches: he announced that J$20 million had already been deposited in the Bank of Jamaica for immediate balance-of-payments purposes; and he promised a longer-term loan of J$50 million and help in building the bauxite-processing plant Jamaica had found so elusive.[103] The Venezuelan president's visit also included a stark reminder of the political realities in the Caribbean—an announcement that representatives of the private sectors of the two countries had reached agreement on the formation of a joint committee of business owners.[104]

The three state visits highlight the complexities of the Jamaican and West Indian situation. Both Guyana and Jamaica enjoy positions of prestige in the Third World; both are articulate spokesmen for the New International Economic Order; both voice a preference for a socialist and anti-imperialist stance in international affairs. Yet both are fragile societies in which deep racial and class cleavages are kept in precarious check by allowing high consumer standards and tolerant social-political rules to operate for the active political parties, trade unions, and other associational interest groups.

This was clearly demonstrated in 1976–77, when after a period of "critical support" radical sectors became more politically aggressive in their challenge to the existing order of things. The defeat they suffered

101. Even the head of the United States Agency for International Development in Jamaica found the courage to tell a Rotary Club luncheon that Castro's visit, far from being a "kiss of death" to the Jamaican tourist industry, would in fact make the country "more titillating, more exciting" to American visitors. (*The Daily Gleaner*, Oct. 29, 1977, p. 20.)

102. *The Daily Gleaner*, Jun. 3, 1978, p. 1.

103. This plant was initially to be a joint Jamaican-Trinidadian-Guyanese project; then it was to be a Jamaican-Mexican venture. Both negotiations collapsed for undisclosed reasons.

104. *The Daily Gleaner*, Jun. 4, 1978, p. 1.

was very reminiscent of the radical left defeats of 1952. It became evident in 1977—as it was in 1952—that nowhere in the British Caribbean did the radical left enjoy substantial internal support. And in the midst of severe economic retrenchments, radical rhetoric tended in 1952 as in 1977 to be counterproductive. Despite the accusations of "destabilization" attempts by Washington, the fact is that, while hardly encouraged by increasing West Indian talk about socialism, the United States could count on forces of the international market place as well as internal West Indian developments to put a damper on radical trends in these societies.[105]

Just as the international constraints operate in Washington's favor, so the internal constraints tend to be structural and as such tend to narrow the freedom of action of radically disposed national elites. The Jamaican (and West Indian) "Bauxite Offensive" of 1974 clearly illustrates the nature of these internal constraints. The U.S. response to Jamaica's Bauxite Offensive increases in significance when one understands that there was a less-than-friendly Nixon-Kissinger Administration in Washington at the time. Yet even as consistent a critic of the United States as Jamaica's Norman Girvan admits that a notable feature of the Bauxite Offensive and the formation of IBA was the absence of confrontation or tension between the producer government and the consumer governments.[106] "The fact is," wrote Girvan, "that during the whole 1974 Caribbean tax offensive, there was no hostile comment (that this writer is aware of) from Government sources in either the United States or Canada."[107]

The reasons are to be found in Girvan's own radical analysis of the Jamaican and Guyanese situations. First, the total incremental foreign-exchange costs of higher priced Caribbean bauxite are so small as to be insignificant in the overall balance-of-payments picture of the United States. Caribbean bauxite is not Middle Eastern oil, nor is the IBA

105. Long-held suspicions of U.S. involvement in a destabilization "plot" against Jamaica seemed to find corroboration in an article in *Penthouse* magazine (Dec. 1977). Even Mr. Peter Abrahams of the official Jamaican news service gave it credence, only to have the opposition force the government to admit in Parliament that the central themes of the story were fabrications. (*The Weekly Gleaner*, Dec. 12, 1977.) The "destabilization" theme was not heard as frequently from that date.
106. Norman Girvan, *Corporate Imperialism*, p. 149.
107. *Ibid.*, p. 150. It is worth noting that in 1973 the then U.S. Ambassador to Jamaica, Vincent de Roulet, was declared *persona non grata* by Jamaica for declaring that he had "promised" that the United States would not intervene in Jamaican politics if no move was made toward nationalization of the bauxite industry. There was no protest from Washington.

OPEC.[108] Second, the Caribbean represents a smaller and smaller share of both the U.S. and the world markets for bauxite and alumina. Jamaica's share of the world market for alumina went from 24 percent to 20 percent from 1970 to 1975, and its share of the bauxite market went from 27 percent to 17 percent. During the same period Guinea increased its production by 836 percent, its share of the world market going from 2 percent to 23 percent. Australia's share of the world market for bauxite went from 14 percent to 24 percent; its share of the U.S. alumina market went from 46 percent to 76 percent.[109] Caribbean leverage on Washington through bauxite continues to decrease. Third, at no time were the supplies of bauxite to the United States in doubt; only price was at issue. Even if she could have afforded a boycott, it is clear that Jamaica could not have secured the solidarity of other producer members of IBA. Finally, and perhaps the crucial point, the price negotiated allowed the companies a comfortable margin of profit, yet was the highest possible Jamaican "take" before the total cost equaled or exceeded the cost of production from alternative sources. Jamaica had reached the limits of its capacity to increase prices, and the companies could live within those limits. Trinidad, which has been eager but unable to join OPEC, is not in a much different situation with its oil industry. In fact, all three arguments made to explain the Jamaica situation also apply to the Trinidad case.

As if to underscore his understanding of Jamaica's position, Prime Minister Manley had engaged in active personal diplomacy in 1974, including visits to Secretary of State Kissinger in Washington and Prime Minister Trudeau in Ottawa just before the Offensive. The move, therefore, was neither as radical nor as spontaneous as it was portrayed as being for internal political consumption.

These international and internal constraints on West Indian government reforms became even more apparent during 1975 and 1976. They presented a unique opportunity for a foreign policy initiative such as the one the new Democratic administration had in mind. The Carter Administration in 1976 launched a diplomatic campaign, the intensity of which had not been seen since Kennedy's "Alliance for Progress." Critical was the level of traveling emissaries, which included his wife, his Secretary of State, his Under Secretary of State for Political Affairs, his Assistant Secretary of State for Inter-American Affairs, and his

108. See Patricia Smallman, "Whatever Happened to Bauxite Market Share?," *The Weekly Gleaner*, Oct. 7, 1977, p. 11.
109. *Ibid.*

Ambassador to the United Nations (Andrew Young). Young's appeal and effectiveness cannot be overstated.[110]

The Carter Administration also made substantial changes in the diplomatic representatives in the area. The British Caribbean had traditionally been the repository for political appointees—some of singular ineptitude[111]—but the Carter appointments of career diplomats seemed to please nearly everyone.[112] In 1976 a "Caribbean Task Force" began functioning in the State Department, and by early 1977 it was clear that Washington's Caribbean "diplomatic offensive" was well on its way. Its fundamental, though not exclusive, goal was to keep West Indian experiments in socialism from drifting to the radical left, and to do so through political rather than military-based policies. Aside from the thinking among Carter and his own staff, this policy had support from two influential sources. Perhaps most important was the long-standing support from the House Subcommittee on Inter-American Affairs headed for many years by Democratic Representative Dante Fascell of Florida. Fascell has long held that relationships with the Caribbean should subordinate military to political considerations and that the United States should play a "supporting" rather than hegemonic role utilizing, where possible, multilateral and regional organizations. The other significant source of support came from the liberal foreign policy "establishment," whose views had received prominent expression in the "Linowitz Report."[113] Even though it did not address itself to the Caribbean specifically, the Report reflected the changing mood in certain influential circles when it advocated (1) the need to respect diversity in ideology and economic/social organization; (2) the independent role of Latin American/Caribbean nations in international affairs; and (3) the global significance of the principal issues of U.S.-Latin American/Caribbean relations.

110. See *The New York Times* coverage of Andrew Young's trip: " 'There really has been a change' Mr. Young has been saying throughout the tour, and the responsiveness of the Caribbean leaders . . . has seemed at times to be more than the visitors expected." (Aug. 14, 1977, p. 15.) "During the trip, hosts and guests sometimes seemed to be bursting with eagerness to cement the new relationship with praise." (Aug. 18, 1977, p. 3.)

111. Philip Kelly, "Recent United States Ambassadors to the Caribbean" (Unpublished manuscript).

112. See Dennis Kux, Chairman of the American Foreign Service Association: "We are pleased with the improvements, especially in the Carribbean, where they clearly reversed the pattern of recent years." (*The Miami Herald*, Aug. 6, 1977, p. 1.)

113. Commission on United States-Latin American Relations, *The Americas in a Changing World* (New York, 1974).

Significantly, the Report recognized that "extensive bilateral concessional assistance from the United States to Latin America is largely a thing of the past," (p. 42) and that the United States should cooperate with other Latin American nations and multilateral development institutions in providing assistance. In this regard the launching in the spring of 1978 of a "Group for Cooperation in Economic Development" was an attempt to implement such a multilateral approach in the Caribbean under World Bank sponsorship. Various foreign governments and international agencies (the IMF, the Inter-American Development Bank, the Caribbean Development Bank) were to coordinate aid activities in the region.

To further underline the shift from military to political thinking, Washington began on the one hand to downplay the significance of the radical threat in the area and on the other hand to emphasize the "opportunistic" nature of the non-Marxist "left." As early as 1972, when asked about the significance of a Conference of Caribbean Revolutionary Groups in Guyana, the representative of the Defense Intelligence Agency (DIA) noted: "It appears to have been a political image building effort by the man in Guyana, Jagan. . . . It just seemed to be a lot of rhetoric and propaganda."[114] The Agency, he told Congress, did not attach much significance to the meeting at all. Similarly, the Deputy Assistant Secretary of State for Inter-American Affairs, after noting that Prime Minister Forbes Burnham of Guyana had declared Guyana to be a Marxist-Leninist state, had nationalized all large foreign-owned enterprises (and many local ones), votes against the United States in the United Nations, and has very close ties with Cuba, could still conclude: "But an independent Guyana seeking its own path to social progress is no threat to this country."[115]

To Terrence Todman, Assistant Secretary of State for Inter-American Affairs, there was a possible "strategic" aspect to some Caribbean radicalism: "A militant anti-U.S. posture could appear to them as the only way to get our attention and realize their ambitions."[116] This awareness of the opportunistic aspects of certain proclaimed socialisms seems to be widespread in the Carter Administration. As one DIA analyst put it: "Burnham's move toward socialism in the first place may have been partially an effort to undercut the popularity of Jagan, who represents

114. Soviet Activities in Cuba. Part 3, *Hearings, SIAA* [Subcommittee on Inter-American Affairs], Sep. 26, 1972, p. 28.
115. Soviet Activities in Cuba. Parts 6 and 7 *Hearings, SIAA*, Jun. 15, 1976, p. 2.
116. *Hearings, SIAA*, Jun. 28, 1977, p. 30.

the majority East Indian population of Guyana."[117] Cynicism is inescapable when one understands that this very "opportunism" is being used as an additional argument in favor of further support to these governments.

But perhaps even more important than the awareness of the selective and strategic radicalism of the non-Marxist left was a genuine new understanding of the varieties of socialist postures in today's world. The Deputy Assistant Secretary of State for Inter-American Affairs told a Congressional subcommittee, "The fact is, that Manley is a Social Democrat, Fidel is a Communist; two people who do not get along in serious politics are Social Democrats and Communists."[118] He proceeded to place the admiration of much of the West Indies for Cuba within this nonthreatening perspective: admiration for Cuba stemmed from the "black English-speaking" Caribbean for Cuba's participation in the "anticolonial and antiwhite" struggle in southern Africa. In general, however, neither Cuba nor the Soviet Union were perceived as posing a major threat, militarily or otherwise.

Washington had finally caught on to the contradictions inherent in the radical politics—both national and international—of the West Indian nations. Except for skilled nudges to the right, Washington appeared satisfied to allow these contradictions to work themselves out, confident that in this *mare nostrum* things generally tend to go its way.

CONCLUSION

The irony of the West Indian situation is that the very successes of majority ownership in industrial enterprises—the Bauxite Offensive or the nationalization of majority shareholdings in Trinidad oil—have contributed to the structural dependency of these nations. As Norman Girvan quite correctly notes, these nationalists moves have made the societies even more a part of the corporate system, since the state benefits to the extent that the companies prosper in the marketplace. Further, in these "rentier states" there will be, in Girvan's words, "a new alliance between the corporate managers of the transnational aluminum companies and the buro-political managers of the Caribbean bauxite-producing states."[119] When the buropolitical managers see their enemies not in class terms but rather in ethnic/racial terms (as in Trinidad and

117. Soviet Activities in Cuba. *Hearings, SIAA*, Jun. 15, 1976, p. 108.
118. *Ibid.*, p. 82.
119. Girvan, *Corporate Imperialism*, p. 115.

Guyana) or across party lines (as in Jamaica), the dominant instinct is survival. Survival often means a nationalist-populist program of jobs through state control of enterprises, public works programs, and other direct benefits to the politically loyal. These programs are sustained by taxation, first of the companies and, as they reach their limits, of the rest of the society.

But since eventually even the new income cannot sustain the ever-increasing national budgets, the outcome is indebtedness. The growth of this indebtedness gives the United States additional leverage on events in these nations. Yet it is a leverage that Washington is satisfied to exercise through multilateral agencies such as the IMF. Bilateral aid, especially through AID, has been and will continue to be used as an expression of solidarity with government programs that meet Washington's approval.

Short of full-scale social and political revolution, which appears nowhere in the offing, these West Indian societies will not be able to break out of the present pattern of structural dependence. The trend that a wide spectrum of the dominant elites of these nations prefer is a state-directed populism with an assigned role for the private sector and an active but nonaligned Third World foreign policy. The evidence seems to be that this is, in fact, as much as the existing West Indian political cultures are willing to bear. The development of socialism, with all the sacrifices that necessarily entails, appeared in the late 1970's as a very remote possibility. This suits Washington well, since the United States perceives populist social democracy to be as effective an alternative to Marxism-Leninism as anything else tried thus far.

Shoes, OPIC, and the Unquestioning Persuasion: Multinational Corporations and U.S.-Brazilian Relations

PETER EVANS

> ... There is a naive and unquestioning persuasion
> abroad to the effect that, in some occult way, the material
> interests of the populace coincide with the pecuniary
> interests of those business men who live within the scope
> of the same set of governmental contrivances.
>   —Thorstein Veblen, *The Theory of
> Business Enterprise* (1904)

Having arrived in Brazil without invitation, pointedly housed by the Brazilians in a hotel rather than an official residence, Jimmy Carter could hardly help noticing that in the spring of 1978 U.S.-Brazilian relations were following a new tack. To some the changes were confusing. When Brazil renounced U.S. military aid, the conservative columnists Evans and Novak began to talk somewhat hysterically about how "Brazil could end up leading an anti-American right-of-center bloc in the Western hemisphere."

Economically as well as politically there were new elements in U.S.-Brazilian relations: while the U.S. International Trade Commission was making life difficult for Brazilian exporters of manufactured goods, Interbrás, the largest of Brazil's state-owned trading companies, was busily carving out markets in the Soviet Union and Eastern Europe, and while officials of the United Auto Workers (UAW) were becoming concerned over the number of Pinto engines coming into Detroit from Brazil, Brazilian businessmen were complaining that the U.S. International Trade Commission was being overzealous in its attempts to protect U.S. domestic industries. At the same time that Interbrás was arranging to assemble refrigerators and air-conditioners in Nigeria and

Peter Evans is Associate Professor of Sociology at Brown University. His most recent publication is *Dependent Development: The Alliance of Multinational, State, and Local Capital in Brazil* (Princeton University Press, 1979).

build hotels in Iraq, complaints were being raised in the U.S. Congress concerning the increases in Brazil's steel exports to the United States.

For U.S. multinationals operating in Brazil the situation had disquieting features. There was "some puzzlement [over] a growing strain of restrictiveness in government attitudes toward their presence in the economy."[1] Uneasiness was reinforced by the emergence of a draft proposal from a group of Brazilian machinery producers aimed at restricting the actions of multinationals, a proposal in which, according to *Business Latin America*, "their language and charges often echo the most vociferous attacks by left-wing critics of foreign capital."[2] For U.S. multinationals, potential worries over nationalism were combined with fears that if political disagreements between the U.S. and Brazilian governments were not resolved, "U.S. trade and investment in the region could be pushed aside to make room for new European and Japanese investors."[3]

Is there a real difference in U.S.-Brazilian relations? After all, U.S. multinationals continue to hold a commanding position within the Brazilian economy. Trade between the two countries still consists primarily of the exchange of raw materials from Brazil for manufactured goods produced in the United States. The basic structures of dependency remain, whether Jimmy Carter stays in a hotel or not. An analysis of U.S.-Brazilian relations should still begin with the models of class structure and trade relations that have been developed by theorists of imperialism and dependency. At the same time, it would be a mistake to dismiss current controversies as merely ephemeral and transitory, for they indicate long-term changes that affect class structures within—as well as class relations between—both periphery and center.

One of the key starting points for the analysis of economic growth in the periphery has always been the role of foreign capital in relation to national development. Imperialism worried even Latin Americans who favored capitalist development because it suggested a split between the interests of capital and the development of local productive forces. As long as capital had its origins and base abroad, it could choose to neglect problems of local accumulation, taking the surplus and using it to foster accumulation elsewhere. Distrust of foreign capital has gone hand in hand with the myth of the "national bourgeoisie," the local entrepreneurial class with a developmental "project." It was presumed that a Latin American "national bourgeoisie" would have an unavoid-

1. *Business Latin America*, (1978), p. 57.
2. *Ibid.*, p. 59.
3. *Ibid.*, p. 131.

able commitment to the development of local productive forces, even though not necessarily to redistribution of the fruits of increased productivity. But, the emergence of a "national bourgeoisie" is seen as a problematic if not unattainable possibility.

In the countries of the center the existence of a "national bourgeoisie" is assumed. The national loyalties of capital are questioned only by cynics, subversives, and an occasional populist. Subsidizing the accumulation of capital abroad is justified as long as the owners of this capital are domiciled at home. The international adventures of large-scale capital are assumed to contribute to local accumulation. Markets will be opened, raw materials provided, profits shipped back—and the center nation, even its working classes, will benefit.

In the periphery, the state and large capital are in part antagonistic insofar as large capital is foreign. The absence of a "national bourgeoisie" places a heavier entrepreneurial burden on the state. Nationalists are wary of openness to the international economy. Foreign trade, like foreign capital, is double-edged, perhaps facilitating local development but perhaps facilitating only dependency and subverting local development. For the center, the international economy is an arena for national aggrandizement and an avenue for the resolution of domestic class conflict. John Hobson and Cecil Rhodes agreed that imperialism allowed accumulation to continue without distribution.

Central to the evolution of U.S.-Brazilian relations over the past decade has been the fact that, despite the continued presence of many features of dependency, Brazil is beginning to take on some "centerlike" characteristics. The Brazilian state takes seriously the possibility that capital can be harnessed to the needs of local accumulation regardless of its foreign origins, and Brazil has begun to push its goods more aggressively in international trade. At the same time, the United States, suffering from balance-of-payments deficits as chronic as those that have plagued Brazil, has begun to wonder whether openness to the international economy is still in its interest. Simultaneously, doubts have begun to arise over whether the fact that the owners of capital are American citizens is sufficient insurance that the expansion of capital will serve national interests.

These tendencies are admittedly only that, and they are still not strong enough to change the fundamental structures of imperialism and dependency. The relations between General Motors and the Brazilian state will always be different from the relations between GM and the U.S. political apparatus. Nonetheless, there is still an undeniable undercurrent in the direction of both an increasing separation of multinationals from their home-country polity and a strengthening of ties between them and certain "semiperipheral" states like Brazil. Similarly, there are increasing parallels between the situation faced by local Brazilian capital and that faced by small domestically oriented capital within the United States. Both find themselves dependent on, yet at the same time disadvantaged by, the resources at the command of international capital.

Exploring these intriguing tendencies requires covering a lot of disparate and apparently disconnected territory. The nature of the current "triple alliance" that binds together multinationals, the state, and elite local capital in Brazil will be our starting point. The contradictions of this "triple alliance" and the essential role of exports in sustaining the Brazilian model must also be examined. A look at the impact of changes in the international economy on U.S. economic growth, American labor, and domestically oriented capital in the United States follows consideration of Brazil's economic problems. Finally, an examination of varieties of "nationalist"[4] reactions to international capital in both Brazil and the United States will provide a political dynamic to complement the economic analysis.

THE TRIPLE ALLIANCE

With Cardoso's promulgation of the idea of "associated-dependent development," students of imperialism began to look more closely at the assumption that international capital was unalterably opposed to

4. "Nationalism" is sometimes taken, especially in Latin America, to refer to policies or ideological positions that speak to the interests of the nation as a whole, that is to the interests of the entire population. In any class-divided society such a definition is highly problematic, and for that reason a definition more restricted to the perspective of the dominant class will be used here: "nationalist" policies are those aimed at maximizing the rate of capital accumulation within the confines of a given nation-state. The term "nationalist" has no direct welfare or distributive implications. As long as "nationalism" is defined in this restricted way, a regime may be nationalist and at the same time repressive and inegalitarian. Yet nationalist policies may be considered to be in the interests of the entire population insofar as the local citizenry are more likely to be able to exercise political leverage over the distribution of the benefits of accumulation that takes place within their own "set of governmental contrivances." "Internationalism" will be used with the same "capitalist" restrictions as nationalism—as referring to policies or ideologies that attempt to maximize the accumulation of capital without regard for the geographical location of that accumulation. For a somewhat different but analogous discussion of nationalism and internationalism, see Franz Schurmann, *The Logic of World Power: An Inquiry into the Origins, Currents, and Contradictions of World Politics* (New York, 1974).

industrialization in all parts of the periphery.[5] Looking over the statistics on foreign investment in the less developed areas since 1945, they realized that there had been a dramatic increase in direct foreign investment in manufacturing. This investment left much of the Third World untouched, but in a few of the larger and better-endowed less developed countries it became part of a substantial thrust toward industrialization.

Countries like Brazil and Mexico changed enough to be considered "semiperipheral" rather than part of the real periphery.[6] Within these countries, multinationals became involved not just in "easy" import substitution but in the production of basic and intermediary goods. The classic image of Third World development as a struggle between a nascent "national bourgeoisie" interested in industrialization and foreign capital interested in keeping the country locked into its traditional place in the international division of labor began to make less and less sense. Accumulation appeared in fact to be based on a "triple alliance" among the multinationals, a segment of the largest owners of local capital, and the entrepreneurial state.

Viewing the elite structure of countries like Brazil as characterized by such a "triple alliance" does not mean eschewing the possibility of "intraelite" conflict.[7] The notion of the triple alliance parallels Sunkel's idea of "national disintegration and transnational integration," in that it suggests an important split between the largest local capital groups and the rest of the local bourgeoisie within Brazil.[8] The largest local capital groups, which Cardoso and Faletto and others have called the "internationalized bourgeoisie," can participate in the process of accumulation propelled by the triple alliance.[9] The participation of the rest of the local bourgeoisie is partial, problematic, and highly depen-

5. Fernando Henrique Cardoso, "As Tradições de Desenvolvimento Associado," *Estudos Cebrape*, 8 (1974), pp. 41–75.

6. Immanuel Wallerstein, "The Rise and Future Demise of the World Capitalist System: Concepts for Comparative Analysis," *Comparative Studies in Society and History* (September 1974) 15 (no. 4), pp. 387–415. See also, Immanuel Wallerstein "Semi-peripheral Countries and the Contemporary World Crisis," *Theory and Society*, 3 (no. 4), pp. 461–84.

7. Peter B. Evans, "Multinationals, State-owned Corporations, and the Transformation of Imperialism: A Brazilian Case Study," *Economic Development and Cultural Change* 26 (no. 1), pp. 43–64. See also Peter B. Evans, *Dependent Development: The Alliance of Multinational, State, and Local Capital in Brazil* (Princeton, N.J., 1979).

8. Oswaldo Sunkel, "Transnational Integration and National Distintegration in Latin America," *Social and Economic Studies*, 22 (no. 17), pp. 132–76.

9. F. H. Cardoso and Enzo Faletto, *Dependência e Desenvolvimento na América Latina: Ensaio de Interpretação Sociologica* (Rio de Janeiro, 1973).

dent on its ability to maintain effective political access to the highest levels of the state apparatus.

In addition to conflicts created by the marginalization of a part of the local bourgeoisie, certain contradictions between the interests of international capital and the needs of local accumulation persist. There will always be a gap between the aims of the nationalist, who puts a premium on the full development of the division of labor locally, and the preferred strategies of international capital. The multinationals' estimation of how full a range of activities and industries it makes sense to implant in Brazil will always fall short of the nationalist estimation. The multinational has no reason to take risks in order to provide Brazil with "externalities" that may benefit the overall process of accumulation without providing any returns to the individual firm. The multinational has options and must exercise them in a way that preserves its flexibility and freedom of action. The nationalist and the multinational must always operate in some tension with each other, even if neither is concerned with questions of welfare or distribution.

The Brazilian state must be "nationalist" in the sense of continuing to pressure the multinationals to put a priority on local accumulation; otherwise its own economic base will be undermined. This kind of nationalism, generated by the objective requirements of local accumulation, might be called "planners' nationalism" or, in Brazil, "CDI nationalism" (after the Conselho de Desenvolvimento Industrial, which must decide which industrial projects should be provided with fiscal incentives). Complementing "CDI nationalism" is the nationalism of the local bourgeoisie—whether of those elements excluded from the triple alliance or jockeying for a better position within it. Nationalism is an ideological weapon useful in protecting its share of the industrial arena. This might be called "ABDIB nationalism" (after the Associação Brasileira pelo Desenvolvimento de Indústria de Base, which contains some of the strongest nationalists among the local bourgeoisie).

The major structural shift in terms of the ownership of industrial assets during the period of the miracle (roughly 1968–74) was, as Newfarmer and Mueller have demonstrated nicely, not a decline in the Brazilian share but a decline in the Brazilian *private* share.[10] From a "CDI nationalist" point of view this is not a disaster, and may even be seen as an improvement, depending on one's estimate of the efficiency

10. Richard Newfarmer and Willard Mueller, *Multinational Corporations in Brazil and Mexico: Structural Sources of Economic and Non-economic Power*, Report to the Sub-committee on Multinational Corporations, Committee on Foreign Relations, U.S. Senate (Washington, D.C., 1975).

of state-owned corporations. Nor does it represent a disaster from the point of view of the large Brazilian private groups that are part of Cardoso and Faletto's "internationalized bourgeoisie" or Sunkel's "transnational kernel." As Cardoso and others have noted, the assets of the very largest Brazilian firms grew during the "miracle" at least as rapidly as—if not more rapidly than—the assets of the largest foreign groups.[11] A political problem has been created, nonetheless, and one whose magnitude would be substantially increased if increased democratization were to broaden the segment of the local bourgeoisie that has access to the state apparatus.

In practice the two kinds of nationalism are often difficult to separate. Together they result in a persistent tension between the Brazilian elite and the multinationals. Nonetheless, the dominant aspect of the relation is one of collaboration around a common interest in the local accumulation of capital. For U.S. multinationals in Brazil, dependent development under the aegis of the triple alliance has been extremely profitable. Most estimates of profit rates for Brazilian affiliates run at least 50 percent higher than profit rates for large manufacturing corporations within the United States.[12] In the late 1960's and early 1970's Brazil provided the multinationals with a profitable arena for expansion at a time when the developed economies were not growing rapidly. Fiscal incentives and an impressive growth in the market for both consumer durables and producer goods made Brazil attractive, as did tight controls on labor and a relatively predictable and sympathetic state apparatus.

By the end of 1976 the value of U.S. manufacturing investments in Brazil approached four billion dollars. Only in Canada, Britain, France, and West Germany were U.S. manufacturers more deeply involved. The triple alliance has grown to such proportions that neither the Brazilian state nor the multinationals can consider dissolving it. Yet the depth of the multinationals' involvement in Brazil makes the contradictions contained in the triple alliance all the more important to them and makes it all the more likely that their attempts to deal with these contradictions will have repercussions for their behavior elsewhere.

The struggles within the triple alliance will not take the form of internecine warfare designed to crush the other participants; it will take

---

11. Cardoso, p. 60.
12. See for example, John M. Connor and Willard Mueller, *Market Power and Profitability of Multinational Corporations in Brazil and Mexico*, Report to the Subcommittee on Foreign Economic Policy, Committee on Foreign Relations, U.S. Senate (Washington, D.C., 1977).

the form of bargaining and negotiation among partners whose interests overlap and who acknowledge one another's worth. A number of bargaining issues might be lumped together under the general heading of "control." Both CDI and ABDIB nationalists would like to limit the power and maneuvering room of the multinationals by forcing them to share control in their ventures—whether by submitting to increased regulation, by allowing local partners to share equity and the decision-making prerogatives that go with it, or by requiring more transfer of technology.

On their side, multinationals must not allow the localization of manufacturing assets within Brazil to lead to what we might call the "Moran effect"—diminution of bargaining power proportionate to reliance on assets fixed within the host country.[13] They must struggle to preserve their relative monopoly on technology. Conversely, as the position of the multinationals becomes increasingly central to the dynamic sectors of the Brazilian economy, greater local control over the multinationals is essential to the Brazilian state's ability to direct the process of accumulation. Cutting back both the legal prerogatives of multinationals by persuading them to enter joint ventures and, perhaps even more important, their technological advantage by including explicit commitments to share technology is on the agenda. Within the general framework of collaboration and common interest, the struggle over control will continue to be intense.

The best recent example of a struggle that centered around the issue of control is the 1977 controversy over the "minicomputer" industry. Brazil established local equity participation and "open technology," i.e., "the effective transfer of technology to Brazilian hands with no restrictive clauses," as the main criteria for approval of incentives for local manufacture of computers.[14] IBM, which has no joint ventures in manufacturing even in the United States, was willing to build its Model 32 in Brazil only if allowed to operate on a wholly-owned basis. Other large computer companies, such as Data General, shared IBM's adverse reaction to the conditions set by the Brazilians.

Had the multinationals been the only actors involved, Brazil's leverage would have been minimal, but unfortunately for them this was not the case. Digibrás, the state-owned holding company in the computer industry, set up a subsidiary, Cobra, which was also state-owned but con-

---

13. Theodore Moran, *Multinational Corporations and the Politics of Dependence: Copper in Chile* (Princeton, N.J., 1974).
14. *Business Latin America*, 1977, pp. 193, 307.

tained some local private capital. Cobra in turn acquired know-how and parts from a U.S. company called Sycor. Once it became apparent that minicomputers might be produced locally by Cobra, CAPRE, the Brazilian agency in charge of regulating the computer industry, was in a position to credibly threaten to bar imports of minicomputers and thus squeeze out any multinational unwilling to enter under its terms. To make the pressure tighter, CAPRE has said that only two firms in addition to Cobra will be allowed to set up local minicomputer manufacture. Thus the multinational that holds out too long may find itself permanently shut out.

One of the most interesting aspects of the nationalist strategy in this instance is that it involves Brazil's use of a "domestically oriented" U.S. firm as an instrument for increasing bargaining leverage against the multinationals. Sycor is a tiny firm, one that could never seriously consider a confrontation with IBM in the U.S. market. Only a few years old in 1976, it had fewer than 2,000 employees and would have been a totally implausible competitor for the Brazilian market on its own. Yet its very "pygmy" status meant that it had much less to lose by sharing its technology with Brazil; and that technology was the vital ingredient necessary for Cobra to put itself in such a strong bargaining position vis-à-vis the computer multinationals.

A very different sort of resolution of the question of control is illustrated by the maneuvers of Dow Chemical in the mid-seventies. Dow entered Brazil late with large projects, yet surprisingly enough was able to enter on a wholly-owned basis.[15] Though it was unwilling to cut local partners in on its equity, Dow was willing to make a major commitment to the development of local technology and budgeted over five million dollars for a local research and development facility, its fourth largest research operation worldwide.[16] By making a gesture toward reducing Brazil's overall technological dependency, Dow has probably also reduced the likelihood that its exclusive control over its own operations will be challenged.

The adaptability of the multinationals will vary from company to company, and pressure on them from the Brazilian state will vary with fluctuations in the local political climate and the degree to which other economic problems appear more important. Primary among these other problems is the imbalance in Brazil's external trade relations.

15. *Ibid.*, 1975, pp. 196, 299.
16. *Ibid.*, 1978, p. 159.

NATIONALISM AND EXPORT PROMOTION

One of the most obvious weak spots in the contemporary Brazilian model is its import-intensive nature. If it is true, as the Economic Commission on Latin America claimed a few years ago, that "for every one percent in the growth of the product, the volume of imports must increase by two percent," then either the pattern of internal growth must shift or exports must continue to grow dramatically.[17] The rise in the price of petroleum exacerbated the problem, but the multinationals' needs for imports of intermediate and capital goods are fundamental to the import-intensive nature of Brazilian development. A study done for the Ministry of Planning argued that two-thirds of Brazil's non-oil trade deficit could be accounted for by the activities of just over 100 multinationals.[18]

From the point of view of the multinationals, the import-intensive nature of their expansion in Brazil is far from disadvantageous. About 70 percent of all U.S. exports of manufactured goods to Brazil were "MNC-related" according to a 1970 U.S. Tariff Commission survey.[18] Since a substantial proportion of "MNC-related" exports goes to the multinationals' own subsidiaries (about one-third according to the 1970 survey), and since the subsidiaries of other multinationals are likely to account for a sizable share of the rest, the expansion of the multinationals' assets in Brazil is directly linked to the expansion of their export-generated profits within the United States.

Although import-intensive industrialization is not disadvantageous for the multinationals, it represents a severe problem for Brazil. During the "miracle," trade imbalances together with a negative service account created a rising current account deficit that was in turn financed by foreign borrowing until debt service was equal to about 40 percent of exports. Something had to be done, and there were two possibilities. The first was to reduce imports, which consisted primarily of capital goods and intermediate products.

The creation of a local capital goods industry and the "deepening" of the process of industrialization was clearly attempted in certain areas,

17. Economic Commission on Latin America (ECLA), *Economic Survey of Latin America, 1974* (New York, 1976), p. 233.
18. *Business Latin America*, 1976, p. 185.
19. U.S. Tariff Commission, *Implications of Multinational Firms for World Trade and Investment and for U.S. Trade and Labor*, Report to Committee on Finance, U.S. Senate (Washington, D.C., 1973).

but success, at least during the early 1970's was limited.[20] The proportion of capital goods supplied by imports increased rather than decreased between 1967 and 1974.[21] In addition, attempts at creating a local capital goods industry raised the question of whether "local" meant domiciled in Brazil or owned by Brazilians.

The expansion of the local capital goods industry could be as profitable for the multinationals as import substitution in the consumer durables. But Brazil's clear preference for a locally owned capital goods sector is an encumbrance for the multinationals, even though it has not yet affected their share of assets. In the spring of 1977, for example, FINAME (the industrial equipment financing section of the BNDE, Brazil's National Development Bank) closed the list of foreign subsidiaries from which Brazilian companies could purchase equipment and be eligible for support in the form of low-interest financing. This ruling would have made it extremely difficult for foreign suppliers not already approved to supply equipment to the lucrative market provided by state-owned firms, and it would have cut foreign suppliers off from the local private market. Fortunately for the multinationals, a group of German and Japanese banks got together and began negotiating a loan to the BNDE, which had responsibility for FINAME. British and American banks were brought in, and eventually a $150 million fund was loaned to FINAME specifically for the use of foreign firms.[22] Nonetheless, the point had been made: insofar as Brazilian funding was involved, preference would go to the local bourgeoisie.

Another striking example occurred when the state-owned railway system asked for bids on an order for 140 locomotives. General Electric, for years the only company producing locomotives in Brazil, naturally expected to get the bid. But GE is a wholly-owned foreign company and has in fact been accused of participating in a cartel that "decimated systematically" local producers of electrical equipment.[23] Instead Equipamentos Villares, a company that had never built a locomotive but that was presided over by Carlos Villares, one of the foremost advocates of ABDIB nationalism, got the bid.[24]

20. Guillermo O'Donnell, "Reflections on the Patterns of Change in the Bureaucratic-Authoritarian State," *Latin American Research Review* 13 (no. 1), pp. 3–39. See also, José Serra, "Three Mistaken Theses on the Connection between Authoritarianism and Economic Development," in David Collier, ed., *The New Authoritarianism in Latin America* (Princeton, N.J., forthcoming).

21. Serra, Table 7.

22. *Business Latin America*, 1978, p. 155.

23. *Wall Street Journal*, January 13, 1978, p. 20.

24. *Business Latin America*, p. 75.

From the point of view of center countries, especially those like the United States that have balance-of-payments problems of their own, one of the compensations for the transfer of increasing amounts of manufacturing capacity to the countries of the "semiperiphery" has been the corresponding increase in the market for imported machinery. For example, a study sponsored by the U.S. Department of Commerce in the early 1970's estimated that Brazilian textile exports of $145 million in 1972 were almost matched by imports of textile machinery amounting to $115 million. The connection between expansion of Brazilian assets and the expansion of export markets was made explicit, for the report admonished U.S. manufacturers to consider "the advantages of mounting subsidiary operations in Brazil for part or complete manufacture and thus provide a launching pad for increased importation." Similarly, the Polo Petroquímico do Nordeste, which was designed to provide local substitutes for imported intermediate products, was viewed by the U.S. Department of Commerce as a potential market for a quarter of a billion dollars of imported equipment.[25] Expansion of capital goods production in the "semiperiphery" removes this compensation. A locally owned capital goods sector would be a double loss.

Local production of capital goods is very attractive from a nationalist point of view, both CDI nationalists and ABDIB nationalists applauding the fuller local division of labor and the opportunities for local capital that it implies. But it is a partial and problematic solution to balance-of-trade problems—partial because it leaves untouched the deficit created by imports of intermediary goods, problematic because it creates a new arena for tension between the multinationals and ABDIB nationalists. Escaping the trade deficit through the expansion of exports is different. Multinationals, local capital, and the state can easily unite around this strategy.

For the multinationals, exporting from Brazil offers the opportunity of replacing lower-profit U.S. production with higher-profit Brazilian production. Supplying markets in other Third World countries from Brazil rather than from the United States gives the multinationals a chance to take advantage of more generous Brazilian export incentives. For example, *Business International* commented that for a Tenneco subsidiary trying to decide how to supply the Nigerian market for tractors and construction equipment, "sourcing from Brazil is attractive because the Brazilian Government, through CACEX [similar to the

25. U.S. Department of Commerce, "Brazil, Survey of U.S. Export and Import Opportunities: Chemical and Petrochemical Industries," prepared by Office of International Commerce (Washington, D.C., 1974).

U.S. Export-Import Bank], provides better credit terms than the U.S."[26] Business Week spoke of Brazil as "a funnel for goods to Black Africa."[27] Massey-Ferguson found that Brazil was a useful "funnel for goods to Asia" as well. Massey discovered that it could sell 53 million dollars to exchange-poor Turkey without taking any exchange risk by manufacturing tractors in Brazil and selling them through Interbrás. Sales to Turkey had previously been made through the United Kingdom but, as a Massey-Ferguson vice-president explained, "We were having trouble getting export credits out of the United Kingdom, and Brazil was anxious to increase its exports."

For the local bourgeoisie—even for those elements that are not properly speaking members of the internationalized bourgeoisie—increases in manufactured exports have been even more of a boon. Industries like textiles and shoes, which were still considered "traditional industries" in the late 1960's, were by the mid-1970's impressive contributors to Brazil's exports. In the brief three-year period between 1971 and 1973, textile exports in general expanded fivefold, and exports of finished textile goods expanded eightfold. The fruits of this expansion accrued in part to relatively small-scale members of the local bourgeoisie. The kinds of labor-intensive, technologically routine goods in which Brazil is most likely to be competitive internationally are exactly the kind of goods that locally owned firms are likely to produce.

State-owned companies are not directly involved in the manufacture of the kinds of goods that Brazil exports, but they may become involved as state enterprises begin to integrate forward, processing the primary products that they now export in raw form. The steps toward forward integration that have already been taken by the Companhia do Vale do Rio Doce are a prime example. In addition, Interbrás, Petrobras's trading subsidiary, has become a major factor in the marketing of a wide variety of Brazilian exports. Perhaps most important from the point of view of state-owned companies, the expansion of exports, by alleviating the pressure to restrict imports of capital goods, removes an important constraint on their own investment plans.

A focus on exports alleviates tensions over the expansion of multinationals. Insofar as the output of the multinationals is clearly aimed at export, it can be more easily justified in nationalist terms and is less likely to be threatening to local capital. As long as multinationals can portray themselves as engines of export expansion, they are more likely to be allowed access to new sectors and less likely to be challenged on

26. Business International, 1976, p. 204.
27. Business Week, November 1, 1976.

issues of control and sharing technology. Finally, of course, export expansion diminishes pressure on the multinationals to restrict their imports of capital and intermediate products just as it does for state-owned companies.

The best illustration of how export promotion provides a mutually acceptable solution to potential conflicts between the multinationals and the Brazilian state is provided by a program called BEFIEX, which ties a generous set of fiscal incentives to balance-of-payments performance. In the auto industry, Brazil was able to get commitments from all the major auto companies to export in total almost six billion dollars worth of their output over a period of several years.[28] For the auto companies the commitment to export amounts to "being thrown into the briarpatch." Given the incentives involved, they are likely to make higher profits on their production for export from Brazil than they could from another location. They will also be in an extremely strong position to demand even more incentives when the initial commitments run out in the mid-1980's, since by that time Brazil will be thoroughly integrated into their programs of "worldwide sourcing." For Brazil, on the other hand, the BEFIEX program represents a substantial contribution to resolution of trade imbalances. The auto industry, which was responsible in 1972–73 for a current account balance-of-payments deficit of $180 million, was on its way to producing a surplus almost that large by mid-1977.[29]

Viewed only in terms of the internal dynamics of the Brazilian alliance, export promotion generates profits, local accumulation, and harmony. Unfortunately for the Brazilian elite, securing the cooperation of the multinationals is only half the issue when export promotion is the goal; external markets are the other half, and that means confronting the internal politics of center countries.

The first thing that is evident in looking at Brazil's trade situation is that, with the exception of the special case of oil, Brazil's balance-of-trade problems originate in her trade relations with the center countries. As Table 1 shows, Brazil ran massive trade deficits in the early 1970's with the United States, Japan, and West Germany—the "core" economies. Very favorable balances with her less developed neighbors and the socialist countries were of insufficient magnitude to counterbalance her deficits with the core. Even in 1974, after the oil price rise, the core

28. Ronald Muller and David Moore, "Brazilian Bargaining Success in BEFIEX Export Promotion Program with the Transnational Automotive Industry" (New York, 1978).
29. *Ibid.*, Table 2.

was still the major source of deficits. Trade deficits with all developed countries were almost double the deficit produced by trade with the Middle East. When the problem of export expansion is looked at over time, the center countries again appear central to Brazil's trade problems. Between 1969 and 1974, exports expanded dramatically with the less de-

TABLE 1

Brazil's Trade Balance Before and After the Oil Crisis, 1972 and 1974
(Millions of U.S. dollars)

Trading partner	Imports	Exports	Balance	Balance as percent of imports
1972				
All developed countries	3,677	3,020	− 657	− 18%
U.S., Japan, W. Germany	2,355	1,447	− 908	− 39
Middle East	374	38	− 334	− 90
Bolivia, Uruguay, Paraguay	29	89	+ 60	+206
Socialist countries	91	288	+ 197	+217
TOTAL	4,775	3,991	− 784	− 16%
1974				
All developed countries	9,576	5,618	−3,958	− 41%
U.S., Japan, W. Germany	6,445	2,862	−3,583	− 56
Middle East	2,404	431	−1,973	− 82
Bolivia, Uruguay, Paraguay	165	251	+ 86	+ 52
Socialist countries	189	415	+ 226	+120
TOTAL	14,162	7,951	−6,211	− 44%

SOURCE: United Nations, Yearbook of International Trade Statistics, Vol. I: 1974 Trade by Country (New York, 1976).
NOTE: Areas are selected and therefore do not add to totals.

TABLE 2

Growth of Brazilian Exports, by Type of Commodity
(*Millions of U.S. dollars*)

Type of commodity	1969	1974	Percent increase
Primary products	2,066	5,804	181%
Manufactured goods	245	2,147	776
TOTAL	2,311	7,951	244%
Manufactured goods as a percent of total exports	11%	27%	

SOURCES: IBGE, *Anuario Estatistico*, 1972: 279–82; 1976: 245–47. Serra, 1978: Table 10.

TABLE 3

Growth of Brazilian Exports, by Destination
(*Millions of U.S. dollars*)

Destination	1969	1975	Percent increase
U.S.	609	1,337	120%
Western Europe	1,069	3,242	203
Bolivia, Uruguay, Paraguay	34	328	865
Africa	24	399	1563
Socialist countries	129	829	543
TOTAL	2,311	8,669	275%

SOURCES: IBGE, *Anuario Estatistico*, 1972: 279–82; 1976: 245–47. Serra, 1978: Table 10.

veloped countries and with the socialist bloc, yet the growth of exports to the core countries lagged behind the overall growth of exports. Dramatic expansion in small markets is not enough: Brazilian exports must increasingly penetrate the world's major markets if export expansion is going to succeed.

The problem of penetrating the markets of the advanced industrial countries is clarified by looking at another trend that is evident in Tables 2 and 3—the increasing role of manufactured goods among Brazil's exports. Primary products remain important, and in years when good harvests occur in combination with favorable market trends, as in 1977, primary exports may even grow more rapidly than manufactured exports. But overall the trend is clear: manufactured products must continue to account for a larger share of Brazil's exports if the pace of export expansion is to be kept up. The World Bank has projected an increase in the share of manufactured goods among Brazil's exports to 37 percent by 1985 and has stressed that "Brazil's growth prospects hinge quite critically on the growth of manufactured exports."[30]

The scenario for Brazil's future export expansion is clear. The huge deficits that have characterized its trade relations with the core countries must be cut back by placing a growing proportion of manufactured exports in these markets. The scenario runs, of course, squarely in the face of what is called "the new protectionism." *Business Latin America* summed up Brazil's predicament succinctly:

Economically the major change can be seen in Brazil's export drive: for the first time it is beginning to step on some toes. When its exports were only primary goods Brazil did not get in anybody's way. But now, by competing in the market for such manufactured products as cars, road-building machinery, radios, shoes and scissors, it is running into some of the troubles that beset other industrial societies. Objections are being raised to Brazil's export incentives, and protective measures have been invoked. This type of response to its exports is the principal sore spot in Brazilian-U.S. relations.[31]

SMALL CAPITAL AND THE INTERNATIONALIZATION
OF PRODUCTION

In Brazil, small locally owned capital has been left largely behind by the internationalization of the Brazilian economy. This might be seen as a plight peculiar to peripheral bourgeoisies, but it is in fact more general. Small pharmaceutical firms in Brazil have a great deal in common with small shoe manufacturers in New England.[32] Even if it is located in the center, small capital is not in a position to engage in direct investment and is not well set up to take advantage of export opportunities.[33] Small capital is, however, often engaged in manufacturing

30. *Business Latin America*, 1978, p. 149.
31. *Business Latin America*, 1978, p. 42.
32. Peter Evans, "Foreign Investment and Industrial Transformation," *Journal of Development Economics*, 3 (no. 4), pp. 119–39.
33. Though the focus here is on small capital, there are obviously also examples of large, domestically oriented capital threatened by imports. Steven Volk's analysis of the steel industry in this volume provides a good complement to the discussion presented here.

exactly the kind of technologically routine products that Brazil is trying to export. The devastating effect that the expansion of exports from the "semiperiphery" can have on small capital in the center is well illustrated by the plight of the U.S. shoe industry.

A quick summary of the U.S. shoe industry's decline in the face of competition from imports over an eleven-year period is provided in Table 4. Over 70,000 jobs disappeared between 1966 and 1976, along with 30 percent of the effective capacity of the industry. Nor was it the case that those who remained employed benefited from increased earnings based on more mechanized operations or the elimination of inefficient plants. The average earnings of those who were able to retain jobs in the industry remained stagnant in real terms and declined relative to earnings in other manufacturing industries. Value added per employee in footwear declined from 52 percent of the average for manu-

TABLE 4
*The Decline of the U.S. Shoe Industry
and the Rise of Imports*

	1966	1976	1976 as a percent of 1966
Total employees	241,500	169,000	70%
Number of companies	675	376	56
Effective capacity (000 pairs)	782,952	568,404	73
Census production (000 pairs)	641,696	413,087	69
Imports (000 pairs)	96,135	369,814	384
Value of shipments (millions of $)	2,473.5	3,482	141
Value of imports (millions of $)	158	1,448	916
Average weekly earnings[a]	$71.81	$70.22	98

SOURCE: American Footwear Industries Association, *Footwear Manual*, 1977, Tables 10, 11, 37, 38; AFIA Statistical Reporter, Quarterly Report, 4th Quarter, 1977.

[a] The figure for 1966 is gross average weekly earnings in current dollars. The figure for 1976 is gross earnings deflated by the change in the consumer price index from 1966 to 1976.

facturing industries in 1964 to 47 percent in 1974. In short, the U.S. shoe industry was not becoming a more modern and less labor-intensive industry but was simply losing out to overseas competition. The most important structural change in the industry during the period 1966–76 was an impressive increase in the degree of concentration. At the beginning of the period, 517 small companies shared just over a quarter of domestic input, whereas 16 large companies shared just over 30 percent. By the end of the period, 21 large companies produced half the industry's output, whereas the 292 companies left in the smallest size category had only about one fifth of the market. Three hundred companies disappeared entirely.

The structure of imports also changed over the period. Japan and Great Britain, both important center-country sources of shoe imports as of 1966, were no longer important factors by 1976. Italy and Spain remained major sources over the whole period, but Taiwan, Korea, and Brazil, three countries that accounted for less than one percent of the dollar volume of footwear imports in 1966, accounted for over 40 percent by the end of the period. In short, the real gains were made by the "semiperiphery."

For the several hundred small entrepreneurs who were driven out of business and the 70,000 workers who lost their jobs, the shift of manufacturing investment to the "semiperiphery" has been a disaster. As similar examples accumulate, it becomes harder for the multinationals and their supporters to argue that overseas investment combined with free trade is the optimal economic policy from the point of view of the "national interest." As Luciano Martins has pointed out, the evolution of the international economy during the 1960's and 1970's "has made it increasingly difficult for multinational corporations to portray their private interests as being the 'general interests' of the United States."[34]

Over the last two decades multinationals have increased their overseas investments at a much more rapid rate than their domestic investments. This tendency has accelerated particularly during the 1970's. In 1960, foreign capital outlays of U.S. multinationals represented 11.5 percent of total domestic outlays in manufacturing industries; by 1974, foreign outlays were 30.9 percent of domestic outlays. Foreign outlays grew at a rate of 16.4 percent a year from 1960 to 1974, whereas domestic outlays grew at only 8.5 percent. In the period from 1969 to 1974 the discrepancy between domestic and foreign expansion was even

34. Luciano Martins, *Nacao e Corporação Multinacional* (Coleção Estudos Brasileiros, no. 4; Rio de Janeiro, 1975), p. 99.

greater: foreign capital outlays expanded at 18.3 percent a year and domestic ones at only 7.8 percent.[35] At the same time that foreign plants were being expanded, the U.S. share of world manufactured exports was declining by about a third.[36]

What would have been the effect if the U.S. government had tried to impede the internationalization of production by preventing U.S. capital from moving abroad? Disregarding the question of whether it would have been technically possible to impede such capital flows, the answer seems to be that capital (which is to say in this case multinationals) would have been worse off, whereas U.S. labor probably would have been better off. Using Peggy Musgrave's estimates of aggregate income effects, we find that, without foreign direct investment, labor would appear to increase both its absolute level of income and its proportionate share of income. Were it possible to analyze returns to small capital independently from returns to large capital, small capital would probably show results similar to labor's. As it is, it is only possible to discuss returns to labor, returns to capital, and overall national returns. Musgrave's conclusions are, first, that foreign investment has "significant distributional effects working to the detriment of labor," and, second, that "the net rate of return on investment abroad at the margin and as seen from a national point of view is negative."[37]

Most of the argument regarding the effects of foreign investment has focused on employment effects rather than on income effects. Studies which find positive effects on employment tend to do so by assuming that foreign markets will be lost without direct investment. In addition, the employment that might be generated by the domestic investment of the same funds is left out of the equation.[38] Using more moderate assumptions, Frank and Freeman, in a study sponsored by the U.S. State Department, concluded that about one million jobs had been lost as a result of foreign investment between 1966 and 1973.[39] Studies like these

35. Subcommittee on Multinational Corporations, Committee on Foreign Relations, U.S. Senate, *Hearing on Multinational Corporations in the Dollar Devaluation Crisis and the Impact of Direct Investment Abroad in the U.S. Economy, Part 13* (Washington, D.C., 1976) p. 116.

36. *Ibid.*, p. 117.

37. Peggy Musgrave, *Direct Investment Abroad and the Multinationals: Effects on the U.S. Economy.* Prepared for use of the Sub-committee on Multinationals, Committee on Foreign Relations, U.S. Senate (Washington, D.C., 1975), pp. xvi, xvii.

38. See for example, Robert Stobaugh *et al.*, "U.S. Multinational Enterprises and the U.S. Economy," in Bureau of International Commerce, U.S. Department of Commerce, *The Multinational Corporation* (Washington, D.C., 1972).

39. Subcommittee on Multinational Corporations, Hearings, p. 107.

make life difficult for the multinationals. In 1950, when three-quarters of the world's automobile production originated in the United States, and when the United States could export automobiles to Brazil, "What's good for General Motors is good for the United States" had a plausible ring to it. Now, as we watch Detroit's output stagnate while GM and Ford are rapidly expanding their production elsewhere in the world, and, even worse, as we watch engines from Brazil going into Detroit Pintos and radios from Brazil going into other Fords, the correspondence of interest is harder to see.

It is not that the multinationals are left without arguments. Professor Stobaugh put their case succinctly to the U.S. Senate's Subcommittee on Multinationals: ". . . U.S. investment, foreign direct investment, is part of a cycle for generating new products and new knowledge into the U.S. and we are exporting that knowledge and those new products and we are getting monopoly profits in this economy from it and in turn we are buying mature [technologically routine] products with the money we made from those exports and services and goods."[40] In short, we are much better off exporting computers and importing shoes than we would be protecting our domestic shoe industry at the expense of our computer exports. This is a plausible argument, and one that might be able to generate considerable legitimacy if the United States had a favorable trade balance and low unemployment. Under present circumstances, however, legitimacy is harder to come by.

A "NATIONALIST" COALITION IN THE CENTER?

Newfarmer and Mueller have estimated that 25 firms control over half of all U.S. manufacturing investment in Latin America.[41] These firms benefit from a number of favorable tax laws, receive certain special services like (Overseas Private Investment Corporation) insurance, and expect the general support of the U.S. government apparatus. As long as a "Hickenlooper" perception of the direct connection between their interests and the general interests of the United States predominated, these 25 firms could comfortably expect the full support of the state.[42]

A "Hickenlooper" vision of foreign investment assumed not only that the interests of the multinationals were synonymous with those of the

40. *Ibid.*, p. 65.
41. Newfarmer and Mueller, p. 43.
42. By "Hickenlooper" perception, I mean the assumption that the U.S. state apparatus should serve to back up the interests of multinationals in their disputes with Third World states that was epitomized in the famous Hickenlooper admendment.

United States but also that the enemies of the multinationals were the enemies of capitalism and therefore of the "American way of life." Hence when the multinationals become involved in disputes or conflicts with a vehemently anticommunist government such as the Brazilian one, it is hard to invoke ideological fervor. Even more seriously, it is difficult to invoke interest-based support, even from other owners of capital. Foreign investors lack even the kind of political support that defense contractors can draw on. The defense contractor can count on the support of labor, anxious to preserve its jobs, and local governments, anxious to preserve their tax base. Overseas factories generate neither kind of support.

Why should we not expect to see small owners of capital—owners of shoe companies, for example—band together around a "nationalist" program that would involve protectionism for domestic industries, the withdrawal of tax and other privileges from foreign investment, and perhaps in the most extreme case a withdrawal of U.S. military and political support from the authoritarian regimes whose repressive labor policies make export platforms possible? If we were seeking a "nationalist" element among small capitalists, the shoe industry would be an obvious place to look for it.[43] The industry has been characterized by large numbers of small firms, and has been directly and severely damaged by imports. Even the largest firms in the industry have not been able to embark successfully on a strategy of direct foreign investment. Yet for all this, the "nationalism" of the shoe industry has not gone beyond specific, self-interested protectionist measures.

One would expect that the most obviously hurt among the owners of shoe companies would be those who have been driven out of business. In reality, many of these have experienced shifts in roles that are far from disastrous. Some managed to sell their companies for large sums of money and are now living in comfortable retirement. The younger and more entrepreneurially oriented are more likely to have transformed themselves into importers. (Since the commercial aspects of the business are paramount, even for a firm involved in manufacturing, working as an importer involves a number of the same skills that are required for running a small manufacturing firm.) A few have been

43. The interviews with shoe industry executives on which the following discussion is partially based admittedly represent only a very small number of New England manufacturers. Since they were not systematically selected, they are not necessarily representative. None of them, for example, was active in the American Footwear Industry Association. Nonetheless, the results of these interviews seem quite consistent with the comments of outside observers regarding the relative lack of organized political activity on the part of small, domestically oriented capital.

kept on by the firms that bought out their companies. (One is reported to be designing shoes in Italy.) There may well be personal disasters, but they do not appear to be characteristic enough to generate any political impact.

What about those still in the industry, still confronting the massive impact of shoe imports? First of all, the largest firms have to be excluded from any "nationalist" coalition. The four largest footwear companies had higher profit levels in the period 1970–73 than between 1963 and 1966.[44] Most of them are heavily involved in retailing as well as manufacturing and have been able to combine domestic production with imports. A few have made direct investments overseas. In 1977, when lobbying for curbs on shoe imports from Taiwan and South Korea was intense, the U.S. Shoe Corporation, one of the largest in the industry, "quietly started up a Far East operation in Taipei, Taiwan."[45] Others have found that trying to take over managerial control of overseas sources is more trouble than it is worth, and that they can profitably take advantage of foreign factories without owning them.

Among smaller manufacturers, those in the "volume" or "commodity" end of the business—that is, those who produce long runs of low-priced shoes—have been most hurt. Most in the industry would admit that firms in this end of the business will probably have to either change their lines or go bankrupt. There are other kinds of shoe manufacturing, however, in which domestic manufacturers have more of an advantage. In certain styles, such as heavy leather boots and casual leather shoes, American designs predominate. In higher-priced leather shoes, direct labor may account for only 15–20 percent of the value of the shoe. Once the foreign manufacturer has paid for freight, normal duties, and warehousing, it would be hard for him to have a cost advantage even if his labor cost him nothing. In the higher-priced, more fashion-dominated segments of the market, there is a strong advantage in being close to the retail market. A small domestic manufacturer can respond to a retailer in 25–35 days; a Brazilian or Taiwanese company may require six months.

In short, there are a number of niches in which the small local manufacturer has a good chance of survival, or at least a chance that is no worse than normal for small manufacturers. They may well fail, just as any small manufacturer is likely to fail, but they are not likely to see themselves as deprived of a chance to compete by the new international

44. American Footwear Industry Association (AFIA), *Footwear Manual 1977*, Table 14.

45. *The Wall Street Journal*, March 3, 1978, p. 2.

economic order. Furthermore, even those who see themselves as engaged in a battle for survival in which the major opponents are foreign lack an ideological framework that might led them into "nationalist" politics. One entrepreneur, whose company had been forced by foreign competition to drastically (albeit successfully) shift its product line, was completely unsympathetic to efforts to protect the shoe industry. He felt that U.S. companies could not compete with the Orient in the volume end of the business and "had no business trying." Tariffs, quotas, and subsidies "make footwear more expensive for the man in the street, increase taxes, and by increasing inflation make it more expensive for someone in Germany to buy an IBM computer." What is striking about his analysis is that it mirrors exactly the "internationalist" position that one might expect from the manager of a multinational. Discovering such an archetypal "internationalist" in the person of a small domestically oriented entrepreneur gives some indication of the general ideological hegemony of the internationalist position.

Even shoe manufacturers who are adamant about the need for protection are not likely to place their demands in the context of any general political program. For those in the higher-priced lines, "the decline of American craftsmanship" is the prime culprit. American workers can no longer, for some reason, match the finesse of the Italian craftsmen. Skilled and willing workers in general are getting harder to find. Seeing the source of their problems in the inadequate skills and motivation of their workers, they are led away from any analysis that might put them in opposition to the multinationals.

Trying to compete in the volume end of the business is more likely to lead to a "nationalist" analysis. One manufacturer, who had watched foreign competition transform his company's position from one of having profits of $500,000 in 1969 to one of having losses of over $100,000 in 1976 and 1977, said bluntly, "As long as the State Department actively supports governments which believe in the suppression of their people, American manufacturers won't be able to compete." Even in this case, however, stoicism rather than political activism was the result.

Shoe manufacturers see the world in individualistic terms. They have little faith in the efficacy of politics or collective action in general. The small-scale entrepreneur, even when threatened by structural changes that might appear to an outsider to call for political action, characteristically either sees solutions in terms of increased individual initiative or is resigned. Testifying before congressional committees or working through the industry association is not viewed as efficacious. Nor is there any evidence that these small manufacturers see their plight in terms of a struggle with the multinationals. They are aware that large firms in the industry can take advantage of imports and have no interest in protectionism, but the idea of a generalized split between domestically oriented and internationally oriented capital has no place in their worldview.

A quick look at the shoe industry suggests that the idea of a "nationalist" coalition built around small, domestically oriented capitalists who have been objectively hurt by the evolution of the international economy is fanciful. Any search for the political consequences of the economic changes associated with the "new international economic order" must focus somewhere besides domestic capital. But this is not to say that the disappearance of several hundred shoe manufacturers and other similar changes have been without political effect.

Some of these effects can be seen in congressional debates. On several recent pieces of legislation, which should have been completely noncontroversial, the "internationalists" have discovered a surprisingly vehement opposition. Routine measures such as approval of funds for the IMF or a tax treaty with the United Kingdom have run into unexpected trouble. Perhaps most striking was the fight over the renewal of the Overseas Private Investment Corporation (OPIC). In the House, the OPIC bill was originally brought forward on the "suspension calendar," which is reserved for noncontroversial legislation. After two days of debate, it was so deeply in trouble that its sponsors whisked it off the floor rather than bringing it to a final vote. The debate over the bill provides a good indication of the erosion of the "internationalist" position. There were three main points of attack: first, that the ventures funded by OPIC might be connected to plant closings and the loss of jobs in the United States; second, that OPIC benefited only the largest firms and did nothing for small business; and, third, that the ventures funded by OPIC did not speak to "developmental" goals because they were sometimes frivolous, because they were generally in the larger, more advanced Third World countries (often those with poor records on human rights), and because they benefited only the elite within those countries.

Representative Leo Ryan of California led the fight, arguing that "what we really have here is assistance in highly developed countries, giving them even more help than they need to take jobs away from our own people here."[46] Others followed his lead, asking "is it not also a fact that many of the products we see flooding the American market

46. Congressional Record, October 2, 1977, p. H12058.

right now and putting our domestic people out of work—TV parts, steel, leather goods, garments—are produced by foreign factories that really are insured by this program?"[47] Some were more perplexed than aggressive, like Representative Danielson of Los Angeles, who said "I have lost three tire plants. . . . The Business Round Table people told me that they would give me an answer. As of today, I have no answer. Maybe my friend the gentlemen from California [Mr. Ryan] has put his finger on it. Maybe these jobs are being sent abroad."[48]

The appeal to small business also proved a useful tool in the hands of opponents to the bill. Representative Long of Maryland introduced an amendment that would have required OPIC to provide "at least 50 percent of all its insurance to small business (as defined by the Small Business Administration)."[49] When the bill's sponsor argued that the amendment would "make the program completely unworkable," Long's retort was immediate and obvious: "I think the gentleman has just made the most damning indictment of the OPIC program that I have heard yet. The gentleman says that there is no room in overseas business or in the overseas market for small business. What could be worse than that?"[50]

The "aid" aspects of OPIC were also subject to attack. Ryan and others pointed to investments such as fast-food chains in Brazil, ITT Sheraton Hotels in India, Safari Lodges in Kenya, and Avis Rent-a-Car services for Malaysia as ". . . not what we had in mind when we created OPIC to help poor countries."[51] Human rights advocates pointed out that ". . . what we see OPIC doing is giving more and more of its money . . . to companies which invest in countries where there are serious and gross violations of human rights."[52] Rep. Long of Maryland capped it off. "This type of industry which we would be guaranteeing is going to benefit some people, surely. It is going to benefit the ruling class."[53]

The supporters of the OPIC bill won in the end. But the debate indicated the fragility of the traditional "liberal-internationalist" coalition that had seen Jacob Javits and Hubert Humphrey getting together behind OPIC. When supporters of the bill argued that the American investments it fostered would increase exports and American jobs, they were not as convincing to their colleagues as they had been five years earlier. The concentration of OPIC insurance on a few *Fortune* "500"

47. *Ibid.*, October 3, 1977.
48. *Ibid.*, February 23, 1978, p.H1450.
49. *Ibid.*, November 3, 1977, p.H12112.
50. *Ibid.*
51. *Ibid.*, p. H12054.
52. *Ibid.*, p. H12057.
53. *Ibid.*, February 23, 1978, p. H1443.

firms appeared more galling. The skepticism over the developmental effects of a direct investment was apparent throughout. If it had not been for the concerted lobbying efforts of a large number of OPIC personnel and for the fact that OPIC was not asking for any money, the outcome might have been different.

The debate did not bring forth a "nationalist coalition." It did show that representatives from liberal, middle-class districts (like Ryan), free traders (like Long), human rights advocates (like Harkin of Iowa), representatives of districts with factories closing (like Danielson), and even representatives of conservative rural districts (like Evans of Georgia) could all find common ground in their opposition to state support of the activities of the multinationals.[54] The vehemence of the opposition to OPIC was even more surprising because of the spontaneity of its emergence. Ryan picked up on the issue almost by chance, not because there were any interests among his constituency that felt strongly about OPIC. Most of his constituents had probably never heard of it. Anti-OPIC arguments struck responsive ideological chords. One representative was reported to have said, "How can I support OPIC when farmers in my district can't get loans?" Long's small business amendment gathered support not because domestically oriented capital was lobbying behind it but because, in the words of one observer with long experience on Capitol Hill, "Congress (especially the House) reacts viscerally to anything that involves small business."

Labor became involved in the battle over OPIC only after Ryan had turned it into a fight. That labor became involved at all represents part of a gradual awakening of the AFL-CIO's traditional "internationalist" stance. The AFL-CIO has often found it much easier to get along with advocates of an "internationalist" position like Jacob Javits than with representatives of small business, whose power and profits are more directly threatened by unions. But as factory closings spread in proportion to the expansion of foreign direct investment, the arguments of the "internationalists" begin to pall.

Even if small domestically oriented capital is congenitally unsuited to mounting collective political action, its plight has political effect. Small business in the abstract has a political charisma reminiscent of that of the "national bourgeoisie" in countries like Brazil. When the plight of small business can be connected with job loss, a potent ideological combination is created.

54. *Ibid.*, p. H1454.

None of this is to say that close relations between the multinationals and the U.S. state apparatus have ended or are about to end. Certainly the Department of Commerce and the other parts of the executive branch that are charged with servicing the needs of the multinationals will continue to do their work. With a serious lobbying attempt, the multinationals can probably still get through almost any piece of legislation that they need. What was striking about the OPIC debate was that there was a debate at all. An unquestioning persuasion is one thing, a questioned ideology is another. The fact that the "internationalist" ideology should be so strongly questioned at a time when ruling circles are rife with representatives of what is surely the epitome of the "internationalist" perspective, the Trilateral Commission, must be cause for concern among the multinationals.[55] Even worse, their political difficulties in the United States have political reverberations in countries like Brazil.

REVERBERATING NATIONALISM

The apogee of pro-U.S. sentiments among those who control the Brazilian state apparatus was passed ten years ago, when Castelo Branco was president and Roberto Campos controlled the Treasury. In those days, the United States was attractive as a bastion of anticommunism. North American support had been critical in assuring the military's smooth ascension to power. North American aid, trade, and investment were mainstays to the model of development that the military was attempting to install.

In the late 1970's the shifting character of the international economy has made reliance on the United States appear less attractive. After watching its balance of payments pushed into the red by chronic trade deficits with the United States for 30 years, Brazil now finds itself treated as a dangerous competitor suspected of being guilty of unfair business practices. These fears might seem more fair if directed toward Germany and Japan. For Brazilians they can only seem unjustified and hostile. Brazil, after all, not only runs negative trade balances with the United States but remains a minor source of manufactured exports to the United States. A Brazilian observer listening to the OPIC debate could hardly help being disconcerted at hearing Brazil used throughout

55. Jeff Frieden, "The Trilateral Commission: Economics and Politics in the 1970's," *Monthly Review* 29 (no. 7), pp. 1–19.

as an example of one of those "highly developed countries" that were "getting more help than they need to take jobs away from our own people here."

In defense of OPIC, Representative Bingham of New York conceded readily that "too much of OPIC activities have centered in countries like Brazil" and pointed out that "Just the other day, for example, OPIC announced that there would be no more general guaranteeing of insurance issued for Brazil and other countries where the per capita income is over $1,000."[56] Representative Long attacked OPIC vehemently for having assisted the Brazilian steel industry:

In 1977 OPIC financed a steel project in Brazil, a country that has received over $940 million in total foreign assistance for its steel industry. . . . I have seen one of their plants. They are pathetic. They are getting a subsidy from their government in addition to ours. But once they have a steel mill, they are going to produce steel and export it abroad, no matter how uneconomic the operation is, and they are going to stop buying from the United States. The steel industry in Brazil has increased its exports of steel into the United States by over 160 times between 1959 and 1974.[57]

Such rhetoric would not be disturbing if it were only that. But when it is accompanied by concrete actions, such as the imposition of countervailing duties on scissors and yarn and pressure toward the removal of export incentives in the shoe industry, it becomes an indication of a potentially serious confrontation between domestically oriented U.S. capital and a central feature of Brazil's export expansion. The issue is particularly salient in the late 1970's since waiver privileges for Latin American exports to the United States will have to be renegotiated by the end of the decade.

At the same time that economic friction with the United States is growing, militant anticommunism (internationally at least) appears to make less economic sense. As Table 1 indicated, when solving trade imbalances is the question, the socialist countries are part of the solution and the United States is part of the problem. Not only are the Soviet Union and Eastern Europe good markets for Brazilian exports, but the former Portuguese colonies in Africa, now socialist, are a promising part of Brazil's potential economic hinterland. Internally, anticommunism remains necessary to the maintenance of class privilege; but inter-

56. *Congressional Record* February 23, 1978, p. H1441, and November 2, 1977, p. H12056.
57. *Ibid.*, February 23, 1978, p. H1451.

nationally, a rigid interpretation of what it means to be a member of the "free world" no longer makes sense.

For U.S. multinationals operating in Brazil, the political advantages of American "citizenship" have become much more ambiguous than they were ten years ago. For one company, Westinghouse, American "citizenship" was an insurmountable obstacle to winning a multi-billion-dollar nuclear reactor contract for which they would otherwise have been by far the strongest competitor. No other company can claim to have been so directly hurt, but there is the uneasy feeling that, as one multinational manager put it, the current state of U.S.-Brazilian relations represents a "negative tangible" for the U.S. multinationals trying to operate in Brazil.

Business Latin America's assessment that "U.S. trade and investment in the region could be pushed aside to make room for European and Japanese investors" should probably be taken either as paranoia or as a self-serving attempt to goad U.S. policymakers into taking a more thoroughly internationalist stance. The fact remains that protectionism, in combination with Carter's human rights and nonproliferation policies, is an embarrassment to the multinationals and enhances the likelihood of nationalist policies on the part of the Brazilian state.

It would be too crude to suggest that the Brazilian state, in a simple *quid pro quo*, will retaliate against the multinationals trying to operate within its territory. In the first place, Brazil remains committed to a developmental model based on the "triple alliance," and for that reason must have the support of multinationals in order to carry out its chosen project of accumulation. Any overt discrimination against the multinationals of a given center country—especially against those of the United States, which, despite everything, account for almost three times as much investment as those of either West Germany or Japan—would limit the bargaining flexibility of the state and threaten the overall success of the "triple alliance."

Policy with regard to the regulation, restriction, or control of multinationals is made on the basis of immediate and pressing needs, not on the basis of emotional or ideological responses to debates in the U.S. Congress. If GM is asked to agree to a program of exports, it is because Brazil must find a solution to its balance-of-payments problems, not because Brazilian officials are upset over accusations of torture. If IBM is not allowed to set up a wholly-owned subsidiary, it is because the Brazilian navy may have a vested interest in Digibrás or because local investors with political connections may see a possibility for profitable

participation in the computer industry if IBM is excluded, not because
the American Yarn Spinners Association succeeded in getting countervailing duties imposed on Brazilian yarn.

The connection between the fraying of the edges of "internationalist"
policies in the United States and the possibility of increased nationalist
pressures on U.S. multinationals is more subtle and indirect. The existence of U.S. policies that are unsympathetic to Brazil's aspirations
(whether unsympathetic to the necessity of export expansion or unsympathetic to the degree of repression the model requires) legitimates
equivalent Brazilian responses. Depriving GE of its rightful share of
local locomotive orders seems more legitimate when U.S. congressmen
are applauding the decision of OPIC not to issue further insurance in
Brazil. The interests of Equipamentos Villares may be the more proxi-
mate cause, but the resurgence of defensive nationalism in the United
States contributes to the legitimacy of nationalist choices in Brazil.

For any rational Brazilian policymaker, the response to rumblings of
U.S. nationalism must involve more than questions of legitimation. Just
as multinationals must continually assess the "stability" of Third World
governments (for which read continuance of regimes favorable to international capital), so countries like Brazil must consider seriously the
possibility that future behavior of U.S.-based multinationals depends
in part on the U.S. political climate. In 1977 Westinghouse was prevented from providing Brazil with a nuclear reactor. Is it beyond the
realm of possibility that in 1984 Congress might prevent IBM from allowing Brazilians access to its computer technology? If such a possibility exists, then the decision to shut IBM out becomes more rational.

U.S. nationalism reinforces Brazilian nationalism, and Brazilian nationalism, as long as it is restricted to careful bargaining, reinforces the
involvement of the multinationals in the "triple alliance." How will
Westinghouse respond when it sees GE lose an important locomotive
contract? How will both GE and Westinghouse respond when they
see IBM cut out of the Brazilian computer industry? Brazil is not only
a market that is growing much faster than the markets in most developing countries, it is also an economy in which profit rates are exceptionally high. If it is necessary to shift worldwide sourcing in such a
way as to make the Brazilians happier, why not. If this means that a
given multinational will produce a little more in Brazil, import a little
less from the United States, and export a little more back into the United
States, why not? The Brazilian state looks at the balance-of-payment
impact of each large multinational individually; the United States does
not. Refusal to cooperate with the Brazilian state might result in a de-

nial of CDI incentives; the United States does not even have a precise definition of what cooperation entails.

TRANSNATIONAL ECONOMICS AND NATIONAL POLITICS

The argument in this paper has rambled from Brazil's trade with Bolivia through the political opinions of New England shoe manufacturers to congressional attacks on Safari Lodges in Kenya—all purporting to clarify the nature of U.S.-Brazilian relations in the 1970's. The logic that underlies this combination of disparate and somewhat incommensurable sorts of evidence needs to be reiterated.

The economic transformation of certain parts of the periphery is the starting point. None of the analysis that has been presented could be extended to Afghanistan, Niger, Zambia, or Paraguay. Only a few countries have experienced the kind of dependent development associated with both indigenous industrial capacity and the formation of a "triple alliance" among state, local, and multinational capital. In these countries, multinationals can be harnessed to projects of local accumulation, but only in the presence of continued nationalist pressure. Continued nationalism, in the sense in which the term has been used here, is a structural feature of the "triple alliance."

Expansion of manufactured exports to center countries is vital to the model of economic growth that has emerged under the aegis of the "triple alliance"—vital because of the economic necessity of resolving the external imbalances created by import-intensive industrialization, and because export expansion is a mode of resolving these imbalances in a way that is both attractive to the multinationals and not threatening to local capital.

At this point, a division appears between the interests of U.S. multinationals and the interests of U.S. capital, whose primary concern is the expansion of the U.S. domestic economy. Independently of the question of exporting back into the United States, serious questions can be raised about whether the accumulation undertaken by the multinationals in the semiperiphery is at the expense of accumulation in their home economies. Existing evidence suggests at least that U.S. labor has suffered. As smaller domestic capitalists are increasingly threatened by the influx of foreign manufactured products, the contradictions between the policy preferences of the multinationals and domestic interests become more severe.

Under these conditions, programs like OPIC test the limits of the "naive and unquestioning persuasion" that support of business must be in the national interest as long as that business is owned by U.S. citizens. OPIC represents a public subsidy available only to companies engaged in building up the economic capacity of countries other than the United States, primarily useful in practice to a tiny number of the largest multinationals. At a time when plant closings in response to foreign competition are routine, when unemployment is a problem, and when balance-of-payments deficits are chronic, convincing politicians that such subsidies are in the national interest requires some skill. Analysis of opposition to programs like OPIC provides a measure of U.S. political reactions to the growing willingness of multinationals to shift production outside the United States.

The postulated result is an increasing disjuncture between the multinationals and the political apparatus of their home state. This point needs to be made very carefully. It has not been argued here that the capitalist class in the United States is divided into "internationalist" and "nationalist" segments, locked in struggle over control of the U.S. state. Small domestically oriented capital has all the political weaknesses that are traditionally attributed by Marxists to the petty bourgeoisie. Because some small entrepreneurs continue to find profitable niches even in the most severely affected domestic industries, there is little collective sense of shared fate. Even small domestically oriented manufacturers are imbued with the internationalist ideology of free trade.

The present disjuncture between the multinationals and their home political apparatus appears to have occurred without any significant general campaign on the part of small domestically oriented capital and, for that matter, with only a very limited amount of pressure from organized labor. The degree to which the ideologically hegemonic position of the internationalist stance has been eroded is impressive precisely because it has occurred in anticipation of pressure from affected interest groups more than as a result of such pressure. The state will, of course, continue to act in the interests of international capital. Even in Congress the internationalist position will be victorious most of the time. The argument is not that the U.S. state has turned "nationalist" but rather that the internationalist front has begun to develop some cracks.

The tentative upsurge of nationalist sentiments in the United States has the effect of increasing nationalist pressures within Brazil, both because U.S. actions make Brazilian nationalism more legitimate and because they stimulate anticipatory defensive policies. The response of the multinationals will be to seek accommodation with the Brazilian demands and thereby increase the distance between themselves and U.S. domestic interests. As long as certain background conditions prevail, the rapprochement between the multinationals and the Brazilian state that has already been achieved will be self-reinforcing.

The background conditions are important. It has been assumed here that profit levels and the expected growth rate will continue to be superior in Brazil. Were center-country protectionism or some other change in the international economy to lead to real stagnation and lower profit rates in Brazil, then the whole dynamic would change. The Brazilian working class could also upset the process. An expansion or even a chronic repetition of a strike wave such as that experienced by São Paulo in the spring of 1978 would change the scenario substantially. If the effective repression of working-class demands were to falter, neither current levels of profitability nor the current restricted definition of nationalism could be taken for granted and the attractiveness of Brazil to multinational managers would be put in question.

The necessary assumptions with regard to the evolution of the North American environment are more conservative. It has been assumed that current problems with the trade balance and with the maintenance of employment in basic manufacturing will continue, and that therefore relations with the international economy will remain problematic. In addition it has been assumed that attempts to cope with structural adjustment within the U.S. economy will continue at their current rudimentary levels.

The assumptions about the future of the North American environment are conservative primarily in that they include no predictions of increased militancy on the part of U.S. labor. Since 1960, U.S. labor has experienced less growth in compensation per hour than any working class in the developed world. How long this can continue without stimulating increased labor militancy or a shift in the direction of more explicitly socialist politics is impossible to tell. Should either of these occur, the process of detachment of the multinationals from their home state might accelerate.

No matter how carefully qualified or tentatively stated, the implications of the argument remain radical. "What is good for General Motors is good for the United States" has been an enduring central premise of the extant U.S. "pact of domination." Such ideological premises have been more difficult to impose in Latin America because such a large segment of capital was foreign. Instability of bourgeois rule has been the result, but the international hegemony of the United States has compensated for local instability. Once "nationalism" can be defined even in the United States in a way that is distinct from the interests of a major segment of capital, Pandora's box is open.

When Representative Long questions whether the valuable services
that OPIC performs for the multinationals are in the national interest,
he is questioning a fundamental ideological premise. What Veblen had
in mind when he spoke of the "naive unquestioning persuasion" was,
after all, the duping of one class by another. In its desire to take advantage of profitable opportunities in semiperipheral countries like Brazil,
international capital may end up exposing its ideological flank more
seriously than it realizes.

The Private Sector, Business Organizations, and International Influence: A Case Study of Mexico

ANGELA M. DELLI SANTE

> But the independent and uncoordinated action of individual corporations, as important as it is, is not enough. Strength is in organizations, in careful planning and long-term implementations, in consistent action for an indefinite period of time, with sufficient financial support, which can only be possible through unified action and through national organizations. . . .
> For this reason, the role of the Chamber of Commerce is vital. . . . It is in a strategic position with an enviable reputation and a wide base of support. . . . There are hundreds of local Chambers of Commerce that can play a vital helping role.
>
> —Lewis F. Powell, *The Powell Memorandum* (1973)

The purpose of this paper is to study the ideological activities of corporations and business organizations—both national and transnational—in Mexico. The functions of various corporations as economic units of production and distribution, and the influence they have had on the economic structures of the "underdeveloped" or dependent capitalist countries, have been widely studied; yet, the role of these corporations and their business organizations on the superstructural level has been largely neglected. Some work has been done on the political side, analyzing the way both the corporations and their organizations function as pressure groups; but few studies have explored the role of business in general, and the transnational corporation (TNC) in particular, on the ideological level of the class struggle.

Angela Delli Sante is a graduate of Rutgers University and the National Autonomous University of Mexico (UNAM). She is associated with the National School for Professional Studies of UNAM, located at Acatlán, Mexico.

Although a theoretical discussion of the nature of ideology is beyond the scope of this paper, let me briefly clarify the way I use the term "ideology" here: by ideology I mean the complex and coherent set of ideas one has of the world, of one's self as a human being, of one's relations with other human beings, and of the institutions—social, economic, and political—in which one is immersed. Ideology is not a static set of coherent explanations of the world, but rather an acquired set of concepts subject to change through the continuing activity of human beings in both the practical and the theoretical-intellectual spheres. It is important to note that since one's concept of the universe—one's ideology—forms part of the subconscious as well as of the conscious mind, all of one's behavior is influenced by it, and hence social change is intimately linked with it.

For the materials in this paper to take on their full meaning, one must understand the dual nature of ideology. In a class society, one's concept of the world is ultimately linked with either of the two fundamental classes: the dominant class, or the antagonic subordinate class. When the ideology of the dominant class has become assimilated and essentially accepted by this subordinate class, ideology serves as an instrument to impede social change. In other words, when the dominant class has achieved hegemony, then, ideology acts to guarantee the reproduction of the entire social, economic, and political system, as well as the position of privilege and dominance of that class. However, even in such a case man's activities in the class struggle produce an elementary awareness of the contradiction between what the dominant ideology expounds and what the real conditions of the subordinate class are. This initial level of class consciousness opens the door to the possibility of constructing an alternative ideology antagonistic to that of the dominant class. The elaboration of this new ideology is not easy, and does not come about automatically; rather, it comes about when there is unity between the daily class confrontation (i.e., practical experience), the nascent class consciousness, and the theoretical knowledge developed by the class leaders identified with the subordinate class. Once the ideology of the subordinate class is structured, it constitutes a revolutionary concept of the world, and thus a potential threat to the hegemony of the dominant class. When this happens, ideology takes on a different nature, now constituting a necessary, though not sufficient, instrument for producing social change. The struggle over ideology we are concerned with in this paper is precisely the struggle over ideology as a guarantor of hegemony or a destroyer of it, as a preserver of the capitalist system or as a source of radical changes capable of transforming that system.[1]

This paper attempts to analyze the function of TNCs in the ideological struggle in Mexico, dealing mainly with the way in which the TNCs have gradually become the producers and distributors of the dominant capitalist ideology as the nature of the capitalist system itself has evolved, as the contradictions within dependent capitalist countries such as Mexico have become more acute, and as socialist ideologies have expanded. Capital accumulation today depends upon the expansion of TNCs, which in turn depends in part upon the control of ideological tendencies antagonistic to the capitalist ideology. Thus in the ideological terrain, TNCs function on two levels in dependent capitalist countries: first, they perfect and consolidate the capitalist ideology among members of the capitalist class itself; and second, they attempt to advance their ideology among members of the working class. Their involvement in both these spheres has grown, and the production of ideological programs and materials now constitutes a particularly necessary part of their activities. We will consider some of these programs and materials through a study first of the American Chamber of Commerce of Mexico (AMCHAM-Mexico; hereafter simply AMCHAM) and then of the campaign mounted against the formerly liberal newspaper *Excelsior*. We will also note some of the links that have always existed between U.S. foreign policy and the U.S. private business sector in Mexico.

THE DEVELOPMENT OF THE IDEOLOGICAL ROLE
OF AMCHAM

The Early Years: 1917–33

In its official publication, *Mexican-American Review*, AMCHAM has constantly reiterated the importance of its existence both in the past history and in the future prospects of American interests in Mexico.

1. For a more complete treatment of these theoretical issues, see Angela Delli Sante, "La Intervención ideológica de la empresa transnacional en países dependientes: el caso de México," in *Revista Mexicana de Sociología*, 39, no. 1 (Jan.–Mar. 1977), pp. 303–23. Above all, see Antonio Gramsci, *La Formación de los Intelectuales* (Mexico City, 1970); idem, *El Materialismo Histórico y la Filosofía de Benedetto Croce*, ed. Juan Pablos (Mexico City, 1975), pp. 11–63; George Lukács, *Historia y Consciencia de Clase* (Mexico City, 1969); Adam Schaff, "El Marxismo y la problemática de la sociología del conocimiento," in Claude Lévi-Strauss et al., *El Proceso Ideológico* (2d ed.; Mexico City, 1973); and Adam Schaff, "El Condicionamiento Social del Conocimiento Histórico," in *Historia y Verdad* (Mexico City, 1969).

As the president of AMCHAM wrote in one issue, referring to private enterprises:

External forces may lead Mexico to adopt a more benign form of economic industrialism, with constant growth of the infrastructure, more foreign investment and, in general, *a larger role for private enterprise.* But transnationals will have recognized their past errors and will be operating much more in harmony with the real situation in Mexico. . . . The state of business toward the end of this century depends in no small measure on whether *we* decide to move with the tides of history or against them.[2]

Both AMCHAM's role and that of the TNCs and business organizations in general have undergone major changes in this century as foreign investment in Mexico has moved from raw-materials exploitation to manufacturing and commerce.[3] Of course, it has not only been structural changes in capitalism that have modified the role of AMCHAM and the type of activities it undertakes; so have the advances of world socialism and the national liberation movements, as we will see further on. Despite the changes, however, certain constants have remained: first, the close relationship between AMCHAM and the U.S. government, on the one hand, and the U.S. and Mexican capitalists and their business organizations, on the other; and second, AMCHAM's role as a pressure group.

According to AMCHAM's own accounts, the establishment of a constitutional government in Mexico and the U.S. entrance into the First World War—both in 1917—were the main motives for U.S. businessmen in Mexico to join their efforts for their own defense.[4] First, the recognition on the part of the Mexican constitutionalist government that private property must be restricted on behalf of the collective social interest (included in Article 127 of the 1917 Constitution) provoked much uneasiness and opposition among the business community—especially in the oil, mining, and agricultural sectors, where foreign invest-

---

2. Al Wichtrich, "Business and the Future," *Mexican-American Review*, Jan. 1977, p. 16 (italics mine). See also "The Years Ahead" in the Nov. 1977 issue, pp. 45–67.
3. On foreign investment, see Bernardo Sepúlveda and Antonio Chumacero, *La Inversión Extranjera en México* (Mexico City: Fondo de Cultura Económica, 1973), p. 50, where they point out that raw materials production, services, communications, and transport accounted for 91.3 percent of foreign investment in 1911, as opposed to 8.7 percent in industry and commerce. These figures were almost reversed by 1970—10.7 percent and 89.3 percent, respectively.
4. See *Mexican-American Review*, commemorative issues of AMCHAM's 50th and 60th anniversaries, Nov. 1967 and Nov. 1977.

ment was mostly concentrated.[5] Second, the entrance of the United States into the war affected the commercial sector in its international business relations. Because of the developments, many businessmen saw the need to protect their interests and organized in national and/or sectoral associations. For example, between 1919 and 1920 the National Association of Mexico (AAM), and the National Association for the Protection of American Rights (NAPAR), were founded, and they used all possible means to protect their investments. NAPAR even sent representatives to Versailles to seek support from the Allies against the Carranza government (1916–20) and to Washington to testify before a Senate committee set up to investigate the Mexican situation; AAM went as far as to promote a revolt against President Obregón (1920–24) aimed at turning back the tides of the nationalist programs.[6]

During this period, the interests of the oil and mining companies predominated, and their pressure organizations were the most active and aggressive. The Oil Producers Association of Mexico (OPAM), formed in 1918, represented British and American companies. During the period 1918–25, OPAM succeeded in obtaining concessions from the Mexican government with the direct help of the U.S. Department of State.[7] In addition, it played a prominent role in opposing President Calles in 1926 when he announced the Petroleum Law. The intervention of the U.S. government can also be measured by the fact that Ambassador Morrow was able to "help" the Mexican Minister of Industry formulate the regulations necessary for the application of the 1926 Petroleum Law two years later.[8] Likewise, the mining companies formed their sectoral pressure groups in 1917, the most important of which was the Committee of American and Mexican Mining Interests (CAMMI). CAMMI had branches in almost all the states where the companies operated; and although it usually dealt directly with the local authorities, in more complex situations it resorted to its legal representatives in Mexico City, its New York headquarters, and/or the U.S. government itself.[9] CAMMI

5. *Constitución Política de los Estados Unidos Mexicanos*, 42d ed. (Mexico City, 1969), pp. 18–30.
6. Lorenzo Meyer, *Los Grupos de Presión Extranjeros en el México Revolucionario: 1910–1940* (Mexico City, 1973), p. 42.
7. *Ibid.*, pp. 63–67; James Daniel, *Mexico and the Americans* (New York, 1960), pp. 212–24.
8. Meyer, *Los Grupos de Presión*, pp. 63–67; responding to pressures from the oil companies, Ambassador Morrow worked for three weeks with the Mexican minister to adjust the 1926 law, p. 63.
9. *Ibid.*, p. 68.

was dissolved when the National (Mexican) Mining Chamber was formed in 1925, and its members joined the new organization.[10]

The economic predominance of the oil and mining companies enabled them to exert great influence over Mexican internal economic and political affairs; for the same reason, their interests prevailed over those of the "less important" enterprises in the manufacturing and commerce sectors.[11] But these latter sectors had their own organizations, which in time grew to have greater influence. Early in 1917, a small nucleus of American businessmen began to take steps to coordinate their efforts, steps that led to the formation of AMCHAM in November. From the beginning a direct link between the U.S. government and AMCHAM was established through the participation of George A. Chamberlain, U.S. Consul General in Mexico, in the formation of the new organization's charter. This link was further strengthened when the U.S. Ambassador and Consul General were named Honorary President and Vice-President—a practice that has continued to the present.[12]

The relationship found immediate application when AMCHAM, in compliance with U.S. foreign policy, led a full-fledged campaign to support the U.S. war effort through the sale of War Savings Bonds and Liberty Bonds, and through the blacklisting of companies suspected of doing business with the Central Powers. Direct ties were also established with American business organizations as early as 1918, when AMCHAM became a member of the U.S. Chamber of Commerce. AMCHAM's role in the ideological struggle was only implicit at that time, yet one of its first steps to organize U.S. businessmen around common criteria was the establishment of its own periodical, *The Journal*, in February 1918. In the 1920's, too, AMCHAM, along with the U.S. Embassy in Mexico, financially supported one of Mexico's conservative newspapers, *El Universal*, which had openly "demonstrated a favorable attitude toward foreign capital and North American politics in general."[13]

10. *Ibid.*, pp. 44–45.
11. Taxes levied on oil and mining concerns accounted for about 7.6 percent of Mexico's GNP in 1910, 11 percent in 1920, 9 percent in 1934, and 7.6 percent in 1940. The contribution of these concerns to the Federal budget (again through taxes) was on the order of 42 percent in 1922, 11 percent in 1929, and 42 percent from 1935 to 1944. (The American Consul General calculated 60 percent for 1936.) See Meyer, *Los Grupos de Presión*, p. 27.
12. See *Mexican-American Review*, commemorative issues of Nov. 1967 and Nov. 1977.
13. Meyer, *Los Grupos de Presión*, p. 72.

During this early period, parallel to the formation of foreign business organizations, the Mexican government itself was taking measures to reorganize Mexican businessmen. By November 1917 the Confederation of Chambers of Commerce of the United States of Mexico had been formed, and a year later, in September 1918, the Confederation of Industrial Chambers of Mexico was founded. Both associations were closely linked to the Mexican government, which spelled out their functions: to promote the expansion of commercial and industrial activities, and to serve as government advisers.[14] Some ten years later, in 1928 (once free from government auspices), Mexican bankers founded their own association—Asociación de Banqueros de México (ABM). And a year later, as a result of the discussion of the new Federal Labor Law, an intersectoral organization was formed—Confederación Patronal de La República Mexicana (COPARMEX). This last organization not only offered legal and labor-relations advice, but was from the beginning the most important Mexican instrument for consolidating and transmitting the capitalist ideology—a role it fulfilled until 1975, when the Consejo Coordinador Empresarial (CCE), a successor organization, was formed and became the new national ideological leader. All these associations, though they have always carried out programs of their own, were to build strong ties with AMCHAM, as we will see in the course of this paper.[15]

Turning back to the initial period of AMCHAM's establishment, since membership was restricted to U.S. citizens, and since U.S. businessmen's membership in the Mexican business organizations was not yet obligatory, there was no institutionalized meeting point for Mexican and American capitalist ideologies. However, as early as 1919 the newly formed Mexican chambers of industry and commerce began to collaborate with AMCHAM by forming a Mexican-American Import-Export Arbitration Committee. A year later they jointly planned an International Trade Conference, which was held in 1921 and attracted "one thousand representatives from the United States, Great Britain, France, and Germany."[16]

From 1920 to about 1934, AMCHAM's activities were fairly limited,

14. Marco Antonio Alcazar, *Las Agrupaciones Patronales en México* (Mexico City: Colegio de México, 1970), pp. 33–34.
15. The programs of the Mexican business associations are separate, and cannot be discussed here for reasons of space; however, it should be noted that they are not necessarily subordinate to U.S. programs.
16. *Mexican-American Review*, Nov. 1977, pp. 4–5.

since the lead was still being taken by the oil and mining companies. However, it had already begun to function as a pressure group, attempting to defend its members' particular interests. One of its first activities in this role was to lobby against the provision of the U.S. income tax law that required U.S. citizens overseas to pay taxes both in the United States and in the foreign country where they were residing. But its main concern was to convince U.S. businessmen to stay in Mexico—to keep the market possibilities open for the future—despite social unrest, fear of confiscation, and internal market demands in the United States that were leading many companies to return home. Although labor was not yet a pressing problem for AMCHAM members, AMCHAM did become involved in one of the most important issues in U.S.-Mexican relations—the situation of the Mexican migratory workers. In 1930, "it cabled President Hoover and congressional leaders in Washington to oppose the Harris Bill, which would have restricted Mexican emigration to the United States, a position that continues in substance up to the present time."[17]

AMCHAM's activities during this period caused it to be considered a reliable business organization by the Mexican government—so much so that it was even honored with an invitation in 1929 to give its opinion on a new Weights and Measures Bill then under consideration.[18]

The Years of Conflict: 1934–40

The period ushered in by the election of Lázaro Cárdenas as president (1934–40) was particularly problematic for the private sector, since the new president initiated a series of reforms that *in appearance* were adverse to that sector. Of course, the reforms responded to the insurgent movements of the Mexican peasants and the consolidation of the working class, which through its unions was becoming a determining force in the Mexican scene. These reforms covered a wide range of areas: great land holdings were confiscated and later distributed to the peasants in the form of "*ejidos,*"[19] labor rights were respected, educational facilities were extended, peasant organizations were strengthened, and the formation of central and national labor confederations was promoted by the government. However, Cárdenas was by no means a socialist; he

17. *Ibid.*, p. 7; and *ibid.*, Nov. 1967, pp. 45, 80.
18. *Ibid.*, Nov. 1967, p. 43.
19. An *ejido* is a form of organization for agricultural production in which the land is granted to a community of farmers for their use. Production is on either an individual or a collective basis.

was instead a fairly representative member of the Mexican liberal-reformist tradition seeking to stabilize Mexico's political institutions, achieve "economic independence," and establish that vague condition of "social justice" without destroying the class structure of Mexican society. In other words, Cárdenas was a prisoner of the ambiguity of the ideology of the petit bourgeoisie. This meant that though he placed great emphasis on "social justice," especially for the peasants and the working class, he did not take a stand completely in their favor; rather, he consolidated the political doctrine of the previous revolutionary regimes, which in broad terms considered the state apparatus to be a neutral arbiter between capital and labor. According to this ideology, the interests of each class were not seen as antagonistic.

Although Cárdenas's programs were construed as being adverse to capitalist interests at the time of their implementation, in fact they had the long-run effect of creating the necessary infrastructure for capitalist accumulation and expansion in Mexico, and laid the foundations for the development model of today.[20] During the middle and late 1930's, however, both Mexican and international capitalists failed to see these potential long-term benefits and instead reacted to what they perceived as an immediate threat. Local and foreign investors, along with the clergy and conservative members of the military, thoroughly opposed the "radicalism" of President Cárdenas. In some instances, these groups counted upon the support of members of the U.S. government in their attempts to force the Mexican government to modify or halt its policies. With the expropriation of oil properties in 1938, these activities were intensified. In an attempt to destroy the newly nationalized industry, the U.S. government collaborated with the private sector by allowing a boycott of machinery and other goods exported to Mexico to take place, and by supporting the partial suspension of silver purchases from that country.[21] These pressures reached their height with an open attempt at armed insurrection. The unsuccessful revolt, financed by both local and international funds, was led by General Saturnino Cedillo two months after the expropriation took place. Secondary sources and docu-

20. See Ariel José Contreras, *México 1940: Industrialización y Crisis Política* (Mexico City: Siglo xxi, 1977), pp. 155–73; Tzvi Medin, *Ideología y Praxis Política de Lázaro Cárdenas* (Mexico City: Siglo xxi, 1976), pp. 226–27; Arnaldo Cordova, *La Política de Masas del Cardenismo* (Mexico City: Édicionas Era, 1974), pp. 177–201.

21. Meyer, *Los Grupos de Presión*, pp. 78–79; Daniel, *Mexico and the Americans*, pp. 250–310; Ricardo Martinez, *De Bolivar a Dulles* (Mexico City: Nuestra America, pp. 151–57; Tzvi Medin, *Ideología y Praxis*, pp. 140–45.

ments found in the National Archive of Mexico provide evidence not only of the participation of foreign investors in the Cedillo affair, but also of the involvement of some U.S. government officials. For example, despite President Roosevelt's "hands off" policy, some members of the U.S. government knew of, and in some instances supported, the activities of foreign investors who collaborated with Cedillo.[22] Nonetheless, the pressures exerted by various national and international groups neither impeded the decision to expropriate the oil industry in Mexico nor led to its modification once it had been taken. This example served as a drastic reminder of those social, economic, and political principles derived from the revolutionary movement that all of Mexico's contemporary governments must at least minimally adhere to in order to maintain their legitimacy.

In reaction to the uncertainties prompted by the activities of the Cárdenas regime, some reorganization took place within the various industrial and commercial chambers making them become more efficient in fulfilling their ideological function in the class struggle. For example, in 1936 AMCHAM changed its Charter to allow Mexicans and capitalists of other nationalities to become members. The Mexican government itself unwittingly helped by passing a law regulating the functions of the Mexican Chambers of Commerce and Industry and making membership in these chambers obligatory for all private enterprises, including foreign ones. This law and AMCHAM's new Charter increased the possibility of uniting the national and international sectors of the capitalist class through cross-fertilization of programs and policies in both the ideological and the political spheres. In retrospect, AMCHAM's appraisal of this period is as follows: "For the American Chamber of Commerce, the decade was busy, tortuous, difficult. Yet, it ended on a brighter note, as the Chamber headed into an optimistic future and finally threaded its way toward stronger cooperation and stronger ties."[23] This "brighter note" was nothing less than the beginning of the rise of U.S. capitalism to predominance in world capitalism, and the beginning of the close and supportive role that the governments of both Mexico and the United States were to play for the benefit of the manufacturing and commercial sectors of the bourgeoisie.

22. For original unpublished documents that support these statements, see Archivo General de la Nación, Ramo Presidentes, Archivo Privado del General Cárdenas (1934–1940), Class. 559, exp. 23,559.3, exp. 28,404.1, exp. 4227; Class. 151.3, exp. 1019, Class. 563.3, exp. 53.1; Class 564.3 exp. 3; Class. 559.1, exp. 70; Class. 559.1, exp. 53.1; Class 563.3, exp. 31; Class. 599.1, exp. 60.
23. *Mexican-American Review*, Nov. 1967, p. 45.

War and Early Postwar Years: 1940-49

According to AMCHAM, the approaching end of the Cárdenas era and the new war in Europe and the Far East had propitious implications. In retrospect, the oncoming period was classified by AMCHAM in the following way: "Yet the government's popular 'Mexico for the Mexicans' policy and the general lack of dialogue between the companies and their 13,000 oil workers did not quench the enthusiasm of the AMCHAM-Mexico. . . . The peso was weakening, but for American businessmen the stage was set for U.S. entry into World War II and the impetus this was to bring to Mexico's manufacturing and trade as Cárdenas responded to Franklin D. Roosevelt's discreet hands-off policy with respect to the oil expropriation. The 'Good Neighbor policy'— coinciding with the 30-year-old AMCHAM-Mexico—was ushering in a new era of good feeling and active cooperation in the economic and political spheres."[24]

"Active cooperation" during the Second World War was far more important than it had been during the First World War, and it took the form of several treaties between Mexico and the United States involving political, economic, and military matters.[25] AMCHAM's collaboration in the economic sphere was principally as liaison between the Mexican government and Mexican businessmen on the one hand, and the U.S. government on the other. According to AMCHAM's own account: ". . . The nation [Mexico] began its heroic task of producing foodstuffs, oil, and other raw materials to feed the war machine. The American Chamber of Commerce was to play a major role in that activity."[26] As an example of AMCHAM's new role, in December 1940, Henry A. Wallace, Vice-President Elect and Ambassador Extraordinary to Mexico, met with Chamber officers to request their cooperation in working out a hemispheric supply plan. Shortly thereafter, Nelson Rockefeller, then coordinator of Latin American Affairs in the U.S. State Department, sent a delegation to seek the Chamber's cooperation in forming a local advisory committee. Interestingly, seven of the eighteen businessmen selected to participate in that committee were AMCHAM members. Partly as a result of AMCHAM's participation, in May 1941 the Douglas Agreement was signed, providing for the purchase by U.S. government agencies of all of Mexico's surplus materials considered to be useful for the war in exchange for machinery and raw materials to keep the Mexican economy going.

24. *Ibid.*, p. 50.
25. *Ibid.*, pp. 51-59; see also Daniel, *Mexico and the Americans*, pp. 310-59.
26. *Mexican-American Review*, Nov. 1977, p. 15.

The link between the U.S. government and AMCHAM was further strengthened when Floyd D. Ransom, the Chamber's president in 1941, "was appointed special representative of the Federal Loan Agency, Defense Supplies Corporation, Metals Reserve, and managed an office that directly liquidated nearly one billion dollars worth of purchases of Mexican materials during the war period. . . ."[27] Similarly, the link between the capitalists of Mexico and those of the United States was also strengthened during the war as supplies from Europe were cut off and Mexican businessmen turned to AMCHAM to find out where they could buy comparable supplies in the United States. Moreover, "In order to increase food production, U.S. technicians swarmed into Mexico and began, with the enthusiastic cooperation of their Mexican counterparts, to tinker with a number of Mexican social and economic mechanisms."[28] This radical substitution of European supplies and tinkering "with social and economic mechanisms" was to lead to the control by U.S.-based TNCs of Mexico's most dynamic and profitable industries.

On the ideological plane, too, AMCHAM's activities in particular were many and varied. For example, AMCHAM recommended the establishment of a U.S. library in Mexico as a follow-up to the "Good Neighbor policy." Rockefeller accordingly arranged for a grant, and the Benjamin Franklin Library was inaugurated in Mexico City in April 1942. Then, two years later, the Mexican-American Cultural Relations Institute was founded—also under the sponsorship of AMCHAM. This Institute offered—and continues to offer today—not only English courses but also a host of other activities, many of which transmit the philosophy and ideology of the free enterprise system.[29] Finally, the U.S. government, anxious to keep Mexico firmly in the Allied camp, sponsored a film program during the war with the collaboration of an AMCHAM ex-president, Sam Bollings Wright. According to Mr. Wright: "When World War II came along they called Mr. Nelson Rockefeller to Washington, and Mr. Roosevelt asked him it he wouldn't take all of Latin America. And his job was to keep Latin America pro-ally. Mr. Rockefeller came here and he turned Mexico over to me. I had 37 movie projectors going all over Mexico trying to keep Mexico pro-ally. We showed pictures (The News Parade) to over 3 million people."[30]

27. *Ibid.*, p. 17.
28. *Ibid.*
29. For AMCHAM's activities, see the files in private companies or in AMCHAM's own library. I had access to the files of a prominent TNC in Mexico.
30. Peter Baird and Ed McCaughan, "The Golden Ghetto," in North American Congress on Latin America's [NACLA] *Latin America and Empire Report*, 8, no. 1 (Jan. 1974), p. 5.

The Postwar Years: 1950–69

After the war, the capitalist and socialist spheres of influence were sharply delineated, and for geopolitical as well as economic reasons Mexico was tightly drawn into the capitalist sphere directly under the influence of the United States. Naturally, the close wartime collaboration between the United States and Mexico, and their extensive common border, constituted important factors linking both countries. But even more important was the constant flow of direct and indirect foreign investment from U.S. capitalists which was directed into the Mexican manufacturing industry, and the gradually growing dependence which developed as the Mexican government increasingly resorted to loans from international financing organizations dominated by U.S. capital. During this period, the development model known as the "mixed economy" was firmly established in Mexico.[31] Economic development was measured strictly in terms of per-capita income, industrial output, GNP, export and import rates, and private capital investment; it certainly was *not* measured in terms of income distribution or social equality. This model was to continue the pattern already established, which featured a high concentration of income in the hands of a relatively small percentage of the Mexican population and a high level of unemployment and underemployment among the majority of the Mexican work force.

Of course, this development model was in no way as automatic and logical as both Mexican and U.S. capitalists try to make it appear. Rather, the Mexican state was to play its traditional postrevolutionary role as arbiter between capital and labor, while providing strong stimuli for private accumulation and initiating a conscious policy of halting the radicalization of the working and peasant classes, curbing the reforms initiated by President Cárdenas, and controlling any independent growth of the Labor Union Confederations. In fact, from 1945 to the second half of the 1970's the reforms initiated by Cárdenas were utilized to ameliorate social unrest and to create the "favorable investment climate" needed by the capitalist class to consolidate the economic and political conditions required for the development model adopted.

By the early postwar years, the Mexican business associations had already been legally reorganized along sectoral lines, separating commerce and industry and organizing the different activities within them, according to specializations. A new national chamber of manufactures, Cámara Nacional de la Industria de la Transformación (CANACINTRA), was formed principally in order to rally support

31. "Mixed economy" denotes industry formed with private and state capital.

for the Mexican government's nationalist capitalist policies among the smaller industries not normally directly linked with the huge TNCs. Of course, as a consequence of these reorganizations each sector now had to deal separately with the government—a situation that businessmen did not like, both because many had cross-sectoral interests in commerce and industry (not to mention banking and insurance) and because many considered the new rulings detrimental to the interests of the capitalist class as a whole and an example of excessive intervention by government in private enterprise. However, this attempt on the part of the government to weaken business's potential for concerted action by stimulating sectoral identification has not been completely successful. Nonetheless, in certain instances CANACINTRA, for example, has diverged from the policies adopted by the rest of the business organizations. One such instance involved the general notion held previously by all the private-enterprise associations that the proper role of government is to keep social order, create a climate in which private enterprise can develop, and otherwise limit its activities to providing essential services: CANACINTRA has broken the ideological lockstep *at times* by accepting the idea of the government as a "partner" in the basic tasks of "development" and by showing itself willing to side with the government in exchange for protection and concessions.

It should be made clear, however, that disagreement and friction among the different factions of the dominant class—including the national and international bourgeoisies—and among the sectoral organizations do not necessarily add up to "antagonism," and that in the long run it is global class interests that prevail over any other considerations. In the ideological sphere this takes the form of a united ideological front —although, as just noted, at times some slight differences are present, especially when sectoral interests are at stake. In other words, despite the existence of certain divergent points of view, the frequent examples of sectoral and intersectoral joint actions by both national and international organizations show these organizations to be powerful, united pressure groups. Marco Antonio Alcazar, in his study on pressure groups, has analyzed five important cases of such joint actions,[32] but for our purposes in this paper one example will suffice. In the 1950's and early 1960's, especially during the presidency of López Mateos (1958–64), the Mexican government tried to exert some control over the production and distribution of component parts used in the assembly of automobiles in Mexico. But the automobile interests were able to find

32. Alcazar, *Las Agrupaciones*, pp. 71–101.

ample support among the business associations as a whole—not only among those related to their particular industry—to pressure the Mexican government to reduce state interference in that sector. Although the government did win in the end, it was only after a prolonged fight that involved not only national and international pressure groups but the U.S. government as well; moreover, the victory was never more than a partial one. In this case, the U.S. government once again joined forces with the huge TNCs to pressure the Mexican government to take decisions that would favor U.S. TNCs involved in automobile production.[33]

Recently the automobile industry was again able to show its power as a pressure group in Mexico. In 1977, the concerted action of various sectoral pressure groups, including both the national and the international bourgeoisies, forced the government to reverse a decision placing ceiling prices on vehicles used for private transportation.[34] This is just another example of the difficulty the Mexican government has in controlling the capitalist class even now that it has been legally divided into sectoral organizations. Particular problems are the overlapping membership in the sectoral chambers, the leadership the largest firms exert through their economic power, and the divisions within the Mexican bourgeoisie and the Mexican government itself.[35]

We should note here that the vast majority of the working class of Mexico and its political and ideological leaders could hardly have envisioned all the inherent contradictions involved in the adoption of the so-called "mixed economy" development model during the initial postwar period. Even had they done so, however, they would have been lulled by the apparent prosperity of the late 1940's and 1950's, when the money reserves that had been saved during the war were released, when jobs were created owing to the installation of new manufacturing

33. For an excellent study of the joint efforts against the Mexican government in this case, see Douglass Bennett and Kenneth Sharpe, "Las Corporaciones Multinacionales Vs el Estado en México: El Caso de la Industria Automotriz," a paper presented in the seminar "Estado y Burguesía Nacional en América Latina," in El Centro de Estudios Sociológicos of El Colegio de México, on June 30, 1977. Also, with reference to this period, a General Motors executive stated in a personal interview in Mexico City in January 1978: "You can be sure that the industry used every means in its power so as not to conform to the pressures of the Mexican Government. But, in 1962, it was a victory for the government."

34. This concerted action was discussed in personal interviews with an executive of the Ford Motor Company of Mexico in 1977 and with a General Motors executive in 1978. Both agreed that multiple sources of pressure had been put on Mexico's ex-president Echeverría and current President López Portillo.

35. For a detailed study of Mexican business organizations, see Robert J. Shaffer, *Mexican Business Organizations* (Syracuse, N.Y., 1973).

plants, and when public works and the construction of government buildings activated internal expenditures and strengthened the internal market.

During this period, too, the role of AMCHAM began to change in conjunction with the influx of U.S. capital, the general "euphoria," the new regulations requiring obligatory membership in chambers of commerce and industry, and the beginning of policies initiating closer collaboration and association between U.S. businessmen and their Mexican counterparts. As one of AMCHAM's past presidents stated: "Whereas up to the early 1950's the Chamber had functioned 'as a closed institution dealing exclusively with U.S. affairs,' luncheon meetings from 1952 on were characterized by the presence of leading Mexican officials and leaders of the Mexican private sector."[36] The luncheon meetings referred to in the quote continue to the present and represent a firm attempt to organize and unify the national and international sectors of the capitalist class in Mexico and to clarify doubts about official Mexican policy that might exist in either sector.[37] Besides establishing these regular working luncheons, AMCHAM also pressed for the formation of a Mexico-U.S. Businessmen's Committee during the initial postwar years and organized a host of specialized committees covering a wide range of services such as government liaison, legal advice to investors, and education.

However, the euphoria of the early postwar years was not to last long. By the beginning of the 1960's, the contradictions in the Mexican model of development had begun to become evident and the successful revolutionary movement in Cuba had already had strong repercussions on Mexican intellectuals. Given this situation, AMCHAM took steps to close ranks and restructure its internal organization to meet the requirements of its new ideological role, which was to become explicit and intensified by the early 1970's. AMCHAM began its new role by hiring a set of professional, paid officers. (Previously the staff and officers had chiefly been concerned with keeping up the services offered—in line with the "business of business is business" maxim.) In recognition of the intensified ideological role AMCHAM was to play from the 1960's on, McNeil Stringer, AMCHAM president in 1961–62, states: "An education committee was formed in 1962 to educate not only students, but

36. *Mexican-American Review*, Nov. 1977, p. 21.
37. During 1977, for example, approximately six such luncheon sessions took place at the University Club, with the presence of important members of the Mexican government and the national bourgeoisie as speakers.

business as well, in the prime ideological question of our time, the conflict between Communism and Free Enterprise."[38] Shortly thereafter, a public relations program divided into two basic areas was initiated: the first area was oriented toward employees (the working class as well as the managerial sector of the capitalist class) and was designed to teach them about the free enterprise system in general and their own companies in particular; the second area was oriented toward the general Mexican public and set out to show "the contribution of U.S. business to the Mexican economy and the Mexican community wherever possible, and by all available means."[39]

Further actions along these lines included the adoption in 1965 of the BEDEL (Bases Esenciales de La Empresa Libre) program, originally developed by Dupont in the U.S. This program was designed to prepare instructors to educate company employees in the principles of the free enterprise system. By 1966, BEDEL had already trained 170 instructors from 108 companies; AMCHAM calculated in 1977 that the 370 businessmen who took the course in 1970–71 had already reached around 25,000 employees. The BEDEL program also provided for some 30,000 books to be "distributed to schools and libraries throughout the republic."[40] By 1970, BEDEL had become a permanent program of AMCHAM and had been expanded to include, among other things student plant tours. In that year the program name was changed to FOREM (Formación de Empresas, "Formation of Companies").

Of course, FOREM is only a blueprint that individual companies can use in designing their own programs or combine with special packages developed by their home offices or corporate headquarters. For example, one of the particularly interesting programs under FOREM is that carried out by Chicle Adams of Mexico. According to Pedro Borda, Industrial Relations Manager of the company: "We have a very sophisticated induction program . . . which basically calls for new employees spending at least two days, sometimes more, learning about the company. Every employee and worker also has to go through a six-hour course called FOREM sponsored by the AMCHAM, which explains what free enterprise is all about."[41] For its excellent work in the ideological field, Chicle Adams has received AMCHAM's Pochteca Award

38. *Mexican-American Review*, Nov. 1977, p. 23.
39. *Ibid.*, p. 24.
40. *Ibid.*, p. 29, more detailed information of formation of BEDEL is in the Nov. 1965 and July 1967 issues of *Mexican-American Review* (pp. 38–39 for the former and 83 for the latter).
41. *Ibid.*, Jan. 1977, p. 9.

(given in recognition of companies' "social responsibility" programs) and also the Golden Quill prize for excellence in communication of the International Association of Business Communications.

Of course, AMCHAM does not attempt to influence the course of events in Mexico only through its own activities and publications. AMCHAM members are also members of the Mexican direct formal associations that all firms and individuals in business—even little shops and market stalls—are required by law to join.[42] Specialized chambers at the local level are in turn included in the national sectoral chambers, which are considered to be advisory organs to the government. Therefore, through their membership in the Mexican chambers, American affiliates have influence over the policies and decision-making processes of the entire business community and of the Mexican government itself. The power this entails becomes especially clear when we consider that the biggest firms, through their internal structure and economic power, dictate the general lines of the policies that the business organizations press for.[43] Cross-membership, then, provides an enormous possibility for far-reaching ideological influence.

The Intensification of the Explicit Nature of
AMCHAM's Ideological Role: the 1970's

Although both TNCs and AMCHAM have always engaged in ideological activities, the changing world and Mexican scenes in the early 1970's led them to adopt a much more active role in the ideological sphere that can be classified as an explicit, open, and aggressive policy geared to defending the free enterprise system at all costs. Needless to say, their Mexican counterparts also intensified their own activities in the class struggle on the ideological level; however, we have not included an analysis of their activities here because of space limitations.

42. Cross-membership is the principal means of direct contact between the national and international bourgeoisies. Even banks are affiliated with AMCHAM in spite of having their own association. (In 1973, 24 banks were members of AMCHAM.) See the *Mexican-American Review*, Sept. 1973, p. 52. It is calculated that sectoral and intersectoral confederations of Chambers of Commerce and Industry have approximately 400,000 member firms. There are also special associations dedicated to export-import activities, about 20 bi-national committees promoting private enterprise to and from the countries represented, around 14 foreign Chambers of Commerce, and myriad civil associations that incorporate executives and professional people linked to international business. See Shaffer, *Mexican Business Organizations*, pp. 90–96; and Departamento de Comunicaciones de la Confederación de Cámaras Industriales, *Confederación de Cámaras Industriales* (Mexico City, Oct. 1, 1977), vol. 28, no. 685.

43. The officers of AMCHAM are important high executives of the TNCs, and major economic support for AMCHAM comes from U.S. corporations.

Changing World Conditions

On the world scene, by the early 1970's the hegemony of the United States had clearly been weakened by the growth of socialist thought and organization, general discontent with world capitalism, and competition from other capitalist countries. Moreover, several nations had issued laws restricting the expansion of TNCs, and organizations such as OPEC had been formed. It was also evident that the United States was nowhere near victory in Vietnam.

In Latin America, by 1970 it was clear that the Alliance for Progress, begun in 1961, had not been able to lessen inequalities in the area or alleviate the widespread discontent among the working classes, peasants, and intellectuals. Nationalizations and expropriations were no longer simply theoretical concepts but were beginning to represent very real challenges to the TNCs.[44] For example, Cuba, firmly on the way toward socialism, had nationalized all foreign corporations; Chile, with an elected socialist president, had taken steps in the same direction; and Peru, with a military nationalist government, had already nationalized several U.S. enterprises and was preparing further expropriations. In addition, the subregional Andean Integration Agreement, ratified in 1969 and originally designed to protect the Bolivian, Chilean, Ecuadorian, Peruvian, and Colombian national economies by establishing new rules limiting some activities of TNCs, had definite anti-imperialist overtones, at least initially. Indeed nationalist rhetoric and policies in Peru had created an uncomfortable situation for TNCs there, owing not only to the establishment of controls over profit distribution but also to the potential for conflict created by heightened class consciousness on the part of the proletariat catalyzed by the passage of new laws since 1968.[45] As for the general spread of discontent with capitalist domination and

44. Although "nationalism" and nationalist policies do not necessarily represent a break with the capitalist system, TNCs have traditionally reacted negatively to both nationalist rhetoric and nationalist policies. For discussion of this problem, see Meyer, *Los Grupos de Presión*; Richard J. Barnet and Ronald E. Müller, *Global Reach* (New York, 1974), p. 188; T. H. Moran, "Two Conflicting Perspectives, Nationalism and 'Dependencia,'" in Jon P. Gunneman, ed., *The Nation State and Transnational Corporation in Conflict* (New York, 1975), pp. 20–25; Baird and Mc-Caughan, "The Golden Ghetto"; and Hugh Stephenson, *The Coming Clash* (New York, 1973), pp. 55–64.

45. On the rising level of class consciousness among Peruvian workers, see *Dinámica de la Comunidad Industrial* (Lima: DESCO, 1974); Confederación Nacional de Comunidades Industriales, *Resolución del Primer Congreso Nacional de Comunidades Industriales* (Lima: CONACI, 1973). For a similar situation in Cuba, see Richard Fagen, *The Transformation of Political Culture in Cuba* (Stanford, Calif., 1969).

ideology, one need only recall the student movements and the spread of guerrilla warfare in Latin America during almost the entire decade 1960–70, the organization and mobilization of the Peruvian peasants during that same period, and the popular movements in the Dominican Republic in 1965 that were repressed with the help of the U.S. military forces.

In addition, other so-called "underdeveloped nations" were openly beginning to unite in order to seek better conditions in their relations with the imperialist centers. This new form of politics, known as "Third World Diplomacy," represented a challenge to the degree of interference of imperialist nations in the economies of these countries and to the level of surplus labor appropriated by TNCs.

Within the United States, too, capitalist hegemony was beginning to be weakened as youth began to question the moral, legal, and political system and as racial minorities became radicalized in their demands for equal treatment.[46] It should be mentioned that although labor in the United States is far from being politically radicalized, it, too, had begun to manifest some opposition to the capitalist system and particularly to the TNCs, as they exported jobs and created unemployment within the United States itself. This opposition was manifested in many ways— among them labor's support of the Hartke-Burke bill in the early 1970's.[47]

Although this very general survey is scarcely sufficient to describe the change in U.S. capitalist hegemony that had taken place by the end of the 1960's, it does illustrate the situation the TNCs faced in the early 1970's. The U.S. Chamber of Commerce, a representative of private enterprise, responded in 1971 with the *Powell Memorandum*, and two years later with a far-reaching program based upon it; in the meantime, the TNCs in Latin America created the Council of the Americas and their own ideological programs.[48]

46. See Gyorgy Adam, "Las Corporaciones Transnacionales en la Década del Setenta," in Paul M. Sweezy et al., *Teoría y Práctica de la Empresa Multinacional* (Buenos Aires: Ediciones Periferia SRL, 1974), pp. 73–107; and Massimo Teodori, ed., *The New Left* (New York, 1969).

47. Luciano Martins, "The Politics of U.S. Multinational Corporations in Latin America," in Julio Cotler and Richard R. Fagen, eds., *Latin America and the United States: The Changing Political Realities* (Stanford, Calif., 1974), p. 375.

48. See Lewis F. Powell, Jr., *The Powell Memorandum, Confidential Memorandum: Attack on American Free Enterprise System* (Aug. 23, 1971), printed and distributed by the Chamber of Commerce of the United States as a supplement of the *Washington Report* (Washington, D.C., Oct. 1972). Also see Chamber of Commerce of the United States, "Business Response to the Powell Memorandum," in *Washington Report*, 12, no. 24 (Nov. 26, 1973). The *Powell Memorandum* outlined the way the Chambers of Commerce and private enterprise in general could

In Mexico in the early 1970's, however, the TNCs and AMCHAM in no way simply followed the dictates of the U.S. Chamber of Commerce. The new policies of AMCHAM, as summarized by its president during 1971–72 in his speech "It's Time to Tell It Like It Is," responded as much to the objective reality of Mexico as to the world scene. On the economic level, by the 1970's TNCs in Mexico had established firm roots and were thus more interested than ever in a favorable investment climate and an attitude of consumerism on the part of the Mexican population. Their investments in the country had nearly doubled between 1960 and 1970, and total U.S. investment in Mexico was one of the highest in Latin America.[49] Not only had the absolute amount of U.S. investment increased, but so had the percentage of total investment held by U.S. investors. Whereas in 1940 only 61 percent of all foreign investment in Mexico came from the United States, in 1970 the figure was approximately 83 percent.[50] What is more, 89 percent of all U.S. investments were found in the most dynamic sectors of the economy—manufacturing and commerce.[51] And remittances to the home country —already high—were expected to increase in the next few years.[52]

Consequently, when the critical situation of the Mexican economy led President Luis Echeverría (1970–76) to initiate policies designed to bring the activities of TNCs under greater government control and to force the TNCs to integrate into the Mexican economy, the reaction of international business was decidedly negative. In 1972, for example, a law was passed attempting to control foreign investment and regulating the transfer of technology by requiring corporations to use technology available in Mexico rather than import it. Also, to control imports and stimulate exports, companies were required to export in order to obtain permits to import certain materials. Of course, it was not only

---

combat the penetration of socialist ideology in different spheres of U.S. society. On Lewis F. Powell, see *U.S. News and World Report*, Nov. 1 and Nov. 8, 1971; *New York Times*, Oct. 22, 1971. The Council of the Americas, a private association, was founded in 1971 by David Rockefeller. It included some 200 American corporations with investments in Latin America. The Council was "to act as a pressure group in Latin America, be an intermediary between Latin American elites and the United States, and organize discussions about social, political, and economic situations." See Fátima Fernández Chrislieb, "Imperialismo y Medios de Información Colectiva en México," in *Estudios Políticos*, 2, no. 6 (Apr.–Jun. 1976), p. 7.

49. See Olga Pellicer de Brody, "Mexico in the 1970s and Its Relations with the United States," in Cotler and Fagen, eds., *Latin America and the United States*, pp. 327–33.

50. *Ibid.*, p. 327.

51. Sepúlveda and Chumacero, *La Inversión Extranjera*, p. 50.

52. Pellicer de Brody, "Mexico in the 1970s," p. 328.

President Echeverría's economic nationalism that caused consternation
among American investors, AMCHAM, and the local bourgeoisie linked
to American capitalists. By the early 1970's, the Mexican working class
had already begun to demonstrate a heightened level of class consciousness (sparked by a reduction in real salaries despite several raises) that
was producing labor movements oriented toward rejecting the system
of government-controlled unions and demanding better living conditions. Several independent unions were formed, breaking in part the
almost monolithic control of the CTM (Confederación de Trabajadores
Mexicanos). Some of these independent unions were formed under the
leadership of Marxist and socialist militants, whereas others took the
traditional liberal-reformist stand—which at any rate is still perceived
as a challenge by the TNCs, some national capitalists, and the leaders
of the CTM.[53] President Echeverría reacted by initiating a series of
policies designed to favor labor and to keep the economic and social
situation under control—i.e., to guarantee the continuity of the so-called
"shared development" policy.[54]

As for the rural problem, by 1970 it was already clear that Mexican
agrarian policies and "agribusiness" (as understood by the TNCs) had
failed to solve the grave social and economic problems of the countryside and to raise the overall low productivity rate. Land invasions were
frequent in northern Mexico. Peasants were demanding land, food, jobs,
and higher salaries.[55] These demands were coupled with a rising level of

53. For the overall economic situation of that period see Comisión Económica para
América Latina, *Estudio Económico de América Latina* (New York, 1972). For a
detailed study of President Echeverría's economic policies, see Héctor Mata et al.,
"Economía Política y Movimientos Populares en el Régimen de LEA (1)," *Investi-
gación Económica* (Mexico City), no. 3 (Jul.–Sept. 1977). On the workers, see
Daniel Molina, "La Política Laboral y el Movimiento Obrero (1970–1976)," *Cua-
dernos Políticos* (Mexico City), no. 12 (Apr.–Jun. 1975), p. 85; Silvia Gómez Tagle
et al., *Tres Estudios del Movimiento Obrero en México* (Mexico City: Colegio de
México, 1976); Peter Baird and Ed McCaughan, "Labor and Imperialism in Mexico's
Electrical Industry," North American Congress on Latin America, *Report on the
Americas*, 11, no. 6 (Sept.–Oct. 1977). For an excellent study of periodicals dealing
with this situation, see Cristina Bernal García and Patricia Salcido Cañedo, "El
Proletariado, sus luchas y la política laboral en México," *Revista Mexicana de Cien-
cias Políticas y Sociales* (Mexico City), no. 83 (Jan.–Mar. 1976), pp. 301–11; also see
Juan Felipe Leal, *México estado, burocracia y sindicatos* (Mexico City: El Caballito,
1975); and Mario Huacuja and José Woldenberg, *Estado y Lucha Política en el
México Actual* (Mexico City: El Caballito, 1976).
54. Molina, "La Política Laboral," pp. 72–73.
55. Armando Bartra, "Seis Años de Lucha Campesina," in Mata et al., "Economía
Política," pp. 157–208; North American Congress on Latin America, "Harvest of
Anger: Agroimperialism in Mexico's Northwest," *Latin America and Empire Report*, 10, no. 6 (Jul.–Aug. 1976).

political consciousness on the part of the agricultural proletariat, which began challenging the control of the National Farmers Confederation (CNC–Confederación Nacional Campesina) by creating independent peasant unions. The ideological leadership of these new organizations (like that of most of the new urban proletarian associations) came from Marxists and other socialists, as well as from some liberal reformists. The government was forced to expropriate land in Sonora for the peasants—a policy that landowners, including TNCs in agribusiness, reacted against with an industry stoppage in 1975.[56]

It was not simply economic nationalism, labor unrest, and the increased level of class consciousness in both rural and urban areas that created what was termed an "unfavorable investment climate" in Mexico in the early 1970's; other factors included the growing discontent and radicalization of students, who in 1968 and 1971 had demonstrated their rejection of the authoritarianism of the Mexican state, President Echeverría's support for the Cuban socialist government and for Chile's recently elected socialist president, Salvador Allende, and his "Third World" policies.[57] Echeverría's support for the "Third World" countries coincided with his policy of "Democratization" ("Apertura Democrática") in the internal sphere. This policy was reflected in the growth of an environment of open questioning of the capitalist system, "consumerism," and the role of TNCs in dependent capitalist countries; the questioning took place in the Mexican press and on Mexican television, and Marxists and other socialists and progressive liberal intellectuals contributed to it. Another reflection of internal "Democratization" was the appointment of a Marxist intellectual as the new dean of the National Autonomous University of Mexico (UNAM), Mexico's largest public university.

It was in this general context that the TNCs adopted the new policy of open defense of the free enterprise system so clearly expressed in AMCHAM's publications and internal documents.[58] The following sec-

56. NACLA, "Harvest of Anger," p. 24.
57. President Echeverría spoke openly of the need for the "Third World" nations to form a united front against imperialism. As to the support for Chile, President Allende's visit to Mexico was enormously popular and successful. It was amply covered by radio, television, and the press. This was all personally witnessed by me as a resident of Mexico.
58. For examples of how the TNCs perceived this entire situation, see Frank Loretta, "It's Time to Tell It Like It Is," speech given on March 2, 1973, before the members of AMCHAM-Mexico, reproduced in Angela Delli Sante, *The Private Sector, Business Organizations, and International Influence: Mexico, A Case Study*, Appendix 1, Internal Document of the Center for Interdisciplinary Studies, ENEP, Acatlán, National Autonomous University of Mexico, 1978; and editorials in the

tion of this paper analyzes the meaning of this new policy and looks at some of the principal activities undertaken on the basis of it.

"It's Time to Tell It Like It Is"

In 1971, AMCHAM, "taking its lead from the *Powell Memorandum*, . . . began a major offensive designed to counter the barrage of attacks against U.S. capitalism,"[59] especially since "trade relations and investments dating back more than 50 years were in great jeopardy."[60] In 1973, Frank Loretta, president of AMCHAM, stated that in late 1971 "the AMCHAM-Mexico, in a fundamental change in its traditional posture, decided to undertake a vigorous campaign of truth and fact to demonstrate the positive benefits of the private enterprise system and direct foreign investment."[61] According to Loretta this "aggressive" move was directed "to convert the doubters, to *pacify* the antagonists, and to convince the open-minded that their destinies are secure and promising under a system that guarantees economic and political freedom of choice and action."[62]

Once again, the link between the U.S. government and the private sector was strengthened when in the fall of 1972 "a high-level meeting was called in Acapulco, where representatives of AMCHAM, the Council of the Americas, and the U.S. Embassy in Mexico gathered forces in an attempt to exert public pressure on the Mexican government. Acting as spokesman of the group, the U.S. Ambassador (John Joseph Jova) demanded a clarification of the role of foreign investment. They soon received official word that, as always, they were quite welcome in Mexico, though they would be expected to share the responsibilities as well as the benefits of Mexican development."[63]

This action and others taken by AMCHAM show that claims of AMCHAM's "nonpolitical" involvement in Mexican affairs are false. With respect to these claims, on January 17, 1977, the president of AMCHAM, Al Wichtrich, declared before a congressional subcommittee on Interamerican Economic Relationships that "the American Cham-

---

Mexican-American Review issues of May 1973, Sept. 1973, and Mar.–Apr. 1976. See also Ejecutivos en Relaciones del Estado de Morelos, *Estudio Cuestionario Sobre Asuntos Laborales*, unpublished document of this organization, dated Oct. 1975.

  59. Baird and McCaughan, "The Golden Ghetto," p. 14.
  60. *Mexican-American Review*, Nov. 1977, p. 35.
  61. See Frank Loretta's speech "It's Time to Tell It Like It Is," in Delli Sante, *The Private Sector*, Appendix 1, p. 1.
  62. *Ibid.*, p. 7.
  63. Baird and McCaughan, "The Golden Ghetto," p. 14.

ber of Commerce in Mexico and we (American citizens) are not in a position to tell the Mexican government what to do. . . . As I have mentioned before, it is a sovereign country. We try to show them where perhaps they are making a mistake and try to prove, you know, how they should adopt certain attitudes, perhaps, foreign investment would be more welcome, this sort of thing."[64] This statement certainly contradicts various public and private AMCHAM declarations made between 1972 and 1977, and it also apparently contradicts another of Mr. Wichtrich's statements made in the course of the same hearings to the effect that the Mexican economy should be integrated with that of the United States.[65]

Indeed, AMCHAM's intention to intervene in Mexican politics was clearly stated in a December 1976 bulletin circulated to all its members:

What the Mexican economy achieves during 1977 will depend more than ever on what happens in the political sphere. On the other hand, however, it is necessary to recognize that the political decisions of the new administration, although difficult to predict, *will be determined also, as never before, by the attitude of the private enterprise sector* . . . because economy and politics do not exclude one another, as some people would like to think: they are complementary roads that arrive at a definitive establishment of social tranquillity, a tranquillity that all of us are interested in preserving.[66]

AMCHAM went on to take an openly political stand in this document by criticizing the Echeverría regime, while manifesting hope in López Portillo and urging private investors to support his policies.[67] In addition, in its effort to organize the capitalist class the document further advocates a united front in negotiations with the state as the only solution to the problem of the private investor:

One of the principal problems that has affected private enterprise in Mexico is its fragmentation, its lack of ability to present and to execute programs of action in a realistic form and on a continuous and coordinated basis. . . .

Until now, the majority of the private business associations have had to

---

64. *Recent Developments in Mexico and Their Economic Implications for the United States, Hearings Before the Subcommittee on Inter-American Economic Relationships of the Joint Economic Committee of the Congress of the United States*, 95th Congress; 1st Session, January 17th and 24th, 1977 (Washington, D.C., 1977), p. 81. In 1973, Mr. Wichtrich was also careful to stress the nonintervention policy of AMCHAM-Mexico in a personal interview with me.

65. *Recent Developments*, pp. 61–67.

66. AMCHAM, Comité de Importación y Exportación, *Boletín*, 1, no. 12 (Dec. 1976), p. 1 (italics mine).

67. *Ibid.*, pp. 5–7.

speak for themselves, and in uncoordinated and confused manner. This of course has invariably permitted the Federal Government to take the initiative in its relations with the private corporation. . . .[68]

AMCHAM's explicit role in the ideological sphere is today the result of a far-reaching program known as the "Communications Program," which is designed to orient not only the capitalist class but the workers, and the government of Mexico as well. This program was adopted in 1972, and its chosen targets are "government, the media, and the employees of the transnational companies themselves."[69] In its official publication, AMCHAM states:

During the early decades, the Chamber—and U.S. business in general—had been content to maintain a low profile. . . . Little by little, the focus was shifted and AMCHAM-Mexico began to react to the growing challenges of the times—one of which was the emergence of Castro and the nationalistic fever that swept through developing nations in Latin America. New leaders of AMCHAM-Mexico recognized that the former passive role had to be replaced by a positive and vigorous defense of the principles for which the Chamber stands—Mexico-U.S. trade, private enterprise, foreign investment . . . The emphasis was on specific programs to tell the story of free enterprise and to place the Chamber in more effective contact with opinion leaders— the press, the private sector, the academic community, the government.[70]

The "Communications Program," the outgrowth of AMCHAM's previous experiences in educational and public relations activities during the 1960's, focuses on "the growing challenges of the times"—socialism and nationalism—and therefore represents a direct attempt to tell the Mexican people and the Mexican government what to do. To get the program started, an impressive team of experts was recruited, including among others Austin Parker of the McCann Erikson advertising agency, McNeil Stringer, who as president of AMCHAM in 1961 "had sounded the warning bell," Ben Candland, a retired editor of a major news magazine, Truls Fagrell, a public relations expert, Al Wichtrich, AMCHAM's current president, and the presidents of three major transnational companies.[71] Obviously, following the lines of "Powellism," this program was designed to create a "positive image" of businessmen.

Among its initial activities was the gathering of attitude surveys "to find out what the man in the street really thought about U.S. business."[72]

68. Ibid., p. 6.
69. Mexican-American Review, Nov. 1977, p. 42.
70. Ibid., pp. 21–23.
71. Ibid., p. 39.
72. Ibid., p. 35.

The results brought back "an alarming amount of misinformation in circulation," but a rather general opinion that "foreign investment was considered very important to the country."[73] With these results in mind, a full-fledged campaign was launched in order to "restore confidence in the free enterprise system." Printed and filmed supporting materials were prepared to counteract the negative publicity given by the press and other media; the FOREM program was further stimulated; prizes such as the Pochteca Award for service to the community were instituted; seminars and courses for company executives were intensified; and "all around" employee educational programs were initiated and encouraged. Needless to say, the *Powell Memorandum* itself was widely circulated among Mexican businessmen, and the Mexican bourgeoisie was strongly encouraged to join in the fight to save the free enterprise system.[74]

Of course, AMCHAM's own publications, which are constantly increasing in number, and its collaboration with Mexican business journals, are intended to support not only the private enterprise system in general but also foreign investment in Mexico. In fact, as part of the "Communications Program," special materials to illustrate the benefits of foreign investment for the Mexican economy and for Mexicans in general have been sent to AMCHAM members.[75] Naturally, these materials are geared toward easing any opposition that might come from the nationalist-oriented bourgeoisie and thus securing the "favorable investment climate" so desired by the huge TNCs.

However, AMCHAM's tactics to "communicate carefully and deeply" are not limited to the business community, employees, and the general public; rather, they reach into the higher education institutions in Mexico, as suggested in the *Powell Memorandum*. The establishment of a Bicentennial Chair in the National Autonomous University of Mexico in 1976 is an example of one of AMCHAM's most ambitious projects of direct influence in higher education. Appointed to this chair was Dr.

73. *Ibid.*
74. See Fernández Chrislieb, "Imperialismo y Medios de Información Colectiva en México," p. 12; and "Echos of the *Powell Memorandum*," in *Noticias* (Mar.–Apr. 1976), p. 1. (*Noticias* is an information bulletin normally published monthly by AMCHAM.) For a general survey of AMCHAM programs, prizes, etc., see *Mexican-American Review* issues from 1972 to 1977; also see the files of private companies who are members of AMCHAM and have kept invitations, publications, bulletins, etc. I had access to the 1977 file of an important TNC in Mexico.
75. Examples of such materials are the "Get Smart Cards" in the Stanford Research Institute series on the *Impact of Foreign Private Investment on the Mexican Economy*. See the letter of January 1977 sent out to members of AMCHAM and signed by Vincent M. Curcio, Jr., Chairman of the Board.

Noel T. Osborne, a University of Colorado graduate and former Fulbright scholar, who was and remains director of the doctoral program in Business Administration and coordinator of the Economics Area of Postgraduate Studies in the School of Commerce and Business Administration of the UNAM.[76]

In contrast to the belligerent tone of the *Powell Memorandum* and AMCHAM's emphatic appeals to the business community to become involved in "social responsibility for business survival," Dr. Osborne's approach is representative of that of the technocratic intellectuals who pretend to divorce science from ideology.[77] As he stated in a published interview:

I don't think that we should attempt to get involved in the ideological arena. Neither is confrontation a productive avenue of approach. But there is something that we can do, we can make an excellent impact by staying away from ideology—from the differences between socialism and capitalism—by getting U.S. and Mexican economists to talk to each other and by using our contacts to build mutual research between the two groups, projects that can be studied without concentrating on the ideological issues.[78]

Clearly, what Dr. Osborne is advocating here amounts to the formation of a concept of the world (an ideology) largely on a subconscious level. Additionally, Dr. Osborne's experience in Mexican higher education has not been limited to UNAM but has included a position in the Autonomous University of Guadalajara. As far as results go, he considers that these can be measured according to the following criteria: "We have helped some 30 students to go to the United States for completion of postgraduate work in economics and business. As far as I know, all but one of these are now back in Mexico, and most are teaching at least part-

---

76. *Mexican-American Review*, May 1977, pp. 5–7; Osborn is paid in part, at least, by AMCHAM-Mexico. See also "El Programa de Doctorado en Administración en la Facultad de Contaduría y Administración," *Gazette UNAM*, 2, no. 20 (Mar. 9, 1978), p. 6.

77. My studies in epistemology over the past three years and the teaching of this subject at the UNAM for the past four semesters have led me to reject such a separation. Indeed, the bibliography supporting my position is too vast to be included here. However, I recommend at least Adolfo Sánchez Vázquez, "La Ideología de la 'neutralidad ideológica' en las ciencias sociales," *Historia y Sociedad*, no. 7 (Mexico City: Imprenta Juan Pablos, 1975); Miriam Limoeiro Cardoso, *La Construcción de conocimientos* (Mexico City: Editorial Era, 1977); Adam Schaff, *Ensayos sobre la Filosofía del Lenguaje* (Barcelona: Editorial Ariel, 1968); idem, *Historia y verdad*.

78. *Mexican-American Review*, May 1977, p. 7.

time in Mexican universities. This is where you begin to have great impact, when people you have trained begin to train others."[79]

As for junior high and high school institutions, AMCHAM sponsors the DESEM program, Desarrollo Empresarial Mexicano, designed to transmit the private enterprise philosophy and give adolescents training in running companies. DESEM started in 1975, and since then some 1,300 secondary schools have participated in the program. "DESEM's importance," states an AMCHAM leader, "lies in the fact that we are literally fighting for the survival of a way of life that permits the maximum exercise of individual liberty!"[80]

Of course, AMCHAM does not work alone; it is a guiding and structuring organization. During the 1970's many individual companies—well aware of the class struggle on the ideological level, and stimulated by FOREM—have continued their programs aimed at blurring the lines of class differences. Many of these programs have been highly praised by AMCHAM and have been used as examples for other enterprises in Mexico. The programs include a wide range of activities such as manager-employee parties and sports events, the building of cultural centers, social work in communities, the sponsorship of special certificates and awards for efficient work in offices and communities, the publication of internal newsletters, etc. directed at creating an image of the company and its workers as one happy, harmonious family, the use of closed-circuit television, and the holding of periodic meetings between managerial staff and union officials. By these means the TNCs in their ideological functions strive to neutralize the class consciousness of the working class.[81]

During a February 1976 seminar held by AMCHAM on the subject of "Public Affairs Involvement," eight companies presented case histories intended to encourage those companies still in the process of designing their own programs. Although an exhaustive review of the presentations at that seminar would be beyond the scope of this paper, I want to mention some aspects of those programs that are particularly

79. *Ibid.*
80. *Ibid.*, July 1978, p. 62; also, interview with AMCHAM functionary in Sept. 1978. The courses last one year, from October to June.
81. *Ibid.*, Apr. 1976, pp. 6–14; *ibid.*, Mar. 1978, pp. 14–27, 43–57. I have also reviewed internal publications of important TNCs and have interviewed TNC executives to discuss these programs. The interviews took place in 1973, 1977, and 1978, all in Mexico City with executives of three different TNCs. Also see Monica-Claire Gambrill, *Estudio Exploratorio Sobre Empresas Neo-Capitalistas e Ideología Sindical*, unpublished master's thesis for the Centro de Estudios Sociológicos of El Colegio de México, 1975.

illustrative of the type of activities patronized by AMCHAM that reach the subconscious of the working class and are even being exported to other parts of the world.[82]

One of the most important case histories presented dealt with Hojalata y Lámina, S.A., a Monterrey-based steel plant, and its intention of building a plant in a community "steeped in tradition" and "hostile" to outsiders. This firm sensed that a confrontation might develop and accordingly "began by quietly making a study of the community and its people. It learned about the social structure and what they wanted out of life."[83] On the basis of this survey, the firm, with the cooperation of the local people, introduced potable water, spent 1.5 million pesos to build a primary school, and hired social workers to teach hygiene and health care to the houewives. Hojalata y Lámina considers that the expenses are worthwhile, since "a new arrival can be made welcome" and "such a program would appear easily justified in the *light of increased production and profits that are the results of its successful application*."[84] In this case, the company is indirectly working to create a "favorable investment climate" which here involves making outsiders and foreigners accepted in the community—in other words, constructing in the community a new concept of the world, a new ideology.

Another revealing case history involves Chicles Adams, which was confronted with a strike in the middle of merging four companies into one (La Campana, La Colonial, Chicle Adams, and Parke Davis). Since the strike would have caused a great deterioration in labor relations, the company decided to better its relationship with the workers by inviting them to "share in setting goals and objectives for the corporation." As a result the entire labor relations department was restructured to include a communications program designed to "involve families of workers and *make them feel part of the organization*. . . . New employees are given orientation materials, and long-time workers are honored with seniority pins and, after 20 years, invitations to a special banquet at which a certificate of appreciation is awarded."[85] Although Chicles Adams's labor relations policies are not very different from those

---

82. The Ford Motor Company program has even been bound for export. Since 1975, the "U.S. Chamber adopted the program in its entirety as a model for overseas AMCHAMs around the world, and copies of the thick yellow binder, in which it is encased, began to circulate in such faraway places as Uruguay and Hong Kong." *Mexican-American Review*, Nov. 1977, p. 41.
83. *Ibid.*, Apr. 1976, p. 8.
84. *Ibid.* (italics mine).
85. *Ibid.*, pp. 10–11 (italics mine).

in other corporations in the United States and elsewhere, I mention them precisely to stress the fact that the "corporate family" approach is one of the most common and apparently efficient means of attempting to blur the ongoing class struggle and hide from the workers the true nature of their exploitation.

Another significant program mentioned, and one I have studied in great detail, is that of the Ford Motor Company of Mexico. This program includes the construction of primary schools in rural areas, a rural training program for farmers, an emergency aid program to help disaster victims, and plans on constructing dormitories for elementary school students in rural areas in 1979. All of these activities are geared toward creating Ford's image as a "good corporate citizen." As a Ford executive explained: "What we are looking for is that that fellow has a favorable image of Ford. We are planting the seeds."[86] The school construction program, for example, initiated in 1967, had by 1976 resulted in the building of more than 101 schools attended by some 82,000 children. Ford *only* requires that the name of the company be printed on the front of the school and that the local Ford dealer become a permanent member of the school board.[87] The question to be asked now is: How easily can students who attend a "Ford" school grow up doubting the good will of that company, or for that matter of the system it represents? As for the rural training program started in 1967, the agronomists who form part of the traveling training force have been distributed in 16 states; it has been calculated that this program has reached 35,000 peasants. Indeed, this program is so cleverly designed that all the salaries are paid by the Mexican government, *except that of the General Coordinator of the program*, who is paid by Ford. The ideological content of this program has been made clear by the Ford Motor Company itself: "The entire program is based on an eminently pragmatic philosophy, and this is the discipline in which the Ford agronomists have been particularly trained in a special course they take before they go into the countryside for field work. In this way, one has the security that there will be no wasted efforts, no lost time, and no education that does

86. Personal interview with an executive of Ford Motor Company, July 1973 and Sept. 1978.

87. Ford de México, *Apuntes para una Historia de la Industria Automotriz* (Mexico City, 1973), p. 49; *Mexican-American Review*, Apr. 1976, p. 6. Incidentally, Ford does not buy the land or school supplies, nor does it pay for teachers or maintenance. *Mexican-American Review*, Mar. 1978, p. 15; today there are 109 schools.

not have useful and practical application individually and collectively."[88] In other words, no time is to be "wasted" on political or social education. That this type of assistance in rural communities can be useful for solving some immediate problems of production cannot be denied. However, the solution to Latin America's acute and complex agrarian problems can only be achieved through a total restructuring of the means of production. This type of reorganization can only be brought about by intensive ideological and political organization. The technocratic and production-oriented help that private corporations give is not capable of bringing about long-range change. Moreover, it can in fact be an obstacle to that change, since it can foster the further growth of the capitalist-individualist ideology in rural areas, making farmers and peasants less receptive to Marxist and other socialist organizers, and therefore to long-term collective solutions to the agrarian problem.

AMCHAM's Contemporary Reach

AMCHAM's ties with international business organizations through its membership in the U.S. Chamber of Commerce, the International Chamber of Commerce, the Association of American Chambers of Commerce of Latin America, etc. also give it wide influence over the strategy and tactics of the ideological struggle on a hemispheric level.[89] Moreover, AMCHAM's ties and parallel policies with the U.S. and Mexican governments and with the sectoral and intersectoral Mexican business organizations have become such an intricate binding web that a detailed account would necessarily be beyond the scope of this paper. Nonetheless, we should note with respect to the U.S. government that the web has been tightly woven through the participation of U.S. officials in seminars and work sessions organized by AMCHAM during the 1970's, as mentioned in the official publication, *The Mexican-American Review*.[90] With respect to the Mexican government, we have already noted that important Mexican officials participate in the Chamber's special

88. Ford de Mexico, *Apuntes*, p. 49; *Mexican-American Review*, Mar. 1978, pp. 15–17; for another educational program in rural areas on junior high school, high school, and college levels, see the Ralston Purina project in *ibid.*, pp. 17, 19. The vice-president of that company in Mexico stated: "This exposure to the free enterprise system at the level of the family farm has opened eyes and changed attitudes among the country's youth toward both Purina and the United States" (*ibid.*, p. 19).

89. Baird and McCaughan, "The Golden Ghetto," pp. 14–15. Recall the Ford project being exported all over the world by AMCHAM.

90. The examples are too frequent to be listed separately. However, see *Mexican-American Review*, monthly, 1970–78.

luncheon programs, and that officers of AMCHAM frequently consult with members of the government.[91]

The latest organizational development in the unification of the entire capitalist class in Mexico was the formation of CCE (Consejo Coordinador Empresarial), a "peak" association, in May 1975. The CCE includes all the executive boards of the most important business organizations: CONCANACO, CONCAMIN, ABM, AMIS, Consejo Mexicano de Hombres de Negocios, and COPARMEX. It can thus be considered the highest pressure group and class organizer in Mexico. Its objectives are:

to coordinate the activities and attitudes of all those organizations that (at a given moment) cannot agree among themselves, due to the fact that they were created to represent different sectoral interests . . . . It also serves as a forum for the representative national private enterprise organizations, in order to exchange information and to unify points of view, and . . . [it] offers the possibility to concert efforts in those tasks that are of common interest for businessmen or socially and economically beneficial for the country . . . . Thus, one of the fundamental goals of CCE is the defense and dignification of businessmen and their social function. The CCE has taken upon itself the job of unifying businessmen around these common ideals, influencing public opinion, and defending the regime of freedom embodied in our Magna Carta.[92]

Though it is difficult to determine to what extent AMCHAM participated directly in the formation of the CCE, there is clearly an indirect link, since the objectives of the CCE mirror the concepts and language of the *Powell Memorandum* and Frank Loretta's speech, "It's Time to Tell It Like It Is." Besides, through the cross-membership of TNCs and Mexican corporations in AMCHAM and the associations represented in the CCE, it is clear that the influence of AMCHAM can make itself felt.[93]

---

91. Among the many examples of meetings between AMCHAM-Mexico officers and members of the Mexican government, see the reminiscences in the *Mexican-American Review* (Nov. 7, 1977, p. 49) of George Blake, president of AMCHAM in 1973: "The experiences that stand out in my memory certainly include the several meetings with President Echeverría, meetings with government ministers, and a forum luncheon we presented with the then Minister of Finance who is now President López Portillo."

92. Consejo Coordinador Empresarial, *CCE* (an 8-page brochure published by this organization in Mexico City, ca. 1976), pp. 1–6; CONCAMIN, *Confederacion de Camaras Industriales*, 28, no. 685, Mexico City (Oct. 1977), p. 59.

93. Note that the officers of AMCHAM often become officers of the Mexican associations, thus producing a direct link in policy formation. The case of Alberto Escobedo, who was General Manager of AMCHAM for several years before leav-

The Anti-Excelsior Campaign

The anti-*Excelsior* campaign, which represents one of the most interesting examples of the application of the *Powell Memorandum* in Mexico, was the concerted action taken by U.S. corporations, Mexican businessmen and bankers, and AMCHAM to destroy a legitimate means of mass communication. This campaign was designed to silence Mexico's most widely circulated and (during the period of 1970–76) most liberal nationwide daily, the newspaper *Excelsior*.

Excelsior supported Echeverría's nationalist policies and rhetoric, and also served as a sounding board for a wide range of Marxist, socialist, and liberal ideas in Mexico during Echeverría's term (1970–76). Even the liberal wing of the Catholic Church was frequently represented in its pages. From the beginning of Echeverría's term, in contrast to other Mexican national newspapers, which were directly identified with right-wing policies and openly defended the TNCs, *Excelsior* adopted a frankly critical stance with respect to Mexico's dependent capitalist status. Many editorials and articles analyzed the capitalist system and its lack of possibilities as a solution for the "underdeveloped" world, and detailed the adverse effects of the TNCs on both the economic and the ideological development of the Third World countries. In fact, the entire concept of measuring "development' in terms of GNP, per-capita income, the balance of payments, industrialization, and similar indices— a concept that had generally been accepted during the 1960's by most Latin American governments and bourgeois economists—was highly criticized in *Excelsior*. Linked with these criticisms were editorials, special essays, and articles that analyzed the concept of the "consumer society" in general and the role Mexican television and radio played in stimulating that type of society. Needless to say, the criticisms of Mexican television programs and the advertisements shown on them constituted a direct blow at the TNCs (since they are the basic economic support for this means of mass communication) and at the most internationally oriented sector of the Mexican capitalist class, which holds a monopoly over Mexican television transmissions.[94] It should also be

---

ing in 1973 to become General Director of COPARMEX, is but one example. See *Mexican-American Review*, Nov. 1977, p. 23; *ibid.*, Sept. 1973, p. 52. Of AMCHAM's 2,236 members in 1976, well over half were Mexican corporations.

94. TNCs indirectly control Mexican television through their sponsorship of the programs offered. They thus transmit the ideology of the capitalist system, and their profits naturally depend in part upon their use of this means of mass communi-

noted that the criticisms of Mexican television and radio appearing in the pages of *Excelsior* were not the exclusive creations of the editors but even came from important Mexican government officials.[95] Thus the action taken against *Excelsior* represented an attempt to interfere not only with a legitimate means of communication but with the policies of the Mexican government itself.

In the early 1970's, *Excelsior* also gave wide support and ample coverage to the socialist experiments in Latin America and the rest of the world. Nonetheless, its content and style were hardly such that one would be warranted in classifying it as a "Marxist" or socialist newspaper; rather, one might say, in a word, that *Excelsior* was a *liberal* newspaper. But when a newspaper with such wide circulation (in 1973 the daily circulation was approximately 160,000; the Sunday, 170,000) criticizes the TNCs and the system they form part of, it definitely constitutes a means for creating awareness of the "real world" and for stimulating further development of consciousness of the ongoing class struggle. This type of consciousness is indeed *essential* for bringing about social change, since it at least represents doubt—a questioning of the system in which one lives—and opens up the possibility of receptiveness to ideologies antagonistic to that of the internationally dominant class. Thus *Excelsior* represented a threat to the interests of the TNCs in the early 1970's, just as it did to those of the Mexican government in 1976, when the government forced the editorial staff to resign.[96]

---

cation. In Mexico the TNCs are closely linked with the most internationally oriented sector of the Mexican bourgeoisie, which monopolizes this medium. See Enrique González Pedrero et al., "El Caso de México," in *El Estado y la Televisión,* in *Nueva Política,* 1, no. 3 (Jul.–Sept. 1976), pp. 186–266.

95. For examples of criticisms of television and radio made by government officials, see *Excelsior,* Jun. 29, 1972, pp. 7, 5: "Moya: Radio and T.V. no han asumido su responabilidad" (Moya Palencia was Minister of the Interior at the time); and *Excelsior,* Jun. 28, 1972, pp. 1, 10, 14, 16; "Deforma la Educación las series de Radio y T.V.: Méndez Docurro" (Minister of Communications and Transportation). Also see the statements made by Bravo Ahuja, Minister of Education, which appeared on pp. 1 and 15 of *Excelsior,* Jun. 30, 1972 in "Apoya B. Ahúja a Moya y Docurro en Lo Dicho de T.V."

96. When President Echeverría's government itself was highly criticized in the paper, the very editorial staff responsible for the ideological orientation during the early 1970's was forced to resign. See Sergio de la Peña, "Un Sexenio de Lucha de Clases en México," *Historia y Sociedad,* no. 10 (Mexico City: Editorial Juan Pablos, 1976), p. 44; Vicente Leñero, "El Atentado Contra *Excelsior,*" a 16-page pamphlet freely circulated without date or publisher; *idem.,* "Lo que ha occurrido en *Excelsior* desde el 8 junio de 1976," *Proceso,* 53 Nov. 7, 1977); Alan Riding, "Mexican Editor Ousted by Rebels," *The New York Times,* Jul. 9, 1977; *idem.,* "Paper in Mexico

The TNC campaign against *Excelsior*, which took place principally from January 1972 to March 1973, consisted of two almost simultaneous actions: a flood of literature sent out to business firms, at least in the Mexico City vicinity; and a defamatory campaign on radio and television.[97] Although the general purpose of this campaign was aimed at forcing *Excelsior* into bankruptcy, each part had certain specific purposes.[98] The literature campaign, which consisted of letters, articles pamphlets, and books, was initially aimed at convincing corporations to suspend their ads in *Excelsior* by undermining the image of the newspaper and its editors, and by creating panic among businessmen. Letters, articles, and pamphlets came first (from February to December of 1972), followed by more pamphlets and two books (from December 1972 to at least August 1974). These materials were always written in vulgar, calumnious, inciting, and insidious language. The campaign on radio and television was aimed directly at destroying the public image of the editors and the newspaper, but indirectly, too—through criticizing the issues dealt with in *Excelsior*—at creating a negative public image of the Echeverría government and the liberal wing of the Church.

There are several aspects of the printed campaign that should be noted. First, the campaign urging businessmen to boycott advertising in *Excelsior* was based on two principal arguments: one was that *Excelsior* was a communist newspaper dedicated to undermining the very system of freedom and individual liberty that the free enterprise system stood for, and that therefore it should not be financially supported by private corporations; the other was that *Excelsior* was not an adequate medium for advertising since it was negative and depressing in tone.[99] As an example of the type of literature used in the campaign, I include here a brief section of the first letter sent out, dated February 1, 1972.

Ends Liberal Tone," *ibid.*, Aug. 22, 1977, p. 6; *idem.*, "Liberal Editor in Mexico Begins New Magazine and Criticizes President Despite Pressure from Government," *ibid.*, Nov. 7, 1976, p. 11; Heberto Castillo, "La Batalla de *Excelsior*—Lucha por la Libertad," *Excelsior*, Jul. 8, 1976, p. 7; and Fátima Fernández Chrislieb, "Un Punto de Vista: la Prensa Mexicana y su relación con el gobierno," in the Cultural Section of *Uno-Más Uno*, "*Sabado*", Feb. 17, 1977, p. 10.

97. For this study I had access to seven three-page letters that apparently represented all the letter types used in the campaign. My information on the television and radio campaign came basically from personal interviews: with an editor of *Excelsior* in 1973, with two former editors in 1977 and 1978, and with a prominent figure in Mexican television who directs several programs each week.

98. This was made clear from the publications by José Luis Franco Guerrero called "Las Malévolas Noticias de *Excelsior*," which formed part of the campaign (dated Oct. 28, 1972; Nov. 12, 1972; Nov. 27, 1972; Dec. 16, 1972; and Dec. 25, 1972).

99. Letters dated Feb. 1, 1972; Feb. 23, 1972; May 16, 1972; Jun. 16, 1972; Jul. 7, 1972; Sept. 5, 1972; Sept. 13, 1972.

Dear Sir:

We know that you are a frequent advertiser in *Excelsior*, and that you are because you are convinced that the ads you take out in that newspaper are favorable for your business. This is not really true. You are contributing to the support of a newspaper that has as its principal goal the creation of a favorable environment for the establishment of a socialist regime. Of course, in that type of society, the first enterprises that will be on the list for confiscations, expropriations, and nationalizations will be the very companies now supporting *Excelsior*.

We will tell you why: The people who now manage this newspaper are doing it with political ends in mind. Their purpose, which has been subtly covered up, is to impose upon our country a government that will destroy private property, national and foreign investments, individual freedoms, free enterprise, and in fact everything.[100]

This first part of the campaign was successful, since many important international and national firm, banks, and business organizations did suspend their ads *en masse* on August 31, 1972.[101] Although some corporations continued to advertise in *Excelsior* until a later date, the bulk of the advertising on which the newspaper depended for its income was suspended from August 31 until the second or third week of December, at which point all regular advertisers except Sears Roebuck renewed their ads (Sears did not renew its ads until June 1973).[102] As a result of the suspension, *Excelsior* lost approximately 100,000 pesos per day—overall, a loss of some 10,000,000 pesos (roughly $800,000). For a newspaper that in 1973 brought in about 20,000,000 pesos in revenue monthly and spent between 17,000,000 and 18,000,000, a monthly reduction of 3,000,000 pesos in revenue obviously represented a significant loss.[103] The repercussions of that loss over an extended period could realistically have brought about the collapse of the newspaper. However, this did not happen for two reasons: *Excelsior* had its own print shop, which had just begun to do commercial printing of graphic arts, and this brought in additional income; and the Mexican government helped the newspaper in two ways. First, state-controlled corporations, such as

100. Letter dated Feb. 1, 1972 (my translation).
101. Interview with an *Excelsior* editor, July 1973; the letter of Sept. 5, 1972, stated clearly that some firms had suspended their ads. Among them were Sears Roebuck, Viana y Cía., Paris-Londres, El Palacio de Hierro, El Puerto de Liverpool, Hnos. Vázquez, Salinas y Rochas, and some banks.
102. The evidence here is based on my own reading of *Excelsior* from August 1972 to June 1973, and on an interview with an *Excelsior* editor in July 1973.
103. Interview with an *Excelsior* editor, July 1973. Also see Franco Guerrero, "Las Malévolas Noticias de *Excelsior*," Dec. 25, 1972, pp. 2–4, where the loss is referred to without exact figures.

Dina Renault, Nacional Hotelera, and Vam (Rambler vehicles), did not suspend their ads; and second, Mexican government financing institutions, such as SOMEX (Mexican Society of Industrial Credit), took out what can be considered excessive advertising. These institutions paid the full rate for their ads instead of the discount rate the regular customers paid.[104] In addition, some Mexican capitalists not directly linked with international capital decided to show open support of the government by siding with it in its efforts to help *Excelsior* financially. One example was the full-page ad taken by the Compañía Alimenticia "Del Centro" on September 14, 1972, from which the following excerpt has been translated:

> Present, Mr. President
>
> . . .
>
> Present with our food industry
> One hundred percent Mexican capital,
> financing, and technology.[105]

It should be noted that once the customary ads were renewed, SOMEX and other government financial institutions reduced their advertising.

All of my research indicates that the anti-*Excelsior* campaign was essentially organized by U.S. subsidiaries in Mexico, which counted upon the support of certain sectors of the Mexican bourgeoisie and reactionary elements in the Church. The facts that have led me to this conclusion are the following. First, among the literature sent out to business firms urging those that had not yet decided to boycott *Excelsior* to do so, the September 5, 1972, letter openly stated that the decision to suspend ads had originally been taken by a large group of business firms such as El Palacio de Hierro, El Puerto de Liverpool, Viana y Cía., Hermanos Vázquez, Sears Roebuck (of the Dupont group), and Aurrerá (of A&P). Moreover, the letter stated emphatically that the decision had been taken by the executive directors of the firms involved *as a joint decision* in a meeting where all had been present. It also mentioned that a prominent Mexican banker had taken part in the discussions and had urged that the decision to suspend the ads be accepted. In other words, the original plan for the anti-*Excelsior* campaign was a joint decision taken by the U.S. and Mexican bourgeoisies sometime immediately before February 1, 1972—the date when the very first letter was sent. Second, the degree of participation of U.S. corporations in the campaign

104. Interviews with *Excelsior* editor, July 1973, and Aug. 1977, when he had been expelled.
105. *Excelsior*, Sept. 14, 1972, p. 20.

was clearly pointed out by an executive of an important U.S. TNC that did not suspend its ads in *Excelsior* during the boycott. This executive stated that, owing to the refusal of his company's executives to join the boycott, pressure had been exerted on the company both in Mexico and at the U.S. home office by other U.S. corporations that had subsidiaries in Mexico. He explained that it was not until the home office was convinced of the political implications of the boycott that it accepted the independent policy adopted by its Mexican subsidiary at the instigation of its Mexican executives.[106] That the boycott organizers had actually been able to exert influence on the U.S. home office of one of the dissident firms is a clear indication that U.S. corporations played a significant role in the organization of the entire campaign. Small Mexican firms could not have had such influence over TNCs.

There is also sufficient evidence to indicate that AMCHAM was one of the principal organizers of this "concerted action." For one thing, Sears Roebuck (of the Dupont group) was one of the original companies to take the joint decision to organize the suspension of ads; as we have seen, Sears did not renew its ads until much later than the rest of the regular advertisers. Frank Loretta, AMCHAM president during the 1972–73 period, was and is an executive of Dupont; coincidentally, during the campaign he remained in office for an extended period, breaking the customary AMCHAM policy of changing presidents annually. More important, we know that Mr. Loretta himself, while president of AMCHAM, did exert verbal pressure on at least one important U.S. TNC when it showed prolonged indecision about whether or not to join the boycott.[107]

After the conclusion of the first phase of the written side of the anti-*Excelsior* campaign, which came about with the end of the advertising boycott in December 1972, we have no certain evidence that TNCs and AMCHAM continued to be directly involved. Of course, a content analysis of the letters and pamphlets sent during both phases clearly shows that there was a central source behind them. Also, the book *El Excelsior de Scherer*, one of the two that formed part of the second phase of the printed campaign, is written in a language similar to that of the pamphlets. Despite the fact that these coincidences suggest the

106. Interviews in June 1973 and Oct. 1977 with an important executive of one of the dissident TNCs. This Mexican executive maintained that *Excelsior* was clearly not a Marxist newspaper and that it was indeed one of Mexico's most important newspapers, as well as one of the best sources for advertising.

107. Personal interview with an executive of one of the undecided firms, Sept. 1977. Mr. Loretta urged executives of that firm to suspend the company's ads, stating that *Excelsior* was a communist newspaper.

same source for the entire literature campaign, we cannot say with certainty that the international bourgeoisie and AMCHAM continued to be involved once the ads were renewed in *Excelsior* in December 1972.[108]

The radio and television campaign against *Excelsior* took place basically from May 1972 until about March 1973. This segment of the larger anti-*Excelsior* campaign was clearly organized to retaliate against the criticisms of the mass media and of advertising presented in the paper during the first years of Echeverría's term. The form this retaliation took was, first, a refusal to accept any advertising for *Excelsior* on all the Mexican radio and television stations, and, second, an active media campaign to criticize the contents, editors, and editorial policy of *Excelsior*.[109] Condemnatory interviews with ex-members of *Excelsior*'s cooperative were filmed and shown from time to time on different programs. One prominent television commentator explained, in a personal interview, that he had had to dedicate two programs to the anti-*Excelsior* campaign or lose his job. Like the written part of the campaign, the broadcast undoubtedly required a significant amount of financial support, as well as planning and central organization. Once again the question is: Who organized these activities?

The answer is both the national and the international bourgeoisies—specifically a sector of the Mexican National Radio and Communications Chamber (Telesistema Mexicano) in collaboration with many of the TNCs and national organizations.[110] Telesistema (now Televisa) is a Mexican monopoly composed of channels 2, 4, and 5 (and as of this writing also 8) that is tightly linked with the international bourgeoisie. In order to create a negative image of *Excelsior* with the obvious intention of reducing its readership, but also in order to reduce the credibility of the nationalist and Third World policies of the Echeverría regime, this consortium used its channels as a forum for some of the ex-

108. It is interesting that even liberal thinkers such as Daniel Cosío Villegas were attacked in the overall anti-*Excelsior* campaign. One entire book mailed out widely in 1974 was dedicated to criticizing him: Leonicio Ibarra, *Danny el Sobrino del Tío Sam (Biopsia de un Cínico)* (Mexico City, 1974).

109. The impact of this strategy becomes clear when we remember that Mexican newspapers customarily advertise on radio and television. During the boycott of *Excelsior* ads, only derogatory comments about the paper and its editors were permitted on the air. Sources: Interviews with an *Excelsior* editor and with a television commentator in July 1973.

110. Information from an *Excelsior* editor (1973, 1977) and a prominent television commentator in July 1973. See Juan Závala Echeverría, "Sobre el Asalto a Excelsior," *Estudios Políticos*, 2, no. 7 (Jul.–Sept. 1976), pp. 123–26; and Patricio Marcos, "Un Golpe de Mano Televisivo," *Estudios Políticos*, 2, no. 6 (Apr.–Jun. 1976), pp. 105–9.

cooperativists who opposed the editors of *Excelsior*. Of course, behind Telesistema's decision to undertake this campaign were the foreign corporations and their Mexican partners, who together sponsor the majority of programs shown on Mexican television. It should be noted that the nucleus of these television sponsors included some of the very firms that had suspended their ads in *Excelsior* from August to December 1972.[111]

The importance of the broadcast part of the campaign can only be grasped if we remember that one of the most overt and effective ways TNCs influence the psychology of individuals in a host nation is precisely through its use of mass communications, especially television. Through these means, TNCs attempt to build the "happy consciousness" (or the "consumer ideology") in dependent nations and thus to guarantee the state of dependency necessary for maximizing global profits.[112]

In conclusion, there can be no doubt that the anti-*Excelsior* campaign in its totality formed part of that "vigorous defense coupled with constructive countermeasures" aimed to educate and "pacify the antagonists" which AMCHAM decided to adopt in 1972 in response to the "growing challenges of the times" (socialism and nationalism) and which required the intensification of the work of the capitalist class in the ideological sphere of the class struggle.

CONCLUSIONS

In the past, foreign investors were openly supported by foreign armies. In recent history, as the cases of Guatemala (1954), Cuba (1961), Santo Domingo (1965), and Chile (1973) illustrate, arms are still resorted to, especially when the contradictions within dependent capitalist countries become acute and the expansion of TNCs is significantly threatened; however, in general, optimum capital expansion depends not on military intervention but rather on the existence of a favorable investment climate, an attitude of consumerism, and an acceptance of

---

111. In addition to sponsoring programs, TNCs have invested in the Mexican television system itself. See Armando Mattelart, *La Cultura como Empresa Multinacional* (2d edition; Mexico City: Ediciones Era, 1976), p. 68.

112. There is a huge amount of literature on the effects of television on the psyche and, consequently, on ideology. For basic reading, see T. Adorno et al., *El Estado y la Television*; Mattelart, *La Cultura*; Ludovico Silva, *Teoria y Práctica de la Ideología* (Mexico City, 1974); and Jesús M. Martínez, "Para Entender los Medios: Medios de Comunicación y Relaciones Sociales," in R. Echeverría et al., *Ideología y Medios de Comunicación* (Buenos Aires: Amorrortu, 1973).

foreign investment in dependent capitalist countries.[113] In order to
guarantee these conditions, modern capitalism requires the existence of
a docile and politically uneducated labor class. As a Del Monte vice-
president, William Druel, clearly pointed out: " 'the countries have to
remain competitive if Del Monte is to stay,' and 'labor is one of the
main factors that has to be kept under control.' "[114] Keeping labor under
control means not only pressuring the state apparatus of dependent
capitalist countries to control strikes, labor protests, and demands for
salary increases but also controlling the growth of dissident ideologies.
In other words, until working class unification takes place, making
foreign military intervention necessary, TNCs will engage in a constant struggle on the ideological level to secure acceptance of the international capitalist ideology among both certain sectors of the local
bourgeoisie and the working class of dependent capitalist countries.
As Seymour Deitchman stated so succinctly: "proper use of 'nonma-
terial' tools represented by sound knowledge and actions in the nonmilitary sphere can obviate the need to involve large military forces."[115]

Without a doubt, the results of this Mexican case study support the
foregoing analysis of the nature of contemporary capitalism. In fact,
this paper has pointed out many of the nonmilitary policies, programs,
and tactics that TNCs (independently or in collaboration with their
spokesman, AMCHAM) have undertaken in order to strengthen the
capitalist class in Mexico and to limit the receptivity of the Mexican
population to antagonistic ideologies. We have seen that as the contradictions within Mexico became more apparent—as it became increasingly evident that TNCs had not been able to solve the grave
problems of unemployment, underemployment, social inequalities, ignorance, and misery in the country, and as Mexicans began to recognize
this situation—the TNCs and AMCHAM intensified their activities in
the ideological class struggle. It became imperative to attempt to eliminate those sources of conflict that might reveal the real impossibility of
TNCs to solve the problems of dependent capitalist countries such as

113. "The Central Strategy of the Global Corporation is the creation of a global
economic environment that will ensure stability, expansion, and high profits for the
planetary enterprise. The implementation of that strategy depends upon the control
of three basic components of corporate power: financial capital, technology, and
marketplace ideology." This was summarized by Barnet and Muller, Global Reach,
pp. 152, 172–84.
114. NACLA, "Bitter Fruits," Latin America and Empire Report, 10, no. 7 (Mar.
1977), p. 13.
115. Quoted in John Saxe-Fernández, "From Counterinsurgency to Counterintelligence," in Cotler and Fagen, eds., Latin America and the United States, p. 358.

Mexico.[116] In their attempt to keep the Mexican population in ignorance of the gross negative effects of TNCs on the economic and social conditions in the country, these corporations attempted to exercise their influence over the mass media, the educational system, and the working class. Indeed, the campaign to silence *Excelsior* is particularly illustrative of the tactics TNCs use to keep any type of criticism of the capitalist system from circulating among a broad public. Likewise, the Ford school-building program and the support of Dr. Osborne at UNAM point up the extent to which these corporations and AMCHAM try to influence the ideological orientation of the educational system. Finally, the programs sponsored under FOREM are clear examples of the type of activities TNCs have designed to transmit the capitalist ideology and the private enterprise system to the working class of Mexico in order to lessen its potential combativeness.

This paper has also illustrated a tendency that has been manifested in Mexico at least since the Mexican Revolution: the intensification of the attempts by TNCs to intervene both in the political sphere (as pressure groups) and in the ideological sphere (as producers and distributors of their particular interpretation of the capitalist ideology) when nationalist economic policies are under consideration or have been adopted. In other words, pressures will be intensified even when nationalist capitalism is stressed, or when the state attempts to modify some of the "rules of the game" by restricting investment or reinvestment, or by attempting to control the appropriation of profits.

Needless to say, the attempts to generate a favorable climate for foreign investment and to control the development of revolutionary ideologies are not exclusive to Mexico. The policies and programs of the TNCs and AMCHAM in Mexico form part of the global policies of American Chambers of Commerce and find theoretical support in the *Powell Memorandum*, which spells out the general strategy for private enterprises in organizing the capitalist class itself and in combatting the expansion of Marxist and socialist ideologies within society.

It is also worth stressing that the political and ideological struggles of the foreign investors and AMCHAM have been closely linked with U.S. foreign policy as it has been manifested in Mexico. Close ties have

---

116. For studies pointing out the limitations of TNCs in dependent capitalist countries, see Irma Adelman and Cynthia Taft Morris, *Economic Growth and Social Equity in Developing Countries* (Stanford, Calif., 1973); Barnet and Muller, pp. 123–84; and F. Fajnzylber and T. Martínez Tarrago, *Las Empresas Transnacionales—Expansión a Nivel Mundial y Proyección en la Industria Mexicana* (Mexico City: Fondo de Cultura Económica, 1976).

always existed between U.S. investors and the Department of State, and this paper has given some examples of those ties—e.g., the fact that the honorary president of AMCHAM has traditionally been the U.S. Ambassador in Mexico. Moreover, we saw a particularly good example of coordinated action in the top-echelon meeting in Acapulco between AMCHAM officials and the U.S. Ambassador in response to the nationalist policies of the Echeverría government.

Although the data presented in this paper have not included many important sources of U.S. government support for the TNCs in their ideological struggle in dependent capitalist countries, one should definitely recall that the private sector's work is constantly being complemented by the U.S. government through its embassies and its policies of counterinsurgency and counterrevolution. In addition, direct ideological support for private investment comes from the United States Information Agency (USIA). One of the principal roles of the USIA is to create a favorable image of the United States in the eyes of foreigners, and this favorable image includes the transmission of the private-enterprise system and its ideology as the basis of the U.S. way of life.[117] Among other organizations forming part of the mechanism for fulfilling U.S. foreign policy one finds the AID, the FBI, the CIA, and the Peace Corps, all of which help to coordinate the activities of both the local and the international bourgeoisies in their attempts to control the working class in dependent capitalist countries. It should be clear that all these organizations are involved in transmitting the capitalist ideology and in reducing the possibilities for growth of revolutionary ideologies and organizations.[118] As for the policies of counterinsurgency and counterrevolution—fundamental aspects of contemporary U.S. national security policy—they include not only military and police training for members of dependent capitalist countries, but also economic aid and ideological indoctrination.[119] Without a doubt, then, the private sector

117. Fátima Fernández Chrislieb, "Imperialismo y Medios de Información Colectiva en México," pp. 5–12.
118. NACLA, "El Aparato Contrarrevolucionario de los Estados Unidos: La Ofensiva en Chile," reprinted in *El Día*, Jan. 13, 14, 15, 1976; *idem.* "La Guerra Secreta" in *Simposio Barbados II, Movimientos de Liberación Indígena en América Latina*, published by Centro Antropológico de Documentación de América Latina (Barbados, 1977). For the FBI's activities in Mexico, see Fausto Fernández Ponte, articles on the first page of *Excelsior*, Dec. 1, 1977; Dec. 2, 1977; Nov. 30, 1977. For CIA activities in Mexico and other countries, see Philip Agee, *Inside the Company: CIA Diary* (New York, 1975).
119. John Saxe Fernández, "From Counterinsurgency to Counterintelligence," pp. 341–67; Octavio Ianni, "Imperialism and Diplomacy in Interamerican Relations," in Cotler and Fagen, eds., *ibid.*, pp. 23–51; William W. Whitson, ed., *Foreign Policy*

—TNCs and their spokesman abroad—does not carry out its ideological fight independently. Although at times its programs appear to contradict foreign policy, they are ultimately part of the incredible network that involves both private and public organizations in dependent capitalist countries and in the United States itself.

There is yet a further conclusion that may be drawn from this research: TNCs, AMCHAM, and U.S. government agencies in Mexico are not alone in their ideological struggle; indeed, they work along with certain sectors of the local bourgeoisie and even at times (as seems to be the case today) with the Mexican state itself. Naturally, I do not wish to give the impression that AMCHAM, TNCs, and U.S. government agencies are in total control over what happens in the ideological struggle in Mexico. Nor have I intended to affirm that all the centralized private initiative for combatting Marxist and socialist ideologies in that country necessarily originates in AMCHAM. Nonetheless, U.S. capitalist organizations in Mexico *do not only react* to what occurs there *but indeed initiate* policies designed to produce certain results.

In summary, then, the activities individual corporations undertake to give themselves the appearance of "good corporate citizens," and many of the programs and policies of AMCHAM-Mexico, do constitute a definite intervention in the internal affairs of Mexico. Although the type of intervention exercised today is but a variant on the historic role these institutions have played since they entered Mexico, that variant, which began during the postwar years and was intensified during the early 1970's, is far more penetrating than earlier traditional roles as pressure groups. This is so because intervention today also occurs in the terrain of the ideological struggle and is hence more subtle than the old form, since it attempts to control not only institutions or organizations but the very subconscious of the general population and the working class. And yet we may end on an optimistic note: history has shown that complete control of ideological growth is not possible, since human beings are engaged in the daily class struggle and therefore are always open to the possibility of rejecting the dominant ideology and replacing it with a revolutionary concept of the world—a precondition of social change. The road ahead is difficult, but not impossible.

and U.S. National Security (New York, 1976); Klaus Lindenberg, *La Función Política de las Fuerzas Armadas en América Latina* (Instituto Latinoamericano de Ciencias Sociales, Santiago, Chile, 1971).

Mexican Gas: The Northern Connection

RICHARD R. FAGEN AND HENRY R. NAU

Energy is a relatively new and potentially fundamental element in U.S.–Mexican relations. For the United States, on the one hand, energy remains a gnawing, unrelenting *problem*. By mid-1978, the United States was in its fifth year of the energy crisis but still without a domestic energy policy. For the new administration in Washington, this fact represented, as *The Economist* put it, "a major setback for Mr. Carter, who made energy legislation the centre piece of his efforts at home this year."[1] In the absence of a domestic energy policy, foreign oil imports soared, reaching 47 percent of total oil consumption in 1977 (up from 36 percent just four years earlier) and precipitating an unprecedented balance-of-payments deficit. More and more of this oil came from potentially insecure Arab OPEC (Organization of Petroleum Exporting Countries) sources.

For Mexico, on the other hand, energy suddenly became a potential *solution* to its serious economic and political difficulties. In the middle of 1976, Mexico was embroiled in its worst economic and—judging from fleeting rumors of a coup—political crisis in recent history. By the end of 1977, after one year of the new administration in Mexico City, the country had made what most international observers characterized as "important progress" toward economic and political stability.[2] The reason, at least in part, was the announcement of enormous new oil and gas reserves in the Chiapas-Tabasco region of southeastern Mexico.

The principal market for this oil and gas, if economic considerations alone prevail, is the United States. From the U.S. point of view, Mexico

Henry R. Nau is Associate Professor of Political Science at George Washington University in Washington, D.C. Among his publications is *Technology Transfer and U.S. Foreign Policy* (New York, 1976). We would particularly like to thank Professors Mario Ojeda and Trevor Farrell for their written comments on an earlier version of this paper. The Rockefeller Foundation, through a fellowship on International Conflict, supported Professor Fagen's research and writing; the George Washington University Committee on Research contributed to Professor Nau's work.

1. December 17, 1977, p. 35.
2. See *Washington Post*, January 3, 1978.

is a relatively secure, non-OPEC source of foreign energy. And the United States, regardless of the course of its domestic energy politics, will remain heavily dependent on foreign imports for at least another decade.

Economic considerations alone, however, do not always prevail—at least not in the narrow sense of the term "economic." Energy is a profoundly political concern, and domestic issues on both sides of the border (as well as a host of international issues that are not directly energy-related) shape and condition policies and their outcomes. The initial phase of Mexico's "northern connection" well illustrates the continuing importance of this proposition.

The opening link in the potential U.S.–Mexican energy connection was the proposed export of Mexican natural gas to the U.S. border via an 800-mile pipeline from Chiapas. This issue broke on the U.S. and Mexican domestic scenes at a particularly critical and perhaps inopportune time. The United States was in the midst of a continuing and increasingly frustrating energy debate. Natural gas had suddenly taken center stage as a key tactical issue in the Congressional conference committee's consideration of a final compromise on a national energy bill. As the *New York Times* pointed out in December 1977,[3] the question of natural gas prices "is the pivot of the whole energy package. If a successful compromise can be struck on gas, then it appears likely that the Congressional conferees could quickly resolve their differences on the other major question outstanding . . . the oil equalization tax."

So it appeared in December 1977. At that moment a letter of intent, signed by the Mexican Government and six U.S. gas-transmission companies, to import Mexican gas at a price of $2.60 per thousand cubic feet (Mcf) was due to expire. The U.S. Government had yet to approve the sale. The Mexican price was pegged to world oil prices on the U.S. East Coast and was substantially above both the ceiling on natural-gas prices recommended in the Administration's energy proposals and the price of natural gas then imported from Canada. Not surprisingly, the Mexican gas connection got caught in the cross fire of the debate on U.S. natural gas and broader energy issues. At the same time, the Mexican authorities and especially the officials of the state-owned petroleum company, PEMEX, were banking (literally as well as figuratively) on Mexican energy resources priced at world levels to revive the Mexican economy and to restore the country's credit worthiness on world financial markets—a critical factor in Mexico's future development plans. So eager were they to initiate action that

3. Editorial, December 23, 1977.

they began construction of the gas pipeline even before a final arrangement on price had been reached with the U.S. Government. The story is, however, even more complicated than the above fragments suggest. The history of petroleum development in Mexico, long-standing aspects of the Mexican developmental crisis, the tangled web of U.S.–Mexican relations, the structure of U.S. banking and business interests in Mexico, and certain particularistic features of the gas-export project (known in Mexico as the *gasoducto*) are all involved. Although we shall not attempt a comprehensive airing of all of these factors, it should be borne in mind that all are relevant to an understanding of the significance of the northern connection for Mexico, for the United States, and for the relations between the two countries.[4]

THE U.S. ENERGY SCENE

Oil and gas currently supply 75 percent of U.S. energy consumption, up from 56 percent in 1950. The use of oil and gas increased as real costs for these fuels in the United States declined from 1950 to 1970—principally because of the price regulation of natural gas and the declining real prices for oil imports.[5] For various reasons, summarized below by Richard Mancke, natural-gas consumption grew more rapidly than oil consumption, rising from 12 percent of the total in 1945 to 33 percent in 1972:

The key to this Cinderella transformation was the steep reduction in the delivered price of natural gas because large new pipelines allowed even larger reductions in gas transmission costs. In addition to transportation economies, the switch to gas has been accelerated because relative to its principal competitors—coal and crude oil—its wellhead price was low, and it is an especially desirable fuel for processes where clean combustion is desirable.[6]

4. Because our research advantage lies north of the border, we have concentrated on the U.S. economic, political, and energy context rather than on the Mexican. We have, however, attempted at least to suggest what aspects of the Mexican reality have shaped and will continue to shape energy and other relations with the United States.

5. Between 1950 and 1970 real energy cost in the United States decreased by 28 percent. See *The National Energy Plan*, Government Printing Office, Washington, D.C., April 1, 1977, p. 2.

6. Richard B. Mancke, *The Failure of U.S. Energy Policy* (New York, 1974), pp. 106–7. On a per-capita-use basis, natural-gas consumption tripled from 1950 to 1975, while oil consumption increased by about 75 percent. Since 1972 natural-gas consumption has slipped back to 27 percent of the total, largely because of supply shortages. For this and other data used in this analysis, unless otherwise noted, see Federal Energy Administration, *Energy in Focus: Basic Data*, Washington, D.C., May, 1977.

Moreover, beginning in the 1950's, Supreme Court decisions forced the Federal Power Commission to regulate the wellhead price of natural gas shipped in *inter*state markets. This policy reinforced the price advantage of natural gas over other fuels in interstate markets, but also created an *intra*state market in which gas remained unregulated. As the price disparity between these two markets widened with the dramatic energy price increases of the 1970's, more and more gas was diverted to unregulated markets, creating curtailments of supply in interstate pipelines.

Low prices and dual markets encouraged the use of natural gas for less essential purposes (such as boiler fuel in industry, and electricity production by utilities) and attracted industrial users to intrastate markets, where producers preferred to sell at unregulated prices.[7] Today, almost 60 percent of all natural gas is consumed by industry and utilities, although other fuels could be substituted in most cases—the exceptions being natural gas for agriculture, fertilizer and other petrochemical feedstock. The other 40 percent is consumed in residential and commercial heating, where in the short run conversion to oil or other fuels is impractical.[8] A large number of the residential and commercial users reside in the Northeast and Midwest and are supplied by interstate pipelines. Since federal regulations give priority of pipeline supplies to homes, hospitals, and schools, curtailments in interstate pipelines affect the industrial consumers in these regions, and put them at an economic disadvantage compared with their more fortunate counterparts in gas-producing states. If the curtailments are severe enough, schools, offices, and even homes may be threatened, as, for example, when some schools and commercial offices were closed during the gas shortages in the winter of 1976–77. Many of the bread-and-butter aspects of natural-gas politics in the United States can be understood in terms of these regional differences.

Oil in the United States is used predominantly for transportation; in 1976 this sector accounted for 54 percent of all oil consumed. Forty percent alone went for motor gasoline, the consumption of which in fact increased from 1973 to 1977 (from 6.7 to 7.2 million barrels per day). Though transportation uses could be reduced by eliminating non-

7. As a result, after the major energy price hikes between 1973 and 1975, only 19 percent of all new gas-reserve additions was made available to the interstate market. A more recent estimate drops this figure to 13 percent. See *Washington Post*, January 25, 1978.

8. Synthetic gas is the only possible substitute and its price makes it noncompetitive in the short and medium run.

essential travel (car pooling, mass transportation, etc.), there are no short- or medium-term substitutes for gasoline.[9] Moreover, another 20 percent of oil consumption goes for home heating, where oil is also non-substitutable in the short term. Thus the greatest flexibility in both oil and gas consumption lies in the industrial and utility sectors. Even here, however, the prospects for rapid conversion to coal or nuclear power (as foreseen in the Carter Administration's energy plan) are constrained by financial as well as by environmental requirements.[10]

Given the increased consumption of oil and gas and the relative inflexibility of demand, what are the prospects for increased oil and gas production in the United States? Overall U.S. energy production has declined since 1972. Domestic oil production peaked in 1970 and natural-gas production in 1973. From 9.6 million barrels per day in 1970, oil production plummeted to 8.1 million barrels in 1976. Between 1973 and 1976, natural-gas production dropped from 22.6 to 19.9 trillion cubic feet. In 1977 the downward trends were modified. Oil production increased slightly to 8.2 million barrels per day, largely owing to the new influx of Alaskan oil. Gas production was roughly equal to 1976 levels.

Whether these trends could be further reversed, at least in the short and medium run, by higher prices paid at the wellhead continues to be debated. Suffice it to note here that from 1973 to 1976 average wellhead prices for crude oil in the United States increased by two-thirds, from $4.68 per barrel to $7.78 per barrel in current 1975 dollars. Similarly, from 1973 to 1975 wellhead prices for natural gas increased by more than two-thirds, from $0.26 to $0.445 per Mcf in current dollars. Partial deregulation in 1976 further tripled the wellhead price to $1.42 Mcf in current dollars. Despite these increases, oil and gas production have not risen.[11]

In the absence of domestic increases, oil imports have skyrocketed and gas imports have reached a critical stage, with several large and, in the case of liquefied natural gas, long-term import commitments pending decision in the near future. Table 1 shows increases in U.S. oil imports

9. Gasohol (alcohol mixed with gasoline) comes the closest and is attracting increasing attention in some circles. Substitution is limited, however—without major engine modifications—to 10–20 percent of total gasoline consumption.

10. For example, energy investments in the United States from 1973 to 1975 consumed 35 percent of all plant and equipment expenditures, compared with a 25–30 percent range before the energy crisis.

11. It may be too early to draw any final conclusions from these statistics. Lead times are lengthy in the development of new oil and gas resources and exploratory drilling, which has increased dramatically in recent years, could produce future production increases.

TABLE I

U.S. Oil Imports, 1970–77

Year	Total imports (mbbl/d)	Imports (Pct. of demand)	OPEC imports[a] (Pct. of total imports)	OAPEC imports[b] (Pct. of total imports)
1970	3.4	23.3%	37.8%	5.7%
1971	3.9	25.8	43.2	8.9
1972	4.7	29.0	43.6	11.2
1973	6.3	36.1	47.6	14.6
1974	6.1	36.8	53.3	12.2
1975	6.0	36.8	59.5	22.9
1976	7.3	42.0	67.2	32.1
1977[c]	8.7	47.0	70.3	35.4

SOURCE: FEA, *Energy in Focus: Basic Data*, May, 1977, p. 6.
[a] Excludes indirect imports. See Table 2.
[b] OAPEC is the Organization of Arab Petroleum Exporting Countries. This column excludes indirect imports also.
[c] 1977 data from *Monthly Energy Review*, Washington, D.C., May, 1978, pp. 12, 14–15.

(crude and product) from 1970 to 1977. Not only have these imports more than doubled, averaging 47 percent of total oil consumption in 1977, but more than two-thirds of the total now comes from OPEC sources (compared with lesss than one-half in 1973), and over one-third comes from the least secure sources, namely Arab OPEC (compared with 14.6 percent in 1973). This increasing dependence on OPEC suppliers reflects both an overall increase in demand and a reduction in imports from America's two traditional oil suppliers, Canada and Venezuela. As Table 2 shows, Canadian petroleum exports to the United States have declined since 1973 from 1.3 million to 514 thousand barrels per day, while Venezuelan exports have dropped from 1.6 million to 912 thousand barrels per day. In contrast, imports from the OPEC states of Nigeria and Saudi Arabia have nearly doubled (from 600–750 thousand to 1.2–1.5 million barrels per day), while imports have grown at similar rates though on a smaller base from other OPEC states (principally Algeria, Libya, Indonesia, U.A.E. and Iran). The sharp increases in imports in 1976 and 1977 suggest the accelerating import dependence faced by the United States as economic conditions returned to "normal" and domestic energy policies continued to drift.[12]

12. It should be noted that to some extent the 1977 increase was the result of

TABLE 2

U.S. Petroleum Imports by Source
(Thousands of barrels per day)

Source	1973	1974	1975	1976	1977
OPEC					
Algeria	151.2	207.1	288.2	438.3	564.2
Indonesia	237.7	340.9	437.7	569.4	570.3
Iran	433.7	731.0	524.8	546.5	786.4
Libya	308.3	40.3	329.3	529.3	838.0
Nigeria	607.9	912.2	837.8	1,119.2	1,229.7
Saudi Arabia	740.3	675.2	891.6	1,365.8	1,523.8
U.A.E.	83.6	87.8	154.2	323.3	446.4
Venezuela	1,633.7	1,457.8	1,030.1	972.2	911.6
Other ^{a}	194.5	217.0	259.3	216.0	378.1
Non-OPEC					
Canada	1,312.9	1,067.6	845.2	599.3	513.9

SOURCE: Monthly Energy Review, Washington, D.C., May, 1978, pp. 14–15.

NOTE: Includes direct and indirect imports. Indirect imports refer to U.S. imports of petroleum products, primarily from Caribbean and European areas, that have been refined from crude oil produced in other areas. U.S. imports of these products have been prorated to each OPEC country of origin, based on the share of total crude oil supply in the Caribbean and European areas that was imported from each OPEC country.

^{a} Includes Ecuador, Gabon, Iraq, Kuwait, and Qatar.

Gas imports have remained constant since 1973 at around 1 trillion cubic feet per year, less than 5 percent of total domestic consumption. If pricing and other factors continue to favor the use of natural gas, however, these imports could increase sharply in the future. Canada has supplied most of the U.S. natural-gas imports in the past but is unlikely to increase and will probably reduce these amounts in the future, in line with its general energy-conservation policies. Additional supplies are expected to come from the Alaskan fields, totaling about 0.8 trillion cubic feet per year,[13] and from several large imports of liquefied natural

---

commercial inventory buildup sparked by Saudi Arabia's increased production and lower export prices which reflected the price split in OPEC at the time. By the second half of 1977 there was a considerable surplus of oil on the world market.

13. The U.S. and Canadian governments signed an agreement in September 1977 authorizing construction of a 5,500 mile pipeline to carry this gas through Alaska and Canada to the U.S. Midwest. Financing, however, is yet to be arranged and is dependent in part on the outcome of the gas-price debate in the United States. Canada did announce in January 1978, that it might expand its gas exports to the

gas (LNG), averaging some 2 trillion cubic feet per year. None of these projects is due for completion before 1985, and all current LNG projects originate in OPEC countries—Algeria, Indonesia, and Iran. If approved, these projects alone could account for 20 percent or more of U.S. gas needs by 1985.[14]

A new factor in this picture of U.S. oil and gas requirements is the prospect of vastly increased oil and gas exports from Mexico, a non-OPEC country and bordering neighbor of the United States. If Mexican production plans are realized and U.S. markets become the principal recipient of enhanced production, gas exports to the United States could total 0.8 trillion cubic feet per year by 1982 (or the equivalent of gas deliveries from Alaska not expected until 1985). Additionally, oil exports could run as high as 1.1 million barrels per day by 1982 (or, according to recent Mexican announcements, by 1980)—i.e. about one-ninth of current U.S. oil import needs and one-sixth of these needs in 1985 as projected by the Carter Administration's extremely optimistic energy plan. Although these amounts will not provide a one-shot solution to this country's energy problems, they do suggest the enormous opportunities offered by the Mexican connection.

THE MEXICAN ENERGY SCENE

Mexican petroleum has a long history of conflict, and from an early stage this history has involved the United States. While Porfirio Díaz and his *científicos* reigned supreme in the late nineteenth and early twentieth centuries, significant exploration and drilling were already taking place. Commercial exploitation began in 1901 when over ten thousand barrels were produced in the state of San Luís Potosí. Mexican oil production was at first controlled primarily by British interests, but after the First World War U.S. interests became predominant. Even during the tumultuous years of the Mexican revolution, production kept increasing. When the Mexican Constitution was signed in 1917—with its famous Article 27 assuring state control of mineral and subsoil resources—production had already risen to over 125,000 barrels per day, most of which was exported to the United States.

United States by as much as 50 percent. But in return Canada would acquire the option to purchase Alaskan gas once the pipeline is completed. Thus the arrangement will result in an early consignment of Alaskan gas, not an increase in Canadian gas exports. See *Washington Post*, January 18, 1978.

14. See *Washington Post*, November 17, 1977.

During this same period, of course, the United States was making impressive gains in petroleum production. But demand was rising so rapidly north of the border—and so slowly south of the border—that by the early 1920's Mexico was the world's largest exporter of crude oil. Not surprisingly, given the geography and the involvement of U.S. oil companies in Mexican production, the majority of these exports went to the United States.

The relationship had never been as easy one, however, at least not since the Mexican revolution.[15] Production declined in the 1920's, and throughout the early 1930's recurrent tensions arose between the Mexican Government and Mexican workers, on the one hand, and the North American oil companies on the other. In 1937 these conflicts came to a head: Mexican oil workers struck for better wages and working conditions, and the Mexican Government under President Lázaro Cárdenas —rallying a very broadly based coalition under the banners of Mexican nationalism and subsoil rights—moved into the confrontation, finally nationalizing the industry on March 18, 1938. PEMEX, Petróleos Mexicanos, was born, the Mexicans were—or so it seemed—the owners of their oil, and the United States was inhibited from full retaliation by the pending struggle with the Axis and by various normative and political constraints deriving from President Roosevelt's Good Neighbor Policy. (Accustomed as we now are to nationalization of subsoil resources, the audacity of the Mexican action in the late 1930's should not pass unnoticed. Until that time, only the Soviet Union had nationalized its total hydrocarbon resources.)[16]

Boycotted by the oil multinationals, PEMEX began a vigorous program of export to the Axis countries. The transatlantic connection was, however, short-lived. Under pressure from the U.S. Government, a compensation formula was worked out; Mexico sided with the Allies, profited greatly from wartime demand for her products, and moved quickly into that stage of rapid aggregate industrial development known somewhat misleadingly as the "Mexican miracle."

Throughout the years of the greatest industrial, commercial, and agrarian expansion, Mexican petroleum production always managed to stay ahead of consumption. Despite low domestic prices for oil (which

15. For additional material see Lorenzo Meyer, *Mexico and the United States in the Oil Controversy, 1917–1942* (Austin, Tex., 1977). See also the brief historical section in George W. Grayson, "Mexico's Opportunity: The Oil Boom," *Foreign Policy*, no. 29, Winter 1977–78, pp. 67 ff.

16. Bolivia expropriated Standard Oil shortly before the Mexican expropriation. But as Meyer explains, the Bolivian action was less important in both its magnitude and its public policy implications. *Mexico and the United States*, p. 182.

encouraged its substitution for other fuels) and a cautious policy in oil exploration and development, the curves of domestic supply and demand did not cross until 1968. At that point Mexican imports exceeded exports, a situation that persisted until late 1974.[17]

During the early 1970's, cracks also began to appear in the Mexican developmental model. By the mid-1970's Mexico was a nation in which long-standing social conflicts were intensifying, domestic and international confidence was declining, and the overall legitimacy of the complex set of *compromisos* holding the state and civil society together were in danger of crumbling. World inflationary and recessionary pressures were buffeting an already shaky economy and peso, aggregate growth was precipitously down from its historic average of about 6 percent, inflation was rising, and the IMF was negotiating a classic austerity package with the beleaguered Echeverría Government.[18]

The growth of this beleaguerment was nowhere more evident than in the statistics on the external public debt. In 1973 the total debt stood at about 6.5 billion dollars. One year later it was over 10 billion, rising steadily over the next two years to about 20 billion. In addition, the terms under which Mexico was borrowing abroad hardened considerably during this period, with shorter maturity for loans and interest levels at the higher end of the market. When President López Portillo took office at the end of 1976, the then outstanding total of debt service

17. In September 1974, the dollar value of oil exports exceeded the dollar value of oil imports for the first time since 1968. The turnaround is documented (by volume) in the following tabulation:

	1973	1974	1975	1976	1977
Average daily production (1,000 bbls/day)					
Crude oil	452	575	717	800	981
Average daily exports (1,000 bbls/day)					
Crude oil	0	16	94	94	202
Refined products	24	18	7	3	5
Average daily imports (1,000 bbls/day)					
Crude oil	65	17	0	0	0
Refined products	65	45	50	22	10

SOURCE: PEMEX and IMF. See also Adrián Lajous Vargas and Víctor Villa, "El Sector Petrolero Mexicano, 1970–1977: Estadísticas Básicas," *Foro Internacional*, no. 72, vol. 18, April–June, 1978, pp. 747–82.

18. For more details on this period see Richard R. Fagen, "The Realities of U.S.– Mexican Relations," *Foreign Affairs*, vol. 55, no. 4, July, 1977, and Robert S. Drysdale, "What Mexico's President Inherited," *Worldview*, November, 1977.

that he faced in the first five years of his term (1977–81) amounted to
19 billion dollars in loan amortization and interest payments. Equally
formidable was the debt-service ratio, which had climbed steadily from
20 percent in 1974 to 34 percent by the end of 1976.[19]

It was in this general context that the final shocks of the Echeverría
Administration hit:

On August 31, 1976, in a move that caught many by surprise though it had
been talked about for many years the peso was devalued for the first time in
22 years. With the peso floating "like a stone" (according to a phrase often
bitterly repeated in Mexico City and elsewhere), multiple reactions and even
panic ensued. While Mexican and foreign dailies headlined "turmoil," "hysteria," and "crisis," as much as four billion dollars fled the country seeking
safe harbor in Texas banks and elsewhere. Investment slowed down, inflation
accelerated, unemployment rose, and the whole complex set of mechanisms
by which devaluation and resultant dislocations and hardships are passed
disproportionately on to the poorer sectors of society came into play. Twelve
days before leaving office, when Echeverría expropriated tens of thousands of
acres of prime land in the northern state of Sonora and turned them over as
small parcels to peasants, talk of a military coup was heard for the first time
in recent memory.[20]

Onto this scene strode President López Portillo, holding an olive
branch extended to both national and international critics of Echeverría
in one hand, and a hydrocarbon ace in the other. From the first cautious
mentions of Mexico's oil wealth in his inaugural address to the buoy-
ant suggestion eleven months later that Mexico's hydrocarbon reserves
might total 120 billion barrels, there was a steady campaign both at
home and abroad to use the oil and gas to restore confidence in Mexico's
future.[21]

In fact, spurred by rising imports and upward pressure on domestic
prices, PEMEX professionals had already been moving for a number of

19. All figures from IMF sources.
20. Fagen, "The Realities of U.S.–Mexican Relations," p. 694. "Although there
was never a consensus on who was supposed to 'do' the coup to whom, the predominant version was that Echeverría would use the armed forces to maintain himself in office." *Ibid.*
21. The primary spokesperson playing the hydrocarbon ace was the Director of
PEMEX, Jorge Díaz Serrano. He mentioned the 120-billion-barrel potential reserve
figure in a lengthy presentation to the Mexican Congress on October 26, 1977. In
his September 1, 1978, speech to the Mexican Congress, President López Portillo
upped the potential reserve figure to 200 billion barrels. It is important to bear in
mind the difference between potential and proven reserves. And since as much as
30 percent of Mexican reserves are gas and gas liquids, Mexico's potential oil reserves are still less than Saudi Arabia's proven oil reserves of 150 billion barrels.

years toward changes in Mexico's cautious exploration and development policies. Renewed exploration efforts undertaken during the Echeverría presidency had resulted in an increase in Mexico's proven petroleum reserves from 5.5 billion barrels at the end of 1973 to over 11 billion barrels by the time of López Portillo's inauguration. But it was the new president who came out of the closet, so to speak, with an aggressive campaign to tout Mexico's petroleum possibilities.[22]

Judging from the record of his first year in office, the official campaign was strikingly successful. In a matter of weeks after his inauguration, the word in international financial circles was that Mexico seemed to be back on the right track again. Credit eased—even though the real import earnings from oil were still years away—and in the fall of 1977, when the United States of Mexico (the central government) went in search of a 1.2-billion-dollar international loan, it was quickly oversubscribed—an unimaginable outcome except in the context of the predicted petroleum bonanza.[23]

The decision to push petroleum development and export was necessarily reflected in the new administration's initial programmatic announcements. By the end of January 1977, PEMEX had released a series of plans and budgets designed to make Mexico a major producer and exporter of hydrocarbons before López Portillo's six-year term was over. Based on a 15.5-billion-dollar budget for new capital investments for 1977–82, the program called for boosting oil production from less

22. There are many hypotheses about why the Echeverría Administration was so cautious in announcing new hydrocarbon finds. Among the most frequently mentioned are: (1) The president did not want to weaken the case for the much needed domestic reforms by suggesting that an oil boom was just around the corner; (2) Mexico did not want to become a pawn in U.S. attempts to beat down OPEC prices—making more difficult and potentially undercutting other Echeverrista Third World policies; (3) Pemex itself, guided by traditional *técnicos*, was following its longstanding conservative and nationalistic policies of supplying Mexico's hydrocarbon needs, but not developing an export potential. All of these hypotheses may, of course, reflect part of the truth.

23. In addition to the President and Díaz Serrano, the most visible international salesman for Mexico during this first year was Gustavo Romero Kolbeck, head of the Banco de Mexico (the central bank). See for example, "Kolbeck's road show: selling confidence in Mexico to the international banks," *Euromoney*, August, 1977, pp. 16–17. See also, "The great Mexican dream for a few barrels more," *Euromoney*, May, 1977, pp. 89–91, 93, and "Mexico: Everyone likes the professionals' touch," *Euromoney*, October, 1977, p. 83. The first major sign that the times were changing came in March 1977, when a 350-million-dollar PEMEX loan was "taken up enthusiastically" by the international banks (*ibid*). The restoration of confidence, of course, did not derive solely from the promise of massive hydrocarbon export earnings. At least as important was the López Portillo Government's apparent commitment to "sound fiscal management."

than 1 million to over 2.25 million barrels a day, increasing exports more than six-fold to include one-half of total production, and tripling petro-chemical output through the building of 66 new plants. At the then current prices, the export of crude and refined products alone was projected to earn almost 21 billion dollars, more than enough to cover all the capital investments planned.[24]

THE GASODUCTO

At the outset, PEMEX was relatively silent on the role to be played by natural gas, aside from its clear place as a feedstock in the soon-to-be-expanded petrochemical industry. Yet as oil exploration and development moved ahead, key decisions about the uses to which the natural gas would be put could not be avoided. The main reason was geological: the newly mapped Reforma (Chiapas-Tabasco) fields, the main source of supply causing the dramatic jump in proven reserves, promised or threatened to produce much more gas than Mexico could use domestically as either a fuel or a feedstock for petrochemicals, and more than could be pumped back into the ground to maintain pressure in the wells.[25] Gas-oil ratios in some wells were running as high as 6 to 7 thousand cubic feet per barrel of oil (cu. ft./bbl.), with an average of about 1,300. Originally, small surpluses were simply flared (burned off), but early in the year a massive export program for the additional gas came under consideration.

Natural gas, unlike oil, is not an easily stored or transported product. Either it must move overland through pipelines, or it must be liquefied by supercooling (condensing in volume by a factor of 600) and then shipped in specially contructed tankers. In the latter case, it must be regassified on arrival, once more to move through pipelines to its final destination. This liquefaction and regassification process is costly, po-

24. See the *Oil and Gas Journal*, February 7, 14, 28, and March 14, 1977 for more details. The capital investments programmed amounted to about one-third of PEMEX's (original) total budget for the 6 years.

25. In these fields the gas occurs in solution with the oil. If the latter is extracted, the former also surfaces. For more data see *Oil and Gas Journal*, June 27 and September 19, 1977. It should be emphasized that this line of argument and its implications, leading toward export to the United States, were not accepted by all sectors of Mexican opinion. For a left-nationalist critique see, for example, Heberto Castillo, "¡Cómo deseo estar equivocado!," *Proceso*, no. 48, October 3, 1977. See also Heberto Castillo and Rius, *Huele a Gas: Los Misterios del Gasoducto* (Mexico City, 1977) for a collection of critical articles by Castillo and cartoons by Rius and others.

tentially dangerous, and generally considered a process of last resort by producers and consumers alike.

In many cases (Algeria and Indonesia being prime examples), the decision to export natural gas automatically implies a decision to install liquefication plants. Geography and markets allow no other alternative. But in the case of Mexico, all roads lead "naturally" to the United States. Just as an export program was seen as essential, so a pipeline directly from the Reforma fields to the Texas border was seen as the only reasonable means of transport. The PEMEX case seemed compelling.

First there was a series of arguments, foreshadowed in the above discussion, about the lack of alternative uses for the gas. Even after an expanded petrochemical industry had been fed, all foreseeable domestic needs supplied, and millions of cubic feet pumped back into the ground to maintain the productivity of the fields, large quantities of gas would still be left over. The only way to prevent such large gas surpluses would be to curtail oil production drastically—clearly not an acceptable alternative. Flaring the surplus gas was a blatant waste of the national patrimony. It had to be captured and exported.[26]

At this point, the economic case for exporting this gas to the United States moved to center stage: to install the liquefication plants necessary to ship the projected quantities of surplus gas to overseas markets would cost between 7 and 8 billion dollars. Even if it were possible to raise capital in these amounts, the date of first exports would be delayed and earnings per 1,000 cubic feet of gas (Mcf) would be cut from approximately $2.20 (via pipeline) to 27 cents (LNG transactions with Europe). In other words, the same amount of gas exported as LNG would earn only about 12 percent as much as it would if exported via pipeline, according to these calculations.[27] These dramatic figures in favor of pipeline export were based of course on the expectation that a $2.60 per Mcf price could be negotiated with the United States. But even at a lower price, the financial advantage of export via pipeline was seen to be immense.

But the economic arguments in favor of the pipeline became even more compelling when viewed in more detail. At an estimated cost of 1.5 billion dollars and a building time of 24 months, the pipeline would

26. As noted below, these arguments subsequently came back to haunt PEMEX and the Mexican Government.

27. See Díaz Serrano's speech to the Mexican Congress on October 26, 1977, available in Mexico City daily newspapers as well as in a PEMEX pamphlet somewhat misleadingly entitled, "Linea Troncal Nacional de Distribución de Gas Natural."

begin to earn foreign exchange at the rate of 3.3 million dollars a day at the outset.[28] In effect, during the first year of operation the pipeline would bring in 1 billion dollars, a figure that would increase each year up to a maximum of 5.2 million dollars a day when the pipeline reached full capacity. In less than two years the pipeline would have more than paid for itself, and the foreign exchange earned over its first six years would top 10 billion dollars. As a potential contributor to Mexico's balance of payments, the pipeline seemed foolproof. As a project on which foreign private and public banks might wish to lend, it could hardly have been more attractive. Few projects promise to generate a stream of foreign earnings equal to their total cost in as short a period as the first 18 months of their active life.[29]

Although nationalistic voices were raised in Mexico against such a clear physical link with the United States, and although charges of "dependence" and "we will be at the mercy of the gringos" were heard in some forums, the momentum and power—both economic and political— of the PEMEX case (particularly in the context of the indebtedness and economic fragility mentioned earlier) seemed overwhelming. Thus, on October 7, 1977, construction was begun on the southernmost section of the *gasoducto*.[30] As of that date, no pricing agreement had been reached with the United States, no final route to the border had been set, and much of the financing was still under negotiation. But the Mexican Government was so anxious to begin the *gasoducto*, and so sure a satisfactory pricing agreement and all the necessary financing would be forthcoming, that the order was given to begin construction.

ALLIANCES: MARKETS, TECHNOLOGY, CAPITAL, AND PRICE

To begin construction at that point was not as reckless or precipitous an act as it might seem at first glance. On the contrary, it made good sense, given the strength of the international alliance of oil exploration and development firms, gas-transmission companies, capital-goods suppliers, bankers, and Mexican interests *al favor del gasoducto* that had by that time been forged. Although some imperfections in the alliance re-

---

28. Calculated at a daily volume of 1.3 billion cu. ft./day during the first year of operation and at a price of $2.60 per Mcf.

29. These calculations do not take into account the additional investment needed to process (sweeten) the gas before it is transmitted. Even if these investments were included, however, the return-on-investment figures would still be very impressive.

30. The start of construction was announced by Díaz Serrano to the Mexican Congress on October 26, 1977.

mained, and although critical voices both north and south of the border were still to be heard, the interests pushing the pipeline were impressive in their weight and coherence.

To understand this alliance, it is necessary to go back at least as far as the first days of the López Portillo Administration, that is, to the beginning of 1977.[31] The tumult of the inauguration was hardly over when PEMEX contracted the Dallas mineral-evaluation firm of De-Golyer and MacNaughten to cooperate in both the verification of recent Mexican hydrocarbon finds and the elaboration of development and export plans for the Mexican petroleum industry. It was a shrewd and in one sense a daring move. Shrewd, because DeGolyer and Mac-Naughten is world famous and respected in its specialty and thus highly credible to many who might otherwise take PEMEX's data with more than a grain of salt.[32] Daring, because to call in a U.S. firm to play such a prominent, early role in the most sensitive of all Mexican industries risked incurring the wrath of local nationalists—as well as the wrath of various opponents of the López Portillo Administration. But the gamble clearly paid off, for not only were few voices raised in protest at home, but the claim that Mexico now possessed new increments of proven reserves and very high levels of probable and potential reserves was almost everywhere and immediately accepted as honest—within the limits of probability that always attach to such estimates.

DeGolyer and MacNaughten was, however, only the advance guard of a small legion of U.S. firms that were soon to beat a path to Mexico City and PEMEX's door. The exact number of hydrocarbon pilgrims to Mexico City—and conversely, PEMEX pilgrims to Texas—during 1977 is known only to certain Mexican officials, but the contacts were extensive. For example, between February and July the president and high officials of Tennessee Gas Transmission (also known as Tenneco Inter-America Inc.) met the top officials of PEMEX, including Díaz Serrano[33]

31. The other sources cited in this and in the following section have been amplified by information gathered in interviews with high officials of the banking and petroleum communities in New York, Dallas, and Houston during late October and early November 1977.

32. DeGolyer's credibility is enhanced by a company policy insisting that the firm act only as consultant. Equity involvement of any sort in mineral exploitation, development, or shipment is prohibited.

33. Tenneco InterAmerica Inc. is the leading member of the six-company consortium that was attempting to buy and distribute the gas in the United States. The other members of the consortium are Texas Eastern Transmission, El Paso Natural Gas, Transcontinental Gas Pipeline, Southern Natural Gas, and Florida Gas Transmission. The consortium is known as "Border Gas." Data on its meetings with PEMEX come from the Tenneco InterAmerica filings with the Federal Energy Regulatory Commission, Washington, D.C.

no fewer than ten times (usually for two to three days) in Houston or
Mexico City. It was during this period that the main outlines of the
natural-gas deal with the United States were sketched out. On August
2 and 3, the representatives of all six U.S. gas-transmission companies
involved met PEMEX in Mexico City to sign the Memorandum of Intentions, which formalized the understanding that had already been
reached, including a mutually agreed-upon purchase price of $2.60
per Mcf.

Needless to say, a marketing agreement, however firm, is only one
small aspect of an undertaking as mammoth and potentially important
as the *gasoducto*. The design and engineering of the project loomed
large from the very beginning. DeGolyer and MacNaughten cooperated
continuously with PEMEX on all phases of this, and Tenneco Inter-
America also prepared an extensive study for PEMEX, which covered
everything from routing to technological requirements.[34] Multiple con-
sultants and potential bidders were called in. One U.S. firm even went
so far as to suggest that much of the pipeline ought to be laid offshore
in shallow water—hardly a disinterested suggestion since this firm is a
world leader in the relevant technology. The offshore argument was
that, although the pipeline would be more expensive at the construction
stage, it would be finished more rapidly and thus begin to earn foreign
exchange earlier.

By the middle of 1977, despite still unresolved questions and details,
the plans for the construction of the pipeline had taken shape. It was
to be a 48-inch line, beginning in the oil town of Cactus in the state of
Chiapas and running northward some 800 miles, roughly parallel to the
Gulf Coast, to the city of Reynosa, just south of the Texas border.
Initially planned with four compressor stations, it would have a first-
year capacity of 1.3 billion cubic feet of gas per day, almost doubling
in the next six years as more gas became available and more compressors
were added. In the absence of a pricing agreement with the United
States, the final route of the *gasoducto* was announced only to the northern town of San Fernando, from which a spur would link it with an
existing east-west pipeline serving the large northern Mexico industrial
city of Monterrey. At this point, the spur was largely a bone thrown to
nationalist sentiment, for the overall design of the main line made it

34. The Tenneco InterAmerica study for PEMEX was very broadly gauged,
covering Mexico's energy needs to the year 2000, world supply and demand, etc. It
concentrated, not surprisingly, on the rationale for and possibilities of exporting
natural gas.

clear that the *gasoducto* was primarily an export facility, not an addition to the existing national gas-transmission system.[35]

Although the pipeline does not cross particularly difficult terrain and although climatic conditions are not particularly harsh, the scale of the entire undertaking and the technology involved are impressive. The largest-diameter gas-transmission line now existing in the United States is 42 inches. In fact, until 1977, no steel mill in the United States could even produce 48-inch pipe. (The 48-inch pipe used in the Alaska oil pipeline was all imported; the *gasoducto* will require approximately 700,000 tons of pipe.) A length or "joint" of big pipe is 36 feet, and at times two joints are welded together before being laid. Obviously very heavy equipment is required to handle such operations. About 125 miles of the route cross swampy land. There the pipe must be blanketed in concrete so that it will not float on surface water, since natural gas, unlike crude oil, adds very little to the weight of the hollow pipe. The compressor stations needed to maintain line pressure are run by large gas turbines, and much additional equipment and technology are required to remove the sulfur (called "sweetening") and the liquids from the gas before it is pumped into the pipeline.[36]

Besides the pipe, capital goods, and technology that must be imported into Mexico to build the pipeline, a significant degree of expertise is called for. Although by law PEMEX must use Mexican contractors for the actual construction process, joint ventures and service agreements with foreign firms are permitted.[37] Fresh from the rigors and experience of building the Alaska pipeline and tied by geography and history to the large Mexican construction firms, it is thus not surprising that North American firms were the primary if not the only foreign associates involved in the initial stages of pipeline engineering and construction. In fact, early in the design phase, Tenneco InterAmerica signed an engi-

35. Tightrope-walking at the edge of the truth, López Portillo described the routing as follows in his first State of the Nation address on September 1, 1977: "We have decided to construct a pipeline that will go from Cactus, Chiapas, to Monterrey, with a branch that will go to Chihuahua and eventually loop back to the capital. Also, it will have another branch that will go to Reynosa for exporting to the United States."

36. An American company, Elcon, is fabricating two of the gas processing plants that will be installed by PEMEX.

37. Left critics of PEMEX in Mexico point out that the *gasoducto* will in fact be a financial bonanza for the few large Mexican private firms in a position to bid on some of the aspects of construction. Although PEMEX has the "in-house" capacity to do certain kinds of petroleum-related construction, laying 48-inch pipe is not among them.

neering service contract with PEMEX, and each Mexican construction firm to secure a piece of the action has associated itself with a North American firm. Overall engineering, testing, and management are in the hands of a joint venture named BICA, comprised of a large Mexican construction firm, ICA, in association with the Bechtel Corporation.

If Mexico could not go it alone on the capital goods, technology, and know-how required to build the pipeline, the need for foreign assistance in financing the project was even more obvious. When construction was actually begun in October 1977, 1.5 billion dollars was the planning figure used as an estimate of total costs. Earlier in the year, however, when the capital requirements had been estimated at only 1 billion dollars, it had looked as if even this lower amount might be difficult to assemble. With international lenders still very cautious, with the IMF 1977 "additional borrowing" ceiling for Mexico set at 3 billion dollars, and with PEMEX's pricing strategy still uncrystallized—or at least unpublicized—the total financial package looked very uncertain.

Soon, however, the climate began to change. The leading factor was clearly the general restoration of confidence in the Mexican economy, referred to earlier. But also important was the rapidly changing perception of the economics of the pipeline itself. By deciding to price gas at the BTU equivalent of No. 2 fuel oil, offloaded in New York (approximately $2.60 per 1000 cu. ft. at the time the decision was announced), PEMEX in effect added the necessary sweetening to a deal that was already looking good.[38] As noted earlier, at this price the pipeline would pay for itself in dollars in less than two years, even allowing for cost overruns in construction. From the perspective of international lenders, it had become, in the words of one banker, "an absolutely golden deal."

By the middle of the year, the IMF borrowing limits on Mexico seemed to be the only remaining major obstacle. Although Mexico had the right (and might have been willing) to use up to one-half of its three-billion-dollar additional borrowing allotment to finance the pipeline, this would clearly have meant that other projects would have had

38. The BTU (British Thermal Unit) equivalency formula is a way of tying the price of gas to the price of oil—in this case OPEC oil. Under the formula, 1000 cu. ft. of gas are priced the same as an "equal" amount of fuel oil—"equal" being defined as the quantity that would have to be burned to produce the same BTU's as 1000 cu. ft. of natural gas. In addition to yielding a relatively higher price for gas, the formula has the advantage (from the seller's point of view) of indexing the price of gas to the (increasing) price of oil. As we note below, this pricing-and-indexing formula encountered strong opposition in both the U.S. executive and the Congress.

to be displaced—a difficult although not impossible set of decisions. But while these decisions still loomed as a possibility, alternative schemes, bypassing the IMF limits, were also under consideration. The most serious and ingenious—although hardly new—was for the gas-transmission companies themselves to prepay for some percentage of the gas that they would be receiving several years later. This would be entered into the Mexican national accounts as export earnings, not as debt, and thus would technically fall outside the IMF borrowing limits. Using these prepayments, PEMEX could then finance the construction of the *gasoducto*—an effective way of putting the cart before the horse. Because the gas-transmission companies would themselves have to borrow the money for the prepayments, the overall cost to the Mexican Government might have been slightly higher than in the case of a direct loan. But so determined was the Mexican Government to build the line, so anxious were the companies to get the gas, and so willing were the banks to lend, that this alternative financing device was considered very seriously.

As the summer heat eased in Mexico City, Chiapas, New York, Washington, and Texas, however, it became evident that no such strategy would be necessary. The IMF, as one informant said, "waved its magic wand," allowing the pipeline financing to be arranged outside the framework of the 3-billion-dollar ceiling. Quite apart from the multiple and mutually reinforcing signals that they were getting at that time from interested parties, it would have been inconsistent for officials at the IMF not to have done so. The *gasoducto* was golden from their point of view too. It was export-oriented, offered quick foreign exchange returns, clearly could be considered sound fiscal management, did not automatically add to inflationary pressures internally, and even promised to generate some jobs without swelling the public payrolls.[39]

PRICE, POLITICS, AND THE STANDOFF

Although the U.S. Government had still not accepted the Mexican price of $2.60 per Mcf for the gas, as the summer of 1977 drew to a close this appeared to be the only remaining problem. With the private banks lining up to lend, the IMF smiling on the project, and private construction firms and manufacturers gearing up to supply needed goods and services, only one major piece of the financial package remained to

39. In his speech of October 26, 1977, Díaz Serrano estimated that the *gasoducto* would "generate from 24,000 to 35,000 jobs during its construction."

be put in place: U.S. Government funding in support of those capital goods and services that would be purchased in the United States.[40] This funding was announced shortly thereafter. In August, the Export-Import Bank reported that it had negotiated two credits with PEMEX. The first was for 250 million dollars to be used for projects in three general categories: exploration and development, refinery improvement and expansion, and natural-gas processing and petrochemical production. The Eximbank estimates were that this quarter-of-a-billion-dollar credit would provide the core financing for almost 600 million dollars of PEMEX purchases in the United States over the next 18 months. Repayments on the loan would not begin until 1983; and the annual interest rate would be 8½ percent.

It was the second part of the Eximbank-PEMEX package, however, that was central to the *gasoducto*. Excerpts from the Eximbank's letter of intent to the U.S. Senate outline the loan and its rationale clearly.[41]

Eximbank is prepared to extend a direct credit of $340,000,000 to Petroleos Mexicanos (Pemex) to assist Pemex in financing the acquisition in the United States and exportation to Mexico of goods and services, all of United States manufacture or origin, required by Pemex in connection with the construction of an 840-mile gas pipeline.

It is expected that the total cost of U.S. goods and services to be supplied to the project will be approximately $400,000,000, of which 85% will be covered by the proposed Eximbank credit and 15% will be provided by Pemex in the form of a cash payment.

It is expected that the type of goods which U.S. companies will be exporting will include large diameter pipe, valves, meters, large compression equipment and chemical process equipment. In addition, U.S. companies are expected to

40. With the exception of the pipe itself (of which only about one-third could be produced in the United States given existing capacity), the Mexican Government wished to purchase a majority of the imported components for the *gasoducto* in the United States. The reasons were political, technological, and financial. At the same time, PEMEX also wished to diversify the sources of financing quite widely—in part for political reasons and in part to secure the best possible terms commensurate with the specific use to which the borrowed money would be put. As an example, it is obviously cheaper to purchase capital goods made in the United States with Eximbank credit than with a commercial loan floated on Eurocurrency markets. Additionally, Eximbank credits are *only* available for such purposes, whereas Eurocurrency loans can be put to almost any use once secured.

41. Under U.S. law, Eximbank credits of 60 million dollars or more must be reported to the Congress at least 25 working days before final approval. If, at the expiration of that period, the Congress has not dictated otherwise, the Bank may give final approval to the loan.

provide certain technical services, such as engineering design and equipment procurement for the sweetener and natural gas liquids recovery plants.

It is anticipated that suppliers in most of the industrial countries will be submitting bids for the sale of goods and services for the project. Many if not all of such suppliers will be receiving strong support from the official export credit agencies in their countries. Eximbank has received information that the official credit agencies of Canada, Japan and the United Kingdom are willing to provide 85% coverage for the same term as Eximbank is proposing, in certain cases with interest rates lower than the Eximbank rate.

The proposed transaction offers substantial benefits to the United States because of the expected flow of gas through the pipeline to U.S. gas transmission companies for distribution to U.S. customers.

In view of the magnitude of the transaction, the repayment term, the existence of foreign competition and the benefit to the U.S. from the increased gas supply, Eximbank's credit is necessary to secure this sale for United States suppliers.[42]

The course of transnational relations, however, like the course of young love, never runs entirely smooth. The hitch in the "golden deal" turned out to be, not surprisingly, the gas-pricing arrangement sought by the Mexican Government. From the point of view of the banks, the gas-transmission companies, the U.S. suppliers of goods and services—not to mention PEMEX—there was unanimity on pricing: the BTU equivalent of No. 2 fuel oil in New York, or approximately $2.60 per Mcf. PEMEX's interest in this price was obvious. Almost equally so were the interests of everyone else mentioned so far. The larger the amount of foreign exchange earned by Mexico with the *gasoducto*, the more easily loans would be repaid, the more surplus would be available for yet more purchases in the United States, and the more the promise of restored Mexican economic health would become a reality.[43] Even

42. Letter from John L. Moore, Jr., President, Eximbank, to the Honorable Walter F. Mondale, September 9, 1977. Reprinted in *Congressional Record*, Senate, September 14, 1977, S14899–14900. The two loans taken together, totaling 590 million dollars, constitute the largest single credit ever proposed by the Eximbank (as opposed to a package of credits and guarantees).

43. The interest of the gas-transmission companies in the price was different although no less real than the interest of banks and the suppliers of capital goods and services. The transmission companies profit in direct proportion to the *volume* of gas moved. As long as demand stays strong, price is not a critical factor to them. Given gas shortages in the United States and the expectation that expensive foreign gas could be "rolled in" with existing lower-priced gas (and thus not jolt consumers too abruptly), the logic of their situation dictated "gas at [almost] any price." Above all, they did not want to be party to a price hassle with the Mexican

gas producers in the United States were not unhappy with the high price. On the contrary, it provided one more argument for the deregulation of domestic gas. "How can you justify holding our prices down," they could tell the U.S. Government, "when you are willing to let foreign gas enter at such high levels?"[44]

Although from the outset there had been rumblings from the U.S. Government on the projected price of Mexican gas, the first major flap was precipitated in the Congress, not in the executive branch.[45] A month after the Eximbank presented its two PEMEX loans to Congress, Senator Adlai Stevenson of Illinois, the head of the Senate subcommittee with oversight responsibilities, introduced the following concurrent resolution (excerpts):

Whereas, the price currently being proposed for U.S. imports of Mexican natural gas to be delivered from the proposed pipeline is significantly greater than prices prevailing for current non-liquefied imports of natural gas and prices permitted for domestically-produced natural gas;

Whereas financing by the Export-Import Bank of the United States of the PEMEX natural gas project at such unreasonable prices for United States energy imports could set a dangerous precedent for prices of other U.S. energy imports—especially those that might be involved in other export financing by the Export-Import Bank;

Whereas, the American public has a right to be assured that financial resources of the United States are not used to develop and construct foreign energy projects that unwarrantedly increase the cost of U.S. energy imports;

Now, therefore, be it Resolved by the Senate (the House of Representatives concurring),

---

Government. They had much to lose and nothing to gain by such a hassle. It should be emphasized, however, that for all concerned the economics of the pipeline remained attractive by comparative standards even at half the $2.60 price. No one ever argued that they would actually lose money at a lower price.

44. For example, George P. Mitchell, Chairman of the Texas Independent Producers and Royalty Owners Association (TIPRO) argued, "We now have a system in which producers cannot receive adequate incentive to develop the nation's gas resources to the fullest, but one that encourages wasteful usage of gas. So now we're in a position of desperately needing imports, for which we'll pay more than if we had developed our own resources without price controls." He added, however, that "the independents aren't contesting the importation of the [Mexican] gas." See "Tipro wants to intervene in Mexican-gas case," *The Oil and Gas Journal*, September 12, 1977, p. 58.

45. Perhaps sensing that U.S. Government financing was not assured, Governor Edwin Edwards of Louisiana had earlier suggested that Louisiana, Texas, and a number of other states might think about supplying *gasoducto* credits should Washington fail to do so. See *The Oil Daily*, July 8, 1977, p. 8.

That it is the sense of the Congress that the Export-Import Bank of the United States not provide financing to Petroleos Mexicanos (PEMEX) . . . unless and until it is established . . . that the Secretary of Energy has approved the price at which such natural gas supplies may be imported into the U.S.; and . . . the Congress is assured of the reasonableness and fairness of such import prices in light of other prices currently prevailing for non-liquefied natural gas imports and prices permitted domestic producers of natural gas supplies within the United States.[46]

The reaction in Mexico City to the Stevenson resolution was predictable—nationalistic outrage that the *gasoducto* financing might be held up simply because Mexico was asking the OPEC price for gas. But the reactions in U.S. petroleum and banking circles were only slightly milder. Thus Mr. Jack H. Ray, the President of Tenneco InterAmerica wrote to Senator Stevenson in words that could only have been music to PEMEX's ears:

It is generally agreed that the purpose of the United States Export-Import Bank is to foster U.S. exports by supplying credit to foreign customers on terms that match those available from other countries. The EXIM Bank is a successful profit-making government institution which paid a $50 million dividend into the U.S. Treasury last year. . . . Its success has been based on its nonpolitical nature and its adherence to good banking practices. There is no precedent whatsoever to support your suggestion that EXIM be used as an arm to regulate or negotiate energy prices. . . .

Furthermore, the threat of removing EXIM credits really has no leverage toward obtaining lower prices for Mexican gas as PEMEX is not dependent on U.S. credit sources. The $600 million in goods and services can be obtained quite easily from other countries, with credit terms equal to those of EXIM Bank. At least five countries have offered total financing of the project. . . .

As one of the largest gas transmission companies in the United States, we are working as hard as we can to obtain natural gas for our customers at competitive prices and help prevent crippling shortages such as occurred last winter. The large-scale importation of natural gas from Mexico is by far the most promising prospect we have to relieve those shortages and help our overall energy picture. Our negotiations with the PEMEX officials have been tough, and I assure you we have done our utmost to acquire gas at the best price. However, the Mexicans are well aware of the world price of energy and expect to get just that. In reality, it is politically unacceptable for them to accept anything less. Can you picture the President of Mexico announcing

---

46. *Congressional Record*, Senate, October 19, 1977, S17370–17371. It should be noted that a resolution is not binding on the parties involved.

to the people that they must tighten their belts because he is going to sell off their natural resources to the United States at less than world prices and thus subsidize the U.S. economy?[47]

Subsequently, other voices were joined to the chorus. In a lead editorial at the end of November, the *Washington Post* wrote:

Mexico has large resources of gas and oil, and it makes altogether good sense for the U.S. Government to lend the capital to develop them. Since the Eximbank's $340 million loan would support Mexico's purchase of some $400 million in U.S. equipment and services for this pipeline, there's every reason to go ahead with the project. What's a fair price for the gas? Mexico's wealth per capita is one-twelfth that of the United States, and Mexico is entitled to full market value. That means a price no less than that of oil.[48]

The Eximbank, caught between those applying multiple pressures to approve the loan on the one hand and, on the other, impressive legislative and executive branch critics of the price Mexico was asking for the gas, had little room to maneuver in the short run.[49] The chairman of the Eximbank reassured Senator Stevenson that the matter of Eximbank credits would be further considered, and Senator Stevenson decided not to press for the adoption of his resolution "in the hopes that the two governments will resist the pressures of domestic politics and the temptations of short-term commercial considerations and make certain that their national interests are paramount."[50] This informal understanding put off the financing issue for several weeks while the Congress continued to wrangle over energy issues. With no resolution of this debate by the end of December, however, the Eximbank finally approved the credits.

In the short run, however, this approval made little difference, since the price negotiations between the U.S. and Mexican governments were not going well. For a brief period toward the end of November, the Departments of Energy and State thought that a compromise on price

47. Quoted with the permission of Jack H. Ray. Letter of October 28, 1977.
48. *Washington Post*, November 25, 1977, p. A-20.
49. Interviews suggest that the Bank officials felt badly used in this situation, since the credits were being held hostage to concerns that were not organizationally "theirs"—and this on a loan that was not only the largest in Bank history, but also one of the best by conventional banking criteria! On the other hand, they were fully aware of and resigned to the politics of the domestic energy situation in which they were enmeshed. If the Eximbank could be said to have had an "official" position on the credit-price question, it was, "Let's give the credits now and argue about the price later, since it is a good deal at any foreseeable price."
50. *Congressional Record*, Senate, October 26, 1977, S17834.

was within reach.[51] Since $2.16 per Mcf (the current price paid for Canadian natural gas) was unacceptable to the Mexicans, a "face-saving" price of $2.60 was offered to be paid when the gas actually began to flow in quantity on the completion of the *gasoducto*. From the point of view of the Carter Administration, this pricing proposal had two great advantages. First, it postponed the paying of the $2.60 price until 1980 or perhaps even later when—given the expectation of higher prices for natural gas domestically—it would be more in line with other sources of supply. Second, and perhaps more important, it in effect untied the price of Mexican gas from OPEC oil prices since it was possible and in fact quite predictable that by 1980 the BTU equivalent of No. 2 fuel oil in New York would be significantly higher.

Although the details of the story are not entirely clear, it seems that the U.S. proposal was actively and positively considered by certain Mexican officials.[52] But what is not in doubt is that it was unacceptable to Díaz Serrano and López Portillo. Thus, despite a flurry of pre-Christmas activity, during which Díaz Serrano and Mexican Foreign Minister Santiago Roel came to Washington and saw Secretaries Schlesinger and Vance, the negotiations were broken off amidst a storm of Mexican criticism of the U.S. position, in part triggered by Secretary Schlesinger's rather impolitic statement that "soon or later" Mexico would have to sell its gas to the United States.[53] On December 22, President López Portillo ordered PEMEX not to renew the memorandum of intent that had been signed with the six American gas companies. Work was simultaneously stopped on the section of the *gasoducto* leading directly to the Texas border.[54] As the new year dawned, the golden deal was looking less viable than at any time since it had first hit the front pages almost a year previously.

With the *gasoducto* already under construction and the price negotiations suspended, the Mexican Government was in an embarrassing position. Having argued long and forcefully that Mexico would have to either flare or export the gas, PEMEX and the President now had to backtrack and say that it was both possible and correct to use the gas domestically. The *gasoducto* was thus quickly transformed into a pipeline to supply the northern industrial city of Monterrey (a secondary use that it would have had in any event), the volume of gas it would

---

51. Based on interviews with U.S. Government officials conducted in Washington, D.C. in late December 1977.
52. Based on interviews in Washington, D.C. and Mexico City.
53. See *New York Times*, January 6, 1978.
54. See *Washington Post*, December 23, 1977, p. A-4.

carry was reduced to 800 million cubic feet per day and pipe and equipment imports were renegotiated to purchase as much as possible from non-U.S. sources.[55]

The contradictions of building a 48-inch pipeline to supply Monterrey with gas did not pass unnoticed by critics of the *gasoducto*. With a selling price of only 32 cents per Mcf domestically (one-eighth of the asked export price), the deal no longer looked particularly golden. As many critics pointed out, such a huge *gasoducto* to Monterrey would simply encourage the wasteful use of extremely low-price gas, amounting in effect to a continuing government subsidy to large industrial users.[56] It was claimed by some that the cost of transport would in fact exceed the selling price, thus undermining any rationale other than export for the *gasoducto*, despite the nationalistic prose in which the project was being promoted. In the acerbic words of Heberto Castillo: "How long will it take for the *gasoducto* to Monterrey to pay for itself if the selling price of the gas is seven cents lower than its transport costs? Is the *gasoducto* to Monterrey only so that we can lose money? Or is the idea to have a pipeline close to the United States?"[57]

In response to the critics, PEMEX and the Mexican Government presented a case for bringing southern gas to northern Mexico even in the absence of immediate export possibilities. Among the advantages cited were the following.[58]

55. The major imported component of the *gasoducto* is the pipe itself, particularly if it only serves Monterrey, because with reduced line pressure, large imported compressors are not needed. PEMEX placed its largest order for pipe in Japan, with other significant orders in France, Italy, and West Germany (see *Oil Daily*, October 12, 1977). The order that was to have gone to U.S. Steel was withdrawn. U.S. officials had feared strong protests from an industry beleaguered by foreign competition, but in this particular case they did not materialize because the one U.S. plant capable of fabricating 48-inch pipe was already over-committed and did not want—at least at that moment—the additional business. Other capital goods and technology suppliers in the United States who expect to do significant amounts of business with PEMEX under the Eximbank loans and other credits adopted a "wait and see" posture, expecting the current problems to be resolved in the near future.

56. See, among others, José Reveles, "Pemex, atrapado por el gasoducto," *Proceso*, No. 62, January 9, 1978, pp. 16–17.

57. "Pemex en evidencia," *Proceso*, no. 61, January 2, 1978, p. 34.

58. This is a composite argument based on interviews in Mexico City and published statements of government officials. See in particular the press conference of Jorge Díaz Serrano, January 4, 1978, and his report on the occasion of the 40th anniversary of the oil nationalization, March 18, 1978. Both were published in most Mexico City newspapers on the following day. See also various statements by José Andrés Oteyza, Secretary of Resources and Industrial Development (Patrimonio y Fomento Industrial), for example in *El Día* (Mexico City), May 7, 1978, p. 9.

—Natural gas is to be preferred to oil as a fuel in most applications for both technical and environmental reasons. The *gasoducto* will enable Mexico to increase the proportion of natural gas in the national energy mix.

—Mexico badly needs a national gas-transmission network. (There is currently no north-south link.) The *gasoducto* will be the "spinal column" of that network.

—Large industrial energy consumers in the north can easily convert to natural gas from fuel oil. (Dual burning systems were originally installed in many locations.) Conversion will free large amounts of oil for export. Even though this is not high quality oil, with some further treatment it can be sold on international markets for about $11 a barrel. These additional export earnings will make the *gasoducto* profitable even if currently low domestic gas-prices remain unchanged.

—The development and decentralization of industry, particularly along the Gulf Coast where the *gasoducto* will run, will be encouraged by the project.

—Large but widely dispersed fields of dry gas in the north, some of which are new discoveries and some of which are currently in use to supply northern Mexico, can be shut down once the *gasoducto* is in operation. Since dry gas is not associated with oil, there is no reason to tap it until such time as more gas is needed domestically, or export at the proper price to the United States becomes possible. Thus, rationality in the exploitation of Mexico's gas reserves is enhanced.

Despite the arguments of the Government, however, Heberto Castillo and other critics continued to find grounds for questioning the wisdom of the *gasoducto*.[59] Moreover, even some government officials admitted in private that for domestic purposes this was clearly the wrong pipeline, built to the wrong scale, and following the wrong route. But what was never in doubt was the Government's determination to continue the project. Thus, by mid-1978 much of the line was already taking shape and a March 1979 completion date for the *gasoducto* had been announced. Whether it was the best solution to the use of Mexico's resources or not, southern gas was going to flow north, but now the northern connection would be made in Monterrey, not in Texas.

59. See the continuing series of articles by Castillo in *Proceso* (Mexico City). See also, for example, Salvador Saenz Nieves, "La Política de Energéticos y el Ducto Cactus-Reynosa," in two parts, *Oposición*, (Mexico City), February 4 and 11, 1978. The critique of the *gasoducto* is only one element, and ultimately not the most important, in the emerging energy debate in Mexico. For an important left-nationalist statement see "Frente de Defensa de los Recursos Naturales," *Oposición*, March 4, 1978, p. 12.

MEXICAN GAS IMPORTS AND U.S. GAS POLICY

As the above story suggests, by the beginning of 1978 the northern connection for Mexican gas was deeply entangled in domestic politics and economics both north and south of the border. Particularly complex was the U.S. scene, where in somewhat unexpected fashion the question of Mexican gas imports had been dramatically precipitated into the domestic energy debate at the time when the Eximbank loans were first brought before the Congress. To understand the subsequent chain of events, it is necessary to analyze this scene more closely.

Mexican gas imports, and especially the question of price, raised three primary issues for U.S. gas policy. The first and most important had to do with the relationship between the price of imported gas and the price of new gas in the United States—an issue that also included the questions of deregulation and dual gas markets in the United States. The second concerned the relationship between the price of Mexican gas imports and the price of gas imports from other foreign sources, principally from Canada, but also in the future, if LNG projects are approved, from Algeria, Indonesia, and Iran. The third issue involved the links between gas imports and the role of natural gas as a whole in future U.S. energy plans.

The first issue is perhaps the most complex. It takes its simplest form in the regional differences of supply and demand for natural gas that were discussed earlier. Congressional representatives from gas-consuming states in the Northeast, Midwest, West, and Southeast have generally led the fight for continued regulation of gas prices at rates no higher than the 1976 level of $1.42 per Mcf, whereas Congressmen from gas-producing states in the South and Southwest have pressed the case for decontrol and market prices of about $2.50–3.00 per Mcf (the exact level is under dispute).[60] Interlaced with these regional differences are other divisions between free-market advocates and interventionists, supporters of industrial versus consumer interests, etc. In its energy plan, the Carter Administration proposed a compromise between the extremes calling for continued controls in the interstate market and extension of these controls to the intrastate market (eliminating the dual

60. Some advocates of continued control sought to roll back gas prices. A coalition of consumer, labor and liberal groups petitioned the Federal Energy Regulatory Commission in November, 1977 to reconsider, among other things, the 1976 opinion of the Federal Power Commission that increased the price for new gas to interstate markets from $0.52 per Mcf to $1.42 per Mcf. See *The Energy Daily*, November 14, 1977.

pricing system), while increasing the price of new gas to $1.75 per Mcf. The latter price was computed on the basis of the BTU equivalent (at the beginning of 1978) of the average refiner acquisition price (without tax) of all domestic crude oil.[61] As such, this price was considerably lower than the equivalent world oil price. Moreover, the Carter Administration did not propose a general tax on domestic natural gas (unlike domestic oil) to bring the final price to consumers up to world oil-price levels. Instead, the Carter proposals taxed only high-volume industrial and utility users of natural gas, proposing eventually to bring final prices to these customers to about one-third *above* the BTU equivalent price of world oil. Meanwhile, high priority residential and commercial customers would continue to pay domestic gas prices considerably *below* world oil-price equivalents.

The House of Representatives approved the key features of the Administration's proposals for natural gas, including the $1.75 per Mcf price level for high priority gas consumers.[62] The Senate, on the other hand, approved a bill that deregulated new gas prices (for onshore gas, immediately; for offshore gas, by the end of 1982) and allocated regulated old gas to high priority customers only until the cost of new gas to low priority users equaled the reasonable cost of substitute fuel oil. In short, the Senate version ensured that low priority customers would never pay more than the substitute cost or world-price equivalent for natural gas, whereas high priority customers would continue to benefit from prices below world levels only as long as old gas contracts remained in force.

Given this wide divergence of pricing policies for natural gas, the price for Mexican natural-gas imports was unlikely to go unnoticed on Capitol Hill. Pegged to the price of No. 2 heating oil delivered in New York, the Mexican price was already higher than equivalent world crude-oil prices in New York (since No. 2 heating oil is a refined product). Moreover, the Mexican price applied at the Texas border. When transportation costs were added to ship the gas from Texas to New York, some estimates were that the actual price in New York would be as high as $3.50 per Mcf. Approving a price for Mexi-

61. The regulated natural-gas price would then escalate after 1978 on the basis of increases in average domestic oil prices. The latter would increase, as the price of new oil was raised over a three-year period to 1977 world levels and then adjusted thereafter to keep pace with domestic price inflation.

62. On the basis of the bill passed in the House, one estimate projected the same real gas price for residential users in 1985 as in 1977, whereas the price for major businesses would more than triple. See *National Journal*, September 10, 1977, p. 1419.

can gas at this level threatened to establish a precedent for pricing domestic gas at equivalent world oil prices, even though the clear intention of the Carter Administration, as well as the advocates of continued control, was to preserve a domestic gas price for high priority customers *below* equivalent world prices. Indeed, the $2.60 price could in fact have been used as a justification for gas prices above world oil prices. Senator Stevenson, as a staunch advocate of continued gas-price regulation, summarized this argument succinctly in a letter to the editor of the *Washington Post*:[63]

When the costs required to integrate [Mexican] gas into the pipeline system and transport it are added, the cost of Mexican gas in New York would be about $3.60 . . . . [This price] would be far in excess of the $1.75 proposed by President Carter as the wellhead price for newly discovered gas in the United States. That price of $1.75 is the BTU equivalent of the average price for domestic crude oil. The $2.60 price is even higher than the OPEC price for crude oil.

Instead of approving gas prices in excess of OPEC oil prices [the Department of Energy] should insist upon a reasonable price . . . . Natural gas prices in excess of $1.75 produce no more natural gas. They do produce inflation, recession, political instability, and windfall profits.[64]

63. December 12, 1977.
64. These and other arguments made by Senator Stevenson did not pass unchallenged by U.S. supporters of the *gasoducto* and the $2.60 per Mcf price. For example, in a long letter dated January 3, 1978 to Senator Stevenson, Jack H. Ray, the President of Tennessee Gas Transmission (Tenneco InterAmerica) wrote a point-by-point rebuttal. Excerpts, quoted by permission, follow.
    4. *"It would be far in excess of the $1.75 proposed by President Carter . . . . That price of $1.75 is the BTU equivalent of the average price for domestic crude oil."*
    My basic problem with this statement is not your referencing Mr. Carter's proposed price but your implication that the Mexican gas should be no higher than the equivalent *regulated* price of domestic crude oil. If the Mexicans had but one reason to drop the negotiations, it would be the presumption that they are expected to price their energy below its commodity value because the United States Government required its domestic producers to do so.
    5. *"The $2.60 price is even higher than the OPEC price for crude oil."*
    This is a factually true statistic but an irrelevant statement. Gas does not compete with crude oil in the marketplace—but with fuel oil which is a product of refining crude oil. The Mexican natural gas delivered at the United States border would be ready to use and, once more, its delivered price to the consumer should be compared to the delivered price of *fuel* oil to the consumer.
For a related although less specific critique, see "Lesson of the Year," *Wall Street Journal*, December 30, 1977, p. 4. It should be pointed out, of course, that for geographical reasons pipeline gas faces a more limited market than crude or fuel oil and therefore a somewhat different pricing situation.

The effect of the Mexican gas price on the price of other gas imports was also at issue. A decision to pay $2.60 for Mexican gas might have precipitated an immediate request from Canada to raise the price of its gas, selling at the U.S. border for $2.16 per Mcf. It might also have had the effect of easing the way in the future for even higher priced LNG imports, currently estimated at $3.50–5.00 per Mcf.

Although the economics of pipeline and LNG imports are substantially different, incremental pricing is an issue shared by both. None of these imports from whatever source could be marketed in the United States if they had to be priced to their final customers at the import or incremental (marginal) price level, which suggests, critics point out, that these imports are priced well above the marginal utility of natural gas. Instead, the practice in the past has been to allow roll-in of higher import prices with lower domestic prices, passing the gas on to the final consumers at an average price. As long as imports are relatively small, roll-in generally has a limited effect on the final price. But as imports and import prices increase, roll-in may significantly raise average prices, providing further justification for deregulation and still higher prices. Thus, to the extent that a policy of encouraging and approving high-priced gas imports over time raises the domestic price of gas, gas imports can be seen as a backhanded way of continuously raising domestic prices toward world price levels or, in short, deregulating natural gas.

The question of Mexican and other foreign gas imports raised a third and longer-term issue for U.S. policy concerning the role of natural-gas supply and consumption in future U.S. energy plans. The Administration's energy plan called for a gradual transition from oil and natural-gas supplies to coal, nuclear power, and eventually nonconventional energy sources. On the supply side, the plan implicitly assumed that there was not much gas left in the United States (about a ten-year supply at current consumption rates).[65] Hence, a price for natural gas much above $1.75 per Mcf was unlikely to encourage substantial new gas production and would more probably accrue to domestic gas producers as windfall profits. The approval of a higher price than this for Mexican and other gas imports would have raised a number of contradictions for the Administration's plan. First, it might have encouraged greater gas supply but would also have increased dependence on foreign energy, a trend the Administration's plan sought to reverse. Second, if these imports were approved for roll-in pricing (and

65. This view is of course disputed. See *National Journal*, September 10, 1977, p. 1419.

they would not be marketable otherwise), they would have increased domestic gas supplies selling on average below world price levels, thereby subsidizing the continued and perhaps accelerated consumption of an energy supply that the Administration's plan hoped to phase out. Third, paying higher prices to foreign producers, whose costs are frequently less than those of U.S. producers (and that is true in the case of Mexican gas from the Reforma fields), would have granted windfall profits to foreign producers that are denied to domestic producers. It is doubtful that the Administration could have sustained such a policy.

Similarly, on the demand side, a number of contradictions could be identified. The Administration plan, as we noted, called for a tax to discourage the consumption of natural gas by high volume industrial and utility users. If this tax works, these users will have probably switched to other fuels by the mid-1980's or so, when gas imports, approved now, would begin to arrive in substantial volumes. If these imports include LNG, they will involve long-term purchase commitments, since LNG projects, with their high initial investment costs, are only viable on a twenty-year or longer basis. The United States would be locked into buying high-priced foreign gas well into the 1990's. If, meanwhile, low priority customers had switched to other fuels, high priority residential and commercial customers would be left as the principal users of gas and would bear the primary brunt of increasingly higher average domestic gas prices (from roll-in of increasing, high-priced imports with declining, low-priced domestic gas). Yet these are the very customers that the Administration's plan sought to protect from increasingly higher prices.

The exact mix of these various issues in the Carter Administration's thinking about the importation of Mexican gas at the end of 1977 is difficult to reconstruct. But it is clear that all were present, and the sum of concerns and contradictions was sufficient to lead to a resounding "no" to the request to import gas at $2.60 per Mcf. Additionally, there is evidence that the policy thicket in the United States is so tangled that even the passage of an energy bill in the Congress may not clear the ground for a dramatically softer price position by the Carter Administration. For example, Secretary of Energy Schlesinger hinted in November 1977 that the Administration was "inclining" against roll-in pricing—a move that would clearly affect the salability of gas imports since the full force of high prices would be borne by specific consumers rather than by the public in general.[66] And many of the other problems

66. See *Energy Daily*, November 28, 1977, and *New York Times*, December 17, 1977.

suggested above will remain even when (and if) a new package of energy legislation is passed.[67]

SOME IMPLICATIONS OF THE GASODUCTO: THE BROADER CONTEXT

It is tempting to see the *gasoducto*, the alliances that formed around it and against it, and the issues it raised as representative of future U.S.-Mexican energy relations. To some extent the temptation is justified, because the relationships and patterns established at the outset of an emerging scenario often have disproportionate weight in what comes later. But it is also true that significant options are still open, many tough decisions and much hard bargaining remain, and there is still time to extract from the *gasoducto* experience important lessons for the future of U.S.- Mexican energy relations.[68] Caveats aside, however, there are at least four broad *problemáticas* raised by the *gasoducto* story, *problemáticas* that will become increasingly present and controversial as Mexican hydrocarbon exploration and development accelerate and as the United States participates in this development, either as a supplier of capital and technology, or as a market for Mexican exports, or as both.

The Role of Foreign Capital, Technology, and Interests

In his first State of the Nation message on September 1, 1977, President López Portillo made the following fine-sounding declaration: "In the petroleum field we have 40 years of accumulated experience. This gives us a high degree of autonomy from foreigners, both in carrying out programs of exploration and exploitation and in technological matters." In historical terms this was essentially a true statement. After the nationalization of the petroleum industry, Mexico certainly demonstrated that it was able to manage, modernize, and expand the industry using essentially its own resources.[69] The factors that have changed,

67. In the appendix to this article we have discussed aspects of the 1978 energy debate in the United States (and the legislative tangle) that bear on natural-gas pricing and U.S. energy relations with Mexico.

68. As mentioned earlier, it should also always be borne in mind that gas and oil development and export scenarios are not the same—primarily because of the OPEC pricing umbrella under which oil is marketed and the much greater storage and transport options that exist for crude oil as opposed to gas. See discussion of this below.

69. The exception has always been capital goods. From 1973 to 1976, for example, PEMEX was the largest public sector importer of merchandise in Mexico, chal-

however, are the scale, the pace, and some of the technological demands of the expansion that is now underway.

The *gasoducto* experience suggests the following changes in circumstances. Because it is a 48-inch line, the overwhelming majority of the capital goods and much of the technology and know-how must be imported. The share of the construction left to the Mexicans is largely in lighter capital goods, earth-moving, and large amounts of labor. Obviously if the project were delayed, if time were taken to install (for example) the mill capacity to produce 48-inch pipe domestically, a larger percentage of the finished project could be labeled "made in Mexico." But the economics of the situation—at least as conceptualized by those who are running the show—have militated against such trade-offs.

To some extent the situation in oil development is even more dramatic. Close to 50 percent of the recent Mexican finds are offshore, in the Gulf of Campeche. This is a new environment for PEMEX, requiring new combinations of skills, technology, and equipment. The scale—both physically and financially—required for offshore work is gargantuan, as anyone who has seen a multimillion-dollar offshore drilling platform can attest. From the outset, specialized U.S. companies have been deeply involved in working in this area with PEMEX. Because this involvement is a nationalistic embarrassment to the Mexican Government, data are difficult to assemble. But some idea of what is happening can be gleaned from the story of one U.S. corporation that managed to get in on the ground floor.

Brown and Root of Houston, Texas, a subsidiary of the Halliburton Company, is "among the world's largest and most diversified engineering and construction companies, with operations extending throughout the world."[70] Soon after the inauguration of López Portillo, Brown and Root formed a joint venture with one of the grand old men of Mexican petroleum, now retired from PEMEX. Under the name of Proyectos

---

lenged only by CONASUPO, the organization charged with organizing the distribution of consumer goods (largely food) to the *sectores populares* in Mexico. In 1973 PEMEX's imports of merchandise were 353 million dollars, rising to 740 million dollars by 1976. Statistics from IMF sources.

70. From Brown and Root, Inc., *International Operations*, a company pamphlet. This publication lists scores of company projects, from Abu Dhabi and Alaska to Venezuela and Vietnam. Petroleum-related projects predominate, but roads, dams, hospitals, pulp and paper mills, and military bases are all mentioned. Offshore operations range from the Gulf of Mexico to the North Sea, Middle East, and Southeast Asia. Company contracts totaled 4.8 billion dollars in 1976.

Marinos (Marine Projects), they then signed a contract with PEMEX for engineering and project management relating to offshore work in the Gulf of Campeche.[71] Proyectos Marinos's major responsibility will be the construction and installation of offshore drilling platforms. Much of the actual construction will be sublet to local contractors—possibly associated in their own joint ventures with U.S. firms, as in the case of the pipeline. Again, given the technology involved (aside from the skeletons of the platforms themselves), a large percentage of it will undoubtedly be imported, almost surely predominantly from the United States. The U.S. labor force involved in all of this is being held to a minimum and will perhaps never number more than about 100 engineers, supervisory personnel, and technicians. But it would be naive in the extreme to use the number of U.S. personnel as the index of the foreign presence. For many years to come, both as capital-goods suppliers and purveyors of technology and expertise, the United States is almost certain to be very deeply involved in Mexico petroleum development.[72]

Oil, Gas, and U.S.–Mexican Bargaining

The flurry of hard bargaining about the price of gas is only the tip of an iceberg that is still in formation. Given the profundity of Mexico's problems, the size of her petroleum reserves, the energy situation in the United States and elsewhere, and the existing complexities of U.S.–Mexican relations, the new bargaining positions that will eventually emerge are difficult to discern. However, it is interesting to consider the implications for one aspect of U.S.–Mexican energy relations, namely energy-pricing policies, and for one aspect of broader U.S.–Mexican foreign relations, namely the immigration issue.

The most controversial issue in world energy politics today is the pricing of future energy supplies (replacing to some extent the issue of nationalization, which preoccupied energy debates before 1973). How OPEC will price future supplies of crude oil is, of course, critical.

71. Although there is a certain personalistic ring to the joint venture and the PEMEX contract, it should be emphasized that the arrangements described are absolutely legal and correct under Mexican law.

72. Although it is probably scant comfort to Mexican nationalists, even such imaginative and quasi-autarkical nations as the People's Republic of China have turned to the United States for technology and capital goods for offshore work. The largest and most recent sale was for two self-contained drilling rigs for fixed offshore platforms, at a total price of from 20 to 30 million dollars. See the *Washington Post*, November 27, 1977, p. A-23, and April 27, 1978, p. A-20. Unlike the Mexican deals, these are straight cash sales with no joint venture component.

The United States, Mexico, and other countries need not follow OPEC pricing policies, but they can hardly ignore the relationship between domestic and export prices and world market prices.

For the United States, present world oil prices do not appear to be intolerable, although their increase in recent years and prospective increases in the future trigger enormous and sometimes acrimonious debate among affected interest groups, resulting in such tangled complications as the gas-deregulation debate and the unwieldy crude-oil-entitlements program. As these divisions continue and perhaps deepen (and it is unlikely that they will disappear with a new energy bill any more than they did after the Energy Policy and Conservation Act of 1975), they could lead to increased frustration and the threat of toughened stances against foreign suppliers of oil and gas. In the case of Mexican gas, for example, Senator Stevenson argued that the $1.75 price, even though below the equivalent world oil price was "a reasonable price . . . high enough for PEMEX, a low-cost producer with no other markets."[73] The implication was that the base price for imported Mexican gas should be the U.S. domestic market price (since this is perceived to be the only conceivable market for that gas), rather than world market prices. Yet given the realities of Mexican politics and economics, accepting prices below world levels—however defined—for hydrocarbon exports is not something that the Mexican Government can easily do. The domestic situation in both countries thus at present includes a confrontational dynamic.

The larger, long-term, energy-pricing context suggests a potential softening of this confrontational dynamic. Two trends are involved. First, up to now, the United States has resisted letting world energy prices determine domestic prices. However, as the United States and other consuming countries acquire greater confidence in OPEC pricing policies, and as the oil producers gain increasing influence in world economic and diplomatic institutions (for example, Saudi Arabia is now the second largest creditor of the IMF and has assumed a permanent position on the Board of Directors), the disparity between world and domestic pricing levels should diminish. Both the Ford and the Carter Administrations have sought to raise the price of new domestic oil to world levels—the difference being that the Ford Administration would have permitted the higher price to go to the producers, whereas the Carter Administration sought to impose a tax on new oil. Though the Carter Administration's crude oil tax did not survive the energy debate

73. See letter to the editor of *Washington Post*, December 12, 1977.

of 1978, the movement toward higher world oil prices seems inevitable. Natural gas prices will also move in this direction, if the mid-1978 compromise to deregulate gas prices by 1985 holds. Second, as Mexican production and export expand to include a higher component of crude oil as opposed to natural gas, marketing flexibility will increase, and the question of price will be much less subject to bilateral bargaining. Even without membership, OPEC prices are Mexico's prices for crude oil, although lower transportation costs and hence higher profits offer some incentives to sell to the United States.

As has been repeatedly emphasized, however, U.S.–Mexican bargaining on energy policy is by no means a simple or isolated affair. At some level and in some fashion it will undoubtedly get entangled with other issues. An obvious candidate for such entanglement is the immigration issue, which for both Mexico and the United States is not an easy question to address—at least not in anything approaching a public forum. In effect, over the next decade the Mexican attitude, stripped of all pretext, will be, "If you want a favorable hydrocarbon relationship with us, you must continue to offer us 'foreign aid' in the form of a relatively open border."[74] The specific content of a favorable hydrocarbon relationship will necessarily be open to multiple meanings and interpretations as times and circumstances change. So too will the notion of a relatively open border. Furthermore, on the Mexican side, a special hydrocarbon relationship with the United States will continue to be extremely difficult to construct for domestic political reasons. On the U.S. side, for a different set of political reasons, it will not be easy to maintain a relatively open border—at least as an expressed public policy goal as opposed to a living reality. But the logic of the situation dictates that Mexico will make serious efforts to link the two issues in one way and that the U.S. will attempt to link them in another—if at all. Coupled with the domestic explosiveness of the issues, these different perspectives suggest years if not decades of controversy.

In reality, the overall bargaining situation is both more complex and more unbalanced than the above example suggests. Since capital, technology, markets, people, and military power are all disproportionately located north of the Rio Grande, even 200 billion barrels of hydrocarbon reserves will not balance the scales. But at least in the 1970's it has not

---

74. Trade issues are an important additional element in the bargaining scenario. An alternative to accepting additional Mexican immigrants is accepting additional Mexican products. U.S. restrictions on winter vegetables and fruits, as well as many manufactured exports from Mexico, however, continue to be an obstacle to the expansion of trade. See *Washington Post*, May 29, 1978.

been as easy for the United States to exploit successfully these traditional sources of bargaining power and coercion as was the case in the previous two decades. This may turn out to be even more true with Mexico (for reasons of history, proximity, culture, and the increasing importance of Hispanics in U.S. politics) than it was with more distant lands and peoples.

National Security

When Díaz Serrano appeared before the Mexican Congress in October to defend the *gasoducto*, he was asked if it was possible that the United States would under certain circumstances "violate our sovereignty and invade Mexico to guarantee the supply of gas." He responded by saying that he thought that this was a very remote possibility and that he had confidence in "the philosophy articulated by President Carter and his enormous preoccupation with human rights." He then added, "I hope that this philosophy, this way of thinking, expresses the genuine desire of the North American people, and signifies for us a guarantee that we can work in peace."[75]

Mexican anxieties about their increased vulnerability because of the "fixed" nature of the gas pipeline do not necessarily reflect the realities of Pentagon contingency planning. It may in fact be the case that to date no ambitious young lieutenant or captain has presented to his superiors a Plan for Guaranteeing a Continuous Supply of Mexican Gas in an Era of Rising U.S.–Mexican Tensions. Be that as it may, the questions raised are real, deriving from two basic facts. First, as emphasized by U.S. officials from the president and the secretary of defense on down, U.S. dependence on foreign energy supplies is a primary national security concern.[76] Most attention is now being given to the Middle East—

75. *Proceso* (Mexico City), no. 52, October 31, 1977, p. 11. In Mexican cartoons, the *gasoducto* is often portrayed as Mexico's Panama Canal, with all the implications and overtones of vulnerability that the canal represents to Panama.

76. For example, "I am also concerned as commander-in-chief of our country about the serious security implications of becoming increasingly dependent upon foreign oil supplies which may for some reason be interrupted," President Carter, News Conference, October 13, 1977, *Washington Post*, October 14, 1977, p. A-8.

Two weeks later, speaking to a conference of business executives, Defense Secretary Harold Brown said, "The present deficiency of assured energy resources is the single surest threat that the future poses to our security and to that of our allies. . . . We now spend annually over $100 billion on our armed forces. . . . If we hand to others the capacity to strangle us and our allies by cutting off our and their oil supplies, then this expenditure does no more for us than to create a useless, encrusted modern-day Maginot line." *New York Times*, October 27, 1977, p. D-11.

for obvious reasons. But to the extent that Mexico becomes an important supplier of oil and gas to the United States, it too will be involved in that set of concerns, with the "added attraction" of being a potentially much more secure source of energy than most other countries because of its close historical and geographic relationship with the United States. Second, Mexico is now regarded as the primary new source of hydrocarbons in the world, with major production coming on line just as the projected shortages of the mid-1980s are precipitated on a global scale. In other words, the marginal importance of Mexican production is seen as far larger than its proportional contribution to world petroleum supplies would suggest.[77] Even if the national security managers in the United States are not yet busy factoring all of this into energy and contingency planning, they may not be long in doing so.

Sowing the Oil

The question of who will benefit from the Mexican petroleum bonanza is high on the agenda of almost everyone concerned. The experiences of other oil-rich, less developed countries are not particularly encouraging, at least when viewed from the perspective of those committed to reducing inequalities and establishing minimal quality-of-life conditions for today's impoverished citizens. Certainly neither the Algerian nor Venezuelan cases gives cause for optimism; nor does the Iranian situation suggest that solutions are easily found. At the very least, profound structural changes in both the public and private sectors are needed before oil riches might begin to be translated into the kinds of programs that will touch basic socioeconomic problems. As stated in an earlier essay:

Oil may allow Mexico to slip away from the IMF but not from history. Oil exports, the related relaxation of debt limits, and the easing of some aspects of the austerity program give breathing space, another chance for hard-pressed Mexican politicians. But oil by itself cannot respond to peasants' demands for land; nor can it create hundreds of thousands of new jobs each year; nor can it keep millions of Mexicans from crossing the border; nor make rapid

---

77. The CIA estimates that Mexican oil production will be between 3.0 and 4.5 million barrels per day in 1985, with a theoretical "top" of 5 to 6 million bbl/d in that year. See *The International Energy Situation: Outlook to 1985* (Central Intelligence Agency, Washington, D.C., April, 1977), p. 11. For an extended analysis of Mexican oil and U.S. national security, see Richard R. Fagen, "El Petroleo Mexicano y la Seguridad Nacional de los Estados Unidos," *Foro Internacional*, no. 74, vol. 19, October–December, 1978.

inroads on redressing a distribution of income that is one of the most unequal in the world; nor reduce public and private corruption; nor deal with the human and social problems generated by a population that doubles in size every 20 years.[78]

But hope springs eternal, and already—in the context of the *gasoducto* controversy—mention has been made of the benefits that would flow to the Mexican people. Thus Díaz Serrano opened his *gasoducto* defense in the Congress by saying that Mexico's petroleum resources were sufficient not only to resolve her current economic difficulties, but also to create "a new country, permanently prosperous; a rich country where the right to a job would be a reality."[79] If not handled with care, there is substantial irony, if not the seeds of a destabilizing vicious circle, in this rhetoric and these claims. The oil bonanza, with its implied promise of great riches, weakens one of the classic arguments used by Third-World elites when faced with popular demands: "We understand your plight, and if only we had the resources we would respond; in the meantime, be patient, for we are working on the problem."

In short, in every enthusiastic declaration of potential gas revenues, oil exports, petrochemical production, or rapidly expanding reserves, there is an implied political promise to the Mexican nation, particularly to the popular sectors. The statistics suggest to international bankers that their loans are going to be repaid and give the managers of PEMEX confidence in their ability to purchase the goods and services necessary to meet ambitious production goals; and the same statistics suggest to millions of other Mexicans that the coming years will not be as desperate as the present and past. The resolution of these partially conflicting claims on the national patrimony lies in the 1980's. How, in whose favor, and at what rate they are resolved will in large measure determine not only Mexico's future, but also the future of U.S.–Mexican relations.

CONCLUSIONS

Energy problems and solutions in the United States and Mexico are ultimately reflections of more fundamental patterns of politics and economic conditions in these two societies. Energy politics in the United States can be seen as a many-sided contest over the rapidly escalating

78. Fagen, "The Realities of U.S.–Mexican Relations," p. 698.
79. *Proceso*, no. 52, October 31, 1977, p. 10. For useful materials on the debate on these issues in Mexico, see *Foro Internacional*, no. 72, vol. 18, April–June, 1978; and *El Economista Mexicano*, vol. 12, no. 2, March–April, 1978.

economic value of energy resources, both among domestic producers, consumers and other groups, and among U.S. and foreign energy suppliers and importers. Energy politics in Mexico can be seen as a somewhat similar contest over the prospective spoils of a future energy bonanza. Existing structures of political and social life are likely to affect these energy contests at least as much as energy itself is likely to affect basic political and social developments. Thus, in the United States, energy problems do not present a situation that is the "moral equivalent of war," nor do energy reserves in Mexico automatically promise to reduce class conflict or resolve existing injustices.

Energy-related dealings between the two countries will inevitably reflect these broader social and political realities. Not surprisingly, the first attempts to negotiate a changed northern connection were not only somewhat unreal but also largely unsuccessful. Mexican officials made the most of oil and gas discoveries to refurbish their country's image in world financial and diplomatic circles. Meanwhile, massive problems continued at home. In the United States and elsewhere, banks and businesses reacted with characteristic fervor to take advantage of the new and more favorable climate in Mexico City and the boom opportunities offered by the dawning of the petroleum-export age south of the border. At first, the U.S. Government slumbered, preoccupied with attempting to shape a domestic energy consensus, which was regarded as the prerequisite of any effective foreign energy policy. Then, stirred to action by an energy-stalled and increasingly frustrated U.S. Congress, the Carter Administration came down hard on a Mexican gas connection that threatened to contradict important aspects of its domestic energy policy.

Are there policy-relevant lessons to be drawn? Only very tenuously and somewhat indirectly. It is tempting to draw an analogy with another neighboring supplier of energy, Canada. U.S.–Canadian energy exchanges in recent years have benefited from an ongoing process of discussion and interaction among high officials. A framework has emerged in which thorny problems, such as the Canadian decision to cut back oil and gas exports to the United States, have been contained and dealt with in the broader context of U.S.–Canadian relations. Obviously such mechanisms would be useful in the Mexican case.[80] But

---

80. A bilateral commission and set of subcommissions were set up between the United States and Mexico after López Portillo's visit to the United States in February, 1977. These include a subcommission on energy. There are no indications to date, however, that it will play any significant role in addressing or resolving important issues.

the analogy has its weaknesses, for even a cursory examination of the broader context suggests that U.S.–Mexican relations are not the same as U.S.–Canadian relations. In fact, the comparison may be particularly misleading, for factors like massive migration—which play such an important role in U.S.–Mexican relations—have no Canadian counterpart. Thus, all indications are that a long and potentially tempestuous period lies ahead as both Mexico and the United States adjust to the new realities.

Appendix
An Epilogue

Just before dawn on October 15, 1978, the last day of the 95th Congress, the Carter Administration's energy bill finally passed—at least some of it did. After eighteen months of continuous controversy and compromise, the final bill was a barely recognizable descendant of the original plan launched in April 1977. As the *Washington Post* reported, the bill was "battered and dented and stripped not only of its hubcaps but also some of the parts that the designers originally considered essential."[81]

The centerpiece of the legislation when it was originally launched was a crude oil tax to raise domestic oil prices to world price levels. Through this and other tax measures, the bill was expected to save 4.5 million barrels of oil imports per day by 1985. When the bill finally passed, the centerpiece was the decision to deregulate natural gas. While the administration contended this measure would still save 1.4 million barrels of oil imports per day by 1985, others argued that it would actually increase oil imports by 2 million barrels per day. No one really knew, but at the end it did not matter. The bill and especially the natural gas provisions were more important as symbols of national will than as substantive contributions to the energy problem.

Toward the end of the energy debate, Senator Muskie concluded that "energy is the most difficult political, economic and social question to come before Congress in our lifetime."[82] The reasons were not far to seek. Estimates of the amounts of money at stake in the gas debate alone ranged from $9 to $50 billion. Large sums depended upon the precise depth of wells qualifying for the new gas price and upon the manner in which inflation and then annual increases were computed to escalate this price. Under these circumstances, it was to have been expected that the gas issue, which has actually been debated in the U.S. for the last thirty years, would follow an agonizing path through the U.S. Congress.

On October 18, 1977, House and Senate conferees began the task of reconciling the widely diverging energy and natural gas bills passed by the two chambers during the previous summer. By the end of the year, Senate conferees were split 9-9 on the gas deregulation issue. The death of one of the conferees in January and three months of secret meetings eventually produced a 10-7 vote on a compromise plan. Meanwhile, however, House conferees lined up 13-12 in favor of an alternative plan. Another two months of de-

81. *Washington Post*, October 16, 1978.
82. *Washington Post*, September 11, 1978.

bate ensued. Finally, on May 24th, an agreement in principle was reached, only to be followed by two more months of tedious negotiations over specific language.

When the complete text (170 pages in all) surfaced in August, the narrow consensus had evaporated. Horse trading was necessary even to get a majority of conferees to sign the conference report. At the end of August, the *Washington Post* reported bluntly that the White House did not have sufficient votes to pass the gas bill. President Carter then returned early from his vacation to launch one final effort to save the last remnant and new centerpiece of his once comprehensive energy plan.

The opposition was led by an unlikely alliance of Senators coming from gas producing as well as gas consuming states. Producing interests wanted immediate deregulation, consuming interests indefinite regulation. To the dissatisfaction of both, the bill called for gradual deregulation by 1985. The White House reached out beyond Capitol Hill to encircle the opposition. It enlisted the help of business groups, farmers, steel, automobile and textile executives—among others. It appealed to the highest sense of national purpose, calling the bill a test of America's ability to act and the dollar's ability to survive. As might be expected, the President's men also resorted to the most conventional practices of Washington politics, trading votes on the gas bill for issues as remote as steel imports.

In the end the administration prevailed but the margin was microscopic. After the Senate passed the gas bill on September 27th by a margin of 57–42, the House decided on October 13th by only one vote, 207–206, to deal with the gas bill and other energy measures as a single package. This set the stage for final passage, although the Senate continued until the last minutes of the 95th Congress to block other parts of the energy bill and thereby to jeopardize the gas compromise.

Not surprisingly, the bill emerging from this tortuous process was exceedingly complex. The price for new gas was to increase immediately to about $2 per thousand cubic feet (compared to $1.75 in the original Carter proposal) and then rise by 3-½ to 4 percent per year above the inflation rate until 1984 when price controls are to be lifted completely. In the interim, controls will be extended to intrastate as well as interstate gas. After 1984 the Congress or the President may reimpose controls for one 18-month period not to extend beyond the end of 1988. Some gas, from deep wells for example, will be deregulated sooner. Altogether, there are 17 or more (the experts cannot agree) categories of gas prices, and the Department of Energy estimated that, to administer the bill, it would require an additional 300 personnel on top of some 500 recently authorized.

What does all this mean for the U.S.-Mexican negotiations on pipeline gas at the Texas border? From one point of view, passage of the natural gas bill seems to remove a key obstacle to these negotiations. The U.S. government had made it clear that further negotiations were impossible until the domestic gas issue was settled. Moreover, the higher price for domestic gas called for in the compromise bill should bring U.S. prices more quickly in line with the original Mexican asking price of $2.60 per thousand cubic feet. Under the bill, the price of new gas in the U.S. will rise to $2.65 per thousand cubic feet by 1981. Additionally, the U.S., it would seem, will continue to need Mexican gas. No one knows how much new gas will be produced by higher domestic prices. The administration estimates an additional 3 trillion cubic feet by 1985 or the equivalent of about 1.5 million barrels per day of oil. But, under interim controls, others argue that new gas, even if it exists, will be held back and, whether it exists or not, will not be sufficient to meet demand stimulated by artificially low prices.

Supply, demand, and prices, however, are far from the only relevant factors. As the *gasoducto* story reminds us, deals like the Northern connection are not made or unmade solely in terms of one or another version of economic rationality. Rather, here as throughout the energy field, politics is very much in evidence. And given the complexity of the politics practiced both north and south of the border—not to mention internationally—only time will tell how, when, and by whom the next attempt to forge a Northern connection will be made.

Index

copy 2

Political Science

Capitalism and the State in U.S.–Latin American Relations

Edited by Richard R. Fagen

Why does the United States respond as it does to political and economic events in Latin America? How does the United States condition events in Latin America, and how is it in turn conditioned by the results of its power and influence? These ten papers seek the answers to these questions by exploring the deep sources of U.S. foreign policy toward the hemisphere.

Part I deals with general aspects of U.S. foreign policy: class and cultural factors limiting choice; the origins and ideology of the new Anti-Sovietism as exemplified by the Committee on the Present Danger; the changing structure of production in the steel and electronics industries at home and abroad; and U.S. support for authoritarian regimes.

Part II is a collection of case studies of relations between individual Latin American countries and the United States (or international institutions dominated by the United States): Argentina and the International Monetary Fund; Peru and private U.S. banks; Jamaica, Trinidad, and Guyana and the meaning and possibilities of their forms of socialism; Brazil and the multinational corporations; Mexico and the Mexican-American Chamber of Commerce; and Mexico and the clash with U.S. energy interests.

Stanford University Press

ISBN 0-8047-1040-6